# Palm Programming

Christian Immler

DATA BECKER®

**Published by:** DATA BECKER CORP
210 Highland Avenue
Needham Heights
MA 02494

**Author:** Christian Immler

**Layout** Andreas Quednau (www.aquednau.de)

Printed in the United States July 2001

**UPC CODE:** **6-80466-90103-7**

**ISBN #:** **1-58507-052-1**

**Important Note**

The procedures and programs described in this book are given regardless of patent. They are intended for amateur and training purposes only.

All information, technical specifications and programs in this book has been produced by the authors with the utmost care. However, the publishers can provide neither a guarantee, nor accept legal responsibility or any other responsibility, for consequences resulting from incorrect information.

The software and hardware designations and trademarks of companies used in this book shall generally remain subject to the legislation covering trade names, trademarks and protection under patent law.

The text contained in this book are suggestions and examples only. They include selective information only with no claims made for completeness.

In addition, although the text has been created with great care, the publisher and the authors shall accept no responsibility for the completeness or correctness, for the contents of the text or for the success of the users actions after following the information given in this manual. Using the information given in the text is solely at the user's own risk.

The names and addresses given in this text are fictitious. Any resemblance to persons alive or dead is purely coincidental and unintentional.

TABLE OF CONTENTS

TABLE OF CONTENTS

TABLE OF CONTENTS

TABLE OF CONTENTS

# 1. "Hello Palm" – The first Palm program

Thousands of programmers have written programs for Palms and other handhelds based on the Palm OS operating system. In addition to the original Palms, handhelds include the IBM WorkPad, Handspring Visor, TRG Pro, Symbol Organizer, and Sony CLIÉ.

Usually, one program doesn't completely fulfill all requirements, and if one does exist, it's too expensive. One solution is to program your Palm yourself. If you view programming as a creative and intellectual challenge, you will enjoy programming your Palm.

Before we explain about programming a Palm, programming languages, and logic, you will write a short program.

Programming a Palm is similar to programming other computers. Even if you've only programmed your VCR, in minutes you will see the results of your very first program on the small screen of your Palm. Programmers have traditionally started programming with "Hello world!" You will begin with "Hello Palm!" in two different programming languages: HotPaw Basic (also called yBasic) and CASL. Both languages are relatively easy to learn yet powerful enough to be in wide distribution among shareware and freeware users, so you can program all the examples of this book (and lots more) without additional expense.

## 1.1 "Hello Palm" with HotPaw Basic

Using HotSync, install HotPaw Basic (www.hotpaw.com/rhn/hotpaw/) like any other program. Thirty days after installation, the limitation of the non-registered version comes into play: At this point, only four programs display at the same time. However, you have not lost the data in the programs you accessed previously even though they won't display. Simply rename the other programs to use them again.

**Note**

**HotPaw Basic only runs with OS 3.x**

HotPaw Basic does not support older Palm OS versions. If you are not certain which OS version you have installed on your Palm, tap the main program interface in the menu on *Application/Info*. Then tap the *Version* button.

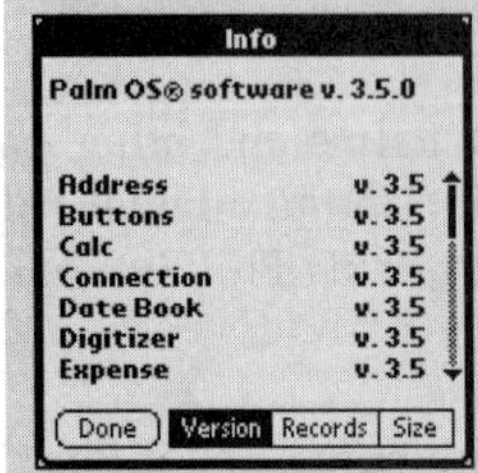


*Display of the OS version*

The Palm OS version appears in the top line.

Do not start Basic right now. Instead, start the standard Memo Pad application of the Palm, using its icon or the Memo button. HotPaw Basic programs are always written on memos. To conserve disk space, HotPaw Basic does not use an editor. (Some users may be familiar with editors from PC programming languages such as Delphi or VisualBasic, but HotPaw Basic uses the Memo Pad Editor that is already on the Palm.)

Create a new memo, from which your first Palm program will ultimately result:

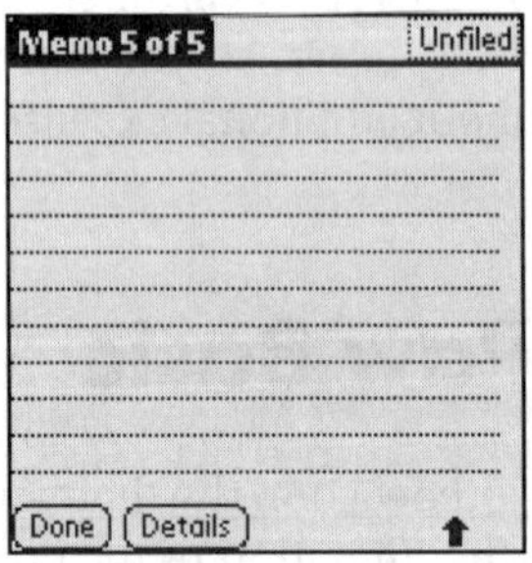


*A blank memo*

**Tip**

**Data entry**

Practices vary. Some users prefer writing with Graffiti; others prefer the onscreen keyboard. Use whatever method you would normally use for writing memos, such as a plug-in keyboard. You can also write the memos on the Palm desktop and transfer them to your Palm by way of HotSync. See Chapter 10 for additional text entry tools.

Write the following program on this memo:

```
#HelloPalm.bas
? "Hello Palm!"
```

**CD**

**Program on the companion CD to this book**

You can also find this program on the companion CD to this book, listed as *0101.bas*. To install the Basic programs from the CD, open them with a text editor and then use the Clipboard to copy the program code to a new memo in the Palm desktop. The next time you do a HotSync, the program will be synchronized to your Palm.

Here's what it looks like:

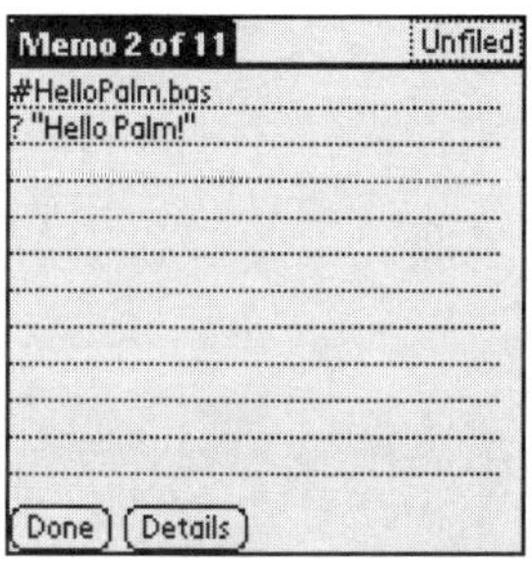


*Your first Palm program*

Exit the memo using the *Done* button. The memo appears in the list.

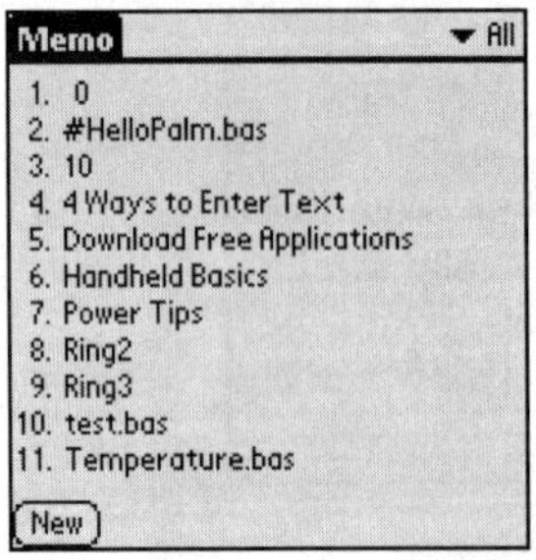


*The program in the list of memos*

Now start the yBasic program, the interpreter of HotPaw Basic.

*Starting screen of HotPaw Basic*

A list of Basic programs appears with a single program entered. yBasic searches all the memos for programs. (A memo counts as a Basic program when the first line begins with a # and ends with *.bas*.)

Highlight this program and then tap *Run*.

*The program runs*

As expected, the program starts up and displays the text *Hello Palm!* on the screen.

Tap *OK* to return to the HotPaw Basic program list.

## How does the Basic program work?

The first program line contains only the program name, which can consist of several words. The # character at the beginning and the *.bas* extension, which HotPaw Basic uses to search the memos for Basic programs, are important.

Do you remember the old Basic from the C64 days? You could use a question mark (?) or the *print* command to output texts to the screen. The same question mark is used today in HotPaw Basic. However, don't concern yourself with the screen output; it is automatically displayed in a dialog box with the *OK* button.

Every Basic program that does not contain the *end* command automatically ends after the last line, just like this one. If a program ends with branches in the middle of the source code, an *end* command must be there (in yBasic always in lower case). At the end of the source code the interpreter automatically assumes an *end* command.

The functions for inputting and outputting data have been enhanced compared to standard Basic. For example, the simple *print* function automatically generates a dialog box with an *OK* button. If you are familiar with Basic, you can convert most existing Basic programs into yBasic for the Palm.

# 1.2 "Hello Palm" with CASL

CASL differs from HotPaw Basic in two fundamental ways. First, you program on the PC and beam the finished programs to your Palm. Having a large screen at your disposal allows you to survey large parts of the source code simultaneously. Second, CASL offers a graphic editor for designing program interfaces, which would not be possible on the Palm. On the other hand, a CASL program is not portable, and you cannot make changes to existing programs on the Palm.

Install the demo version of CASL 3 from the CD onto your PC. After installation, start the CASLide development environment.

In the left window, find the *No Project* entry. Currently no project is loaded.

Click the *New Project* icon and give your new project a name, for example *hallo.cpj*. Confirm the message that appears with *OK*.

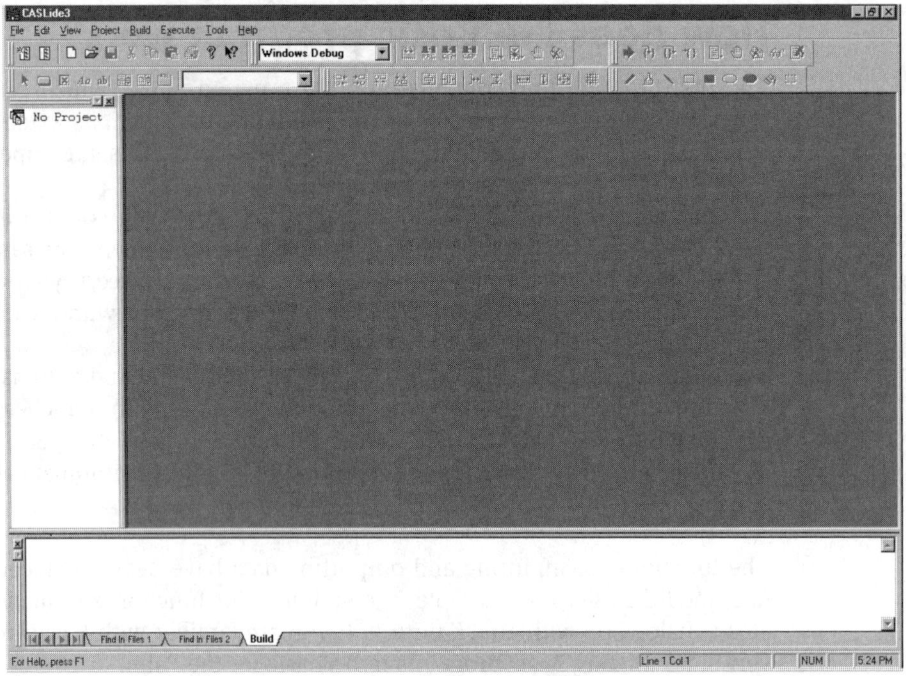

*The CASLide development environment. The toolbars on top could look a little different*

Two windows automatically open, which, at first glance, differ only in their background color.

Write the following program text in the window with the white background:

```
Label hello_label;
End;

Function Startup;
  Put hello_label, "Hello Palm!";
End;
```

Keep in mind that in CASL, each program line must end with a semicolon. The *Put* ... line is indented solely to make things easier to read.

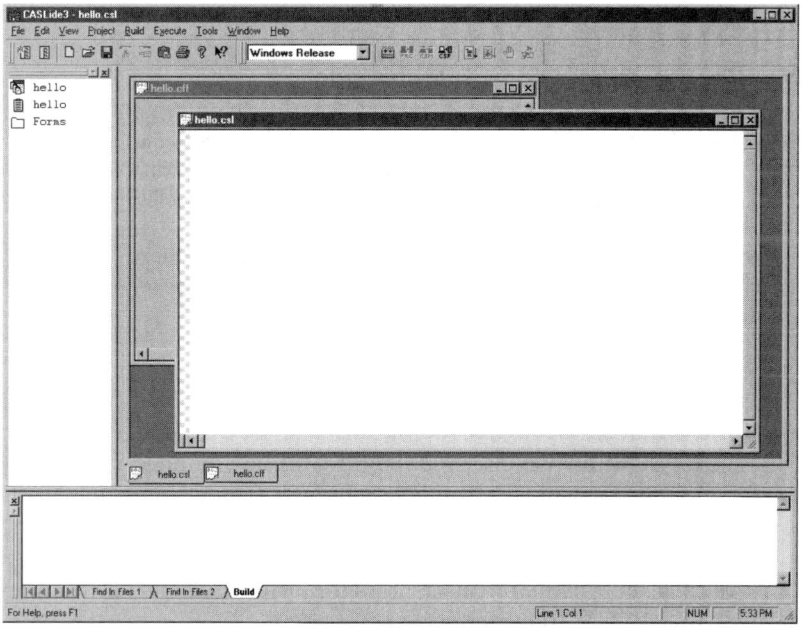

*Two new windows in the CASLide*

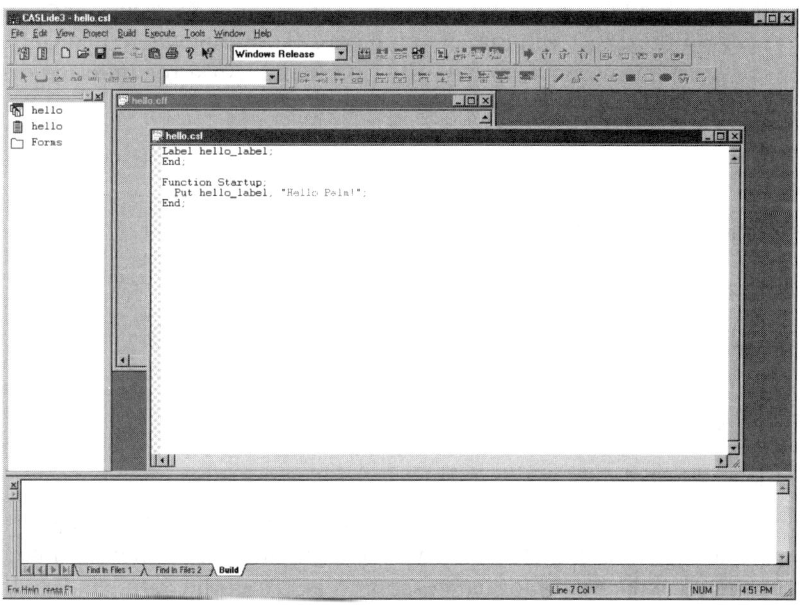

*The program in the CASLide*

**CD**

**Program on the companion CD to this book**

You can also find this program on the companion CD to this book listed as *0102.csl.* To install the CASL programs in the CSL format from the CD, copy them to your CASL work directory and create a new project with the same name. The CSL file will automatically be added to the project.

Do not distribute CASL project files directly in the CPJ format because they contain absolute path specifications to all the files that are used. Also, different computers may have different directories.

Switch the Target Selector, the list box in the upper toolbar, to *Windows Debug*. By doing this you are specifying the system for which the program is to be compiled (= translated from the clear text into machine language). *Windows Debug* stands for "Test under Windows".

Next click the *Compile* icon or press [F7]. This generates a machine-readable program from the source code.

If you have not made any mistakes copying, the message *Total errors = 0* appears in the lower window. If you have a typo somewhere in a CASL command, the compiler will not process this command. An error message displaying the faulty word and its line number appears.

**Tip**

**Most frequent error source in CASL**

Remember that in CASL, each line must end with a semicolon. If the semicolon is missing from a line, the CASL compiler displays a syntax error in the next line. Therefore, if you get this type of error message, always check the previous line.

Click the *Run* icon or press [Ctrl]+[F5].

This starts CASLwin-Runtime, with which you can test the programs on your PC without having to install the Palm OS Emulator. In the next chapter, starting on page 23 additional information about CASL and the Palm OS Emulator is available. Use the information to test any Palm program on your PC.

*The program in CASLwin-Runtime*

The program seems to work, but you want it running securely on the Palm, not on your PC.

CASL programs, like HotPaw Basic programs, require their own runtime modules. These modules contain numerous predefined functions, for example for dialog boxes and buttons, which many programs use; so the compiler does not generate a truly independent running program with all of the particulars. However, it does create a code that accesses the standard functions of the runtime module, making it a significantly smaller program. Use the Palm installation tool to install the *Caslrt_pro.prc* and *Mathlib.prc* files, in the event you do not already have them installed on your Palm. You will find both files in the *Pilotfiles* subdirectory of your CASL installation. If you are using an icon organizer, install the *Caslrt_spt.prc* file in place of *Caslrt_pro.prc*. Icon organizers are employed chiefly in industry. They have additional buttons that require less input at the Graffiti area for use under rough working conditions. In addition, they contain a bar code scanner for reading labels and bar code stamps. The special runtime module supports these functions.

**Note**

**CASL 3 only runs with OS 2.x and higher**

CASL 3 no longer supports older Palm OS versions. Palm OS 1.x only ran on old Pilot 1000, Pilot 5000, and Palm Pilot Personal handhelds without the infrared update module.

Next, compile the CASL program for the Palm.

Switch the Target Selector to *Pilot Release*.

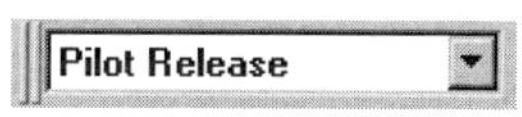

Click the *Compile* icon again or press F7.

Click the *PRC Install* icon. This generates a PRC file, which can run on the Palm as a program. A dialog box appears:

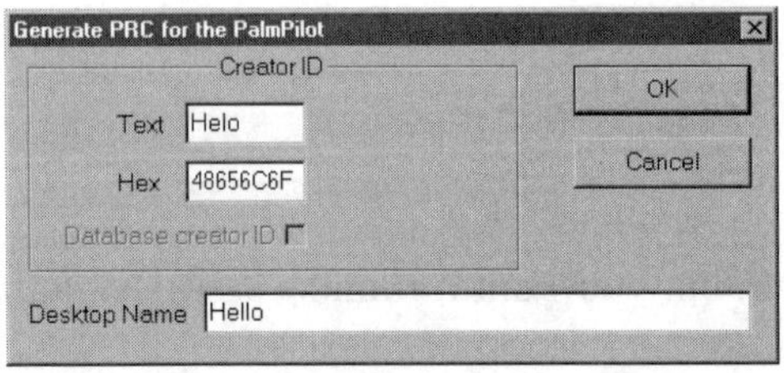


*Creating a PRC file*

Enter the dummy name of HELO in the *Text* field. This name is registered with Palm Computing, Inc. as a dummy. If you randomly used a developer name, complications with other programs that are registered with this creator ID may result. The *Hex* field is automatically filled out.

In the *Desktop Name* field, write the name in which the program is to appear on the Palm. The name of every program with its own icon on the Palm program startup interface also appears in the field. This has nothing to do with the file-name of the installed program file.

Now when you click *OK*, the Palm installation tool is automatically called and the compiled PRC file is installed on the Palm during the next HotSync.

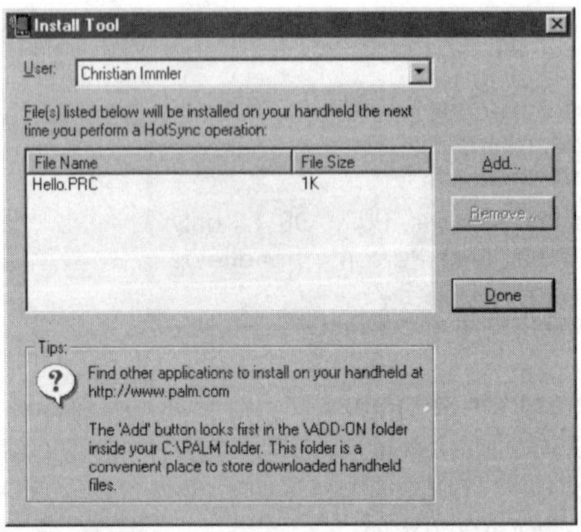


*The new program in the installation tool*

CASL programs appear on the Palm with a castle icon.

Tap this icon to start the program.

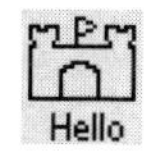

*The "Hello Palm" program on the Palm*

## How does the CASL program work?

CASL programs do not look like Basic programs, nor do they function like Basic programs. The first two lines:

```
label hello_label;
end;
```

define a *label*, a display field on the screen in which something is to be displayed later. Similar to Visual Basic programs, every CASL program needs output forms for its data under Windows.

This *label* is called *hello_label* and does not have a specially defined position or parameters. The CASL runtime automatically defines the label.

Keep in mind that every CASL expression must end with a semicolon.

The last three program lines:

```
function startup;
  put hello_label, "Hello Palm!";
end;
```

define a function. This function writes the *Hello Palm!* string in the previously defined label.

Every function within a program requires an independent name. The special name of *startup* causes the function to be called automatically at program startup.

# 2. Basics: The HotPaw and CASL programming environments

This book explains two Palm programming languages: HotPaw Basic and CASL. Both programming languages are popular with beginners because they are easy to learn and because they offer extensive functionality, even for more complex programs. Additional function libraries and tools are available on the Internet for both languages. You can use these resources to solve nearly every conceivable problem. The shareware versions are only slightly restricted; therefore, you can use them to duplicate all of the programming examples.

The most noticeable differences between these two languages are:

- HotPaw Basic is programmed directly on the Palm.
- CASL is programmed on the PC, and the finished program is beamed to the Palm.

One advantage of CASL is to have a large screen at your disposal, allowing you to view large parts of the source code simultaneously. In addition, CASL offers a graphic editor for designing program interfaces, something that wouldn't be possible on the Palm.

On the other hand, the HotPaw advantage is its portability: You can write a new program or revise an exisiting one wherever and whenever your Palm is with you.Through ScratchPad (see below), HotPaw Basic gives you the opportunity to run single programming statements immediately without first having to write and compile a complete program.

# 2.1 HotPaw Basic – Programming on the Palm

The Basic (**B**eginners **A**ll Purpose **S**ymbolic **I**nstruction **C**ode) programming language has existed on various computer platforms for about 30 years. During this time, hardly an operating system or a hardware platform existed for which no Basic dialect existed. Basic is built on a few very simple statements that can be understood immediately by their names. Using logic, you can understand simple programs even without a background in Basic. In addition, functions defined in an external library vary from system to system. In the case of HotPaw Basic, for example, functions exist for accessing the Palm standard applications.

In Basic programs, usually you do not need to predefine anything, declare any variables, or adhere to other structures. This makes programming very easy; however, it also leads to "spaghetti code", or programs that become incomprehensible even to the person who wrote them.

HotPaw Basic works essentially in accordance with the same rules of syntax as any other Basic language, only with the addition of Palm-specific functions. The following list shows the most important features of this programming language.

- Programs written directly on the Palm or beamed from the PC using memos.
- Over 75 functions and about 30 integrated Basic commands.
- Extensive support of the ANSI/ISO-Basic-standard for simple porting of programs.
- Twice as precise floating point arithmetic with the Mathlib library.
- Input and output of data occurs through predefined standard dialog boxes of the Palm OS.
- Standard buttons and logic elements can be used in custom programs.
- Graphic support including color for the Palm IIIc.
- Different sound functions.
- Special functions for controlling the infra-red and serial ports.
- Access to the Palm standard applications (Date Book, ToDo-List, Memo Pad).
- Access to standard database formats: JFile, HanDBase, DB and List.

You will become more familiar with these functions as you read further. If you are familiar with another variant of Basic on a different system, you may recognize differences using the list.

HotPaw Basic is an enhancement of the older Palm programming language, cbasPad. In contrast to cbasPad, HotPaw Basic only runs with Palm OS 3.x. However, old programs from cbasPad are compatible with HotPaw Basic, with a few exceptions. In Chapter 10, references to the functions you need for a HotPaw Basic program to run with cbasPad are available, in case you are still using an old Palm OS. However, in most cases it is worthwhile to upgrade to OS 3.x because all devices, except for the really old Pilots that come with Palm OS 2.x can be upgraded to OS 3.x.

**Internet**

**Manufacturer Info**

You can find detailed information about HotPaw Basic, additional sample programs, and links on the manufacturer's Web page:
http://www.hotpaw.com/rhn/hotpaw

HotPaw Basic uses the *Mathlib.prc* mathematical function library. This library contains functions for floating point arithmetic in the four fundamental operations of arithmetic as well as trigonometric and logarithmic functions. The HotPaw Basic interpreter does not recalculate every operation; instead, it resorts to the existing functions of *Mathlib.prc*. This freeware library comes supplied with some Palm programs. You can download them free of charge at http://www.probe.net/~rhuebner/mathlib.html.

**CD**

**Program on the companion CD**

You can find the *Mathlib.prc* file on the companion CD to this book. Install the file as you would any other Palm program using the Palm installation tool.

## Operation of HotPaw Basic

Start HotPaw Basic with this icon on the Program startup interface of the Palm. A list appears of all the Basic programs on your Palm.

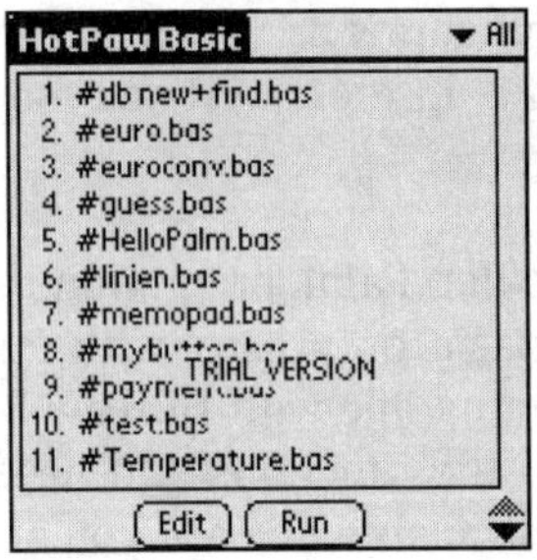


*List of the Basic programs*

The source texts of the individual programs are stored as memos, as a rule one memo corresponds to one program (see below).

To have a memo recognized as a Basic program, the first line, which contains the name of the memo, must begin with the # character and a space and end with the *.bas* string. However, it is possible to have spaces in program names.

To select a program in the list, tap it and then start it with the *Run* button. The *Edit* button opens the selected program as a memo, for the purpose of editing it.

## Rules of syntax

Essentially, HotPaw Basic uses the same syntax as any other Basic version. The most important rules of syntax are:

- Basic keywords (command names, variable names) must be separated from each other by spaces.
- Every program line typically requires a statement.
- Programs execute by line from top to bottom, provided they do not contain any special *go to* statements or loops.
- If a specific sequence of operations is to be considered within a formula, parentheses can be used, as in mathematical formulas. However, open parentheses must always be closed.
- Texts and other strings that are to be output or assigned to variables must be in quotation marks.

In addition, remember these special rules in HotPaw Basic:

- All Basic keywords must be written in lower case letters. In most other Basic dialects, case is not important.

- Line numbers can be used but are not required. If you use line numbers, they must appear in ascending order. You can use blanks in your count to add lines later.
- Multiple statements can appear in a single line separated by a colon.
- Lines may be a maximum of 80 characters long. However, to improve readability, make your lines only long enough to have the complete text fit in a line on the Palm screen.
- Comment lines begin with the # character. These lines will not be evaluated and can contain any comment text, with the exception of the first line, which contains the program name after the # character.

Palm memos can be a maximum of 4,000 characters in length. If you need more characters for your program, you can concatenate several memos. To do this, add the following line to your program

```
#include <#TITLE>
```

An additional memo with a first line that contains the *#TITLE* string is automatically inserted here.

In this way, you can insert several additional memos into the main program using program lines. However, it is not possible to nest *#include* statements. This means that a memo inserted in this way must not contain any additional *#include* statements.

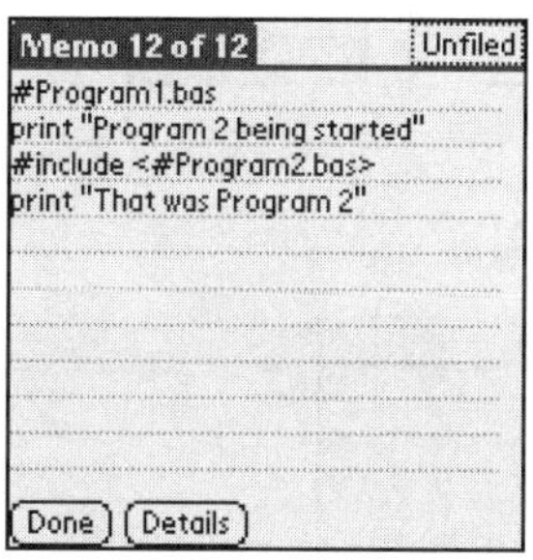


*Program 1*

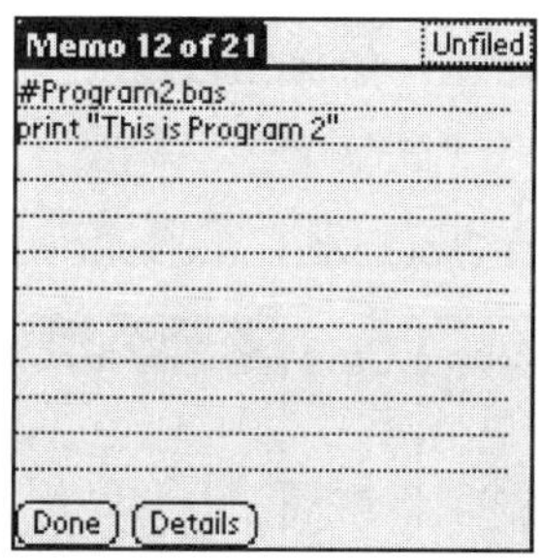


*Program 2*

In this example we start Program 1. It outputs a message. When you confirm the message with *OK*, Program 2 starts and then jumps back to Program 1.

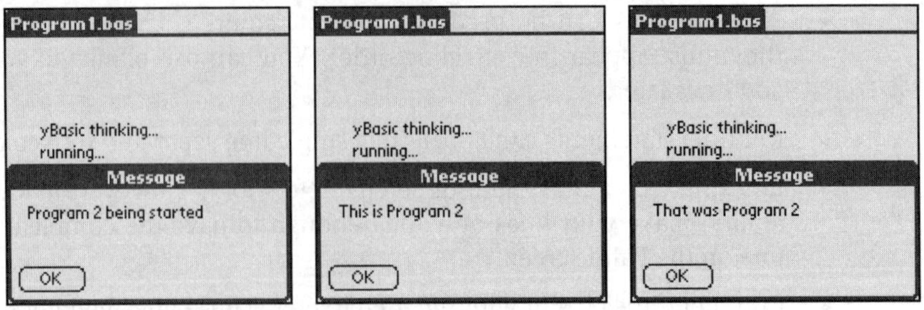


*Sequence of output for the program*

**CD**

**Program on the companion CD**

You can find these two programs on the companion CD to this book as *0201.bas* and *0202.bas*.

Accordingly, the following program would not be possible:

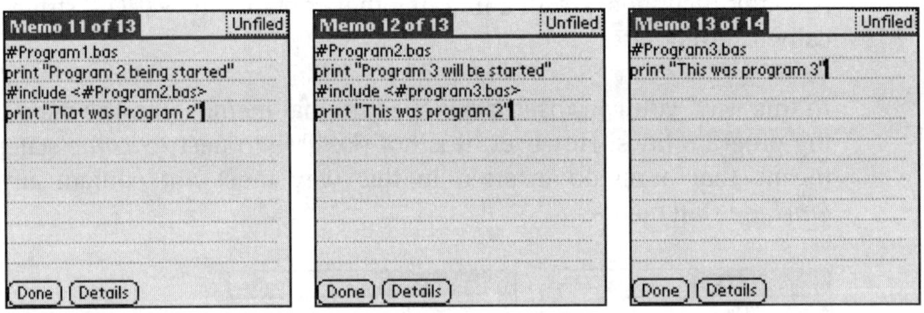


*Sequence of output for the program*

Now when you start Program 1, the following occurs:

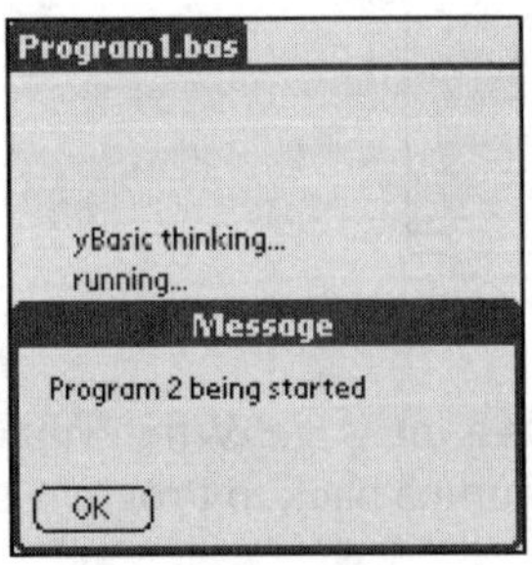


*Program 1 starts Program 2*

*Program 2 attempts to start Program 3*

Program 3 does not start, because the call would be a nested *#include* statement. Thus the message "This is Program 3" does not appear. The entire program continues to run normally without calling Program 3.

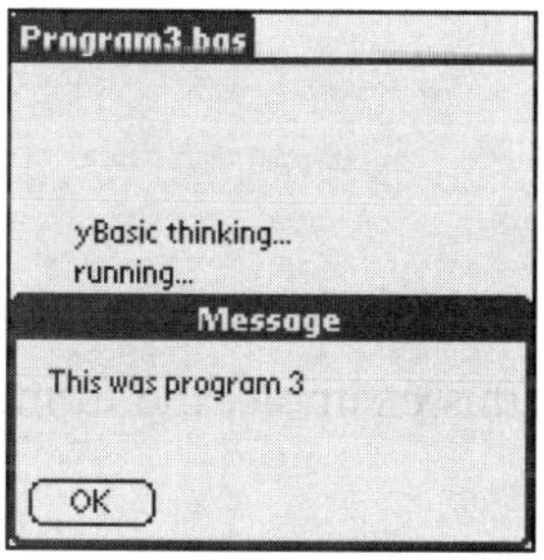


*Program 2 continues running*

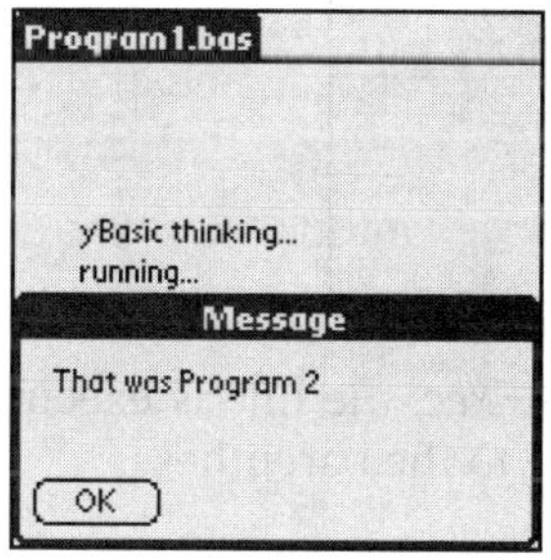


*back to Program 1 again*

## ScratchPad for testing Basic statements

If you want to quickly test a formula or perform a short calculation, don't go to the trouble of writing a program on a memo. HotPaw Basic has something called the ScratchPad, which can immediately perform an input Basic statement, similar to the direct input mode of most PC Basic interpreters.

You can open the ScratchPad from the main menu of HotPaw Basic with *Options/view ScratchPad* or */L*.

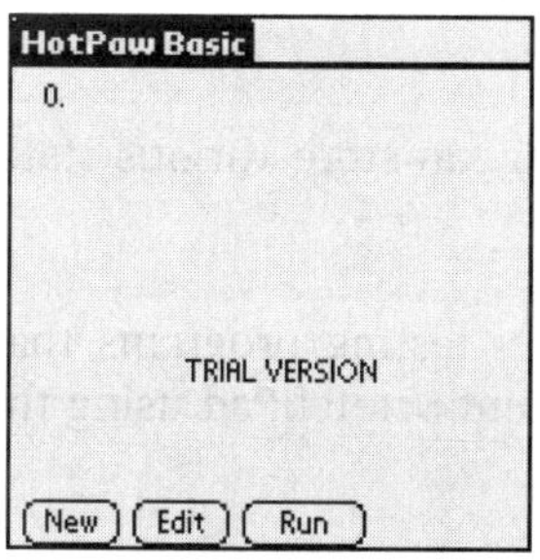


*The ScratchPad in HotPaw Basic*

The first time you start it, no entries appear. Highlight the first line with the 0 and tap *Edit*.

A text editor appears, in which you can enter Basic statements. To test a text line, highlight it.

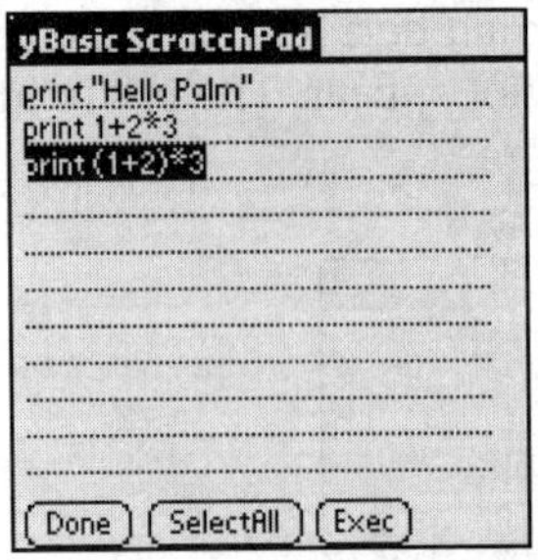


*Highlighted text line in the ScratchPad*

When you tap *Exec*, the line is executed. In this example, the formula is calculated according to the parentheses:

```
(1+2)*3
```

The *print* statement outputs the result in a predefined dialog box. Click *OK* to continue working on the ScratchPad.

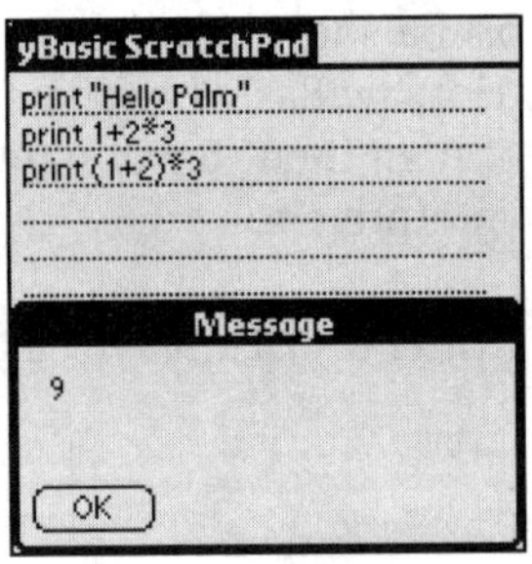


*The executed program line*

Only the highlighted line is executed, so you can store various statements here as a note and test them.

The ScratchPad also gives you the option of testing programs that consist of more than one line. To do this, exit the current ScratchPad using the *Done* button and then create a new one using *New*.

Enter the program text here; remember that each line must have a line number. At the very beginning a line must contain

```
new
```

while

```
run
```

must appear at the end of a line. These two lines must not contain any line numbers.

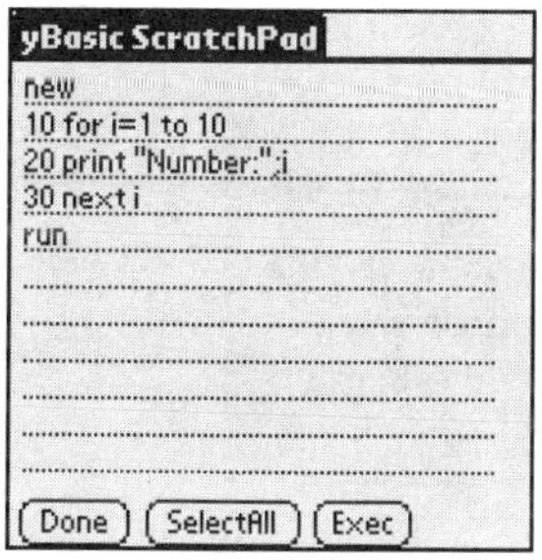


*Short program in the ScratchPad*

To run the program, tap *SelectAll* and then tap *Exec.*

This program consists of a simple loop :

```
10 for i=1 to 10
..
30 next i
```

Everything between these two lines will be repeated, whereby the *i* variable assumes the values of 1 through 10. Thus in the example, ten repetitions take place.

Accordingly, the line:

```
20 print "Number: ";i
```

is executed ten times. Each of these *print* statements brings a standard dialog box on the screen that has to be confirmed with *OK.*

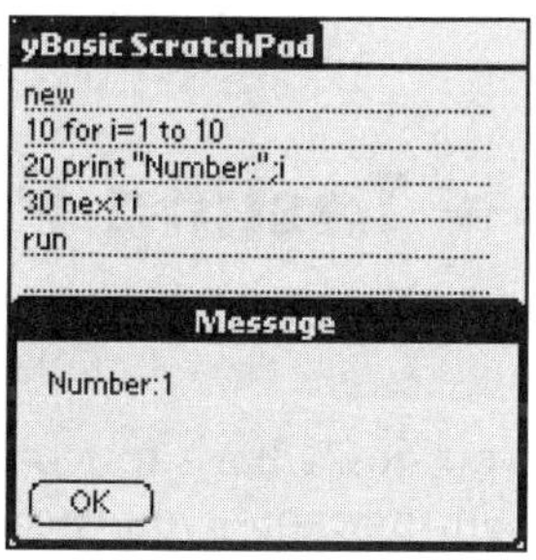


*Running program in the ScratchPad*

The text *Number:* and the number *i* appear in the message. The semicolon between them causes both elements to be output within a *print* statement immediately after each other.

> **Tip**
>
> **Use the Clipboard**
>
> The ScratchPad supports the Palm OS Clipboard. You can copy the tested programs directly to a memo to make "proper" programs out of them. Conversely, you can copy single lines from memos to the ScratchPad to test them.

If you test programs again and again, they might run amuck. For example, if you already see an error at the beginning or if the program runs without purpose for an indefinite time, you can cancel the action two ways:

- Tap *Done* or press the Date Book button.
- If the program is currently showing an input box, choose *Options/Stop* or enter the */X* Graffiti character.

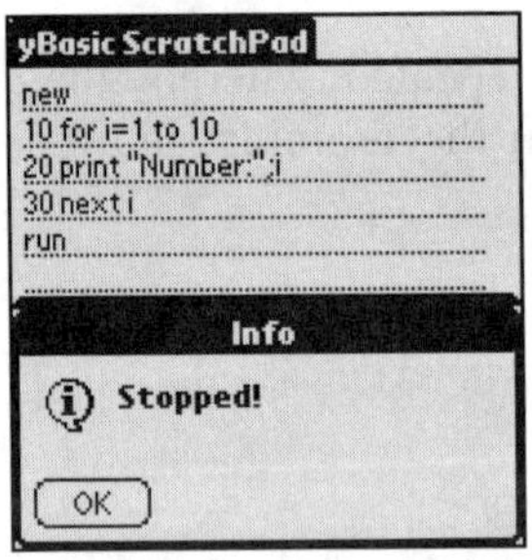


*A program stopped by using Options/Stop*

The second method returns you to the ScratchPad immediately after confirming the message.

## 2.2 The Palm OS Emulator – Testing Palm Programs on the PC

Another advantage of the Emulator is that you don't have to jeopardize your valuable Palm data with defective programs. Furthermore, you can use your PC keyboard for data input on the Emulator.

If you want to test programs on different versions of the Palm, simply start multiple emulator sessions with a different OS ROM loaded in each session (using different ROMs with the emulator is explained later in this chapter). This is certainly a better solution than having to obtain multiple pieces of Palm hardware. Why buy extra Palm devices when you can test the programs right on your PC?

*The Palm OS Emulator*

The Palm OS Emulator (POSE for short) simulates a Palm on the PC. The user interface is absolutely identical to that of the Palm.

The Emulator-specific functions, such as the creating of a screenshot or the installation of applications, are available in a context menu that you access by right-clicking the emulated Palm in the display.

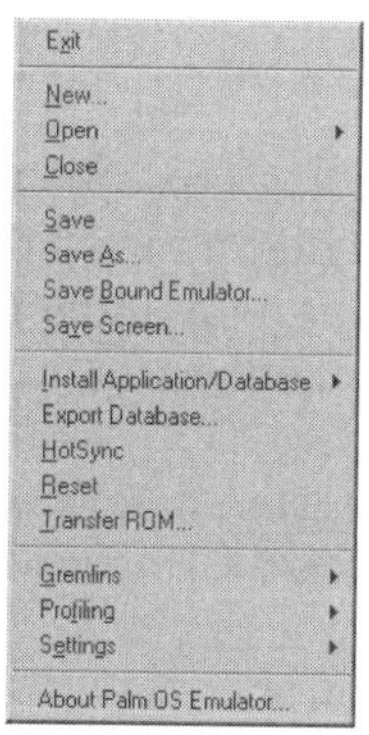


*The Context menu in the Palm OS Emulator*

**Internet**

**Emulator download**

You can find the current version of the Emulator at
http://www.palmos.com/dev/tech/tools/emulator/

Palm OS Emulators are also available for Linux and Macintosh. Although you can test Palm programs with them, this book focuses on the Windows version because the CASL development environment is only available for Windows.

## Transferring the Palm OS-ROM

For copyright reasons, by default this emulator does not contain a ROM with the Palm OS. However, it does contain a function with which you can retrieve the ROM of your Palm from the docking station and integrate it into the emulator.

**Note**

**The ROM**

The ROM is part of a computer's operating system and is in a memory module that cannot be overwritten (ROM = **R**ead **O**nly **M**emory). This module is not just hardware; it contains software protected by copyright, which may not be distributed. Emulators usually have functions for retrieving original ROM modules as files and thereby use the genuine operating system in the emulator.

First, install the *ROM transfer.prc* file, which comes supplied with the emulator, on your Palm. Then disable the HotSync Manager because the transfer program would not be able to control the interface otherwise.

When you start the Emulator without the ROM, a dialog box appears in which you can load a ROM from the Palm using the *Download* button. If the emulator is already running and you still want to load a ROM from a different Palm version, choose the *Transfer ROM* option in the Emulator context menu.

A wizard appears. Set the port, to which the docking station is connected, and the transfer speed.

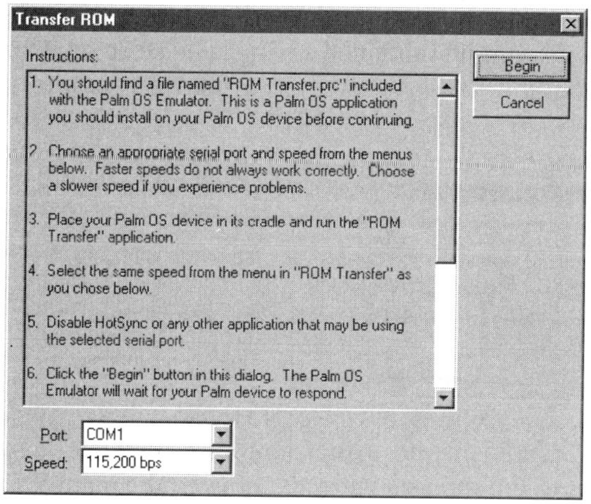


*Selecting the port and the transfer speed*

Plug the Palm into the docking station and call the ROM Transfer program. Set the same transfer speed.

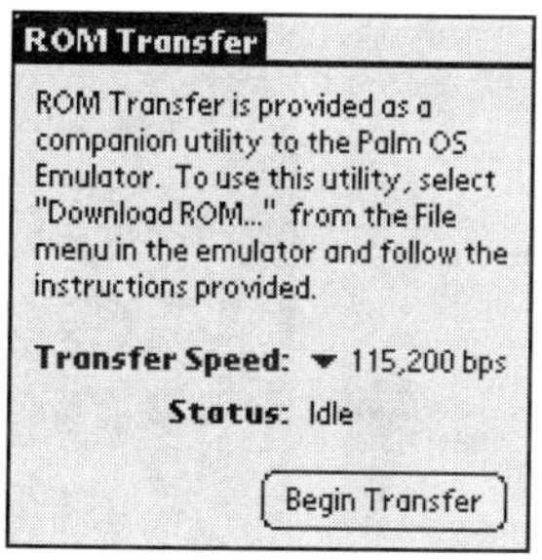


*The ROM Transfer program on the Palm*

Tap *Begin Transfer*. Do not press the HotSync button!

*Transferring the Palm's ROM*

After the download operation has concluded, a prompt asks you to name the ROM save as file.

Now start a new Emulator session.

Next, set which Palm model is to be simulated and designate the amount of RAM. Select the ROM file you just finished saving. The selected Palm model has to match the corresponding ROM, because it is the only way to simulate the Palm exactly.

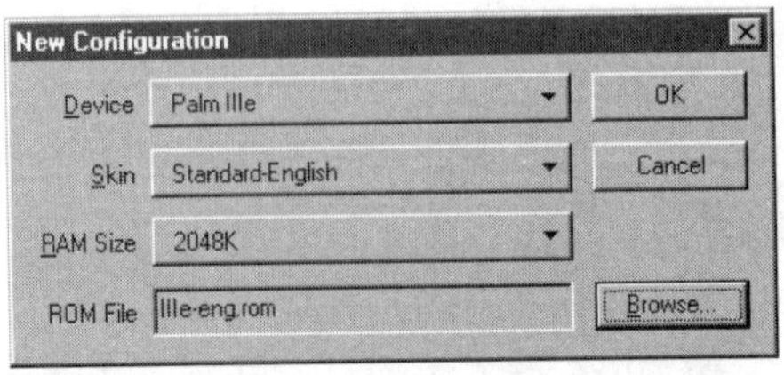


*Starting a new Emulator session*

Depending on which ROM you are using, you can duplicate any device you want, from an old Pilot to the modern Palm Vx, or even the Palm VII.

Emulation options for the TRGpro, the IBM WorkPad and the Visor, are also available, provided you have the correct ROM.

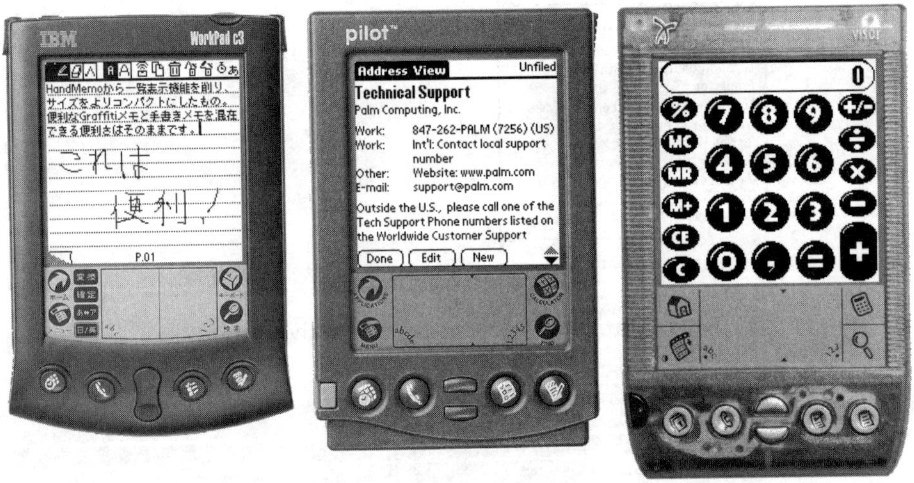


*Variuos emulated devices*

It is even possible to duplicate a Japanese IBM WorkPad on the Emulator, making it easier to test Japanese programs. The Japanese version has additional soft buttons in the Graffiti area for inputting special characters in conjunction with the Japanese Graffiti shorthand, which is only contained in Japanese Palm OS versions.

# Installing Programs in the Emulator

Ordinarily you would use the Palm OS Emulator to test programs without having to install them on an actual Palm. Choose the *Install Application/Database* option in the context menu of the Emulator. You will find a list of the last programs installed. Using the *Other* menu item, install any PRC or PDB files.

If the Emulator is currently displaying the program startup interface, you must call a program first and then return to the startup interface to see the icon for the newly installed program.

You can save several sessions with the Emulator, whereby the complete memory contents are stored in a file with the *.psf* extension, including all installed programs and data. Choose the *Save As* option in the context menu of the Emulator. This process allows you to use different configurations and even different Palms in the Emulator.

# Skins

Skinning is in.

Today's programs offer numerous options for completely changing a program's look and feel. The current Palm OS Emulator has an interface for skins, so you can create your own. Although skins have no practical application, they are attractive.

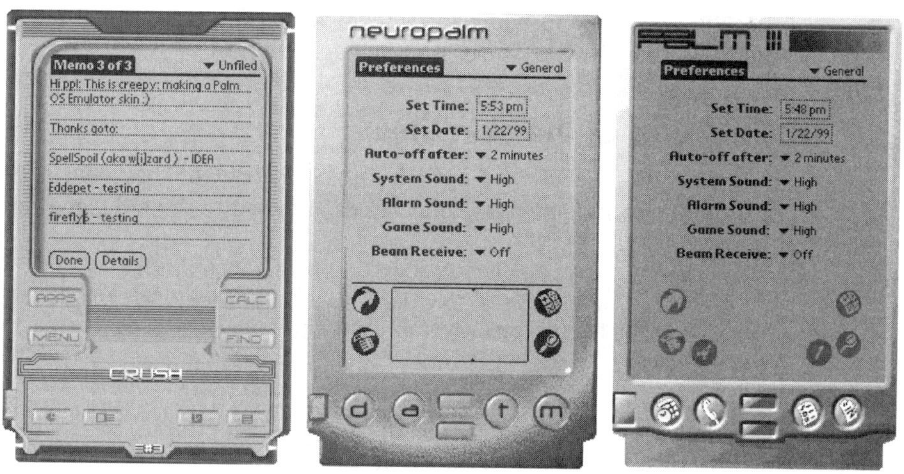


*Different skins*

These skins consist of a file with the. *skin* extension, in which the location of the individual buttons is stored, along with the suitable specification for specific Palm models. Two image files are included, one for the normal size and one for twice the size of the emulator. The two images cannot be fundamentally different because the coordinates of the buttons and display elements are only specified for the normal size, and the coordinates for the double size must be calculated from them.

To use the skins, copy all the files to the *Skins_v1.1* subdirectory of the Palm Emulator. Then choose the *Settings/Skins* option in the context menu of the Palm OS Emulator.

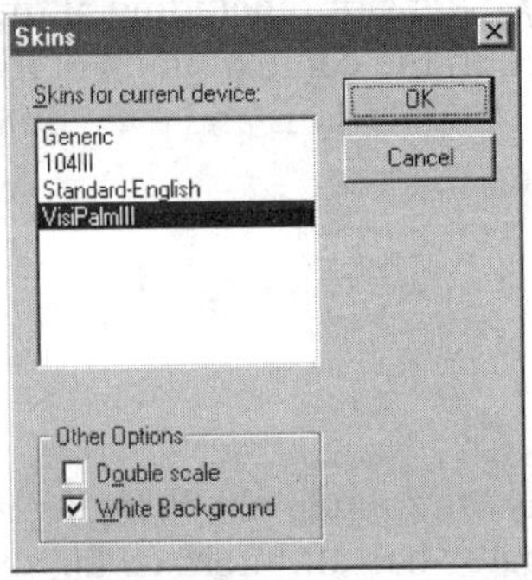


*Selecting different skins*

Select a skin in this dialog box. Only those skins that are suitable for the Palm model currently being used appear. You can also choose the size and set the background color to white for screenshots. (This option will not work for the Palm IIIc, which always uses a white background.)

## Structure of the skin files

The skin files are created entirely in ASCII format. They consist of predefined parameters, which have specific values assigned to them depending on the skin. Note this example:

```
# This is a skin file for the Palm OS Emulator. See the ReadMe.txt
# file in this directory for a description of its contents.

Name            = Pilot
File1x          = Palm_Pilot_16.jpg
File2x          = Palm_Pilot_32.jpg
BackgroundColor = 0x7B, 0x8C, 0x5A
HighlightColor  = 0x64, 0xF0, 0xDC
```

```
Devices          = Pilot1000, Pilot5000, PalmPilotPersonal,
                   PalmPilotProfessional

#                                x     y     w     h
#                              ----  ----  ----  ----
Element1   = PowerButton,         5,  287,   14,   22
Element2   = UpButton,          104,  285,   26,   12
Element3   = DownButton,        104,  307,   26,   12
Element4   = App1Button,         30,  285,   25,   25
Element5   = App2Button,         68,  285,   25,   25
Element6   = App3Button,        139,  285,   25,   25
Element7   = App4Button,        178,  285,   25,   25
Element11  = Touchscreen,        37,   39,  160,  220
Element12  = LCD,                37,   39,  160,  160
```

The lines that begin with a # character are only comments and are not required. A description of the different parameters follows. Use the same case for the names of the parameters that are in this book.

| | |
|---|---|
| *Name* | Specifies the name of the skin that is to appear in the pick list. |
| *File1x* | Filename of the image file for the normal size of the emulator. |
| *File2x* | Filename of the image file for double the size of the emulator. |
| *BackgroundColor* | Background color as three hexadecimal values for R, G, B. |
| *HighlightColor* | Background color with enabled background illumination as three hexadecimal values for R, G, B. |
| *Devices* | Device types with which this skin functions. You can use the following names in the current emulator: *Pilot1000, Pilot5000, PalmPilotPersonal, PalmPilotProfessional, PalmIII, PalmIIIc, PalmIIIe, PalmIIIx, PalmV, PalmVx, PalmVII, PalmVIIEZ, Symbol1700, Visor* |
| *Element#* | The various buttons and display elements are listed. Some elements only exist with certain Palm models. For each element the x and y coordinates of the upper left corner are specified after the name, whereby the zero point is in the upper left corner of the image file. After that the width and height of the element follow. The buttons are variable in size. The sizes of the touchscreen and the LCD field cannot be changed. |

You will find the names of the buttons in the following table:

| Name | Meaning | Comment |
|---|---|---|
| PowerButton | On/Off button | |
| UpButton | Scroll up | |
| DownButton | Scroll down | |
| App1Button | Date Book | |

| Name | Meaning | Comment |
|---|---|---|
| App2Button | Address Book | |
| App3Button | ToDo List | |
| App4Button | Memo Pad | |
| CradleButton | HotSync button | Not contained in the standard skin. Only functions when the skin displays a docking station. |
| Antenna | Pull out antenna | Only with Palm VII, activated by clicking the antenna |
| ContrastButton | Contrast setting | Only with the Palm V series |
| Touchscreen | Entire touch sensitive area including the Graffiti field | Always 160 x 220 |
| LCD | Screen | Always 160 x 160 |

The coordinates are only specified for the normal size. The emulator automatically calculates them for the double size.

**Internet**

**Skins on the Internet**

You can find additional skins, not only for the Palm OS Emulator, but also for different other programs, at http://skinz.org and http://customize.org.

# 2.3 SaveToHost and SwitchHack make programming easier

With HotPaw Basic you can also program on the emulator. Two small tools are explained here that will make your routine programming easier.

## SwitchHack

SwitchHack is a Hackmaster enhancement that lets you easily toggle back and forth between several Palm applications. For example, you can switch between the program and the memo with the source text in HotPaw Basic without having to use the program startup interface.

# 3. Performing simple calculations

Every computer program is based on mathematical calculations, even if the calculations are not apparent. In fact, the word *computer* comes from the verb *to compute,* which means *to calculate.*

## 3.1 The four fundamental operations of arithmetic in the Palm OS

You can perform simple calculations in HotPaw Basic using the ScratchPad. As long as you want to display the results only, use the simple *print* function, which you learned about in the previous chapter. This function outputs the results of the calculation in a standard dialog box.

*Simple calculation with the ScratchPad*

HotPaw Basic uses the four fundamental operations of arithmetic (+ - * /) as well as the modulo function (*mod* = remainder in whole number division) and the exponential function (^ - corresponds to the superscript exponents in normal mathematical notation), and to other Basic dialects as well. Use these basic arithmetic operations just as you would in a mathematical formula. You don't have to pay attention to a special syntax, as used by some other programmable pocket calculators.

Remember that the arithmetic rule "point before line" applies. The operators are executed in the following sequence:

| Operators | Meaning |
|---|---|
| ( ) | The contents of the parentheses are calculated first in a formula |
| - | Minus sign in front of negative numbers |
| ^ | Exponent 2^3 corresponds mathematically to $2^3$ |
| * / mod | Multiplication, division, modulo (mod calculates the whole number remainder in an integer division) |
| = < > <= >= <> | Equals, less than, greater than, less than or equal to, greater than or equal to, unequal |
| not | Logical not |
| and | Logical and (linking of two conditions that both have to be true simultaneously) |
| or xor | Logical or (linking of two conditions, at least one of which must be true), Logical Xor (linking of two conditions, of which precisely one must be true, but not both) |

**Tip**

### The modulo function

Modulo calculates the whole number remainder in the division of whole numbers. For example, if you divide 9 by 4, the result is 2 with a remainder of 1, which cannot be divided integrally. This function is used in the synthesizer technology for generating sawtooth waves. If you represent the results as a function curve, the value increases steadily and then abruptly falls to 0. The entire procedure repeats itself over and over again, for example:
8 mod 4, 9 mod 4 ... 16 mod 4 = 0, 1, 2, 3, 0, 1, 2, 3, 0.

*Examples of calculations with the mod function*

Using parentheses, you can change the calculation of the last illustrated formula. The contents of the parentheses are always calculated first. This result is then used for further calculation. As noted in the following illustrations, this can lead to different results.

*Differing results with parentheses set differently*

With simple numbers, you can input this directly, as shown in the illustrations, by writing the numbers in the program source code. On the other hand, if you want to continue using the result or if you are dealing with changing values, you must use variables in the formulas. To avoid errors when dealing with complicated numbers that occur repeatedly, using variables is a good idea.

*Calculating with fixed input values*

> **Note**
>
> **Decimal point**
>
> HotPaw Basic and CASL use the period as a decimal point.

Variables are single letters or character combinations that symbolize a numerical value. The program can change them at any time. Variable names can be up to 15 characters long. In most cases fewer characters suffice and, in fact, avoid unnecessarily long text lines that clutter up the source code.

To write the same program with variables, you need a few more program lines, but to make up for it, the program is far more diverse.

For multiple line programs, you have to use line numbers on the ScratchPad. Otherwise, the yBasic interpreter cannot process the program and reports an error. There are no problems in reading memos without line numbers.

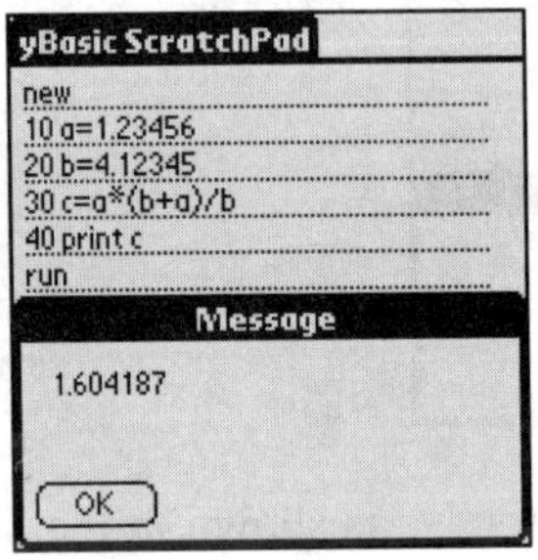


*Program with variables on the ScratchPad*

In this example the variables *a* and *b* are assigned the two numerical values. The result after calculation is in variable *c*. This is output using the *print* statement.

You can also write the program as a proper program, that is, as a memo to save yourself the trouble of entering line numbers and the *new* and *run* statements. However, you must have a program name in the first line. You can copy the program text directly from the ScratchPad to the memo using the Clipboard. The syntax is exactly the same.

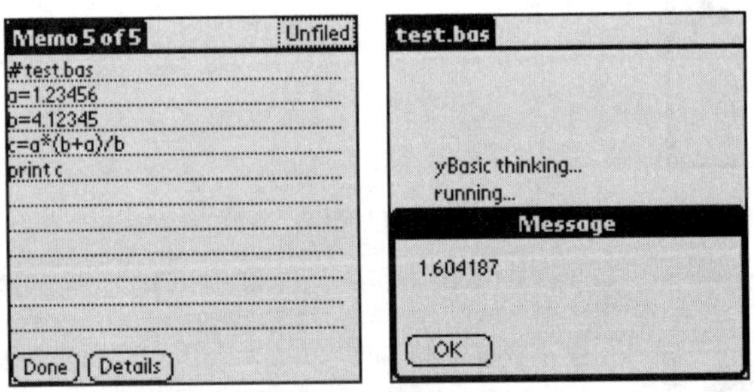


*The program as a memo and the output of the results*

**CD**

**Program on the companion CD**

You can also find this program on the companion CD to this book as *0301.bas.*

## Converting units of measurement

Using a similarly simple formula, convert degrees Fahrenheit (°F) into degrees Celsius (°C). The basic, complicated formula reads:

$$°C = \frac{°F - 32}{1.8}$$

Converted in Basic this becomes:

```
c=(f-32)/1.8
```

Use parentheses to cancel out the point -before- line rule.

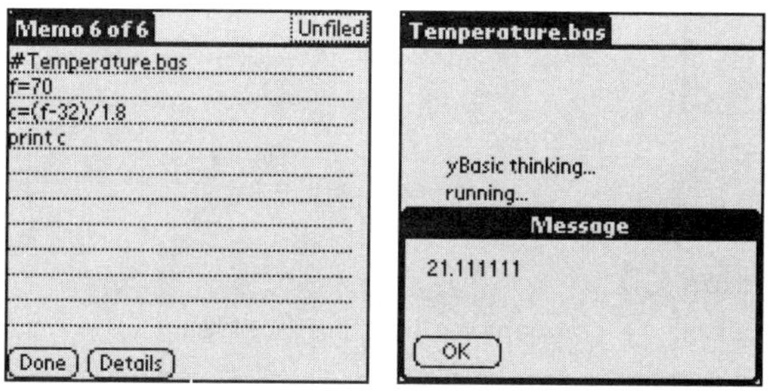


*The program as a memo and the output of the results*

**CD**

**Program on the companion CD**

You can also find this program on the companion CD to this book as *0302.bas*.

In variable *f* there is a value in °F. Using the formula, convert it into °C and then store it in the variable *c*. This is then output, using the *print* function.

However, the program is limited in this form: To calculate another value, the information must be entered in source code by changing the variable *f*. Because this is not a user-friendly solution, you must build an input form into the program to enter the desired value.

# 3.2 Forms for data input and output

For such cases, which occur in almost every program, not only do all programming languages offer the option of outputting values, they also enable the user to enter values during the program run. Programs that run completely on their own without interaction from the outside would always yield the same result and are therefore seldom used.

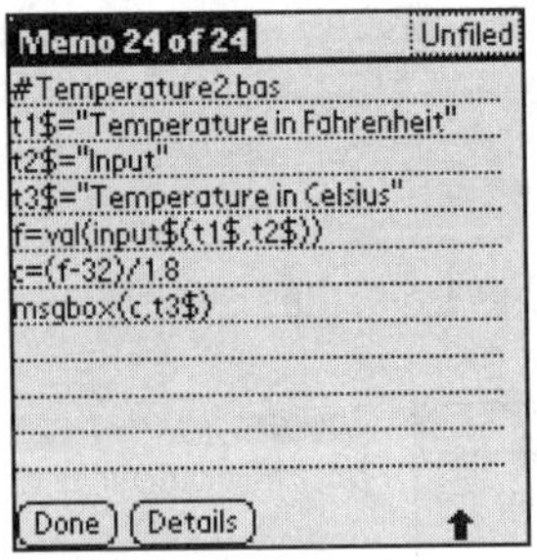


*Program for converting from °F to °C*

**CD**

**Program on the companion CD**

You can also find this program on the companion CD to this book as *0303.bas.*

This program offers an input option for the user. The first three text variables are defined in the first program lines for use in the dialog boxes.

**Note**

**Definition of string variables**

Variables that are used for storing texts and other strings must contain a $ character as the last character of the variable name. A maximum of 63 string variables may be defined in a program.

After the definition of the three text variables comes the prompt to enter a value in °F.

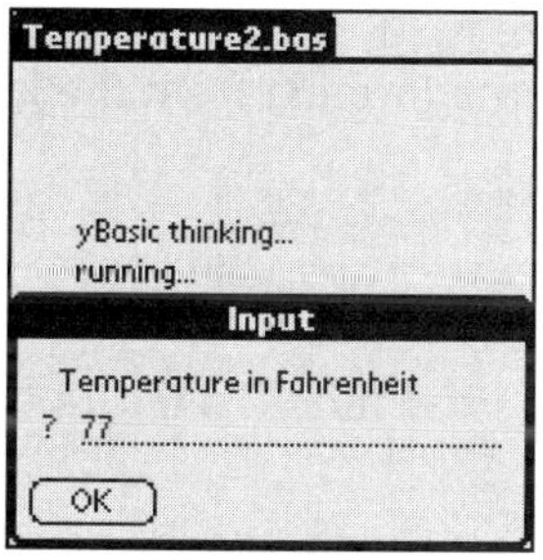


*Input form*

Use the *input$()* function.

### *input$( prompt$,[title$[ , default$ ] ] )*

This function can use three parameters, whereby the last two are optional:

- ***prompt$*** – Explanatory text line in the input form.
- ***title$*** – Text in the window title line.
- ***default$*** – Default value for the input.

In the example

```
f=val(input$(t1$,t2$))
```

the *t1$* variable ("Temperature in Fahrenheit") as *prompt$* and the *t2$* variable ("Input") as *title$* for the window title lines appear.

The *input$* function always returns a string. However, you need a numerical value for the conversion. yBasic uses the *val()* function for conversion.

### *val(a$)*

This function determines a numerical value from the a$ string.

**Note**

**Maximum of eight parenthetical levels**

Nesting functions, as in this example, you can write code that is significantly shorter. However, a maximum of eight parenthetical levels can be nested within each other. More than eight levels results in a Stack Overflow Error. Normally, you won't need eight parenthetical levels. If this is not sufficient, you must work with variables for temporary storage. In the example, it would look like this:

```
f$=input$(t1$,t2$)
f=val(f$)
```

The numerical value of the input temperature in °F is now in the *f* variable. In the next line, this is converted into °C using the formula from the last example, and then it is stored in the *c* variable.

```
c=(f-32)/1.8
```

To output this variable, don't use the simple *print* function but rather the more convenient *msgbox()*.

### *msgbox( message$ [ , title$ [ , n ] ] )*

This function can use up to three parameters and creates output similar to *print*; however, you can write any text in the window title line.

- ***message$*** - Value that is to be output. This can be a string or a numerical value.
- ***title$*** - Text in the window title line.
- ***n*** - If a 2 occurs here, two buttons appear in the output form, *OK* and *Cancel*. If a 1 occurs here or no value at all, only an *OK* button appears.

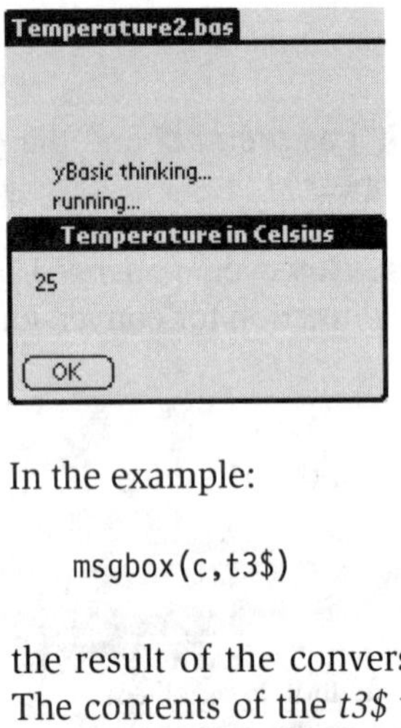


*Output of the converted value*

In the example:

```
msgbox(c,t3$)
```

the result of the conversion, which is in the *c* variable, is output as *message$*. The contents of the *t3$* variable ("Temperature in Celsius") appears in the window title line.

# Loan calculation

Naturally, more complicated formulas are also possible. The next example shows how to calculate a loan. The calculation occurs through a predefined financial function.

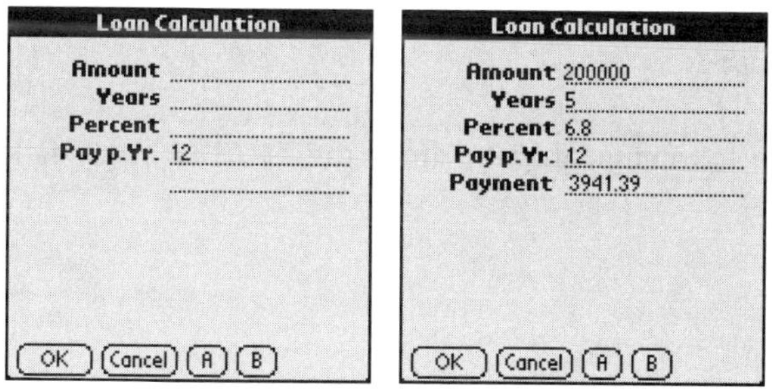


*The program after startup and the output of the results*

The input and output form is of special interest. Use a standard function for forms integrated in yBasic.

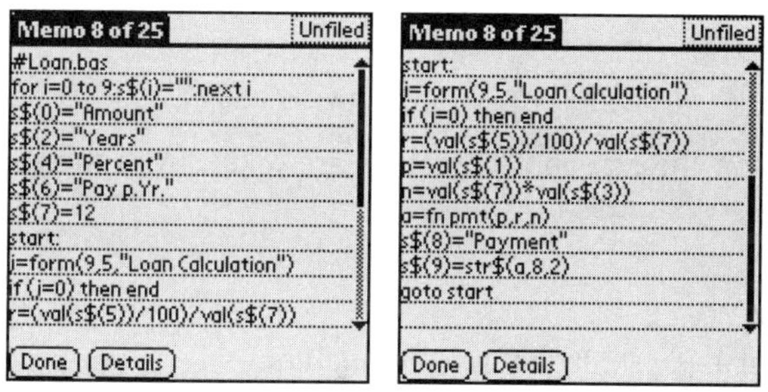


*The program for loan calculation*

**CD**

**Program on the companion CD**

You can also find this program on the companion CD to this book as *0304.bas*.

In yBasic a predefined data field *s$(0) ... s$(63)* occurs. This field can be used together with the *form()* function for inputting and outputting strings.

Only the first ten variables of this field are used in the program. These are all set to a blank string "" in the first program line because variables can contain uncontrolled memory fragments at program startup. yBasic does not know any global variables that can be preserved after the termination of a program and can be used later by other programs.

```
for i=0 to 9:s$(i)="":next i
```

The *form()* function creates a two-column form in which the *s$(i)* variables with even numbers specify the field labels and the variables with the odd numbers specify the value field.

Accordingly, in the following program lines the *s$(0) ... s$(6)* fields are filled with the field labels.

The line:

```
start:
```

serves only as a branch mark and is not used by the program until later.

In the line:

```
j=form(9,5,"Loan calculation")
```

the form is placed on the screen. The values are taken from the *s$(n)* variable field.

### form(9,n,title$)

The *form()* function always needs three parameters:

- *9* - This number specifies the type of form. The 9 stands for a two-column form.
- *n* - A number between 2 and 9 that specifies the number of lines in the form.
- ***title$*** - Text in the window title line.

Note that four buttons with the labels *OK, Cancel, A,* and *B* are automatically created at the bottom border of the form. If the user taps on one of these buttons, a value corresponding to the following table is returned, which can be evaluated by the program.

| Button | Return value |
|---|---|
| OK | 1 |
| Cancel | 0 |
| A | 2 |
| B | 3 |

The return values of buttons *A* and *B* can be evaluated program dependently if necessary.

The program stops here, until the user taps one of the buttons. Up to this point you can make any necessary changes. After you tap a button, the program can evaluate the return value and then continue running.

In the example, the return value is stored in the *j* variable.

```
j=form(9,5,"Loan calculation")
if (j=0) then end
```

If you tap *Cancel*, the value 0 is in the *j* variable and the program terminates. If you tap one of the other buttons, the program continues normally and the calculation starts.

The following program lines calculate the results from the values that the user enters from the form in the *s$(1)*, *s$(3)* and *s$(5)* variables.

```
r=(val(s$(5))/100)/val(s$(7))
```

divides the yearly interest rate by the number of installments and thus determines the interest for each installment.

**Note**

**Form input always contains strings**

Keep in mind that the input fields of such a form always contain strings. If the values are to be used for mathematical calculations, you have to convert them into numerical values using the *val()* function.

The next program line:

```
p=val(s$(1))
```

writes the numerical value of the loan amount from the *s$(1)* input field to the *p* variable.

```
n=val(s$(7))*val(s$(3))
```

calculates the number of total installments to be paid from the number of years and the installments per year.

Use an externally defined function for the actual financial calculation.

### fn pmt(p,r,n)

This function calculates the amount of an installment from the loan amount, the interest, and the number of installments. For this purpose, three parameters are passed:

- ***p*** - Loan amount at the beginning prior to the first payment.
- ***r*** - Interest rate per installment.
- ***n*** - Number of total installments to be paid.

After the calculations are completed, the program writes the *"Payment"* field label and the calculated result in the last field, which has been blank up to now. This must first be converted into a string.

```
s$(9)=str$(a,8,2)
```

### str$(x,n,2)

creates a string from a numerical value and automatically truncates it after the second decimal place.

- ***x*** - The numerical value that is to be converted.
- ***n*** - Maximum number of characters in the string.

After that the program jumps back to the *start* branch mark with the *goto* command

```
goto start
```

The *form()* function is at the *start* branch mark again, which now writes the form on the screen again with the newly calculated values.

### goto n

The program jumps to a branch mark. This consists of a name that cannot match any used variable name. The branch mark must be alone in a line and end with a colon (:). If the program uses line numbers, the parameter *n* can be a line number instead of a branch mark.

## Euro currency conversion

In the next example you won't just convert a single value into another, but into several at the same time. The program converts a price in Euros into different national currencies simultaneously. The conversion itself is simple because the conversion rates are fixed.

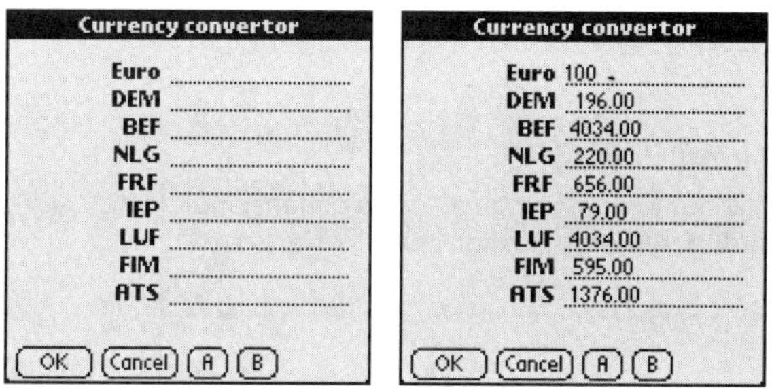


*The program for currency calculation at startup and with calculated values*

Use a *form()* function again for outputting the values.

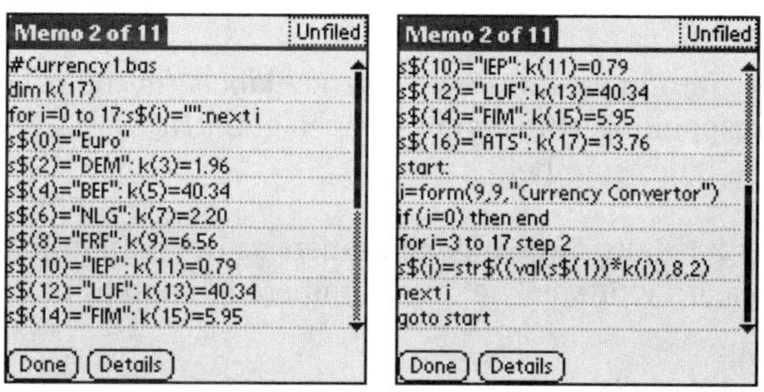


*The source code*

**CD**

**Program on the companion CD**

You can also find this program on the companion CD to this book as *0305.bas*.

In addition to the variable field for input and output, use an additional *k(n)* field in which the conversion rates of the individual currencies compared to the Euro are stored. Such self-defined variable fields must be dimensioned prior to their first use; that is, you have to specify beforehand how many variables you want to use in such a field:

```
dim k(17)
```

### *dim VAR( a [ , b ] )*

This statement dimensions a field (= Array). Such a field can have up to two dimensions. The *a, b* parameters specify the highest value in the first and second dimensions. The lowest permissible value in both dimensions is always 0. Variable fields are often processed with loops. You can always have them begin with 0.

**Note**

**Only one-dimensional string fields**

Variable fields that contain string variables can be one-dimensional only. The predefined *s$(n)* and *r$(n)* fields do not have to be dimensioned.

After the dimensioning of the *k(n)* field, the predefined *s$(n)* field is filled with blank strings up to the value 17.

```
for i=0 to 17:s$(i)="":next i
```

In the following program lines, different currency labels fill the even-numbered variables. The corresponding conversion rates in the *k(n)* variable are written with the next highest index number.

In this way the rates have the same index numbers as the output fields, in which the calculated values are written. The even-numbered variables of the *k(n)* field remain unused.

```
j=form(9,9,"Currency converter")
```

The form is defined as in the last example, only this time with nine lines.

```
if (j=0) then end
```

You can exit the program with the *Cancel* button.

After that comes the actual calculation:

```
for i=3 to 17 step 2
  s$(i)=str$((val(s$(1))*k(i)),8,2)
next i
```

In increments of two, results now fill the *s$(i)* variable field. Because the even-numbered variables contain the currency labels, only the odd variables may be processed.

In each variable the Euro value from *s$(1)* is multiplied by the *k(i)* rate value. The result is converted into a string with two decimal places with the *str$()* function.

In the line:

```
goto start
```

the program jumps back to the *start* branch mark and builds the form with the new values again.

## Currency conversion with variable rates

The conversion rates of the Euro currencies are fixed. However, the conversion rates for other currencies can fluctuate radically on a daily basis.

Most banks now specify the official mean rates compared to the Euro. For example, if you want to convert a DM amount into British pounds or US dollars, you must first convert the value into Euros and then into the other currency according to the current rate.

**Internet**

**Current currency rates**

You can find a table with rates of the most important currencies updated on a daily basis at http://www.commerzbank.de/news/indizes/devise_d.html. The sequence of the rate data listed here also corresponds to the sequence in which the data from the sample program is displayed.

The next program example has similar function but different currencies.

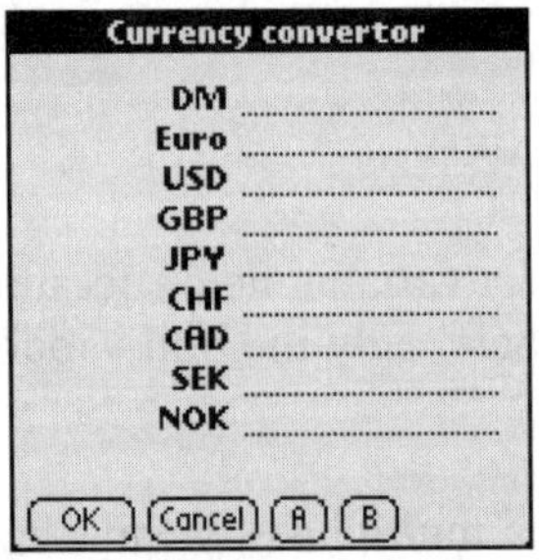


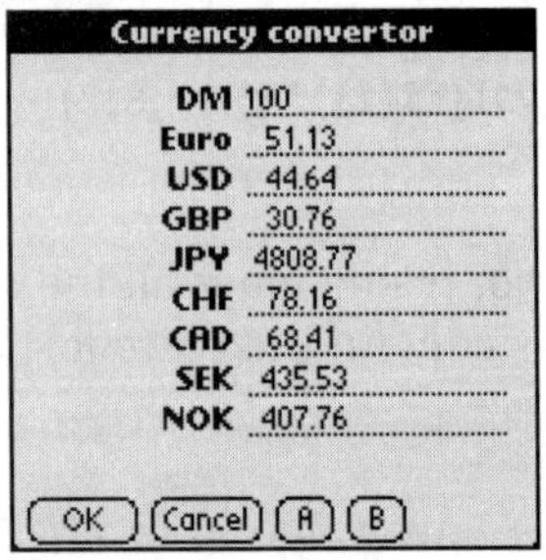


*The program for currency conversion at startup and with the calculated values*

Aside from the other currency labels, the calculation is slightly modified because the DM value is first converted into Euros.

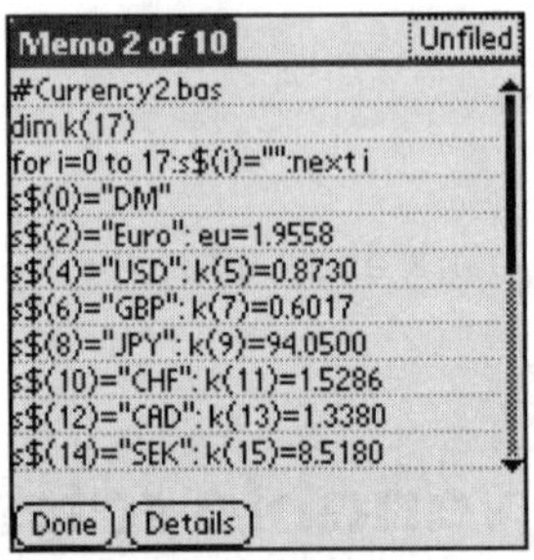


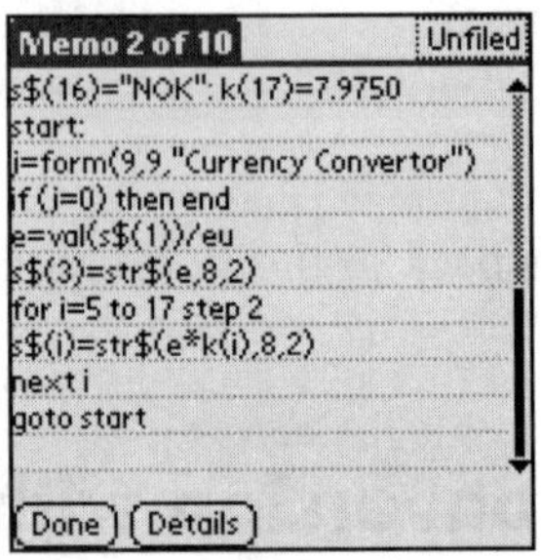


*The source code*

**CD**

**Program on the companion CD**

You can also find this program on the companion CD to this book as *0306.bas*.

The dimensioning of the *k(n)* field and the filling of the variable fields with different rate values proceeds exactly as in the preceding program version. The *eu* variable, in which the conversion rate Euro/DM is stored, is new.

```
s$(2)="Euro": eu=1.9558
```

After the form is created on the screen and the user has entered an amount in DM, it is converted into Euros and stored in the *e* variable.

```
e=val(s$(1))/eu
```

This value, converted into a string and shortened to two decimal places, is displayed in the *s$(3)* form field.

```
s$(3)=str$(e,8,2)
```

Use the *e* variable for further calculation of the individual rates and not the shortened value of *s$(3)* because the *e* variable still possesses complete accuracy.

```
for i=5 to 17 step 2
  s$(i)=str$(e*k(i),8,2)
next i
```

This loop begins now with the value 5 because the rates to be calculated do not start until the third line of the form. The *s$(1)* variable contains the DM amount; the *s$(3)* variable contains the converted value into Euros.

## Rate changes

One disadvantage of this program is that rate changes can only be taken into consideration if you change the source code. In the next version the rates are entered in such a way that the user can change them. A list appears below.

```
#Currency3.bas
dim k(17)
for i=0 to 17:s$(i)="":next i
  s$(0)="DM"
  s$(2)="Euro": eu=1.9558
  s$(4)="USD":k(5)=0.8730
  s$(6)="GBP":k(7)=0.6017
  s$(8)="JPY": k(9)=94.0500
  s$(10)="CHF": k(11)=1.5286
  s$(12)="CAD": k(13)=1.3380
  s$(14)="SEK": k(15)=8.5180
  s$(16)="NOK": k(17)=7.9750
  for i=5 to 17 step 2
  s$(i)=str$(k(i),8,4)
next i
start:
j=form(9,9,"Currency converter")
if (j=0) then end
e=val(s$(1))/eu
s$(3)=str$(e,8,2)
for i=5 to 17 step 2
  s$(i)=str$(e*val(s$(i)),8,2)
next i
goto start
```

> **CD**
>
> **Program on the companion CD**
>
> You can also find this program on the companion CD to this book as *0307.bas*.

The deciding difference to the previous version is that the rate data is writing to the form fields of the right column and thus can be changed directly by the user.

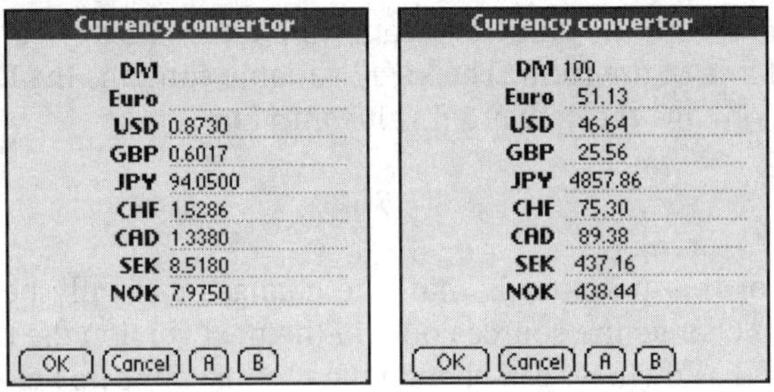


*The modified program for currency conversion at startup and with calculated values*

These lines

```
for i=5 to 17 step 2
  s$(i)=str$(k(i),8,4)
next i
```

write the *k(i)* rate values to the odd-numbered variables of the *s$(i)* data field before the form appears on the screen. An accuracy of four decimal places is used in the conversion into strings.

Now users cannot only enter an amount in DM but also change the rate values.

Naturally, the process only works if the changed values are used for calculation, not the original rates:

```
for i=5 to 17 step 2
  s$(i)=str$(e*val(s$(i)),8,2)
next i
```

Upon closer examination, this program change, which at first glance has such a useful appearance, has a catch: You can only have one value calculated, because after that the results are in the fields of the right column, no longer the rates. You must exit the program with *Cancel* and restart it, whereby the manually entered course changes are lost and the original rates from the source code are retrieved again.

The next program version offers an improvement in this regard. Use the two buttons *A* and *B* from the *form()* function.

```
#Currency4.bas
dim k(17)
for i=0 to 17:s$(i)="":next i
s$(0)="DM"
s$(2)="Euro": eu=1.9558
s$(4)="USD": k(5)=0.8730
s$(6)="GBP": k(7)=0.6017
s$(8)="JPY": k(9)=94.0500
s$(10)="CHF": k(11)=1.5286
s$(12)="CAD": k(13)=1.3380
s$(14)="SEK": k(15)=8.5180
s$(16)="NOK": k(17)=7.9750
abutton:
for i=5 to 17 step 2
  s$(i)=str$(k(i),8,4)
next i
start:
j=form(9,9,"Currency converter")
if (j=0) then end
if (j=2) then goto abutton
if (j=3) then goto bbutton
e=val(s$(1))/eu
s$(3)=str$(e,8,2)
for i=5 to 17 step 2
  s$(i)=str$(e*val(s$(i)),8,2)
next i
goto start
bbutton:
for i=5 to 17 step 2
  k(i)=val(s$(i))
next i
goto start
```

**CD**

**Program on the companion CD**

You can also find this program on the companion CD to this book as *0308.bas*.

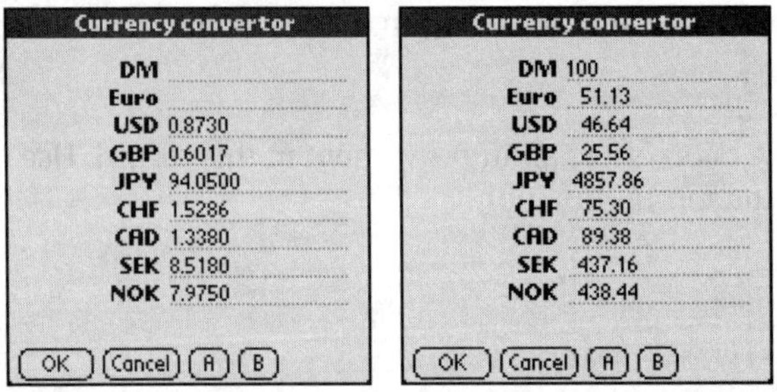


*The modified program at first acts the same in the calculation*

At program startup and during the first calculation, you won't notice any change. However, when you tap the *A* button after the calculation, the rates are displayed again instead of the calculation results.

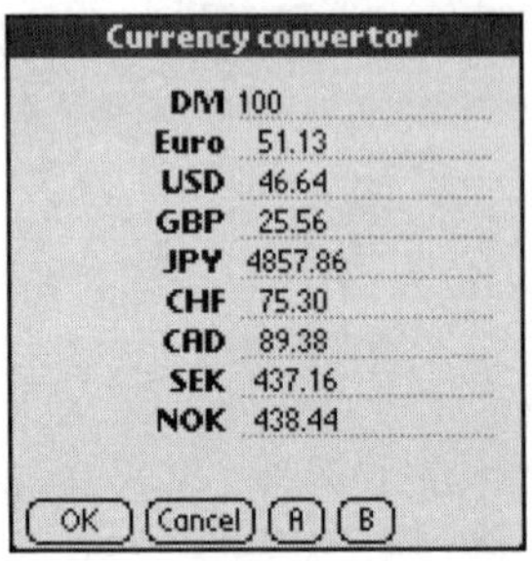


*Display of the rates*

This functions in the following manner:

```
j=form(9,9,"Currency converter")
if (j=0) then end
if (j=2) then goto abutton
```

If you tap the *A* button, the *form()* function returns the value 2, and the program jumps back to the *abutton* branch mark. This is located in the place where the rate data is written in the fields of the right form column.

```
abutton:
for i=5 to 17 step 2
s$(i)=str$(k(i),8,4)
next i
```

As long as the rates are displayed instead of the calculated results, you can change the rates in the form fields. If you tap the *B* button, these changed rates are saved.

```
j=form(9,9,"Currency converter")
if (j=0) then end
if (j=2) then goto abutton
if (j=3) then goto bbutton
```

If you tap the *B* button, the *form()* function returns the value 3, and the program jumps back to the *bbutton* branch mark. It is located in a place the program never accesses during normal operation because there is a *goto* statement in the line before it that is executed without further condition.

```
bbutton:
for i=5 to 17 step 2
  k(i)=val(s$(i))
next i
goto start
```

The changed values are written back from the odd-numbered *s$(i)* variables to the *k(i)* variables, in which the rate data is saved. After that the program jumps back to the place where the form is created on the screen and input is expected.

With this new data the program can continue calculating. To do this, enter a DM value and tap *OK* again.

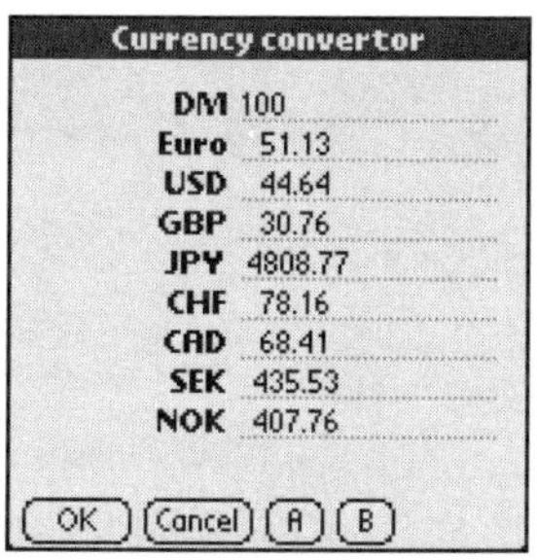


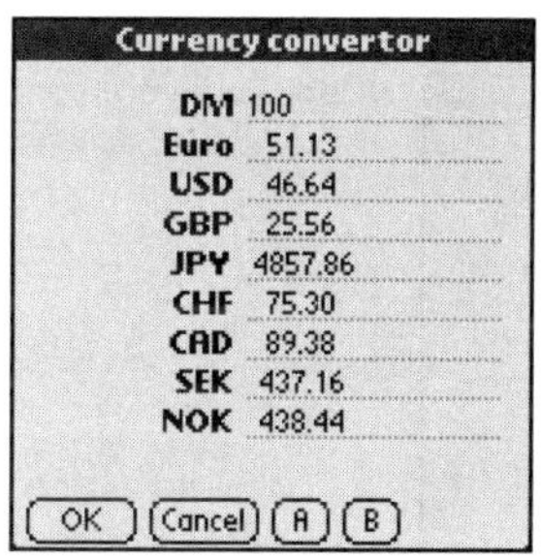


*Changed rates and the result*

On these figures the conversion rates for US$ (*USD*) and British pounds (*GBP*) were slightly modified. Compare the calculation results with the earlier illustrations.

**Note**

**No global variables**

HotPaw Basic is not familiar with any global variables. This means that when you exit a program, all the variables lose their values.

When you exit the program with *Cancel*, all the manual rate changes you made are lost. When you restart the program, the variables no longer contain any usable values and, in any case, must be reinitialized by the program.

## Memos as memory

As a programmer you have to learn to think creatively. A creative solution exists for every problem, even if the solution does not always follow conventional routes. For example, if a programming language does not offer a specific function, you must work your way around the limitation skillfully.

A currency converter of any practical use requires a permanent memory in which you can store the modified conversion rates to be available the next time you start the program. Unfortunately, yBasic does not offer this type of memory.

However, the Palm has other options, such as memos, for storing data permanently. To make use of this memory for the next program version,

first write a simple memo with the conversion rates. You must list them in the same order that the program displays them. In the first line of the memo, give it the name of *Rate table*.

Memo Pad

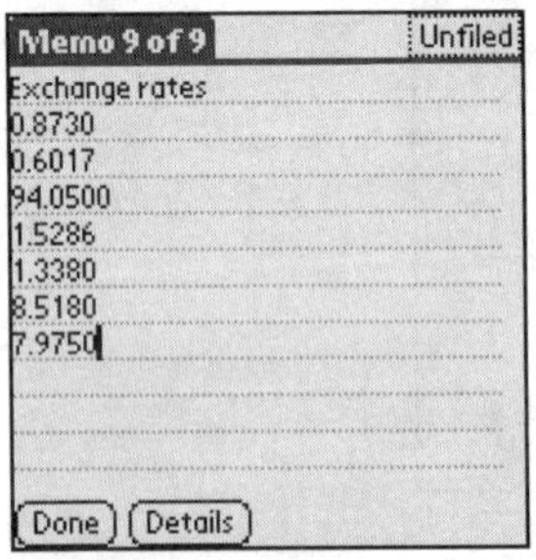


*Memo with conversion rates*

> **CD**
>
> **Program on the companion CD**
>
> You can also find this memo on the companion CD to this book as *0309.txt*.

| Order of the currencies on the memo | |
|---|---|
| USD | US dollar |
| GBP | British pound |
| JPY | Japanese yen |
| CHF | Swiss franc |
| CAD | Canadian dollar |
| SEK | Swedish krone |
| NOK | Norwegian krone |

You can easily modify this memo when rate changes occur. The program imports the rate data from the memo.

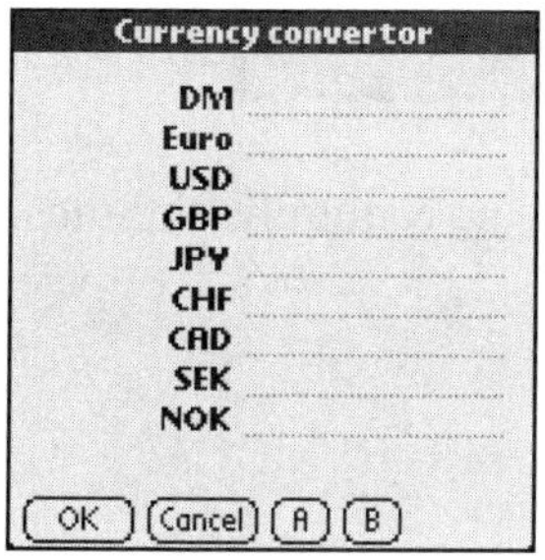


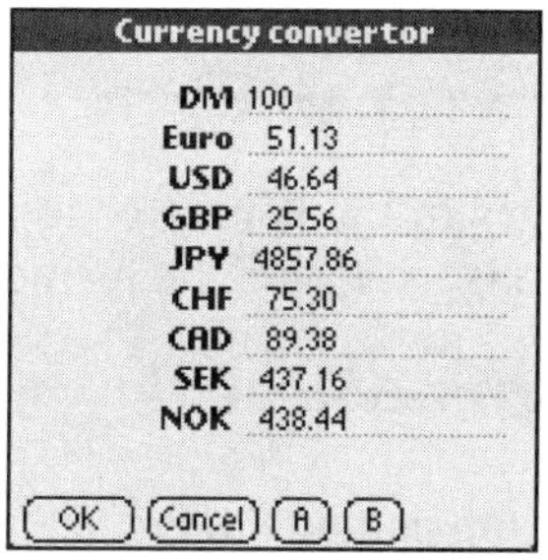


*The modified program still looks unchanged*

```
#Currency5.bas
dim k(17)
for i=0 to 17:s$(i)="":next i
s$(0)="DM"
s$(2)="Euro": eu=1.9558
s$(4)="USD"
s$(6)="GBP"
s$(8)="JPY"
s$(10)="CHF"
s$(12)="CAD"
s$(14)="SEK"
s$(16)="NOK"
m=db.find("memo","Rate table")
if (m<0) then goto error
open "memo",m as #1
  input #1,x$
  for i=5 to 17 step 2
    input #1,x$
    k(i)=val(x$)
  next i
close #1
start:
```

```
j=form(9,9,"Currency converter")
if (j=0) then end
e=val(s$(1))/eu
s$(3)=str$(e,8,2)
for i=5 to 17 step 2
  s$(i)=str$(e*k(i),8,2)
next i
goto start
error:
print "Rate table not found"
```

**CD**

**Program on the companion CD**

You can also find this program on the companion CD to this book as *0310.bas.*

Some critical changes in the source code occur. Naturally, the most interesting item is how the data is read from the memo:

```
m=db.find("memo","Rate table")
```

This line finds a memo named *Rate table.*

### *db.find("memo",title$)*

This function searches the list of memos for the *title$* string in the title line. The function begins searching the memos from the back so that if duplicate names occur, the last one is found first. The function returns the number of this memo. The function returns a negative value if it does not find a memo with the corresponding name.

```
if (m<0) then goto error
```

If you use the *db.find()*function, always build in a route where the program can go in case no matching memo is found. In the example the program jumps to the *error* branch mark, which is in a location in the text that the program never accesses during normal processing.

```
error:
print "Rate table not found"
```

The following error message is output :

*Error message when no matching memo is found*

If the memo named *Rate table* is found, it is opened for reading.

```
open "memo",m as #1
```

The number of the memo is taken from the *db.find()* function.

### *open "memo",m as #n*

This function opens a memo for the purpose of reading it. Two parameters are required for this:

- *m* - Number of the memo.
- *n* - Number of the opened file. yBasic can keep four files open simultaneously *#1* ... *#4*.

After the file is opened, it can be read out line by line.

```
input #1,x$
```

reads the first line of the memo, which contains the header, and writes the contents to the *x$* variable.

### *input #n,x$*

This function reads the current line of a memo. Each time the function is called, it reads the next line of the memo. The function has two parameters:

- *#n* - Number of the opened file.
- *x$* - Variable, to which the line is to be written.

After the header has been read, which the program does not further analyze, the additional lines are read one after the other in a loop and assigned to the *k(i)* variables, in which the rate values are stored.

```
for i=5 to 17 step 2
  input #1,x$
  k(i)=val(x$)
next i
```

> **Note**
>
> **Reading strings from memos**
>
> The *input* function always reads strings from memos. If you need numerical values for further calculations, you have to convert the read values using the *val()* function.

After the last line has been read, the opened file has to be closed again.

```
close #1
```

### *close #n*

This function closes an opened file. After that, another file can be opened under the same number.

- *#n* - Number of the opened file.

Once the program finishes taking data from the memo, it continues running. Whenever a conversion rate changes, make the necessary change in the memo. The program rereads the memo at every program start.

## 3.3 Forms and calculations in CASL

Calculations in CASL run in quite similar fashion to calculations in Basic; however, the input and output differ greatly. For each value that is to be input or output, a corresponding field must be defined on the screen. These forms usually take up the greatest part of the source code.

In the first example, you perform a very simple calculation, namely the conversion of a given value from °F to °C. In Basic this equals a total of three program lines. You could have written the formula in a single line. In CASL the same program is significantly more involved:

```
label cl;
  end;

variables;
  numeric c;
  numeric f=70;
  end;

function startup;
  c=(f-32)/1.8;
  put cl, c;
  end;
```

Remember that in CASL, every program line has to end with a semicolon.

**CD**

**Program on the companion CD**

You can also find this program on the companion CD to this book as *0311.csl.*

**Tip**

**Syntax check in color**

If you copy the program, you can rule out spelling errors by highlighting in color. CASL automatically writes all CASL statements and keywords in blue. In the sample program these are the words: *label, end, variables, numeric, function, put.*

Like most CASL programs, the program consists of three parts:

- Form definition for input and output.
- Variable declaration.
- Functions.

## Form definition

The first section of the form definition is as short as possible.

```
label cl;
  end;
```

Only one *label* is defined. A *label* is a field for text. Every *label* needs a name, in this case *c1*, so that the program can address it, and it must conclude with an *end*. Normally the *labels* contain additional parameters, such as their position on the screen. However, the example above is simple.

## Variable declaration

The second section of the program declares all occurring variables. In this example, only two occur. The *f* variable contains the initial value in °F; the *c* variable contains the newly calculated value in °C.

```
variables;
  numeric c;
  numeric f=70;
  end;
```

The variable declaration always begins with the *variables* keyword and ends with an *end*.

CASL is familiar with three different variable types:

- ***numeric*** - Variable for numerical values.
- ***string*** - Variable for strings.
- ***byte*** - Special form of *numeric* for numbers in the maximum size of a byte (0 ... 255). Can only be used in fields.

In the declaration of a variable, you can also directly assign it a value, which you can change at any time.

## Functions

The last section defines the actual program functions. Every function has its own name and must end with *end*. One of the functions in the program is always called *startup*. This function automatically starts up when the program is called.

```
function startup;
  c=(f-32)/1.8;
  put c1, c;
  end;
```

The example demonstrates a single function only. This function is automatically started at program startup.

The first line of the function executes the calculation, according to the same formula as the Basic program at the beginning of this chapter.

The *put* statement in the following line writes the calculated result c to the c1 *label* defined at the beginning of the program.

### *put <Object>, <Value>;*

This statement writes a numerical value or a string to a *label, text,* or *button.*

## Project settings

Before you compile the program, set the *Physical Screen Size* to 160 in the *Project/Project Settings* menu, to duplicate the exact size of the Palm screen. Make the same settings for the following CASL examples as well.

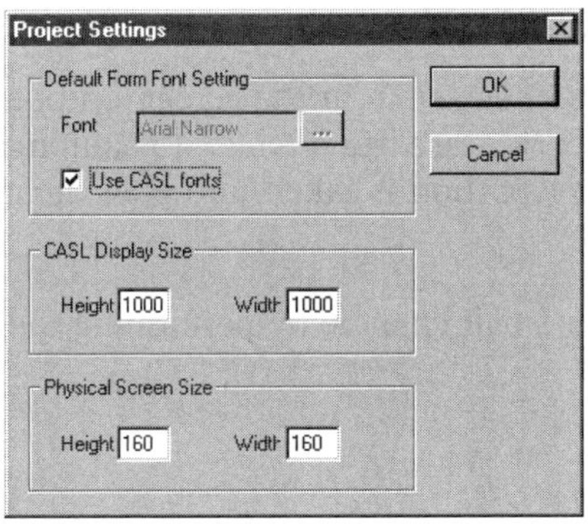


*Settings for the screen size*

When you compile and start the program, only the calculated result appears on the screen.

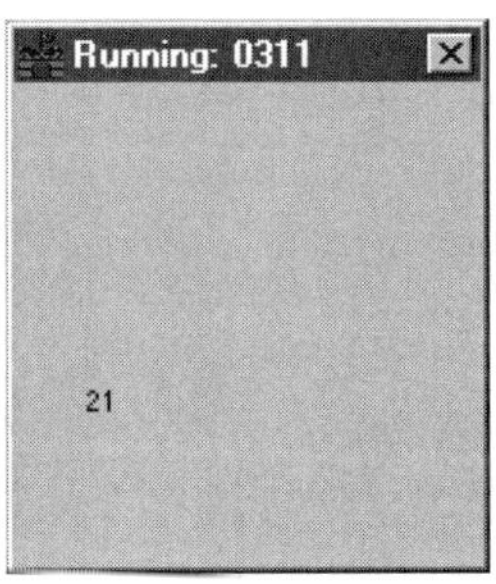


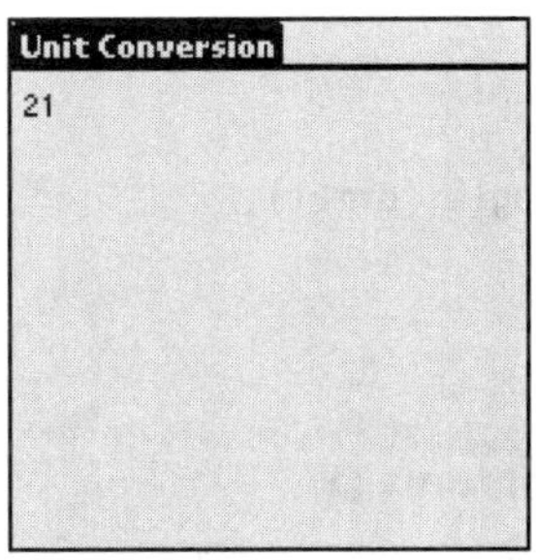


*The program in Windows ...* *... and on the Palm*

The *Unit conversion* title line was specified when the PRC file was created.

The displayed results are unsatisfactory in two respects:

- The results are inaccurate. The same yBasic program calculates a result of 21.1111. You can remedy the first problem relatively easily. CASL calculates every bit as accurately as yBasic. It even uses the same functions for doubly accurate floating-point arithmetic from *Mathlib.prc*.
- The position of the number on the screen in Windows does not match the actual Palm display. You can find a solution for this problem in the next program example.

In addition, a good program would include a display of the original value and the units.

## Formatted screen output

The problem of the shifted display lies solely in the screen output. A *label* always outputs a string. If a number is passed to a *label*, it is automatically converted and only the whole number portion is taken into consideration for this conversion.

You can solve the problem with a small change, by performing the conversion manually.

```
label c1;
  end;

variables;
  numeric c;
  numeric f=70;
  string format="##.##";
  end;

function startup;
  c=(f-32)/1.8;
  put c1, string(c,format);
  end;
```

**CD**

**Program on the companion CD**

You can also find this program on the companion CD to this book as *0312.csl*.

Here a new *format* variable of the *string* type is defined. It contains a formatting specification that is used further back by the *string()* function.

### *string(numeric n, string f)*

This function converts a number into a string in accordance with a special formatting specification. The function uses two parameters:

- ***numeric n*** - The numerical value that is to be converted.
- ***string f*** - Formatting specification.

The formatting specification consists of # characters and a decimal point. The # characters after the decimal point specify the decimal places. The numerical value is mathematically rounded off and not simply truncated to the specified number of decimal places.

*The program in Windows ...*

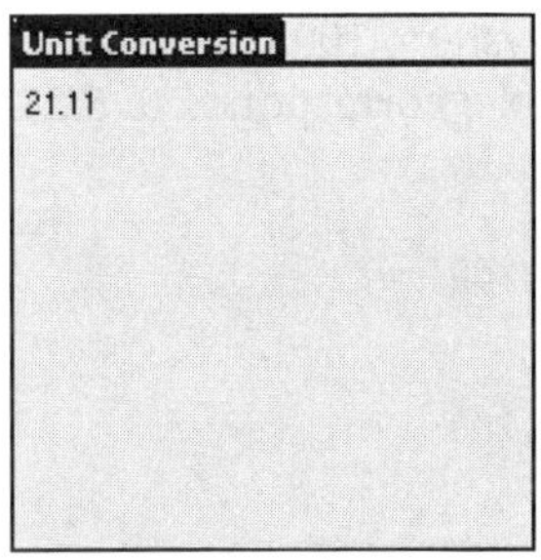


*... and on the Palm*

The program now outputs the calculated value with two decimal places, although it is still just somewhere on the screen and without any explanatory information.

In the next program version you can create clean, formatted screen output.

# Coordinate system

CASL isn't as strictly fixed on a hardware platform as yBasic. In addition to running on the Palm, CASL programs run in Windows and Windows CE. For this reason, CASL uses a virtual screen resolution of 1,000 x 1000 pixels, which is automatically converted to the 160 x 160 pixels of the Palm display when being compiled for the Palm. You can set the size of the Windows window of CASL runtime in the *Project/Project Settings* menu in the *Physical Screen Size* parameter. Set this to 160 x 160 pixels also.

Coordinates are used for positioning the elements, beginning in the upper left corner. The coordinates of an element always refer to its upper left corner.

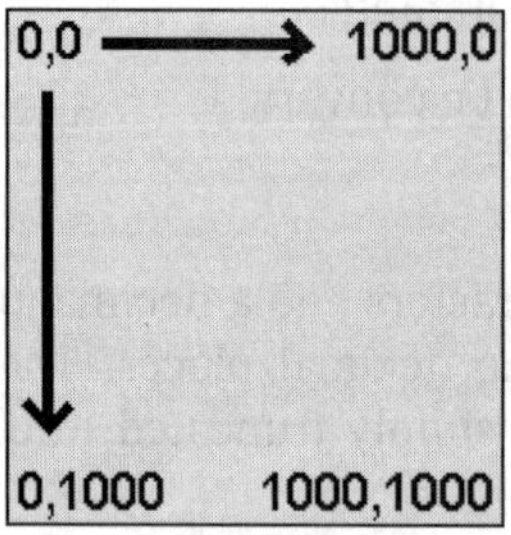


*The CASL coordinate system*

In this coordinate system, 100 units correspond to 16 pixels on the Palm, or conversely one Palm pixel corresponds to 6.25 coordinate units.

```
label f1;
  position 100,200;
  end;
label f2;
  position 300,200;
  display "°F";
  end;
label c1;
  position 100,400;
  end;
label c2;
  position 300,400;
  display "°C";
  end;

variables;
  numeric c;
  numeric f=70;
  string format="##.##";
  end;

function startup;
  c=(f-32)/1.8;
  put f1, string(f,format);
  put c1, string(c,format);
  end;
```

**CD**

**Program on the companion CD**

You can also find this program on the companion CD to this book as *0313.csl*.

Four *label* elements are defined in this program. Each has a *position* parameter, which specifies the location on the screen. In the *display* parameter you can specify a string in the *label* definition that is to be displayed.

The *labels* in the program are specified for the following values:

| Label | Value |
|---|---|
| f1 | Default value in °F |
| f2 | Text "°F" |
| c1 | Calculated value in °C |
| c2 | Text "°C" |

## *label*

In addition to the name, which is necessary, a *label* can have different optional parameters:

| Parameter | Values | Meaning |
|---|---|---|
| char_size | Width, Height | Size in letters |
| display | String | String displayed by default |
| font | Font_Name, Font-Style, Size | Font |
| hidden | | Hidden |
| pixel_size | Width, Height | Size in coordinates |
| position | x, y | Location in coordinates |
| bitmap | String | Displayed graphic |

The actual program function was changed only slightly. In addition to the calculated value c, the original value f is converted into a string and entered in the corresponding *label*.

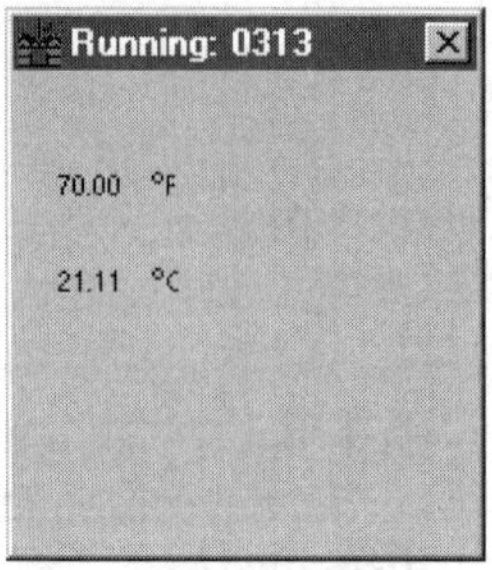


*The program in Windows ...*

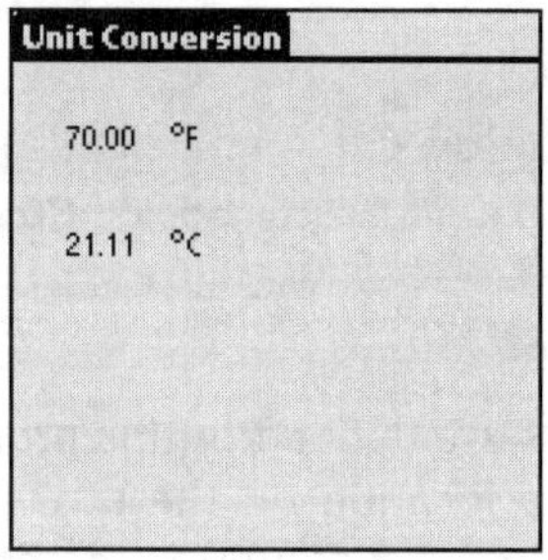


*... and on the Palm*

In the illustration shows that in Windows the coordinate system only covers the gray area of the window, but on the Palm it covers the entire screen including the title bar. Therefore, to avoid unwanted effects, never place your elements all the way on top.

## User input

The program is still unusable for practical purposes because you have had no opportunity to change the initial value of the calculation.

In the next program version, there is an input field for this purpose.

```
text f1;
  position 100,200;
  char_size 5,1;
  end;
label f2;
  position 400,200;
  display "°F";
  end;
label c1;
  position 100,400;
  end;
label c2;
  position 400,400;
  display "°C";
  end;
button calc;
  position 500,200;
  display "Calc";
  end;
```

```
variables;
  numeric c;
  numeric f;
  string format="##.##";
  end;

function calc;
  get f1, f;
  c=(f-32)/1.8;
  put c1, string(c,format);
  end;

function startup;
  show f1;
  end;
```

CD

**Program on the companion CD**

You can also find this program on the companion CD to this book as *0314.csl*.

The first *label*, in which the original, defined initial value was displayed, is now replaced by a *text* element.

### *text*

A *text* is a field that accepts user input. Along with the name, which is necessary, it can have different optional parameters:

| Parameter | Values | Meaning |
|---|---|---|
| char_size | Width, Height | Size in letters |
| display | String | String displayed by default |
| font | Font_Name, Font-Style, Size | Font |
| invokes | Function name | Function that is called during text input |
| hidden | | Hidden |
| no_input | | Prevents input by the user |
| pixel_size | Width, Height | Size in coordinates |
| position | x, y | Location in coordinates |
| scrollbar | Type (*top* or *bottom*) | Location of the scrollbar for multiple line fields |

The size of the *text* element in the example is set by the *char_size* parameter to a width of five characters and a height of one line. In fact the *text* elements are always wider than specified to enable experimentation.

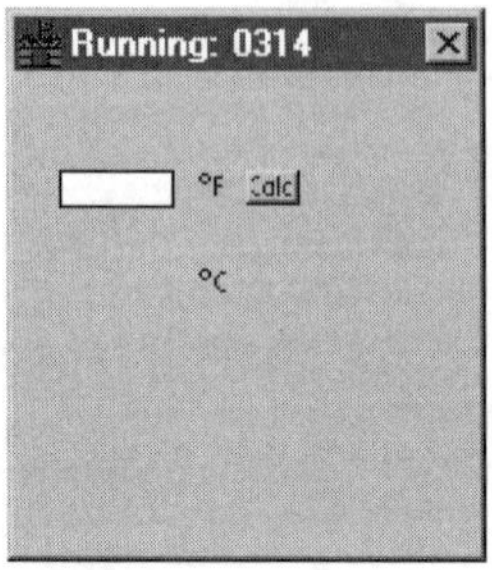


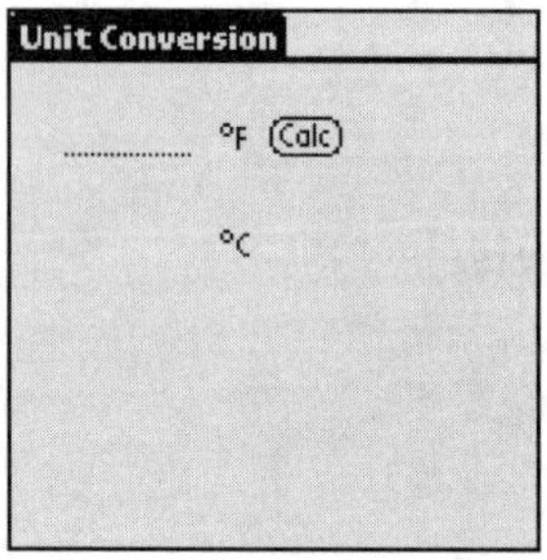


In addition to the input field, a new element appears: the button, which triggers the calculation. After you have entered a value, tap *Calc* and the calculation begins.

Such buttons exist as predefined object types in CASL.

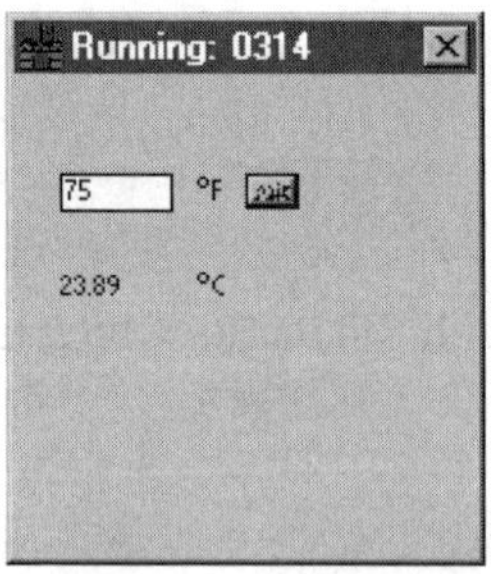


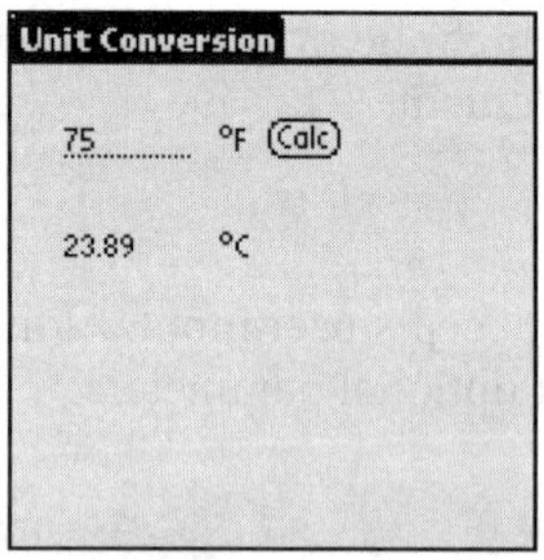


### *button*

A *button* is an element the user taps. When tapped, a button always executes the function that corresponds to its name, unless the *invoke* parameter specifies another function. Along with the name, which is necessary, it can have various optional parameters:

| Parameter | Values | Meaning |
|---|---|---|
| border | *square, bold, dashed, none* | Appearance of the button |
| char_size | Width, Height | Size in letters |
| checkbox | | Checkbox instead of button |

| Parameter | Values | Meaning |
|---|---|---|
| display | String | String displayed by default |
| font | Font_Name, Font-Style, Size | Font |
| invokes | Function name | Function that is called during text input |
| hidden | | Hidden |
| pixel_size | Width, Height | Size in coordinates |
| position | x, y | Location in coordinates |
| bitmap | String | Graphic on the button |
| hardware | key1-key4, PageUp, PageDn | Hardware keys, which can control the button |

In the example the button is called *calc* and calls the function of the same name:

```
button calc;
  position 500,200;
  display "Calc";
  end;

function calc;
  get f1, f;
  c=(f-32)/1.8;
  put c1, string(c,format);
  end;
```

The new *calc* function now performs the calculation, after retrieving the *f1 text* element with the *get* statement and writing the value in the *f variable*.

### *get <Object>, <Value>;*

This function retrieves the current string from a *label, text,* or *button.*

The *startup* function was changed, because no calculation is being performed at program startup. Now the function only makes sure that the input field appears.

```
function startup;
  show f1;
  end;
```

## Automatic calculation

Up until now, when you entered a new value you always had to tap the *Calc* button to convert the value. However, CASL *text* elements can automatically call a function during editing through the *invokes* parameter, that is, when changing the entered value.

You can make use of this feature in the next example where the *text* element calls the *calc* function automatically.

**CD**

**Program on the companion CD**

You can also find this program on the companion CD to this book as *0315.csl.*

Compared to the last example, only two small changes occur; therefore, the full text for the complete program does not appear:

- The *button* element is omitted.
- The *text* element for inputting the value receives an additional *invokes* parameter.

```
text f1;
  position 100,200;
  char_size 5,1;
  invokes calc;
  end;
```

With each changed digit in the input field of °F temperature, a new value is automatically calculated for the °C temperature.

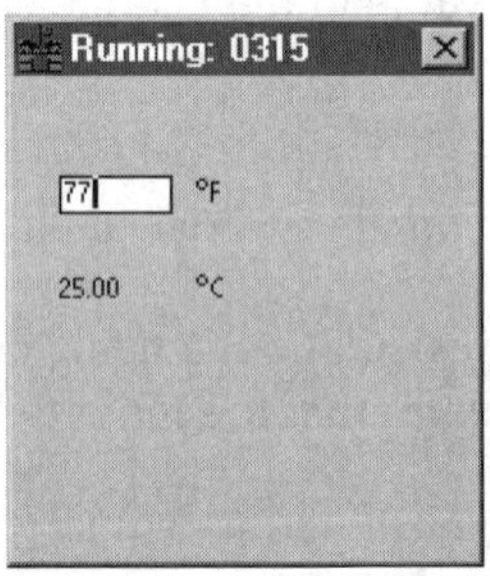


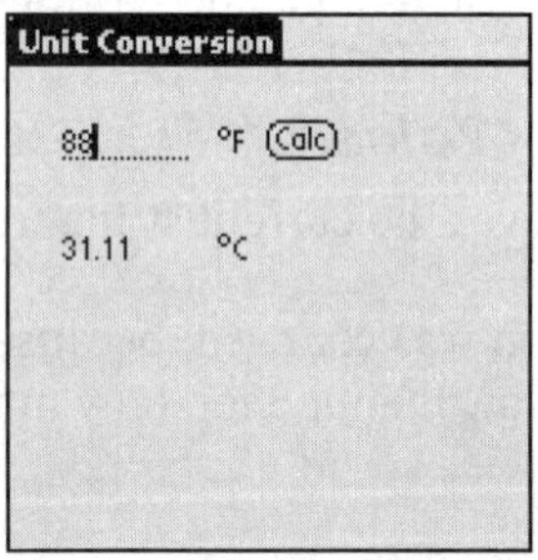


## Currency converter with automatic Calculation

Next, you employ the procedure of automatic calculation in a larger program when inputting a numerical value, as described in the last example. You also program a currency converter in CASL with the same operation as the program you created earlier under HotPaw Basic. However, in this program all values should be calculated upon the entry of an amount in DM. When a change in the rates occurs, the results should be updated.

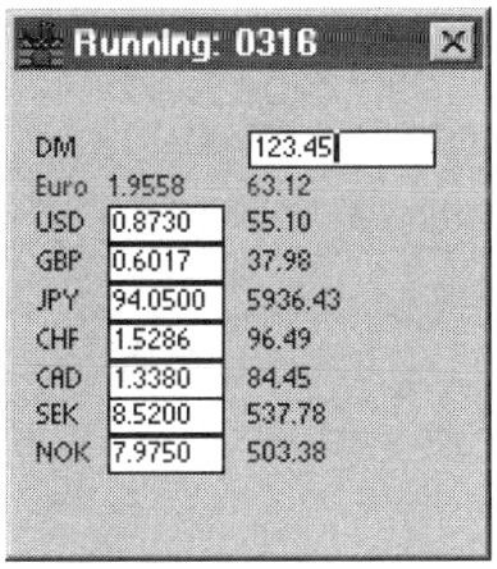


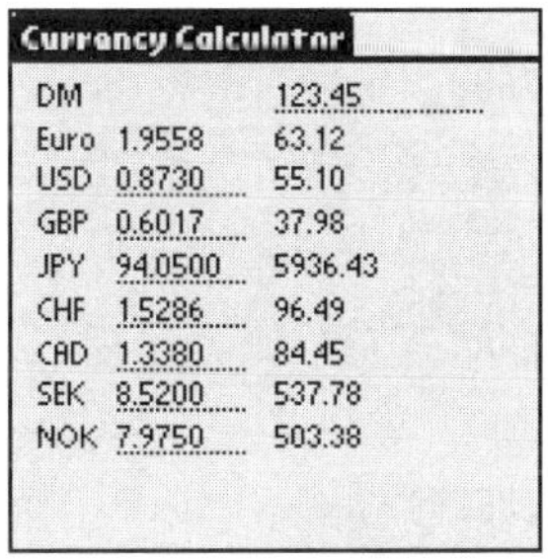


Enter the amount to be converted in the *DM* field in the upper right corner. This amount is converted into Euros in the second line in accordance with a fixed rate. From the Euro amount, the amounts in the third column are calculated using the rates in the second column, which can be changed.

```
label dem1;
  position 50,120;
  display "DM";
  end;
label eur1;
  position 50,200;
  display "Euro";
  end;
label usd1;
  position 50,280;
  display "USD";
  end;
label gbp1;
  position 50,360;
  display "GBP";
  end;
label jpy1;
  position 50,440;
  display "JPY";
  end;
label chf1;
  position 50,520;
  display "CHF";
  end;
label cad1;
  position 50,600;
  display "CAD";
```

```
  end;
label sek1;
  position 50,680;
  display "SEK";
  end;
label nok1;
  position 50,760;
  display "NOK";
  end;
label eur2;
  position 200,200;
  display "1.9558";
  end;
text usd2;
  position 200,280;
  char_size 5,1;
  display "0.8730";
  invokes calc;
  end;
text gbp2;
  position 200,360;
  char_size 5,1;
  display "0.6017";
  invokes calc;
  end;
text jpy2;
  position 200,440;
  char_size 5,1;
  display "94.0500";
  invokes calc;
  end;
text chf2;
  position 200,520;
  char_size 5,1;
  display "1.5286";
  invokes calc;
  end;
text cad2;
  position 200,600;
  char_size 5,1;
  display "1.3380";
  invokes calc;
  end;
text sek2;
  position 200,680;
  char_size 5,1;
  display "8.5200";
  invokes calc;
  end;
```

```
text nok2;
  position 200,760;
  char_size 5,1;
  display "7.9750";
  invokes calc;
  end;
text dem3;
  position 500,120;
  char_size 8,1;
  display "";
  invokes calc;
  end;
label eur3;
  position 500,200;
  end;
label usd3;
  position 500,280;
  end;
label gbp3;
  position 500,360;
  end;
label jpy3;
  position 500,440;
  end;
label chf3;
  position 500,520;
  end;
label cad3;
  position 500,600;
  end;
label sek3;
  position 500,680;
  end;
label nok3;
  position 500,760;
  end;

variables;
  numeric d;
  numeric e;
  numeric e3;
  numeric usd4;
  numeric gbp4;
  numeric jpy4;
  numeric chf4;
  numeric cad4;
  numeric sek4;
  numeric nok4;
  string format="##.##";
  end;
```

```
function calc;
  get dem3, d;
  get eur2, e;
  e3=d/e;
  put eur3, string(e3,format);
  get usd2, usd4;
  put usd3, string(e3*usd4,format);
  get gbp2, gbp4;
  put gbp3, string(e3*gbp4,format);
  get jpy2, jpy4;
  put jpy3, string(e3*jpy4,format);
  get chf2, chf4;
  put chf3, string(e3*chf4,format);
  get cad2, cad4;
  put cad3, string(e3*cad4,format);
  get sek2, sek4;
  put sek3, string(e3*sek4,format);
  get nok2, nok4;
  put nok3, string(e3*nok4,format);
  end;

function startup;
  show dem3;
  end;
```

**CD**

**Program on the companion CD**

You can also find this program on the companion CD to this book as *0316.csl.*

**Note**

**Program does not work with the CASL demo version**

The CASL demo version is restricted to 20 objects, 20 functions, and 40 global variables. However, this program uses 18 *label* and 8 *text* objects, which is 6 objects too many. By calculating two rates fewer, you can run the program with the CASL demo version as well.

The program, which at first glance looks cluttered, is quite simply structured. Become accustomed to having an easy-to-read structure for your own programs from the very beginning and go to the extra trouble to document programs that you want to use for a long time, as shown in the following sections.

In the first part, nine *labels* are defined, which contain the currency descriptions.

```
label dem1;
  position 50,120;
  display "DM";
  end;
...
```

The individual *labels* are at a distance of 80 coordinate units from each other.

In the second column, a *label* for the fixed Euro rate occurs as well as *text* fields for the variable rates of the other currencies.

```
label eur2;
  position 200,200;
  display "1.9558";
  end;
text usd2;
  position 200,280;
  char_size 5,1;
  display "0.8730";
  invokes calc;
  end;
...
```

These fields are at the same distance from each other in a column.

The third column consists of a *text* field for the DM amount to be converted and *label* fields for the values of the other currencies calculated from it.

```
text dem3;
  position 500,120;
  char_size 8,1;
  display "";
  invokes calc;
  end;
label eur3;
  position 500,200;
  end;
...
```

All *text* fields call the *calc* function with the *invokes* parameter. This function calculates all the values and is so fast that it is not worthwhile to write functions that only recalculate the changed value for rate changes.

```
get dem3, d;
get eur2, e;
```

The DM amount and the Euro rate are retrieved first; then the amount in Euros is calculated and written to the *e3* variable.

```
e3=d/e;
put eur3, string(e3,format);
```

This amount is then written to the *eur3 label* field in shortened form.

```
get usd2, usd4;
put usd3, string(e3*usd4,format);
```

Two lines for each currency appear. These lines retrieve the current rate, calculate the amount, format it, and write this amount in the appropriate *label* field.

The *startup* function doesn't calculate anything; it only displays the input field for the DM amount and thus the entire form.

## Variable table

Good program documentation includes a table of all the variables that are used:

| **Label** | |
|---|---|
| dem1...nok1 | Currency descriptions |
| eur2 | Fixed Euro rate |
| eur3...nok3 | Converted amounts in different currencies |

| **Text** | |
|---|---|
| usd2...nok2 | Conversion rates |
| dem3 | DM amount |

| **Variables** | |
|---|---|
| numeric d | DM amount |
| numeric e | Fixed Euro rate |
| numeric e3 | Euro amount |
| numeric usd4...nok4 | Conversion rates |
| string format | String for formatted output of the values |

# 4. Graphic programs for the Palm OS

Even though the Palm display window isn't particularly large, you can address each of the 25,600 pixels individually to display relatively detailed graphics. In general, programs emphasize functional graphics over attractive pictures. For this reason, most Palm programming languages offer convenient functions for drawing lines and geometric forms.

In this chapter you learn more than the pure representation of graphics as well as programming techniques for managing the data necessary to create a graphic. Usually it's not enough to draw the graphic on the screen. The data used in the graphic has to be created and must also be available later if the graphic changes. For example, with business graphics that show the percentages of various numerical values, the entire graphic changes when only one value changes, because the percentages shift.

## 4.1 Coordinates and lines

All of the pixels on the Palm screen are controlled through a coordinate system with a zero point in the upper left corner. You learned about the CASL coordinate system in the last chapter. In this system the virtual coordinates 1,000 x 1,000 are converted to 160 x 160 real Palm pixels. Thus 6.25 coordinate units correspond to one pixel on the Palm. In contrast, HotPaw Basic works with a coordinate system that corresponds exactly to the pixels.

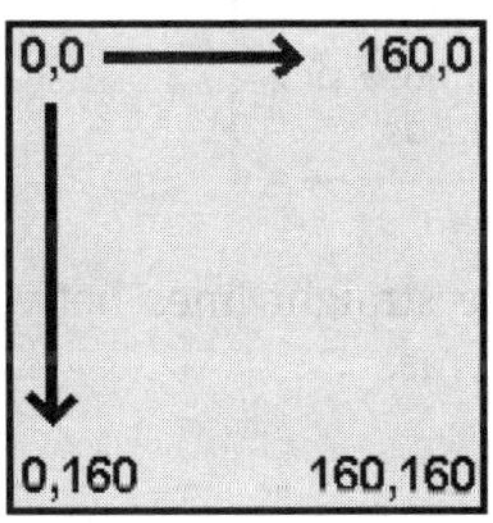


*Coordinate system in yBasic ...*

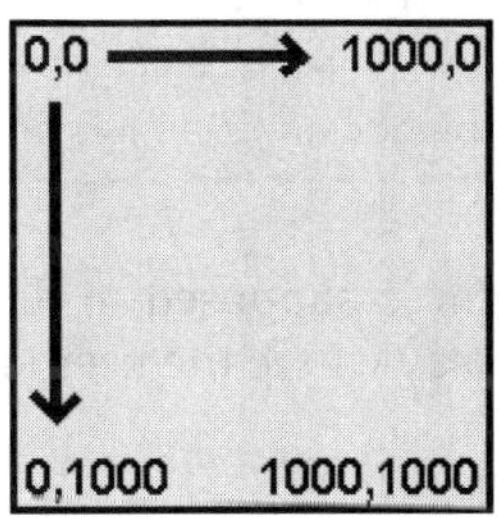


*... and in CASL*

Remember that the coordinate systems always begin in the upper left corner of the Palm screen. At the same time the title bar of the program is also in the upper area, so do not use the upper 15 pixels for your graphics. The following illustration shows a graphics program overwriting screen areas that are actually meant for the title line and control elements with graphics.

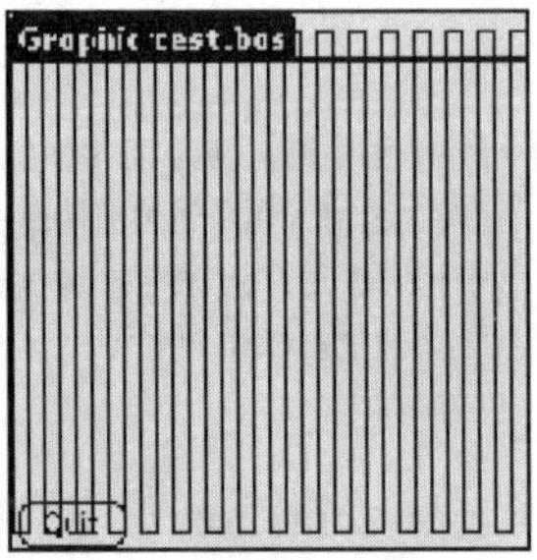


*Graphic overwrites title line*

**CD**

**Program on the companion CD**

If you want to reconstruct this example, you can also find this program on the companion CD to this book as *0401.bas*.

# Simple graphic in HotPaw Basic

Most programming books use a house as an introduction to graphics programming, with which all the fundamentals of vector graphics can be explained visually. To avoid using this example yet another time, create a simple paint program on the following pages. It is, however, a bit more exacting.

**CD**

**Program on the companion CD**

Nevertheless, for the sake of continuity, you can also find a house program for the Palm on the companion CD to this book as *0439.bas*.

The paint program is supposed to draw simple straight lines between the two points on the display where the user taps the stylus.

```
#Draw Program2.bas
draw -1
```

```
start:
x1=fn pen(0)
y1=fn pen(2)
x2=fn pen(0)
y2-fn pen(2)
draw x1,y1,x2,y2,1
goto start
```

*The simple paint program*

**CD**

**Program on the companion CD**

You can find this program on the companion CD to this book as *0402.bas.*

First, in a program that uses graphics, you need to clear the screen of standard messages.

```
draw -1
```

This line clears the screen and the message "yBasic thinking ..."

### *draw -1*

The *draw* function uses the *-1* parameter to clear the graphic screen up to the title line and a *Quit* button in the lower left corner. Therefore, restrict your graphic to the area of 0.15 ... 160.145.

After that, the program prompts you for the coordinates that the user tapped.

```
x1=fn pen(0)
y1=fn pen(2)
```

### *fn pen(0)*

This function waits until the user taps somewhere on the display. The return value of this function, referred to here as *x1*, contains the x-coordinate of the point that the user tapped. The program will evaluate this value.

### *fn pen(2)*

This function returns the y-coordinate of the last point that has been tapped. In contrast to *fn pen(0)*, the function does not wait for the user to tap the screen but returns the y-coordinate of the last screen contact, regardless of how long ago it has been. In this way you can determine the exact coordinates of a tapped point using a combination of *fn pen(0)* and *fn pen(2)*.

The coordinates of the tapped point are stored in the *x1* and *y1* variables.

```
x2=fn pen(0)
y2=fn pen(2)
```

The same procedure is repeated one more time to store the coordinates of the second tapped point in the *x2* and *y2* variables.

Next the program draws a straight line between these coordinates.

```
draw x1,y1,x2,y2,1
```

### *draw x1,y1,x2,y2,1*

This function draws a straight line, which is determined by points *x1,y1* and *x2,y2*.

After the line has been drawn, the program goes back to the spot directly after the screen clear. In this way the next line is drawn on the screen in addition to the existing line.

## Limit the drawing area

In this version of the paint program, it is possible to paint over the title line and the *Quit* button.

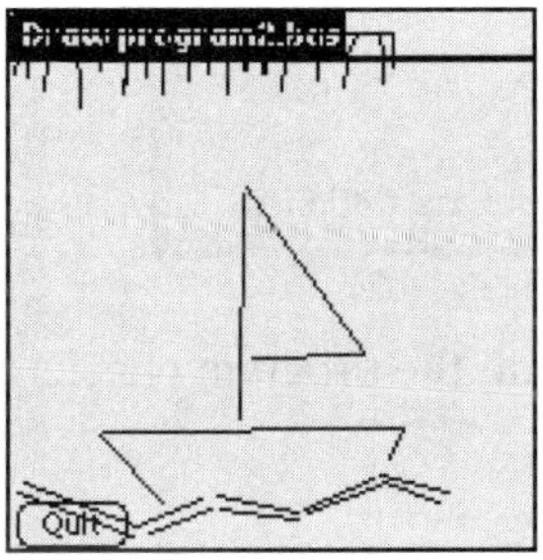


*Painted over title line and Quit button*

(The next program version will allow coordinate input between the y-coordinates of 15 and 145 only.) This reserves 15 pixels on top and below for the standard elements of the user interface. It is not necessary to check the x-coordinate, because the entire screen width can be used.

Whenever the user taps an area outside of this valid graphic area, the program displays a message saying it does not accept the point shown.

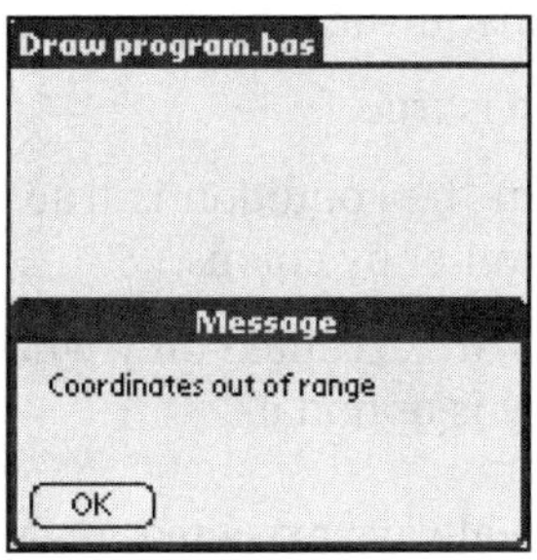


*Message when an invalid point is tapped*

For this purpose, extend the program by a few lines:

```
#Draw Program.bas
draw -1
start:
x1=fn pen(0)
y1=fn pen(2)
if ((y1<15) or (y1>145)) then goto error
x2=fn pen(0)
y2=fn pen(2)
if ((y1<15) or (y1>145)) then goto error
draw x1,y1,x2,y2,1
goto start
error:
print "Coordinates outside of permissible area"
goto start
```

**CD**

**Program on the companion CD**

You can find this program on the companion CD to this book as *0403.bas.*

Depending on the evaluation of a tapped point, the program checks whether this coordinate lies in the valid area:

```
if ((y1<15) or (y1>145)) then goto error
```

Almost all programming languages have an *if...then* statement for such queries, which executes something when a specified condition is true.

### *if <Expr> then <Action1> [ : <Action2> ] [ : else <Action3> ]*

An *if...then* query consists of a condition and at least one action that is to be executed if this condition applies.

- **Expr** - Condition that can be answered unequivocally with true or false.
- **Action1** - Is executed when the condition is true.
- **Action2** - Is executed after *Action1* when the condition is true. In this way several actions can be connected to each other by colons.
- **Action3** - After the word *else*, the actions are executed only when the condition does not apply. This part of the query is optional.

The statements in the next program lines are always executed, regardless of the outcome of the *if...then*-query. If you want to prevent this, after the *then* jump to a different place in the program with a *goto* statement. If the condition applies, the program no longer goes to the line following the *if...then* statement.

This is precisely the procedure our program uses to check user input.

```
if (...) then goto error
```

If the condition in parentheses applies, the program jumps to the *error* branch mark and outputs the message there. If the condition does not apply, the program continues running.

The condition consists of two parts that are connected by a logical OR operation.

```
(y1<15) or (y1>145)
```

This OR operation is always true when at least one of the two subconditions is true. Thus, in the example, if a y-coordinate is smaller than 15 or a y-coordinate is greater than 145, the OR operation is true.

However, an OR operation is also true when both subconditions are fulfilled simultaneously, which is not possible in the example.

If the user taps an invalid point, the program outputs the error message and then returns to the beginning repeatedly. Therefore, it does not matter whether the invalid point is the first or the second point in the query. In any event, the user has to tap two new points to draw the next line.

## Simple drawing program in CASL

Of course, you can also draw graphics in CASL. In the first example, write a simple drawing program with which you can draw lines through coordinate input.

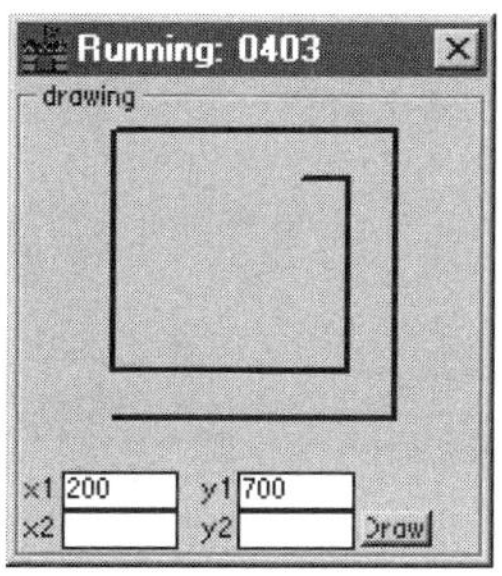


*The program in Windows ...*

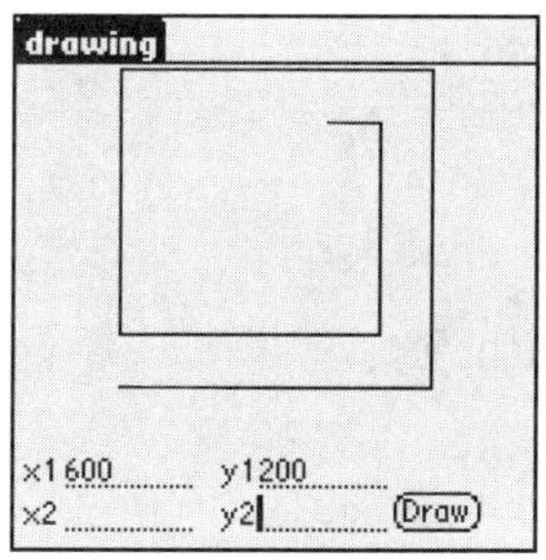


*... and on the Palm*

> **Note**
>
> **Direction of the y-axis**
>
> Keep in mind that the y-coordinates on the Palm are counted from top to bottom and not from bottom to top, as is the case with building measurements or in most CAD programs.

```
frame drawing;
  end;

label x1label, drawing;
  display "x1";
  position 20,820;
  end;
```

```
label y1label, drawing;
  display "y1";
  position 400,820;
  end;

label x2label, drawing;
  display "x2";
  position 20,900;
  end;

label y2label, drawing;
  display "y2";
  position 400,900;
  end;

text x1text, drawing;
  char_size 5,1;
  position 100,820;
  end;

text y1text, drawing;
  char_size 5,1;
  position 480,820;
  end;

text x2text, drawing;
  char_size 5,1;
  position 100,900;
  end;

text y2text, drawing;
  char_size 5,1;
  position 480,900;
  end;

button line, drawing;
  display "Draw";
  position 740,900;
  end;

variables;
  numeric x1;
  numeric y1;
  numeric x2;
  numeric y2;
  end;

function line;
  get x1text, x1;
```

```
get y1text, y1;
get x2text, x2;
get y2text, y2;
set drawing, pen, x1, y1;
draw drawing, line, x2-x1, y2-y1;
put x1text, x2;
put y1text, y2;
put x2text, "";
put y2text, "";
end;
```

CD

**Program on the companion CD**

You can also find this program on the companion CD to this book as *0403.csl.*

CASL uses frames for drawing graphics. Frames are virtual drawing sheets that can also have buttons and other objects. The program can toggle these frames on and off as a whole. In the first program, lines such a *frame* is defined:

```
frame drawing;
  end;
```

### *frame*

In addition to its name, a *frame* can also have two additional optional parameters:

| Parameter | Values | Meaning |
|---|---|---|
| display | String | Title line, if this does not match the frame name |
| hidden | | Hidden |

On this *frame*, four *label* and four *text* fields for inputting coordinates appear:

```
label x1label, drawing;
  display "x1";
  position 20,820;
  end;
...
text x1text, drawing;
  char_size 5,1;
  position 100,820;
  end;
...
```

If such an object is to be on a *frame*, the name of the *frame* must be specified after the object name in the object definition. In addition to these fields, you can find a button in the lower right corner that calls the function for drawing a line when the coordinates have been entered.

```
button line, drawing;
  display "Draw";
  position 740,900;
  end;
```

The user enters the coordinates of the starting point of the line in the top two fields, entering the coordinates of the end point in the bottom fields, each in the CASL coordinate system.

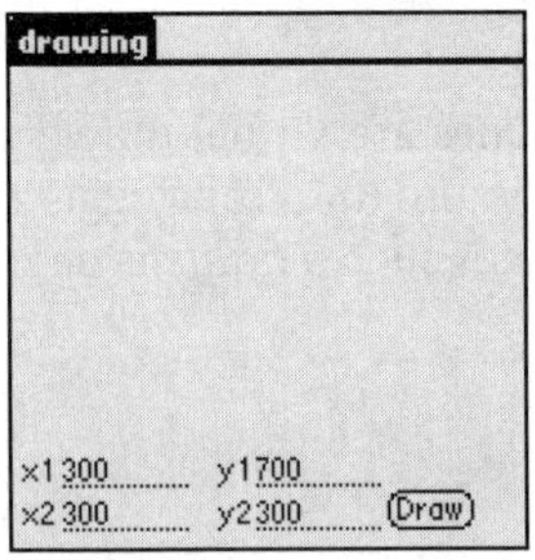


*Input of the coordinates ...*

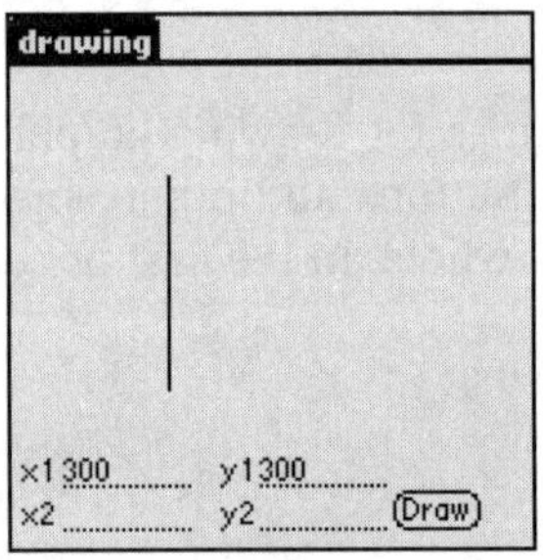


*... and the drawn line*

After that, if you tap the *Draw* button, the program draws the line. The program automatically writes the coordinates of the end point of the line in the fields for the starting point so that you can continue drawing. If the next line is to begin somewhere else, you can also specify different values in these fields. The button calls the *line* function:

```
function line;
  get x1text, x1;
  get y1text, y1;
  get x2text, x2;
  get y2text, y2;
  set drawing, pen, x1, y1;
  draw drawing, line, x2-x1, y2-y1;
  put x1text, x2;
  put y1text, y2;
  put x2text, "";
  put y2text, "";
  end;
```

This function first reads out the four text fields to four numeric variables. Then the program sets the current position of the pen with a *set* statement.

### *set <frame>, pen, <x>, <y>;*

This function corresponds to the movement of a pen in elevated state, that is, without drawing, to a specified coordinate position on the sheet. The word *pen* is not a variable parameter but must appear in the function precisely so.

In the next step the *draw* function draws the line.

### *draw <frame>, <form>, <x>, <y>;*

This function draws a line, a rectangle or a circle between the current coordinate and the specified offset in x and y direction. Thus, *x* and *y* do not specify the coordinates of the line end point but do specify an offset that is added to the current coordinate position.

The parameter form can accept three different values:

| | |
|---|---|
| line | Draws a line. |
| rectangle | Draws a rectangle, whose diagonal corresponds to the offset. |
| circle | Draws a circle or ellipsis that lies exactly in a rectangle whose diagonal corresponds to the offset. |

In this program the user specifies the end point in absolute coordinates and not as an offset. Therefore, the program has to convert the coordinates before drawing the line.

```
draw drawing, line, x2-x1, y2-y1;
```

After the line has been drawn, the function uses simple *put* statements to write the coordinates of the line end point *x2,y2* to the *text* fields for the new line beginning and clears the *text* fields of the line end point.

**Tip**

**Drawing points**

If you want to draw a single point, draw a line with offset 0.0 whose starting point is equal to the end point.

## Additional forms in the drawing program

You can also draw both of the other graphic forms with a small program enhancement:

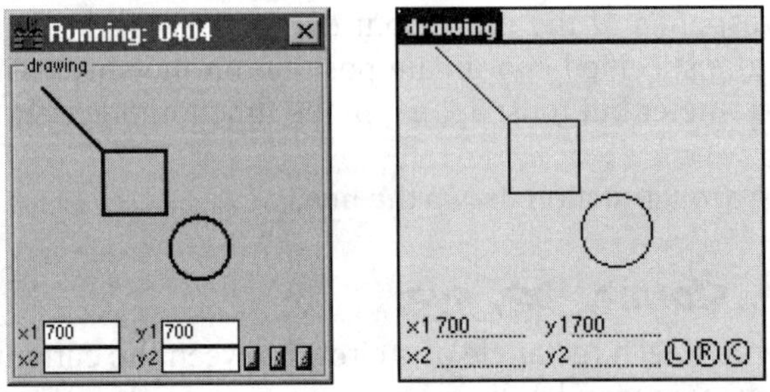


*The enhanced program in Windows and on the Palm*

*Line:*
*x1=100 y1=100*
*x2=300 y2=300*

*Rectangle:*
*x1=300 y1=300*
*x2=500 y2=500*

*Circle:*
*x1=500 y1=500*
*x2=700 y2=700*

**CD**

**Program on the companion CD**

You can also find this program on the companion CD to this book as *0404.csl.*

For this purpose, the *Draw* button at the lower right is replaced by three buttons:

```
button line, drawing;
  display "L";
  position 740,900;
  end;

button rectangle, drawing;
  display "R";
  position 820,900;
  end;

button circle, drawing;
  display "C";
  position 900,900;
  end;
```

These three buttons call three different functions:

```
function line;
  get x1text, x1;
  get y1text, y1;
```

```
    get x2text, x2;
    get y2text, y2;
    set drawing, pen, x1, y1;
    draw drawing, line, x2-x1, y2-y1;
    put x1text, x2;
    put y1text, y2;
    put x2text, "";
    put y2text, "";
    end;

  function rectangle;
    get x1text, x1;
    get y1text, y1;
    get x2text, x2;
    get y2text, y2;
    set drawing, pen, x1, y1;
    draw drawing, rectangle, x2-x1, y2-y1;
    put x1text, x2;
    put y1text, y2;
    put x2text, "";
    put y2text, "";
    end;

  function circle;
    get x1text, x1;
    get y1text, y1;
    get x2text, x2;
    get y2text, y2;
    set drawing, pen, x1, y1;
    draw drawing, circle, x2-x1, y2-y1;
    put x1text, x2;
    put y1text, y2;
    put x2text, "";
    put y2text, "";
    end;
```

These three functions differ only in their names so that they can be called by different buttons and placed in the *draw* statement by the Form parameter.

**Note**

**Forms are drawn filled out**

The *draw* function draws circles and rectangles with the background color filled. This means that they cover up previously drawn objects. Thus the order in which objects are drawn is crucial.

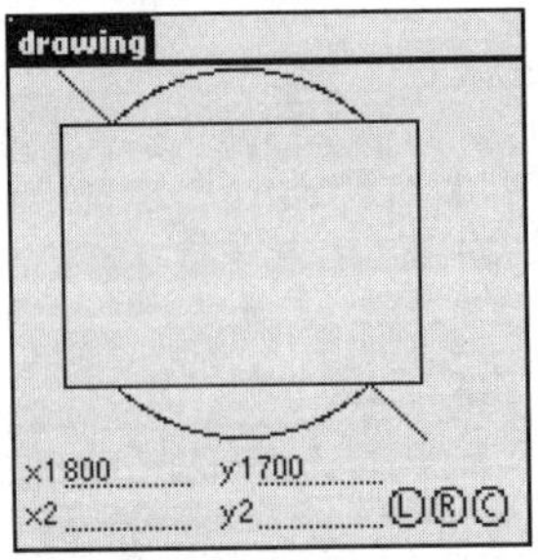


Line - Circle - Rectangle

*The enhanced program in Windows and on the Palm*

*Line:*
*x1=100 y1=100*
*x2=800 y2=800*

*Circle:*
*x1=100 y1=100*
*x2=800 y2=800*

*Rectangle:*
*x1=100 y1=200*
*x2=800 y2=700*

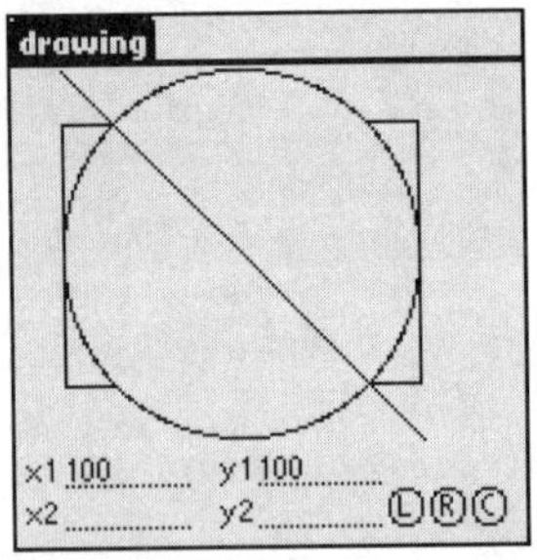


Rectangle - Circle - Line

*The enhanced program in Windows and on the Palm*

*Rectangle:*
*x1=100 y1=200*
*x2=800 y2=700*

*Circle:*
*x1=100 y1=100*
*x2=800 y2=800*

*Line:*
*x1=100 y1=200*
*x2=800 y2=800*

# 4.2 Repetitions with loops

Often you can create complex graphics by repeating simple lines, so detailed coverage on the option of using repetition loops in programming languages follows.

## Classic graphic demos

Computer graphics that were touted as modern in the 70s usually consisted of a haphazard arrangement of lines created by simple programs because nobody took the trouble to hand draw enough lines in exact distance.

The structure of this graphic is quite simple: it consists of just straight lines. The hyperbolic curve results from the overlapping of the lines:

- Draw a vertical line from top to bottom.

- Go to a specific measurement from the starting point to the right and the same amount from the end point to the top and draw a new line there.
- Repeat this procedure until you reach the top with the new line end point.

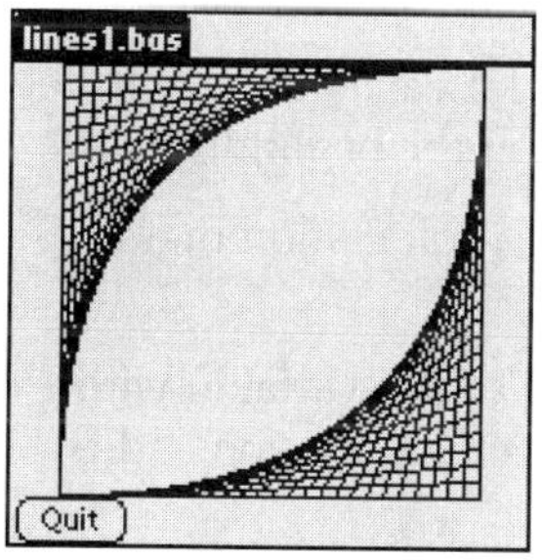


*Computer graphics in the style of the 70s on the Palm*

This example shows you how to use the simple *draw* command, which can only draw straight lines, to represent curves as well. The bottom half of the graphic functions according to the same pattern.

Here's what it looks like in yBasic:

```
# lines1.bas
draw -1
for x = 15 to 145 step 5
draw x,15,15,160-x
draw x,145,145,160-x
next x
w = fn pen(0)
end
```

**CD**

**Program on the companion CD**

You can also find this program on the companion CD to this book as *0405.bas.*

After clearing the screen with the *draw -1* function, a loop starts:

```
for x = 15 to 145 step 5
...
next x
```

This loop counts from 15 to 145 in increments of 5.

### *for <Var> = <Expr1> to <Expr2> [ step <Expr3>] ... next <Var>*

Such a loop requires several parameters:

- **Var** - Variable, used for counting. This can be evaluated within the loop and is increased at the end by the *next* statement.
- **Expr1** - Numerical value or the result of a calculation that begins with the loop. The *Var* variable is set to this value at the beginning.
- **Expr2** - Numerical value or the result of a calculation that is to end with the loop.
- **Expr3** - Incrementation for the increase of the variable with every loop cycle. This value is optional. If it is not specified, the loop adds 1 to the count and continues counting.

All lines within the loop are executed again with each loop cycle.

In the example x assumes the values of 15 to 145 in increments of 5. These values specify the coordinate area in which the graphic is located. The topmost 15 pixels and the lowest 15 pixels of the 160 x 160 pixels large display are reserved for the title line and the *Quit* button. This time use *draw* rather than *lineto* to draw the lines. This function makes it possible to freely specify the starting and end points of a line and doesn't just continue drawing at the last point.

### *draw <x1>, <y1>, <x2>, <y2>, <mode>*

This function draws a line from coordinate point x1,y1 to x2,y2. The current pen position here does not matter. The *mode* parameter makes different drawing modes possible. You can use the values specified in the table for *mode*.

| Mode | Meaning |
|---|---|
| 1 | Draws black line. |
| 2 | Draws gray line. |
| -1 | Deletes line. |
| 4 | Draws rectangle out of black lines. |
| 5 | Draws rectangle out of gray lines. |
| 7 | Draws filled rectangle. |
| -7 | Deletes rectangle. |

```
draw x,15,15,160-x
```

This line draws the upper left part of the graphic. The starting point of the line wanders with the *x* variable from left to right. Its y-coordinate remains constant at 15. The end point of the line wanders in equal increments from bottom to top. The x-coordinate remains at 15. The 160-x formula calculates the y-coordinate in such a way that it moves in the area from 145 to 15.

```
draw x,145,145,160-x
```

This line calculates the lower right part of the graphic in accordance with the same pattern. Thus, with each loop cycle, a line is drawn in the upper left part and a line is drawn in the lower right part of the graphic, saving you the trouble of a second loop for the second graphic.

## The same program ported to CASL

CASL also has this type of loop. It just looks different here. The following example shows you how to convert a yBasic program to CASL so that it yields an identical result.

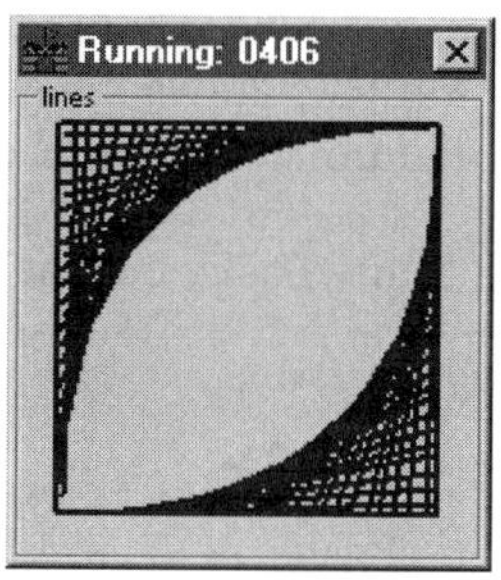


*The program in Windows ...*

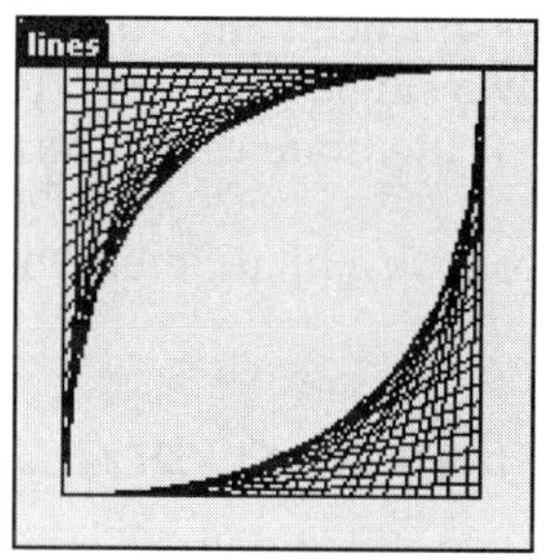


*... and on the Palm*

The CASL graphic looks somewhat less accurate than the same graphic from yBasic because of the different coordinate systems mentioned earlier. One pixel corresponds to 6.25 CASL coordinates. However, the CASL graphic functions always work with integral values so that sometimes a pixel is addressed that is located next to the one that would be correct from the computer's point of view. Therefore, always plan your graphics in the 160-pixel grid, as you would also do in HotPaw Basic, and then convert the coordinates for use in CASL programs into integral CASL coordinates.

```
frame lines;
  end;

variables;
  numeric x;
  end;

function startup;
  for x=93.75, x<=906.25;
    set lines, pen, x, 93.75;
    draw lines, line, 93.75-x, 1000-x-93.75;
    set lines, pen, x, 906.25;
    draw lines, line, 906.25-x, 1000-x-906.25;
  next x+31.25;
  end;
```

CD

**Program on the companion CD**

You can also find this program on the companion CD to this book as *0406.csl.*

This program doesn't need any *button, label,* or *text* fields. Like the Basic program, it uses only a single *x* variable. The function that draws the graphic starts immediately and is therefore called *startup*. No additional functions occur.

In CASL the loops look a bit different than they do in yBasic, but they have comparable functionality:

### *for <Var> = <Expr1>, <Expr2> ... next <Expr3>*

Such a loop requires similar parameters to that of yBasic:

- **Var** - Variable used for counting. This can be evaluated within the loop and is incremented at the end by the *next* statement.
- **Expr1** - Numerical value or result of a calculation with which the loop begins. The *Var* variable is set to this value at the beginning.
- **Expr2** - Condition that must be fulfilled so that the loop continues running.
- **Expr3** - Increase of the variable with each loop cycle. This value must always be specified here.

All the lines within the loop are executed again with each loop cycle.

In the example, you took the exact numerical values from the yBasic program and multiplied them by 6.25.

**Tip**

**Different draw functions**

The *draw* functions of CASL and yBasic behave differently. In yBasic the coordinates of the starting and end points of the line are specified, whereas in CASL, only the offset, or the vector of the line, is specified. This is added to the current pen position in the *draw* function. If you repeated the same draw function in yBasic, it would always draw the same line. In CASL the line would shift farther and farther, because the starting point depends on the current pen position and changes with every line drawn.

The *draw* lines from the yBasic program must be represented by two lines in CASL, *set* and *draw*.

```
set lines, pen, x, 93.75;
 draw lines, line, 93.75-x, 1000-x-93.75;
```

## Squares

Another sample graphic that used to be popular had overlapping squares drawn in it. The next square was always larger than the previous one to demonstrate how surfaces overlap. Although only lines are being drawn, they automatically result in surfaces in the background color and cover each other up. The change in size causes each new rectangle to require more drawing time and effort than the previous rectangle, thus going more slowly. While this is a good way to measure picture construction speed in video cards, it does not have an effect on the small Palm display. What is more, this program is ideal for demonstrating how, with very little effort - only a single program loop - you can change several parameters simultaneously, namely two lengths of the rectangle sides and two coordinates for the location.

*The program in Windows ...*

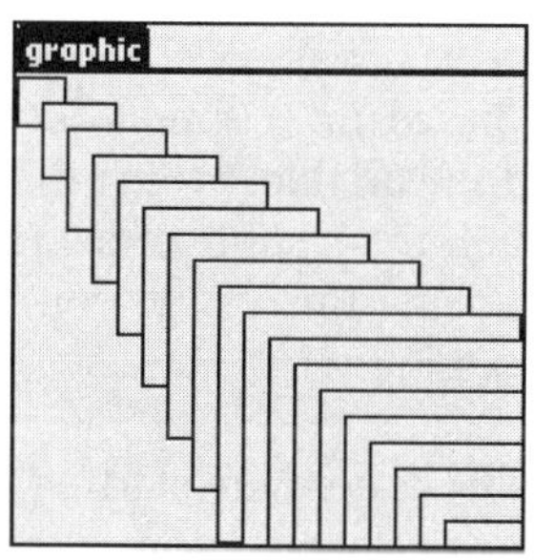


*... and on the Palm*

The CASLwin Runtime program runs so quickly on the PC that you don't see how the individual squares are created. On the Palm you can follow the procedure easily.

```
frame graphic;
  end;

variables;
  numeric x1;
  numeric y1;
  numeric x2;
  numeric y2;
  numeric i;
  end;

function drawGraphic;
  for i=0, i<20;
    set graphic, pen, x1+i*x2, y1+i*y2;
    draw graphic, rectangle, (i+2)*x2, (i+2)*y2;
  next i+1;
  end;

function startup;
  x1=0;
  y1=100;
  x2=50;
  y2=50;
  drawGraphic;
  end;
```

**CD**

**Program on the companion CD**

You can also find this program on the companion CD to this book as *0407.csl*.

The program is based on a simple loop. All the geometrically relevant values have been stored in variables which the functions in the loop access. You might have saved yourself the trouble of using the variables and entered the values directly. However, using this route, you can create a second series of squares in the next step.

The *x1,y1* variables denote the starting point of the first square, while *x2,y2* signify the offset to the starting point of the next square. The *i* counter counts the loop cycles and is also used to calculate the location and size of the current rectangle with *x2,y2*.

Next you have a second series of rectangles drawn by making a small change to the *startup* function:

```
function startup;
  x1=0;
  y1=100;
  x2=50;
  y2=50;
  drawGraphic;
  x1=999;
  y1=100;
  x2=-50;
  y2=50;
  drawGraphic;
  end;
```

**CD**

**Program on the companion CD**

You can also find this program on the companion CD to this book as *0408.csl*.

The program calls the loop twice, using a different set of variable values each time.

*The program in Windows ...*

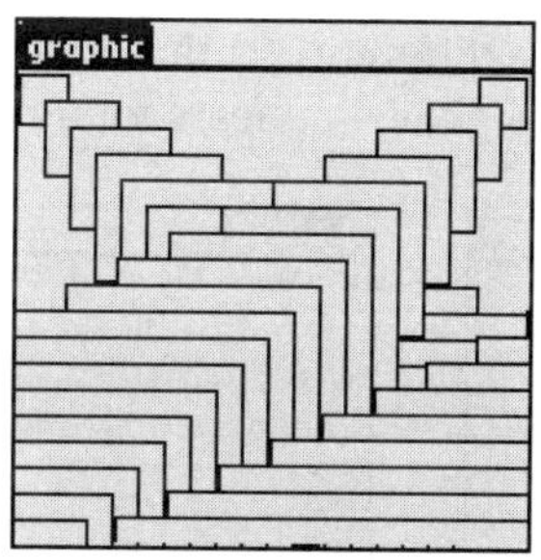


*... and on the Palm*

*Some Palm software may not support this graphic program.*

The results look different in Windows than they do on the Palm. The two run-time modules don't behave quite the same. How can that happen?

Starting with the value $i = 9$, a negative x-coordinate for the left side of each rectangle appears. In some cases the rectangles disappear from the screen on the left. In Windows the graphic data in the negative area is simply ignored; however, on the Palm the data is carried along from the right border back to the left. Thus the parts of the squares that would actually be on the left outside of the screen appear here in the lower right area.

Neither runtime module is disturbed that in this formula graphic data with coordinates greater than 1000 come into being both in x and in y direction. On the other hand, coordinates in negative y direction cause the runtime module on the Palm to crash.

**Tip**

**No negative coordinates**

Avoid drawing in the negative coordinate area with graphic CASL programs. Coordinates greater than 1,000 can be skipped over without problems, while negative coordinates cause defective functions.

## Matrix for drawing programs

The loops you have been using until now can generate linear patterns and sequences. You also use two-dimensional loops for surface patterns and two-dimensional repetitions. Because such a thing cannot occur in a linear program, use nesting loops.

The following program corresponds to the simple drawing program on page 91 of this chapter. The difference is that a dot matrix at a distance of 50 x 50 coordinate units (= 8 x 8 pixels) appears for a better overview while you are drawing.

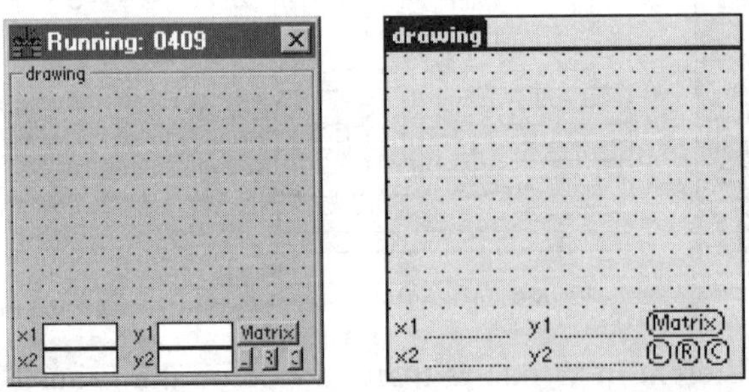


*The program in Windows and on the Palm*

The matrix is displayed at program startup. If you draw a rectangle or an ellipsis, it lies over the matrix and covers it up. The *Matrix* button generates the matrix again over the drawn graphic.

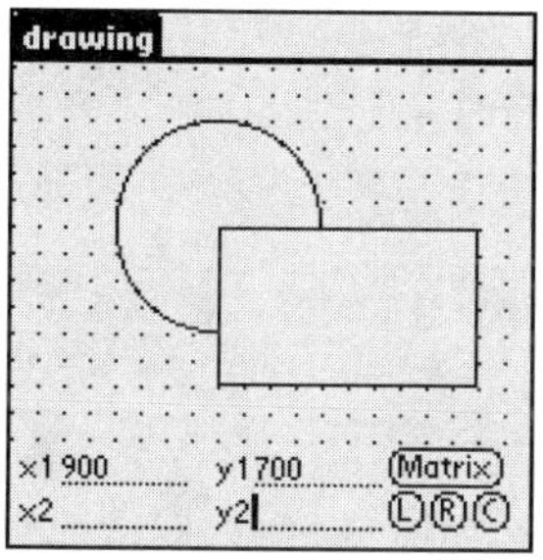


Drawn objects ...

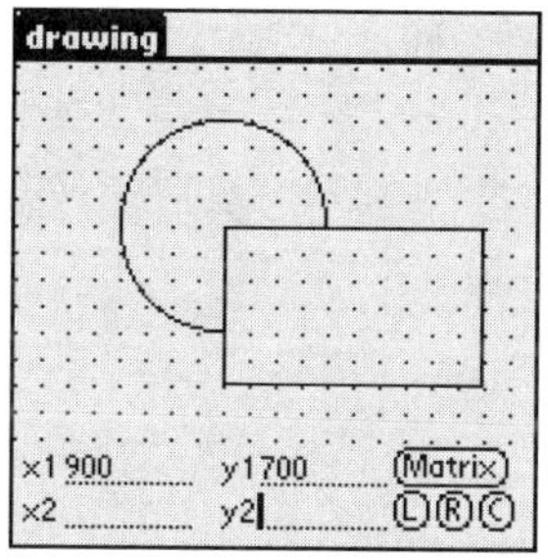


... and the generated matrix

*Circle:*

*x1=600 y1=600*
*x2=200 y2=200*

*Rectangle:*

*x1=400 y1=400*
*x2=900 y2=700*

```
frame drawing;
  end;

label x1label, drawing;
  display "x1";
  position 20,820;
  end;

label y1label, drawing;
  display "y1";
  position 400,820;
  end;

label x2label, drawing;
  display "x2";
  position 20,900;
  end;

label y2label, drawing;
  display "y2";
  position 400,900;
  end;

text x1text, drawing;
  char_size 5,1;
  position 100,820;
  end;

text y1text, drawing;
  char_size 5,1;
  position 480,820;
  end;

text x2text, drawing;
  char_size 5,1;
  position 100,900;
  end;
```

```
text y2text, drawing;
  char_size 5,1;
  position 480,900;
  end;

button line, drawing;
  display "L";
  position 740,900;
  end;

button rectangle, drawing;
  display "R";
  position 820,900;
  end;

button circle, drawing;
  display "C";
  position 900,900;
  end;

button matrix, drawing;
  display "Matrix";
  position 740,820;
  end;

variables;
  numeric x1;
  numeric y1;
  numeric x2;
  numeric y2;
  numeric i;
  numeric j;
  end;

function line;
  get x1text, x1;
  get y1text, y1;
  get x2text, x2;
  get y2text, y2;
  set drawing, pen, x1, y1;
  draw drawing, line, x2-x1, y2-y1;
  put x1text, x2;
  put y1text, y2;
  put x2text, "";
  put y2text, "";
  end;

function rectangle;
  get x1text, x1;
  get y1text, y1;
  get x2text, x2;
```

```
  get y2text, y2;
  set drawing, pen, x1, y1;
  draw drawing, rectangle, x2-x1, y2-y1;
  put x1text, x2;
  put y1text, y2;
  put x2text, "";
  put y2text, "";
  end;

function circle;
  get x1text, x1;
  get y1text, y1;
  get x2text, x2;
  get y2text, y2;
  set drawing, pen, x1, y1;
  draw drawing, circle, x2-x1, y2-y1;
  put x1text, x2;
  put y1text, y2;
  put x2text, "";
  put y2text, "";
  end;

function matrix;
  for i=0, i<=1000;
    for j=100, j<=800;
      set drawing, pen, i, j;
      draw drawing, line, 0, 0;
    next j+50;
  next i+50;
  end;

function startup;
  matrix;
  end;
```

**CD**

**Program on the companion CD**

You can also find this program on the companion CD to this book as *0409.csl.*

Compared to its predecessor, this program was enhanced by one function and one button. The function with its nested loop is important. The button calls this function. The new *startup* function does the same thing, so that the matrix will be drawn at program startup.

The exterior loop counts the *i* variable in increments of 50 to 0 to 1,000. This counts the columns of the matrix. Within this loop, another one counts the *j* variable, also in increments of 50, but only from 100 to 800.

This interior loop sets the drawing pen to the coordinates i,j and draws a line there with the length of 0, in other words it draws a dot. When the interior loop has completed running from 100 to 800, a column of dots is drawn. The exterior loop increases the *I* value and thus the x-coordinate by 50, one column width; then the interior loop draws the next column using dots.

In this way the program can draw two-dimensional patterns using nested loops.

## Charts make numbers more descriptive

Whenever you see statistics, they are almost always garnished with a bar chart or a pie chart. Graphics are much easier on the human eye than columns of numbers are. Every modern spreadsheet program offers comfortable options for creating different charts. Until now few programs like this have been available on the Palm.

The following example shows you how to build such graphics into your programs, using HotPaw Basic.

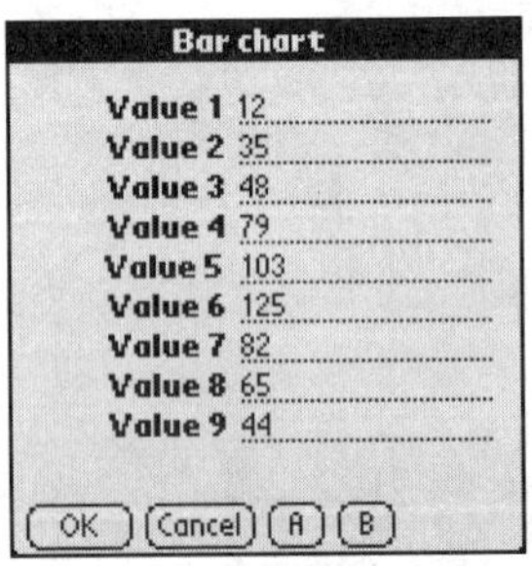


*Value table ...*

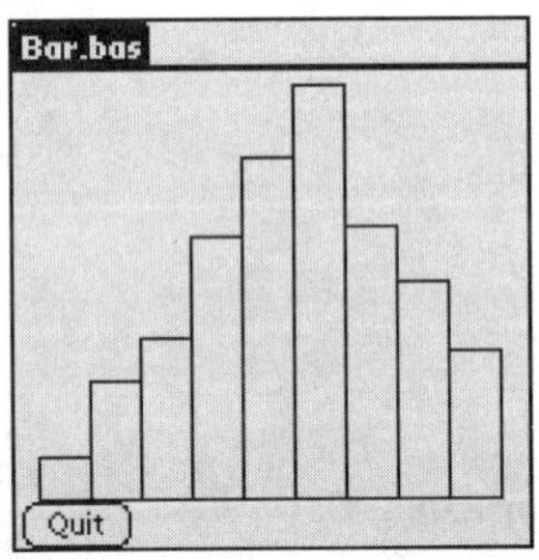


*... and bar chart*

In the sample program, enter the values to be portrayed into a form. These values could just as easily be the results of some calculation that was placed in a variable field. Use nine values because the yBasic standard forms make up to nine values possible. For other purposes you can also display more bars in accordance with the same system.

```
#Bar.bas
for i=1 to 17 step 2:s$(i)="":next i
for i=0 to 16 step 2
s$(i)="Value "+str$(i/2+1)
next i
start:
j=form(9,9,"Bar Chart")
if (j=0) then end
draw -1
for i=0 to 8
y=val(s$(2*i+1))
draw i*16+8, 145-y, 15, y, 4
next i
w=fn pen(0)
goto start
```

> **CD**
>
> **Program on the companion CD**
>
> You can also find this program on the companion CD to this book as *0410.bas.*

The first loop of the program fills the odd numbered variables of the *s$(i)* field with blank strings.

```
for i=1 to 17 step 2:s$(i)="":next i
```

The second loop writes the *"Value"* string in the even-numbered variables of this field, followed by the field number. These field numbers should be numbered in sequence and thus must be calculated using the i/2+1 formula from the even numbers.

```
for i=0 to 16 step 2
s$(i)="Value "+str$(i/2+1)
next I
```

After that an input form appears on the screen in accordance with the known system.

```
for i=0 to 8
y=val(s$(2*i+1))
draw i*16+8, 145-y, 15, y, 4
next i
```

This loop runs nine times for the nine values of the form. First the *y* variable is assigned the value from the form. Because the loop counts from 0 to 8 – the field labels are odd numbers from 1 to 17 – a conversion is necessary.

After that a rectangle is drawn, representing the bar. Use a variant of the *draw* function for that.

### *draw <x>, <y>, <Width>, <Height>, 4*

Always specify the upper left corner of the rectangle with x and y. The width and the height are then plotted to the lower right. In the example, this means:

- **x** - i * 16 + 8: Each bar is 16 pixels wide. The first bar starts at the x-coordinate 8 so that the nine bars are evenly distributed on the 160 pixels wide display.
- **y** - 145 - y: The lower edge of all bars should be at y-coordinate 145, to leave room for the *Quit* button predefined by yBasic. That way the upper edge is at 145 minus the calculated bar height y.
- **Width** – 15 pixels, one less than the mathematical width, because the first edge of the next bar is already on the 16th pixel.
- **Height** - y, the calculated height of the bar.

After the bars are drawn, the program waits for a tap on the display and then goes back to the input form. If the user taps the *Quit* button, the program ends.

## Display problems

This program functions well as long as the data is in the range between 0 and 130. However, most of the data that is to be generally displayed in the next example does not fall in this range.

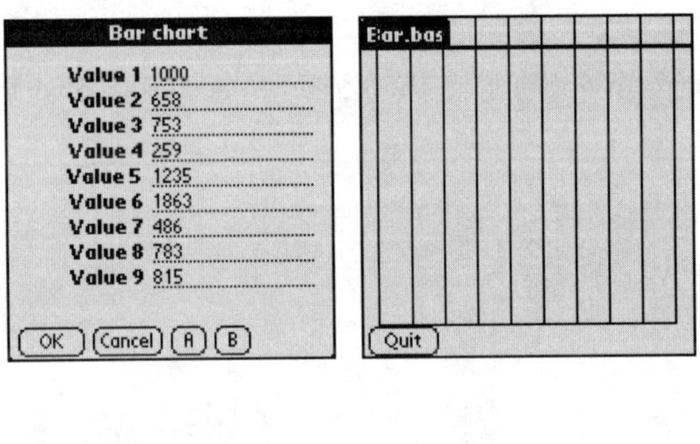


*Values that are too large*

With larger values the upper ends of the bars are no longer recognizable. Thus the program completely loses its reason for being. However, the same thing happens with very small values, which can no longer be distinguished on the bars.

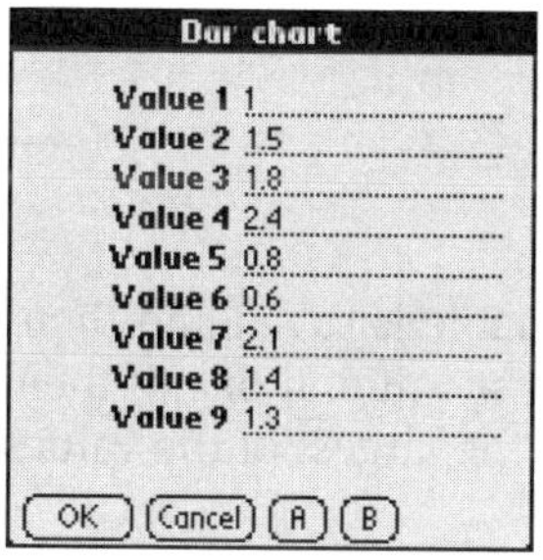

*Values that are too small*

In a bar chart, the absolute values aren't very important for a visual overview. What's important is that you recognize the differences between the values. For this reason, professional presentation graphic programs scale in such a way that the greatest value fills out the display. The other values can then be made out significantly better.

```
#Bar.bas
for i=1 to 17 step 2:s$(i)="":next i
for i=0 to 16 step 2
  s$(i)="Value "+str$(i/2+1)
next i
start:
j=form(9,9,"Bar chart")
if (j=0) then end
draw -1
m=val(s$(1))
for i=3 to 17 step 2
  if val(s$(i))>m then m=val(s$(i))
next i
for i=0 to 8
  y=int(val(s$(2*i+1))/m*130)
  draw i*16+8, 145-y, 15, y, 4
next i
w=fn pen(0)
goto start
```

**CD**

**Program on the companion CD**

You can also find this program on the companion CD to this book as *0411.bas*.

The initializations at the beginning and the input form correspond to the previous program version. Prior to drawing the graphic, the program determines the maximum value among the input values.

```
m=val(s$(1))
for i=3 to 17 step 2
if val(s$(i))>m then m=val(s$(i))
next i
```

For this purpose, the first value in the *m* variable is saved and then the remaining values are read and compared with the first value. If one of them is larger, it is stored in the *m* variable so that at the end the largest of the values is in the *m* variable.

Now the program calculates the bar height *y* in accordance with the following formula:

```
y=int(val(s$(2*i+1))/m*130)
```

The value from the form is divided by the maximum value times 130. The height of the screen area that can be occupied by the graphic is 130 pixels. The *int()* is used here to get the integral part of the calculated value. Decimal places can result from the division, which leads to errors rounding off in the *draw* statement.

### *int( <Number>)*

Determines only the integral part of a number, thus truncating all decimal places without rounding the numbers off mathematically.

The figures show the same number series as before, only displayed with the new program version.

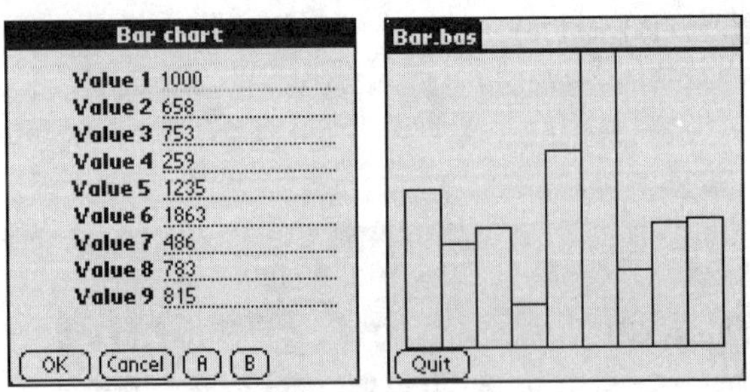


*Large values*

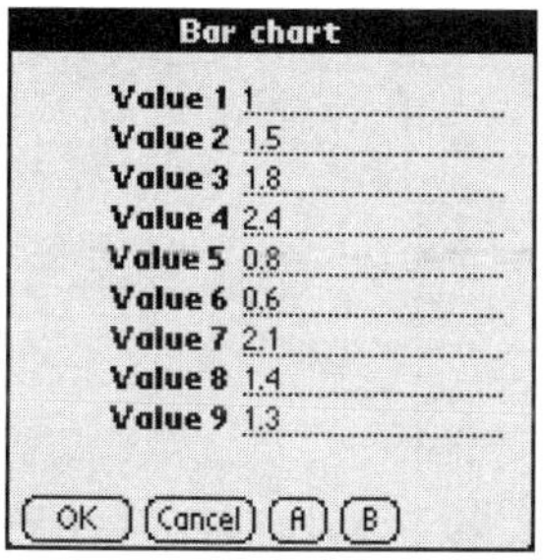


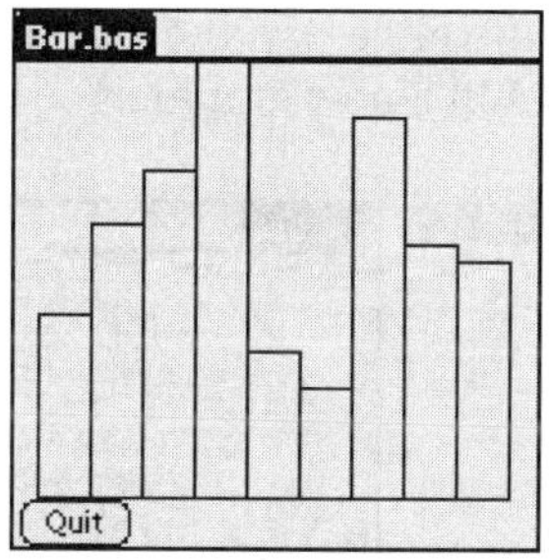


*Small values*

## Pie charts in yBasic

When it is more important to show the percentage distribution than the individual values in statistics, people prefer to use pie charts. In a pie chart, a circle is divided up into "pie wedges" corresponding to the percentages of the value to the total sum.

Modern spreadsheet programs and presentation programs on the PC can automatically generate pie charts. You can do the same thing on your Palm.

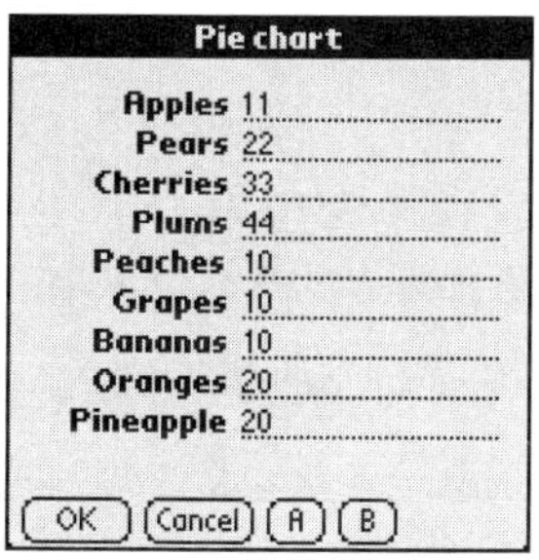


*Value table*

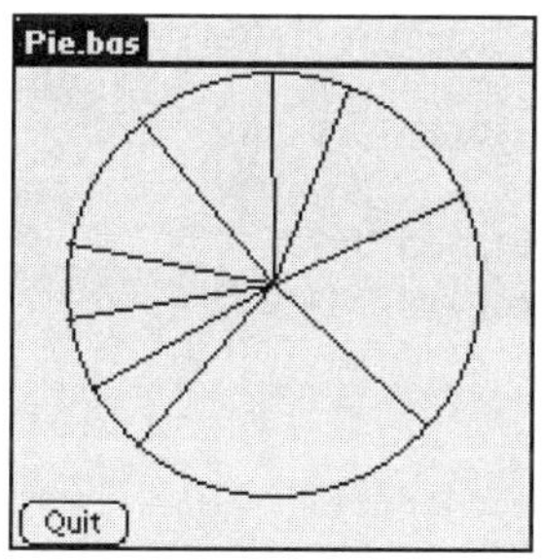


*Graphic*

In this program, enter nine values in a value table similar to the last example. Of course, these values could also be the results of a calculation. (In Chapter 8, which is about databases, you will learn how to graphically evaluate data from a database.)

The values are converted to a pie chart by tapping the *OK* button. As is customary in such graphics, the first value appears by the circle segment beginning on top, then continues clockwise. The next values follow in clockwise fashion. The individual segments correspond in their size to the percentage of the value.

To return to the value table, tap the graphic. You can change values and see the effects of the change in a new graphic.

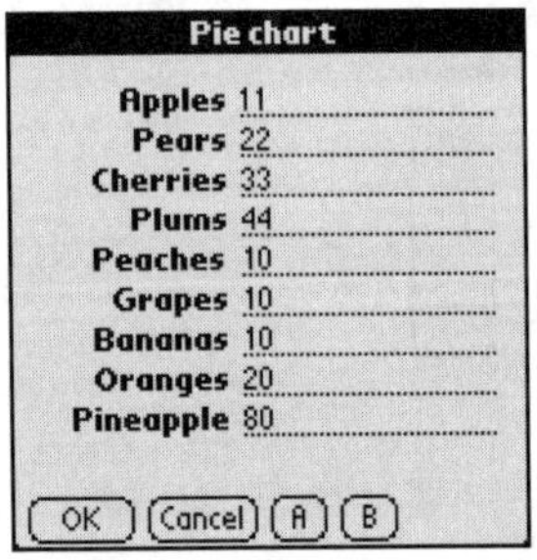


*Changed value table*

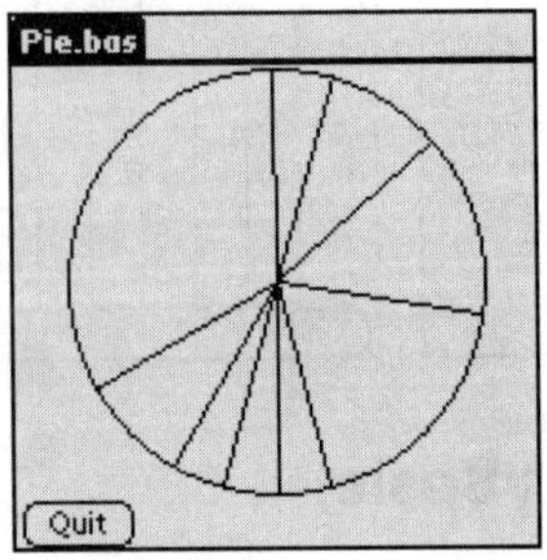


*New graphic*

In the illustration, the last value was significantly increased. That has consequences for the entire graphic because it now takes on a significantly higher percentage.

```
#Pie.bas
for i=1 to 17 step 2:s$(i)="":next i
m=db.find("memo","Field labels")
if (m<0) then goto error
open "memo",m as #1
  input #1,x$
  for i=0 to 16 step 2
    input #1,s$(i)
  next i
close #1
start:
j=form(9,9,"Pie chart")
if (j=0) then end
draw -1
draw circle 80,80,64
s=0:pi=3.14159:y=-pi/2
for i=1 to 17 step 2
  s=s+val(s$(i))
next i
for i=1 to 17 step 2
  y=y+val(s$(i))/s*2*pi
  draw 80,80,80+cos(y)*64,80+sin(y)*64,1
next i
w=fn pen(0)
goto start
error:
print "Field labels are missing"
```

**CD**

**Program on the companion CD**

You can also find this program on the companion CD to this book as *0412.bas*.

For a change, in this example, don't automatically generate the field labels; instead, import them from a memo, as described in yBasic on page 62 of Chapter 3.

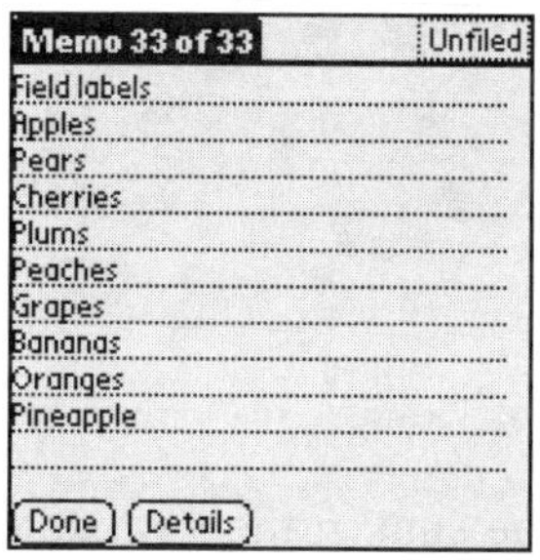


*The memo with the field labels*

After the memo is imported, a form appears in which the user can enter the values.

```
draw circle 80,80,64
```

This function draws the circle in which the pie chart is to be displayed.

### *draw circle <x>, <y>, <r>*

Draws a circle with the *x,y* center point and the *r* radius.

In the next line, the three variables that are important for the program run are initialized:

- **s** - Becomes the sum of all values later, important for calculating the percentages.
- **pi** - The circular number π, which has no fixed definition in yBasic.
- **y** - Angle of the first pie segment. Basically, HotPaw Basic calculates angle functions in radian measure, while the perpendicular line here, in contrast to the common mathematical definition, lies at $-\pi/2$.

**Tip**

**Angle calculation in radian measure**

Like most other programming languages, HotPaw Basic calculates angle functions in radian measure. In this connection a full circle with 360° corresponds to $2*\pi$ in radian measure. The zero direction points to the right, corresponding to the 3 on the clock. Usually angles are then counted counterclockwise so that the perpendicular line corresponds to the 12 on the clock or 90°, or $\pi/2$ in radian measure. However, HotPaw Basic calculates in the mathematically negative sense: angles are counted clockwise. Thus the perpendicular line is at $-\pi/2$.

The following loop:

```
for i=1 to 17 step 2
s=s+val(s$(i))
next i
```

adds all the values of the table and stores the sum in the *s* variable. After that comes the calculation of the pie chart.

```
for i=1 to 17 step 2
  y=y+val(s$(i))/s*2*pi
  draw 80,80,80+cos(y)*64,80+sin(y)*64,1
next i
```

The boundary line angle of the respective segment is stored in the *y* variable. Because the segments all lie one behind the other, these angles are all added to the previous angle. The angle of an individual segment results from the following formula:

```
val(s$(i))/s*2*pi
```

The next line of the program then draws a line from the center of the circular point to the point on the circular line that corresponds to the new total angle.

Here is a variable table for the program:

| Variable table | |
|---|---|
| i | Loop counter |
| j | Return value of the buttons in the form |
| m | Return value of the db.find function for opening the memos |

| Variable table | |
|---|---|
| pi | Circular number π |
| s | Sum of all values |
| s$() | Predefined input form |
| w | Dummy for waiting for tapping on the display |
| x$ | Dummy for intercepting the title line during importing of the memo |
| y | Added angle for segments of a circle |

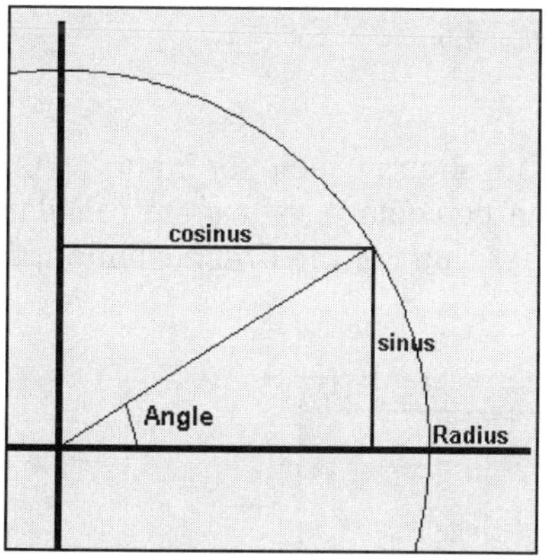


*Calculation of a random point on the circular line from the angle and radius*

**Tip**

**Simplified pie chart function on the Palm IIIc**

HotPaw Basic also offers a simplified function for drawing filled-in circle segments for pie charts. However, this only works on the Palm IIIc. You can find more information about this program later in this chapter in 4.4 starting on page 155.

## Pie charts in CASL

CASL has the same program, but it's more time-consuming. Therefore, you can build in an additional function. The percentage values are automatically displayed in the table. In addition, two new techniques are introduced in CASL with this program, namely arrays of objects and shifting between different frames. You have already used arrays of variables in different sample programs. In principle, arrays of objects function quite similarly.

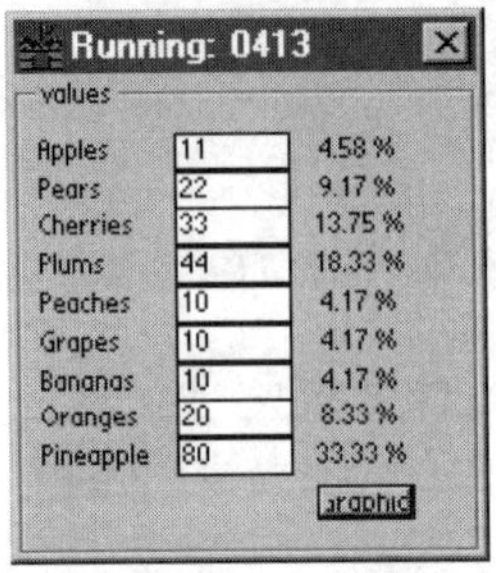


Inputting the values in Windows ...

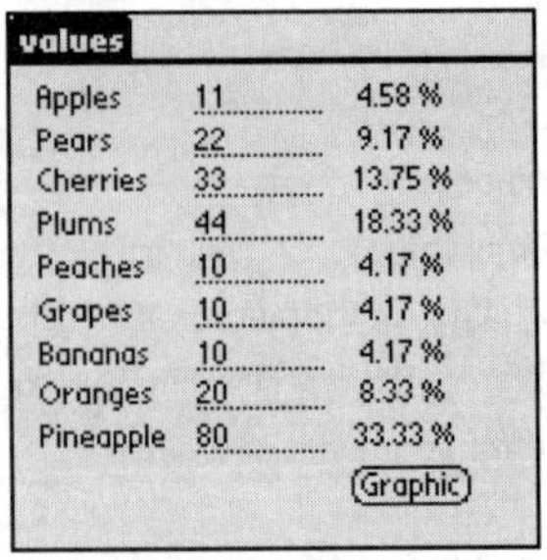


... and on the Palm

Like the yBasic program, this program shows a table for inputting the values. As soon as the values are entered, the percentage values are calculated and displayed next to the input values. When you tap the *Graphic* button, the pie chart appears.

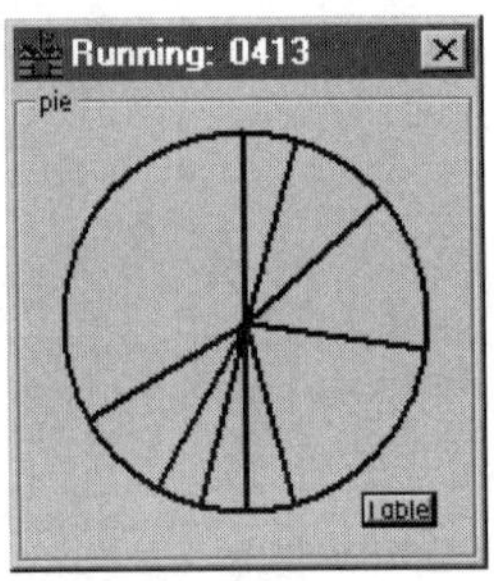


Pie chart in Windows ...

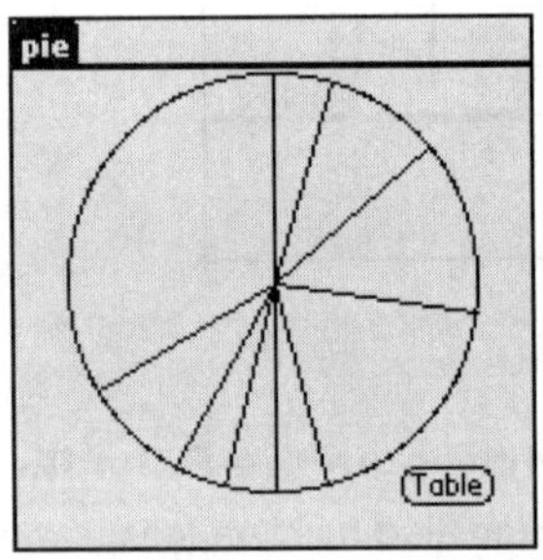


... and on the Palm

The arrangement of the individual segments also corresponds to that of the yBasic program. If you tap the *Table* button, the table for inputting the values reappears.

```
frame values;
  end;
label b[9], values;
  end;
text w[9], values;
  char_size 5,1;
  invokes calc;
  end;
label p[9], values;
  end;
button graphic, values;
```

```
  position 650,860;
  display "Graphic";
  end;

frame pie;
  end;
button table, pie;
  position 750,860;
  display "Table";
  end;

variables;
  numeric i;
  numeric s;
  numeric w1[9];
  numeric y;
  numeric pi=3.14159;
  string format="##.##";
  end;

function calc;
  s=0;
  for i=0, i<9;
    get w[i], w1[i];
    s=s+w1[i];
  next i+1;
  for i=0, i<9;
    put p[i], string(w1[i]/s*100,format)+" %";
  next i+1;
  end;

function graphic;
  hide values;
  show pie;
  set pie, pen, 100, 100;
  draw pie, circle, 800, 800;
  y=-pi/2;
  for i=0, i<9;
    y=y+w1[i]/s*2*pi;
    set pie, pen, 500, 500;
    draw pie, line, cos(y)*400, sin(y)*400;
  next i+1;
  end;

function table;
  hide pie;
  show values;
  end;
```

```
function startup;
  hide pie;
  show values;
  for i=0, i<9;
    move b[i], 50, 120+i*80;
    move w[i], 350, 120+i*80;
    move p[i], 650, 120+i*80;
  next i+1;
  put b[0], "Apples";
  put b[1], "Pears";
  put b[2], "Cherries";
  put b[3], "Plums";
  put b[4], "Peaches";
  put b[5], "Grapes";
  put b[6], "Bananas";
  put b[7], "Oranges";
  put b[8], "Pineapple";
  end;
```

CD

**Program on the companion CD**

You can also find this program on the companion CD to this book as *0413.csl.*

At the beginning, a definition area occurs, as in every CASL program. This time two *frame* objects are defined, *values* and *pies*.

On the *values frame* you can find a *button* and two arrays of *label* fields and one from *text* fields. These arrays correspond to the definition variable fields from several objects that can be addressed through an index number. In the definitions of these objects, the name of the *frame* on which they are to appear must be specified everywhere.

```
label b[9], values;
  end;
```

Defines nine *label* objects on the *values frame*. Later these *labels* can be addressed as *b[0]* to *b[8]*. Until now they have contained neither contents nor exact locations. The program will define both later. The same applies for *labels p[0]* through *p[8]*.

```
text w[9], values;
  char_size 5,1;
  invokes calc;
  end;
```

The *text* objects *w[0]* through *w[8]* are also located in different locations on the screen but have two parameters in common, the *char_size* size and the function that they call: *invokes*. That is why these parameters can be specified in the definition.

```
variables;
  numeric i;
  numeric s;
  numeric wl[9];
  numeric y;
  numeric pi=3.14159;
  string format="##.##";
  end;
```

An array is also defined in the variable definitions, here as a numeric variable field, in which the numerical values of the input values are accepted in the program. In addition, the $\pi$ circular number is set here, which is not defined as a constant in CASL either.

```
function startup;
  hide pie;
  show values;
  for i=0, i<9;
    move b[i], 50, 120+i*80;
    move w[i], 350, 120+i*80;
    move p[i], 650, 120+i*80;
  next i+1;
put b[0], "Apples";
  put b[1], "Pears";
  put b[2], "Cherries";
  put b[3], "Plums";
  put b[4], "Peaches";
  put b[5], "Grapes";
  put b[6], "Bananas";
  put b[7], "Oranges";
  put b[8], "Pineapple";
  end;
```

At program startup you must first see to it that the correct *frame* is visible, namely the one with the input form. When working with several *frame* objects, always make certain that only one is enabled. Use the *hide* and *show* functions.

## *hide <Object>;*

Hides an object. This object can be a single *button* or even an entire *frame*.

### *show <Object>;*

Makes an object or a *frame* visible. Buttons and other objects on hidden *frames* do not become visible until the *frame* has been made visible.

After the *values frame* has been made visible, a loop is started that places the objects predefined as arrays in their proper positions on the screen.

### *move <Object>, <x>, <y>;*

Moves an object to the specified x,y-coordinate, making it possible to arrange objects from an array using a loop. It is not possible to specify the position of arrays directly in the object definition.

After all of the objects are positioned, the field labels are written one after another to the *labels b[0]* through *b[8]*. This also would have been possible beforehand and has nothing to do with the position of the *labels*. It is also possible to move *labels* with contents.

When the user enters a numerical value, all percentage values are automatically recalculated. The *w[i] text* fields contain an *invokes* parameter in their definition, which calls the *calc* function.

```
function calc;
  s=0;
  for i=0, i<9;
    get w[i], w1[i];
    s=s+w1[i];
  next i+1;
  for i=0, i<9;
    put p[i], string(w1[i]/s*100,format)+" %";
  next i+1;
  end;
```

This function consists of two loops that are processed one after the other. In the first loop the contents of the *w[i] text* fields are read out to the *w1[i]* numerical variables array and simultaneously the sum of all nine variables is formed in the *s* variable.

The second loop writes the percentage specifications from this to the *label* fields *p[i]*. The format specification from the *format* variable is then used and a percent sign (%) is appended to the end of this string.

**Tip**

**Linking strings**

In CASL and in yBasic, strings can be appended to each other with a plus sign. This character has nothing to do with a mathematical addition here.

Each time the user changes a numerical value, the program executes the *calc* function. When the user taps the *Graphic* button, the function of the same name starts up:

```
function graphic;
  hide values;
  show pie;
  set pie, pen, 100, 100;
  draw pie, circle, 800, 800;
  y=-pi/2;
  for i=0, i<9;
    y=y+w1[i]/s*2*pi;
    set pie, pen, 500, 500;
    draw pie, line, cos(y)*400, sin(y)*400;
  next i+1;
  end;
```

First, this function switches the *frames*. The *values frame* is covered and the *pie frame* on which the graphic is to appear is displayed.

Here the pen is set to the coordinates of 100,100 and a circle is drawn up to the coordinates 800,800. Keep in mind that in CASL you do not specify the circle center point and the radius but rather two corner points of a rectangle circumscribing the circle. The two points do not lie on the circular line.

The loop then calculates the angle of the individual segment lines and draws them. The formulas are the same as in the yBasic program, only with different coordinates - the CASL coordinate system has 1,000 x 1,000 units.

**Tip**

**Angle calculation in CASL**

Like HotPaw Basic, CASL calculates in radian measure in the mathematically negative sense. The angles are counted clockwise; thus the perpendicular line also lies at $-\pi/2$.

The *Table* button on the lower right in the graphic calls the *table* function, which switches the *frames* again, so that the input form returns to the foreground.

```
function table;
  hide pie;
  show values;
  end;
```

## Graphic display of serial data

Long number columns of the kind that come into being with measured curves of all kinds, stock prices, and currency rates are quite difficult to grasp. However, if you represent the numbers graphically as a curve, you immediately recognize trends or regularities.

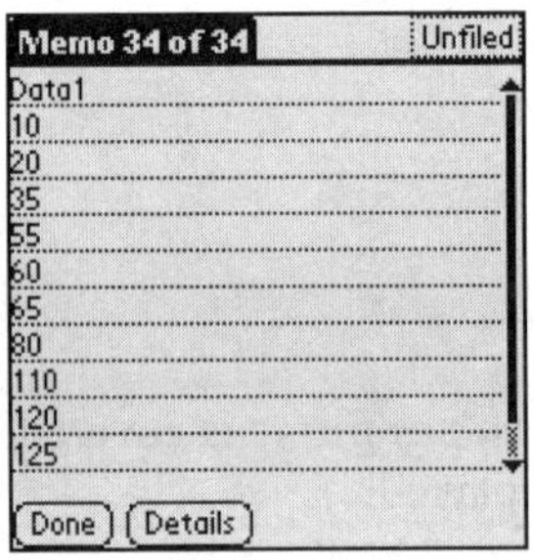


*Measured data on a memo ...*

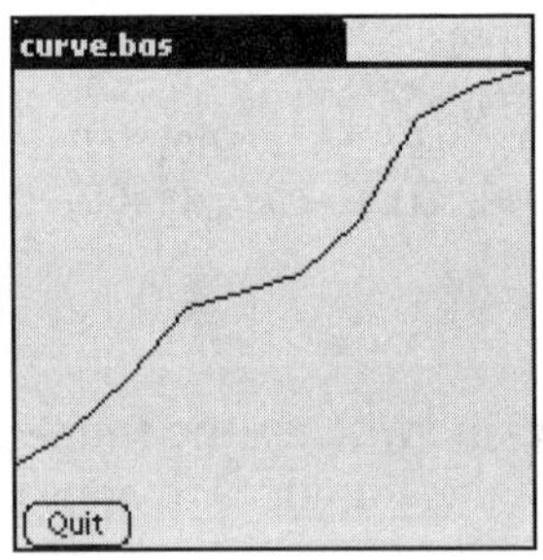


*... and as a simple graphic curve*

Using only the numbers, the drop into the middle range of the curve would not be nearly as noticeable as in a graphic.

The next program reads a series of numbers from a memo and displays them graphically. This series of numbers can contain up to 160 individual values. More values wouldn't make sense anyway, because you would no longer be able to make them out on the 160 pixel wide display.

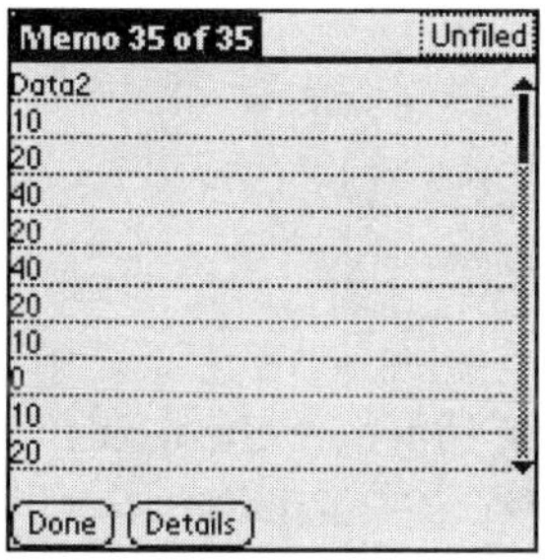


*Memo with 48 data ...*

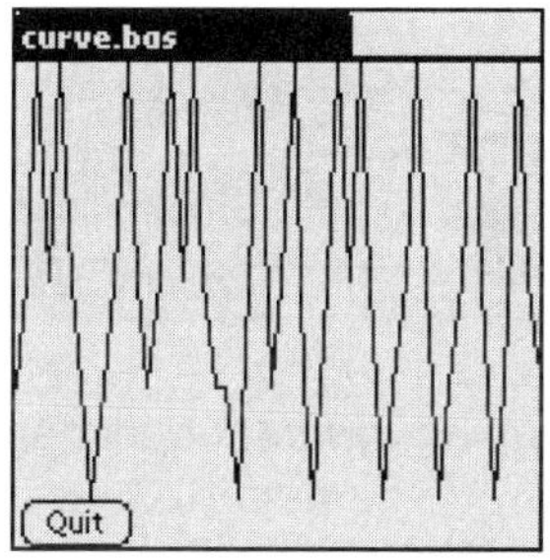


*... and the curve*

If you collect additional values, enter them on a memo and restart the program. The curve was automatically scaled in width and height in such a way that all the measured data can be seen.

```
#curve.bas
dim d(160)
n$="Name of memo"
a$=input$(n$,"curves",1)
me=db.find("memo",a$)
if (me<0) then goto error
open "memo",me as #1
  input #1,x$
  n=0
  while (x$<>"")
    input #1,x$
    d(n)=val(x$)
    n=n+1
  wend
close #1
m=d(0):n=n-2
for i=1 to n
  if d(i)>m then m=d(i)
next i
draw -1
moveto 0,145-(d(0)/m*130)
for i=1 to n
  lineto i*160/n,145-(d(i)/m*130)
next i
w=fn pen(0)
end
error:
print "Memo not found"
```

**CD**

**Program on the companion CD**

You can also find this program on the companion CD to this book as *0414.bas*, with both memos for the curves as *0415.txt* and *0416.txt*.

At program startup an *input$()* query appears, in which the user must enter the name of the memo to be imported. In this way you can store the different data series on different memos and display them optionally.

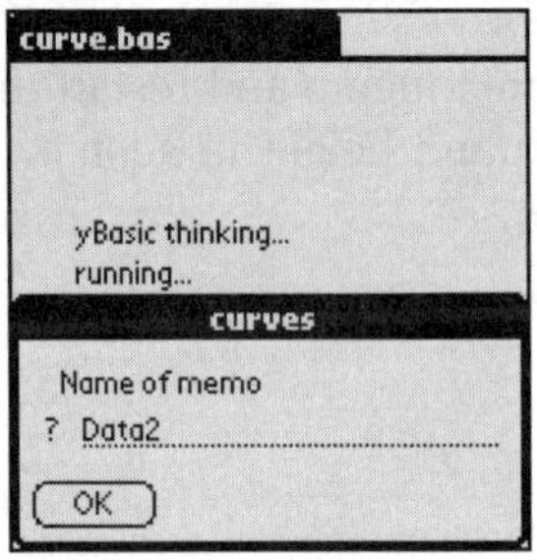


*Inputting a memo name*

The inputting of the memo proceeds somewhat differently this time than in the preceding examples, because it is not known how much data a memo contains.

```
open "memo",me as #1
input #1,x$
n=0
while (x$<>"")
  input #1,x$
  d(n)=val(x$)
  n=n+1
wend
close #1
```

The first line, which contains the name of the memo, is input, but is not subject to further evaluation. Next comes a *while...wend* loop, which continues entering lines as long as they are not blank.

**Note**

**Important!**

Always conclude the memos with the data for this program with a last [Enter] so that the cursor is under the last number. Otherwise, the program cannot detect the end of the memo.

The numerical value of the input string is written to the corresponding field of the *d(n)* array.

### *while <Condition> ... wend*

All of the statements between the *while* line and the *wend* line will be executed as long as the condition after *while* is true. Therefore, make certain that something happens within the loop to make this condition false at some point. Otherwise, the program will run in a continuous loop.

If the condition does not apply from the beginning, the statements in the loop won't be executed at all.

In this case, one line of the memo is input, the numerical value is stored, and the counter for the *d(n)* array is increased. If the loop runs into the blank line at the end, it won't be saved, but the next time the condition is checked, the loop is terminated.

```
m=d(0):n=n-2
for i=1 to n
  if d(i)>m then m=d(i)
next i
```

According to the procedure from earlier examples, the maximum of the input values is now determined, to scale the y-axis of the graphic.

The number of input values that is needed for the construction of the graphic is two numbers smaller than the counter *n*. For this reason, *n* is reduced by 2 for the further calculation.

```
draw -1
moveto 0,145-(d(0)/m*130)
for i=1 to n
  lineto i*160/n,145-(d(i)/m*130)
next i
```

After the screen has been cleared, the pen position is set to the first value of the curve. This is located at the left screen border at the x-coordinate 0. Using the maximum value, the y value is scaled to a height of 130 pixels. For graphic screen controls, 15 pixels each are reserved above and below. The calculated value is subtracted from 145, because the Palm coordinate system goes from top to bottom and thus the y-coordinate 145 corresponds to the lowest border of the area used by the graphic.

The following loop draws the entire curve using simple *lineto* commands. In the process, the x values are distributed equally over the 160-pixel width of the Palm display.

Here is a variable table for the program:

| Variable table | |
|---|---|
| a$ | Name of the memo with the values |
| d(160) | Numerical values of the input data |
| i | Loop counter |
| m | Maximum of the values |
| me | Return value of the *db.find* function for opening the memos |
| n | Number of the edited value |
| n$ | String with text for input form |
| w | Dummy used to wait for tapping on the display |
| x$ | Input line of a memo |

## 4.3 Arranged data structures for complex graphics

In the preceding examples, you have already seen how to create regular patterns as well as more complex graphics with the help of loops. However, these graphics were always a fixed result of some type of calculation and were no longer used in the program except for visual effect.

What about changing a graphic, for example in a game, where it can be important to know what the graphic looks like? While yBasic offers different functions for writing graphics to the screen, it has no function for reading such a graphic. A yBasic program must note in some other way the data of a graphic, which will later be important.

With most graphics it is sufficient to note the logic that comes after the graphic to be able to recreate the elements of the graphic if necessary. Normally you don't have to go to the extra trouble of saving the state of these pixels.

The following examples show how to efficiently work with complex graphic data.

# Jigsaw puzzle

The next program displays a simple jigsaw puzzle made of square tiles. Each tile has a light and a dark side. You can turn the tiles over by tapping them.

*The jigsaw puzzle*

```
#jigsawpuzzle1.bas
dim a%(15,12)
draw -1
for y=0 to 12
  for x=0 to 15
    draw x*10+1, y*10+17,7,7,4
    a%(x,y)=0
  next x
next y
start:
x1=fn pen(0)
y1=fn pen(2)
x=int(x1/10)
y=int((y1-15)/10)
a%(x,y)=1-a%(x,y)
p=a%(x,y)*14-7
draw x*10+1, y*10+17,7,7,p
goto start
```

**CD**

**Program on the companion CD**

You can also find this program on the companion CD to this book as *0417.bas*.

The program consists of two parts: In the first part the program draws the tiles, whereas the second part permits user interaction to turn over the tiles.

Under yBasic you can make practical use of 160 x 130 pixels of the Palm display. With a tile size of 9 x 9 pixels and one pixel space, this results in 16 x 13 tiles on the field.

```
dim a%(15,12)
```

At the beginning you define an array out of integer variables, which store the state of every tile: 0 for white and 1 for black. When dimensioning an array in HotPaw Basic, you specify the highest permissible index number, that is, one less than fields in the array, because the counting can begin with 0. In CASL the exact number of fields is specified for dimensioning.

Variables with a percentage sign at the end of the name can only accept integral values. These integer variables occupy a bit less disk space, which hardly has an effect in normal cases, but can definitely play an important role with larger arrays. This single array already takes up the space of 208 variables.

```
for y=0 to 12
  for x=0 to 15
    draw x*10+1, y*10+17,7,7,4
    a%(x,y)=0
  next x
next y
```

The first part of the program consists of two loops nested within each other, which draw the squares. The enlarged illustration shows you how the coordinates of the individual squares are precisely calculated.

*Section from the graphic with specification of the pixel coordinates*

Use the *draw* function to draw the tiles. If the last parameter is a 4, a rectangle will be drawn without filling.

After the outer loop has run through completely, 208 squares appear on the display, all in white. The entire *a%(x,y)* array is filled with zeros.

After the first part of the program

The second part of the program, beginning with the *start* branch mark, runs continuously, until the user taps *Quit*. Turn over individual tiles by tapping them.

```
start:
x1=fn pen(0)
y1=fn pen(2)
x=int(x1/10)
y=int((y1-15)/10)
a%(x,y)=1-a%(x,y)
p=a%(x,y)*14-7
draw x*10+1, y*10+17,7,7,p
goto start
```

Until now you have only used the *fn pen(0)* function for the purpose of waiting. The return value of this function, referred to here as *x1*, contains the x-coordinate of the point on which the user tapped. The program evaluates this value to determine which tile was tapped.

## *fn pen(2)*

This function returns the y-coordinate of the last point tapped. In contrast to *fn pen(0)*, the function does not wait for the user to tap the screen but returns the y-coordinate of the last screen contact, regardless of how long it has been. In this way you can determine the exact coordinates of a tap on the screen with a combination of *fn pen(0)* and *fn pen (2)*.

If you divide the coordinates by 10 (= width and height of a tile) and take only the integral portion, you get the number of the tapped tile in x and y direction.

Prior to this, the 15 pixels of the upper border, on which there is no tile, are deducted in y direction.

A white tile is supposed to turn black when tapped, and a black one is supposed to turn white. The color is stored as 0 or 1 in the array fields. With the following formula you can switch 0 and 1 with each other without having to query the current state beforehand:

```
a = 1-a
```

Remember that you are dealing with a variable assignment here, not a mathematical equation. From a mathematical point of view, this equation would only be correct for a = 0.5. In yBasic (and also in CASL) variables have values assigned to them using the mathematical equals sign. Thus you have the value 1 - 0 = 1 from a 0 and conversely you have the value 1 - 1 = 0 from a 1.

Depending on the new color of the tile, it should now be repainted. To do so, use the *draw* function with two different parameters:

- 7 - Draws a filled rectangle
- -7 - Draws a blank rectangle. In contrast to parameter 4, not only is the outline drawn here but the contents are also deleted. In this way you are able to draw a blank rectangle over a filled one and remove the former filling again.

Based on the color of the field, 1 or 0 in the array variable *a%(x,y)*, the program has to set this parameter to 7 or -7. Use this formula:

```
p=a%(x,y)*14-7
```

The parameter *p* is then used in the *draw* function and draws the tile.

```
draw x*10+1, y*10+17,7,7,p
```

After that, the program returns to the *start* branch mark and waits for the user to tap the next tile.

## More demanding variant for gamers

While the last example was interesting from a programming standpoint, it may not have been challenging for gamers, so another rule now comes into play:

When a tile is turned over, the four tiles directly adjacent to it are also turned around. In the process, tiles that were previously turned over may be turned back again.

Now try to turn over the tiles from a given pattern in such a way that the entire playing field is the same color, or conversely, to create an appealing picture on the blank field. Thus, a minor change to the rules can make a challenging puzzle task out of a simple jigsaw puzzle.

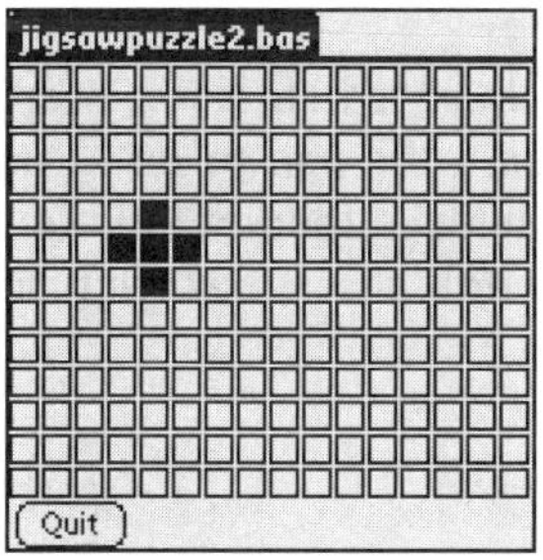


*The first tile turned over ...*

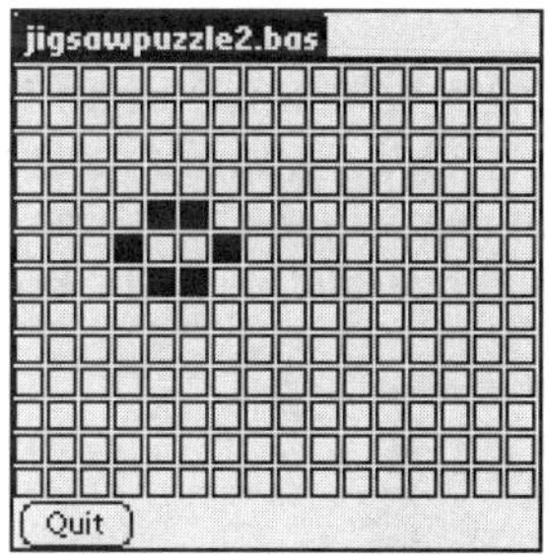


*... and the one next to it*

When you tap a field, the program not only has to turn it over but also the four adjacent fields as well.

```
#jigsawpuzzle2.bas
dim a%(17,14)
draw -1
for y=1 to 13
  for x=1 to 16
    draw (x-1)*10+1,(y-1)*10+17,7,7,4
    a%(x,y)=0
  next x
next y
start:
x1=fn pen(0)
y1=fn pen(2)
x=int(x1/10)+1
y=int((y1-15)/10)+1
x2=x : y2=y : gosub drwing
x2=x+1 : y2=y : gosub drwing
x2=x : y2=y-1 : gosub drwing
x2=x-1 : y2=y : gosub drwing
x2=x : y2=y+1 : gosub drwing
goto start
drwing:
a%(x2,y2)=1-a%(x2,y2)
```

```
p=a%(x2,y2)*14-7
if ((y2>0) and (y2<14)) then draw (x2-1)*10+1,(y2-1)*10+17,7,7,p
return
```

**CD**

**Program on the companion CD**

You can also find this program on the companion CD to this book as *0418.bas*.

The biggest problem with this variant is the border fields. If a user taps one of these fields, there can be no mistake because a tile had to be turned over that was outside of the actual field. With border fields, a total of only four instead of five tiles are turned over, while in the corners only three tiles are turned over.

*Turned over tiles at the edges*

To simplify the problem with the border fields, dimension the array larger in both directions by two fields each. That way a series of invisible tiles exists around the visible field, which can automatically be turned around with it. The actual state of these tiles is not important. They are not included in the display.

```
dim a%(17,14)
```

Accordingly, the loop parameters for the drawing of the individual tiles must be adjusted. The loop no longer counts from 0 to 12 and 0 to 15, but rather from 1 to 13 and 1 to 16.

```
for y=1 to 13
for x=1 to 16
```

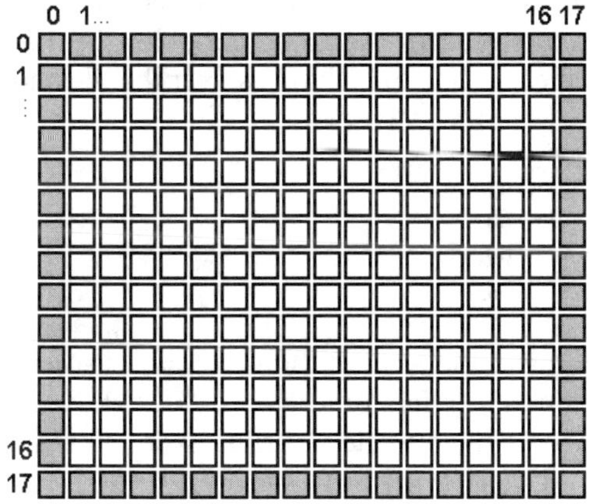


*Numbering of the tiles. The gray shaded tiles cannot be seen*

After the new numbering, the tiles on the screen would have different coordinates, shifted by exactly one tile measure to the right and bottom. To avoid this and still not have to recalculate the coordinates, reduce the number of tiles in both directions by 1 only in the *draw* function.

```
draw (x-1)*10+1,(y-1)*10+17,7,7,4
```

In precisely the same manner, the values of the tapped point must be increased to mark the correct field.

```
x=int(x1/10)+1
y=int((y1-15)/10)+1
```

After the program has determined which tile was tapped, five tiles must be turned over, the one that was tapped and the four adjacent tiles. If you tap a border tile, five tiles are turned in the program, not all of which are visible, however.

If, as in this case, a specific program part is invoked several times, you can define it as a subroutine and then you don't have to enter it more than once in the source code. Basic uses the *gosub...return* statement.

## gosub...return

The *gosub* statement goes to a branch mark defined in the program, a place that the program does not get to in normal execution. The program continues running until it reaches the *return* statement. From here the program goes to the line directly after the *gosub*, from where the subroutine was invoked.

In our example the numbers of the five tiles to be turned over are determined using the tapped tile *x,y* and stored in the *x2,y2* variables. In the process, the *drwing* subroutine is started each time, which turns over the tile and redraws it.

```
x2=x : y2=y : gosub drwing
x2=x+1 : y2=y : gosub drwing
x2=x : y2=y-1 : gosub drwing
x2=x-1 : y2=y : gosub drwing
x2=x : y2=y+1 : gosub drwing
```

The subroutine, which begins at the *drwing:* branch mark, uses the *x2,y2* variables from the main program and differs otherwise only slightly from the previous program version. Here too, only one tile is turned over and redrawn.

```
drwing:
a%(x2,y2)=1-a%(x2,y2)
p=a%(x2,y2)*14-7
if ((y2>0) and (y2<14)) then draw (x2-1)*10+1,(y2-1)*10+17,7,7,p
return
```

**Note**

**No local variables**

In contrast to many other programming languages, HotPaw Basic does not use any local variables for subroutines. This means that a variable that is used in the main program and has a value there can also be used in the subroutine with precisely this value. It is not necessary to pass the variable to the subroutine in particular or to declare it separately. The subroutine has full access to all variables of the main program.

The invisible tiles occupy variables in the array and accordingly can also be turned over logically. However, keep this in mind when you turn things over graphically: yBasic, unlike CASL, doesn't produce any error messages when the program draws in the coordinate area outside of the screen. Thus the tiles to the left and right of the visible area can be turned over without any problems. However, above and below the playing field visible pixels appear that you have kept free for visual effect. Thus, the *draw* function would draw new squares here if a tile in the uppermost or lowermost row is turned over.

To prevent this, a query was built in before the *draw* function so that a tile is only drawn when its coordinate in y direction is greater than 0 and at the same time (=logical AND) less than 14, thus in the visible area between 1 and 13.

## Preset tasks

This program turns into a real brainteaser when it is a matter of turning over a preset pattern in such a way that after that all the tiles show the same color, white or black. These tasks should be saved outside of the actual program to create your own tasks or to exchange them with other users.

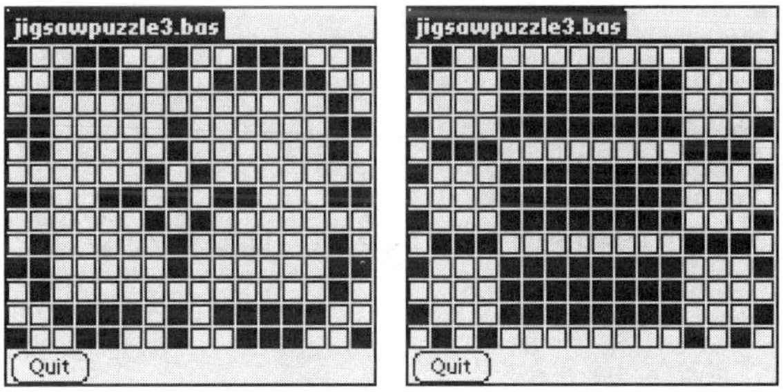


*Examples of tasks to be solved*

To exchange and edit data, save the tasks on memos in simple ASCII format. For each black field, a 1 is there; for each white field, a 0. Each tile line corresponds to one line on the memo.

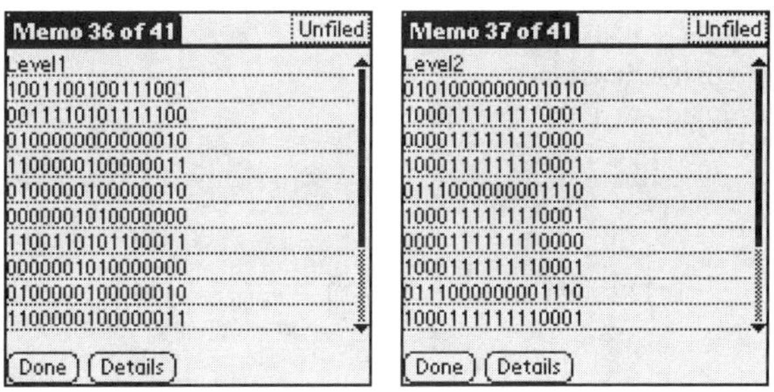


*The same tasks as memos*

**CD**

**Program on the companion CD**

You can also find these memos on the companion CD to this book as *0419.txt* and *0420.txt*.

The next version will enhance the program to input the memos and draw the tiles from the beginning in two different colors.

```
#jigsawpuzzle3.bas
dim a%(17,14)
draw -1
n$="Memo name"
au$=input$(n$,"Task",1)
me=db.find("memo",au$)
if (me<0) then goto error
open "memo",me as #1
  input #1,x$
  for y=1 to 13
    input #1,x$
    for x=1 to 16
      a%(x,y)=val(mid$(x$,x,1))
      draw (x-1)*10+1,(y-1)*10+17,7,7,4
      if (a%(x,y)=1) then draw (x-1)*10+1,(y-1)*10+17,7,7,7
    next x
  next y
close #1
start:
x1=fn pen(0)
y1=fn pen(2)
x=int(x1/10)+1
y=int((y1-15)/10)+1
x2=x : y2=y : gosub drwing
x2=x+1 : y2=y : gosub drwing
x2=x : y2=y-1 : gosub drwing
x2=x-1 : y2=y : gosub drwing
x2=x : y2=y+1 : gosub drwing
goto start
drwing:
a%(x2,y2)=1-a%(x2,y2)
p=a%(x2,y2)*14-7
if ((y2>0) and (y2<14)) then draw (x2-1)*10+1,(y2-1)*10+17,7,7,p
return
error:
print "Memo not found"
```

**CD**

**Program on the companion CD**

You can also find this program on the companion CD to this book as *0421.bas*.

At the beginning, a query for a memo name and a function for opening the memo and inputting the first line have been added. This runs in accordance with the known pattern.

Within the outer loop, which generates the lines of the tiles on the screen, a line of the memo is now read and stored in the *x$* variable.

```
for y=1 to 13
  input #1,x$
  for x=1 to 16
    a%(x,y)=val(mid$(x$,x,1))
    draw (x-1)*10+1,(y-1)*10+17,7,7,4
    if (a%(x,y)=1) then draw (x-1)*10+1,(y-1)*10+17,7,7,7
  next x
next y
```

In the inner loop, one character of the input line is evaluated at a time. Use the *mid$()* function.

### *mid$(<String>, <Position>, <Length>)*

This function reads individual characters or character strings from a string. For this purpose, three parameters are specified:

- **String** - The string, from which the program is to read.
- **Position** - Position of the first read character. The first character in the string here is number 1, not number 0 as is the case with arrays.
- **Length** - Length of the string that is to be input.

In the example, exactly one character is input from the x$ string, which contains one line of the memo. The position is counted off by the loop. The input character ("0" or "1") is then converted into a numerical value by the *val()* function and stored in the *a%(x,y)* variable field, where it specifies the color of the tile.

All of the tiles are first drawn white, as in the last program. After that a query uses the a%(x,y) value to decide whether a black square should be drawn in the tile.

Thereafter, the actual game runs exactly as it did in the previous version.

## Labyrinth

For thousands of years labyrinths and mazes of all different kinds have fascinated people. This special form of graphic has triggered the particular interest of artists, while mathematicians and logicians have also been intrigued. In the computer age both the designing and the solving of such labyrinths have offered notable challenges to programmers.

**Note**

### Labyrinths in science

Labyrinths of different topology are used repeatedly in research projects as test objects for operations of artificial intelligence (AI = Artificial Intelligence) and robotics. Upon observing a labyrinth, a practiced human observer can quickly identify a solution without following the path directly. System solutions are also possible through experimentation for those unable to obtain a clear view of the labyrinth in its entirety. All systems must find solutions that come as close to human "intuition" as possible. To do so, you must attempt to gather information about the topology into a pattern to evaluate it, which is nearly impossible for the human due to limited memory and limited ability to calculate; nevertheless, it can occur through pure intuition. While pure trial and error goes significantly faster with the computer than with human beings, it is not a suitable solution for a labyrinth that is theoretically infinitely large. In this way, approaches are developed for problems of various kinds that are not so easy to represent graphically as a labyrinth.

The next program example randomly generates a labyrinth, through which only one path exists. In the process you can see logical structures for converting such tasks, as well as possibilities for randomly driven operations.

*Different labyrinths*

Each labyrinth has a different appearance with exactly one path through each one from the upper left corner to the lower right corner. Try them out.

**Tip**

### Function principle

This guaranteed path is based on a simple principle. In generating the labyrinth, the program starts at the borders. From a random point on a wall, a new wall segment is drawn in the free space. This new wall segment cannot end at an existing wall. Thus, one wall point (in the matrix of the labyrinth) is always randomly selected and from there a wall is drawn to a free matrix point, until all the matrix points are occupied. Because a wall is never drawn between two walls, no continuous barrier that prevents a solution can occur. Conversely, no wall begins at a free point in space, so that no islands can occur either, which would result in two alternative paths.

You can see this principle exactly if you follow the generation of a labyrinth.

*Steps in the formation of a labyrinth*

```
#laby.bas
wi=19: he=16
dim m(wi+2,he+2)
for x=2 to wi:for y=2 to he
  m(x,y)=0
next y:next x
for x=2 to wi
  m(x,1)=3:m(x,he+1)=3
next x
for y=2 to he
  m(1,y)=3:m(wi+1,y)=3
next y
m(1,1)=4:m(wi+1,1)=4
m(wi+1,he+1)=4:m(1,he+1)=4
for x=0 to wi+2
  m(x,0)=4:m(x,he+2)=4
next x
for y=0 to he+2
  m(0,y)=4:m(wi+2,y)=4
next y
z=2*wi+2*he
draw -1
draw 0,16,wi*8,16
draw wi*8,16,wi*8,(he-1)*8+16
draw 0,he*8+16,wi*8,he*8+16
draw 0,24,0,he*8+16
```

```
while (z < (wi+1)*(he+1))
  x=rnd(wi+1)+1:y=rnd(he+1)+1
  if m(x,y)>0 and m(x,y)<4
    r=rnd(4)+1
    on r goto 110,120,130,140
    110 x2=x-1:y2=y:goto line
    120 x2=x:y2=y+1:goto line
    130 x2=x+1:y2=y:goto line
    140 x2=x:y2=y-1:goto line
    line:
    if m(x2,y2)=0
      draw (x-1)*8,(y-1)*8+16,(x2-1)*8,(y2-1)*8+16
      m(x2,y2)=1
      m(x,y)=m(x,y)+1
      z=z+1
    endif
  endif
wend
w = fn pen(0)
```

CD

**Program on the companion CD**

You can also find this program on the companion CD to this book as *0422.bas*.

The labyrinth is 19 fields wide and 16 fields high. In the beginning these two numbers are stored in the *wi* and *he* variables. This results in 20 matrix points for walls and additionally, for calculation purposes, similar to the jigsaw puzzle in the preceding examples, one matrix row outside for each one. A variable field *m* is dimensioned from this, which contains 22 x 19 variables (0 ... 21, 0 ... 18).

Thereafter more loops follow, filling this variable field with values based on the following table (see next page).

The numbers specify how many walls are connected with the matrix point in question. The outermost row serves only programming purposes. Here there are 4s everywhere, exactly as in the corner points of the field, because no more walls can be built here. The boundary walls of the labyrinth are represented in the variable field by the second row from the outside. Except for the corner fields, this row has 3s.

| 4 | 4 | 4 | 4 | 4 | 4 | 4 | 4 | 4 | 4 | 4 | 4 | 4 | 4 | 4 | 4 | 4 | 4 | 4 | 4 | 4 | 4 |
|---|---|---|---|---|---|---|---|---|---|---|---|---|---|---|---|---|---|---|---|---|---|
| 4 | 4 | 3 | 3 | 3 | 3 | 3 | 3 | 3 | 3 | 3 | 3 | 3 | 3 | 3 | 3 | 3 | 3 | 3 | 3 | 4 | 4 |
| 4 | 3 | 0 | 0 | 0 | 0 | 0 | 0 | 0 | 0 | 0 | 0 | 0 | 0 | 0 | 0 | 0 | 0 | 0 | 0 | 3 | 4 |
| 4 | 3 | 0 | 0 | 0 | 0 | 0 | 0 | 0 | 0 | 0 | 0 | 0 | 0 | 0 | 0 | 0 | 0 | 0 | 0 | 3 | 4 |
| 4 | 3 | 0 | 0 | 0 | 0 | 0 | 0 | 0 | 0 | 0 | 0 | 0 | 0 | 0 | 0 | 0 | 0 | 0 | 0 | 3 | 4 |
| 4 | 3 | 0 | 0 | 0 | 0 | 0 | 0 | 0 | 0 | 0 | 0 | 0 | 0 | 0 | 0 | 0 | 0 | 0 | 0 | 3 | 4 |
| 4 | 3 | 0 | 0 | 0 | 0 | 0 | 0 | 0 | 0 | 0 | 0 | 0 | 0 | 0 | 0 | 0 | 0 | 0 | 0 | 3 | 4 |
| 4 | 3 | 0 | 0 | 0 | 0 | 0 | 0 | 0 | 0 | 0 | 0 | 0 | 0 | 0 | 0 | 0 | 0 | 0 | 0 | 3 | 4 |
| 4 | 3 | 0 | 0 | 0 | 0 | 0 | 0 | 0 | 0 | 0 | 0 | 0 | 0 | 0 | 0 | 0 | 0 | 0 | 0 | 3 | 4 |
| 4 | 3 | 0 | 0 | 0 | 0 | 0 | 0 | 0 | 0 | 0 | 0 | 0 | 0 | 0 | 0 | 0 | 0 | 0 | 0 | 3 | 4 |
| 4 | 3 | 0 | 0 | 0 | 0 | 0 | 0 | 0 | 0 | 0 | 0 | 0 | 0 | 0 | 0 | 0 | 0 | 0 | 0 | 3 | 4 |
| 4 | 3 | 0 | 0 | 0 | 0 | 0 | 0 | 0 | 0 | 0 | 0 | 0 | 0 | 0 | 0 | 0 | 0 | 0 | 0 | 3 | 4 |
| 4 | 3 | 0 | 0 | 0 | 0 | 0 | 0 | 0 | 0 | 0 | 0 | 0 | 0 | 0 | 0 | 0 | 0 | 0 | 0 | 3 | 4 |
| 4 | 3 | 0 | 0 | 0 | 0 | 0 | 0 | 0 | 0 | 0 | 0 | 0 | 0 | 0 | 0 | 0 | 0 | 0 | 0 | 3 | 4 |
| 4 | 3 | 0 | 0 | 0 | 0 | 0 | 0 | 0 | 0 | 0 | 0 | 0 | 0 | 0 | 0 | 0 | 0 | 0 | 0 | 3 | 4 |
| 4 | 3 | 0 | 0 | 0 | 0 | 0 | 0 | 0 | 0 | 0 | 0 | 0 | 0 | 0 | 0 | 0 | 0 | 0 | 0 | 3 | 4 |
| 4 | 3 | 0 | 0 | 0 | 0 | 0 | 0 | 0 | 0 | 0 | 0 | 0 | 0 | 0 | 0 | 0 | 0 | 0 | 0 | 3 | 4 |
| 4 | 3 | 0 | 0 | 0 | 0 | 0 | 0 | 0 | 0 | 0 | 0 | 0 | 0 | 0 | 0 | 0 | 0 | 0 | 0 | 3 | 4 |
| 4 | 3 | 0 | 0 | 0 | 0 | 0 | 0 | 0 | 0 | 0 | 0 | 0 | 0 | 0 | 0 | 0 | 0 | 0 | 0 | 3 | 4 |
| 4 | 3 | 0 | 0 | 0 | 0 | 0 | 0 | 0 | 0 | 0 | 0 | 0 | 0 | 0 | 0 | 0 | 0 | 0 | 0 | 3 | 4 |
| 4 | 3 | 0 | 0 | 0 | 0 | 0 | 0 | 0 | 0 | 0 | 0 | 0 | 0 | 0 | 0 | 0 | 0 | 0 | 0 | 3 | 4 |
| 4 | 4 | 3 | 3 | 3 | 3 | 3 | 3 | 3 | 3 | 3 | 3 | 3 | 3 | 3 | 3 | 3 | 3 | 3 | 3 | 4 | 4 |
| 4 | 4 | 4 | 4 | 4 | 4 | 4 | 4 | 4 | 4 | 4 | 4 | 4 | 4 | 4 | 4 | 4 | 4 | 4 | 4 | 4 | 4 |

For the program this means: another wall can be built.

```
z=2*wi+2*he
```

After the variable field has been filled, an important variable is set. This variable specifies the total number of matrix points that have at least one wall. This will be used later to determine when the labyrinth is finished, namely when all the matrix points are connected with at least one wall. The *wi* variable corresponds to the number of matrix fields in width minus 1, while *he* corresponds to the number of matrix fields in height minus 1. Thus we can use the formula *2*wi+ 2*he* to determine the number of fields on the border without counting anything twice in the corners. All the border fields already lie at walls at the beginning.

```
draw -1
draw 0,16,wi*8,16
draw wi*8,16,wi*8,(he-1)*8+16
draw 0,he*8+16,wi*8,he*8+16
draw 0,24,0,he*8+16
```

Different *draw* functions now draw the border lines. Each matrix field has a width of 8 pixels. In the upper left corner and the lower right corner there is a gap of one field for the entrance and the exit. 16 pixels are reserved for the title bar in the upper screen border.

```
while (z < (wi+1)*(he+1))
...
wend
```

After that the actual generation of the labyrinth starts with a *while...wend* loop, which is executed until the total number of matrix points connected to walls is less than the number of all points in the matrix (width * height).

```
x=rnd(wi+1)+1:y=rnd(he+1)+1
```

Two random functions now determine the x,y-coordinates of a matrix point.

### *rnd(n)*

This function determines an integral random number in the range of 0 ... n-1.

> **Note**
>
> **Random numbers**
>
> Generally you would think that nothing could happen randomly in a program. So how can a program generate random numbers? If you divide a large prime number by some value, beginning at the x decimal place the result will be numbers that can hardly be foreseen. These numbers change without any regularity when you increase the divisor regularly. While this result seems to be random, you can reproduce it at any time through an identical program or by invoking the same program multiple times. If you now take a number made up of some of these digits and divide it by a number resulting from the current second or the contents of any memory location of the computer, you get a result which cannot be reproduced and is therefore termed a random number.

This randomly selected matrix point is checked to determine whether there is at least one wall there. Only in this case can this point be used as the starting point of a new wall. If there are already four walls at that point, the program cannot draw a new one there.

```
if m(x,y)>0 and m(x,y)<4
...
endif
```

For this purpose we use a special form of the *if* statement, which we haven't used in any of our sample programs up to now.

### *if <Condition> ... endif*

If the condition applies, all the following program lines will be executed, if not, the program continues at the *endif* line. To differentiate this from the known *if...then...else* statement, the keyword *then* is missing here.

Several such *if...endif* constructs can be nested within each other. In our program this *if...endif* has another one later.

Thus, if there is already at least one wall at the randomly selected point in the example , *(m(x,y)>0)*, this point can be used as a starting point, if not, the program runs after *endif* to the *wend* line. From there it goes back to the beginning of the *while* loop and determines a new point.

If the point is considered as the starting point of a new wall, another random number between 1 and 4 is calculated, which determines the direction of the new wall.

```
r=rnd(4)+1
on r goto 110,120,130,140
110 x2=x-1:y2=y:goto line
120 x2=x:y2=y+1:goto line
130 x2=x+1:y2=y:goto line
140 x2=x:y2=y-1:goto line
```

Depending on the randomly selected direction, x and y-coordinates have to be calculated for the end point of the new wall to be drawn. There are four alternatives for this, which are differentiated by a *on...goto* statement.

### *on <Number> goto <Line numbers ...>*

Using this statement we can program decisions that, in contrast to the *if...then* selection, have more than two solutions. For this purpose, the following parameters are necessary:

- **Number** – Integral value between 1 and n. Depending on this value, the program goes to one of the specified line numbers. 1 goes to the first line number, 2 to the second and so on. If the number is greater than the number of specified line numbers, the program continues running without going anywhere.

- **Line numbers** – List of line numbers to which the program can jump.

> **Note**
>
> **Specification of line numbers**
>
> In a yBasic program you can use line numbers for individual lines without the entire program having to have line numbers. The specified line numbers must always be at least as large as the actual number of the line in the program, but can also be larger. All line numbers have to be specified in ascending order, but with spaces of any size.

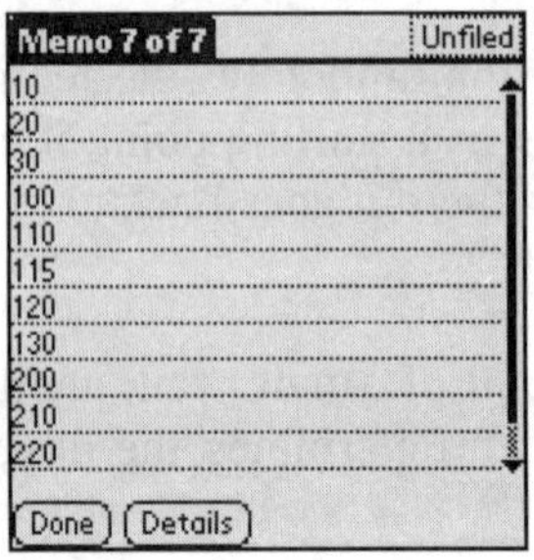


Valid line numbers

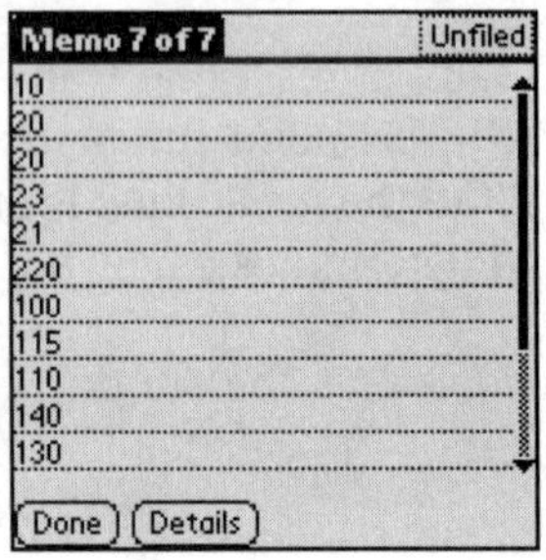


Invalid line numbers

Depending on the selected direction, the four different lines in the program each calculate new coordinates for the end point and then all return to the *line* branch mark.

```
line:
if m(x2,y2)=0
...
endif
```

The program first uses another *if...endif* query to check whether no wall occurs at the planned end point. Only then can a new wall be drawn, because otherwise there could be a barrier that splits the area into two parts and thus prevents a solution.

If the new point has been blank up to now, the program can draw the wall.

```
draw (x-1)*8,(y-1)*8+16,(x2-1)*8,(y2-1)*8+16
m(x2,y2)=1
m(x,y)=m(x,y)+1
z=z+1
```

After that the counter for the new point *m(x2,y2)* is set to 1, for the first wall connected there. The counter for the starting point is increased by 1, as is the z counter, which counts the total number of connected matrix points.

In this way the program randomly builds one wall after another until the entire field is full.

## Path through the labyrinth

The traditional solution to navigating a labyrinth successfully begins with the recommendation to keep one hand on the wall, paying careful attention not to change hands. If navigators at the entrance in the upper left corner touch the wall with their left hand, after many detours, arrival at the exit in the lower left corner is guaranteed – if the individual touches all the walls that are connected with a border point on top or on the right.

According to the construction principle used here, the labyrinth is divided into two parts, walls connected to the upper or right border and walls that are connected to the lower or left border.

The program does not save the individual walls, only the number of walls at each matrix point. This way it is not possible to reconstruct the labyrinth unambiguously for a search algorithm. yBasic does not allow you to retrieve the screen contents afterwards to determine where a wall is located. If that were possible, a program could find the path through experimentation or using methods of artificial intelligence.

*A labyrinth logically divided into two parts*

This program will use a method that doesn't even need detours yet finds the optimum path immediately. First, you must give the program some additional information when generating the labyrinth.

If you take a good look at the sample labyrinth from the last illustration, you will determine that the optimum path runs exactly between the light and the dark parts. Therefore, in finding your way, you must always proceed with a light wall on one side and a dark wall on the other side.

Thus the new additional information consists in specifying with each point whether it is connected to the upper right part or the lower left part. After that the program will find its way.

*Labyrinths and solution paths*

```
#laby2.bas
wi=19: he=16
dim m(wi+2,he+2), n(wi+2,he+2)
for x=2 to wi:for y=2 to he
  m(x,y)=0: n(x,y)=0
next y:next x
for x=2 to wi
  m(x,1)=3:m(x,he+1)=3
  n(x,1)=1:n(x,he+1)=2
next x
for y=2 to he
  m(1,y)=3:m(wi+1,y)=3
  n(1,y)=2:n(wi+1,y)=1
next y
m(1,1)=4:m(wi+1,1)=4
m(wi+1,he+1)=4:m(1,he+1)=4
n(1,1)=1:n(wi+1,1)=1
n(wi+1,he+1)=2:n(1,he+1)=2
for x=0 to wi+2
  m(x,0)=4:m(x,he+2)=4
```

```
next x
for y=0 to he+2
  m(0,y)=4:m(wi+2,y)=4
next y
z=2*wi+2*he
draw -1
draw 0,16,wi*8,16
draw wi*8,16,wi*8,(he-1)*8+16
draw 0,he*8+16,wi*8,he*8+16
draw 0,24,0,he*8+16
while (z<(wi+1)*(he+1))
  x=rnd(wi+1)+1:y=rnd(he+1)+1
  if m(x,y)>0 and m(x,y)<4
    r=rnd(4)+1
    on r goto 110,120,130,140
    110 x2=x-1:y2=y:goto line
    120 x2=x:y2=y+1:goto line
    130 x2=x+1:y2=y:goto line
    140 x2=x:y2=y-1:goto line
    line:
    if m(x2,y2)=0
      draw (x-1)*8,(y-1)*8+16,(x2-1)*8,(y2-1)*8+16,1
      m(x2,y2)=1
      m(x,y)=m(x,y)+1
      z=z+1
      n(x2,y2)=n(x,y)
    endif
  endif
wend
w = fn pen(0)
x=1:y=1:r=4
draw 0,20,4,20,2
while (x<wi+1)
  if (n(x+1,y)<>n(x+1,y+1))and(r<>1) then x2=x+1:y2=y:r=4:goto path
  if (n(x+1,y+1)<>n(x,y+1))and(r<>2) then x2=x:y2=y+1:r=3:goto path
  if (n(x,y)<>n(x+1,y))and(r<>3) then x2=x:y2=y-1:r=2:goto path
  if (n(x,y)<>n(x,y+1))and(r<>4) then x2=x-1:y2=y:r=1:goto path
  path:
  draw x*8-4,y*8+12,x2*8-4,y2*8+12,2
  x=x2:y=y2
wend
w = fn pen(0)
```

**CD**

**Program on the companion CD**

You can also find this program on the companion CD to this book as *0423.bas.*

At the beginning, in addition to the *m(x,y)* variable field, in which the number of connected walls is saved for each point, a second variable field, *n(x,y)* is dimensioned. A 1 occurs here if the point is connected with the upper or right border; a 2 if it is connected to the lower or left border.

```
dim m(wi+2,he+2), n(wi+2,he+2)
```

In the following loops, in which the *m(x,y)* values for the border points are entered, additionally the *n(x,y)* values are also defined for all border points.

After that the creation of the labyrinth runs, as in the preceding example, with one small addition:

```
n(x2,y2)=n(x,y)
```

Every time a new wall is drawn from a point x,y to a new point x2,y2, *n(x2,y2)* is also set to the same value as *n(x,y)*. The newly connected point belongs to the same side as the point at which the new wall begins. According to the construction pattern used here, no walls without connection to a border can occur.

After the user taps the display once, the program would normally end here. However, the new program goes further and finds the solution path.

The path is drawn step by step from one field to the next. The following variables are used for calculation:

| Variable | Meaning |
|---|---|
| x | x-coordinate of the last field crossed by the path |
| y | y-coordinate of the last field crossed by the path |
| x2 | x-coordinate of the field for the new path segment |
| y2 | y-coordinate of the field for the new path segment |
| r | Direction of the last path segment:<br>1 to the left<br>2 to the top<br>3 to the bottom<br>4 to the right |

At the start you are at coordinates 1,1 in the upper left. The path comes from the left through the entrance.

```
x=1:y=1:r=4
draw 0,20,4,20,2
```

The first unchangeable line piece is also drawn right here from the entrance to the first field. The *2* parameter at the end of the *draw* function stands for dotted lines instead of solid lines.

This is followed by a *while...wend* loop, while the program searches for the path.

```
while (x<wi+1)
  ...
wend
```

This loop runs until the x-coordinate attains the value 20. Because only 19 fields occur in x direction, the path must reach the border to the right, next to the labyrinth through the only exit.

In finding the path, distinguish two types of coordinates: The coordinates of the path field and the coordinates of the four matrix points around the path field. Four possible directions are added to this, which are termed *r*. The figure illustrates the individual points and coordinates.

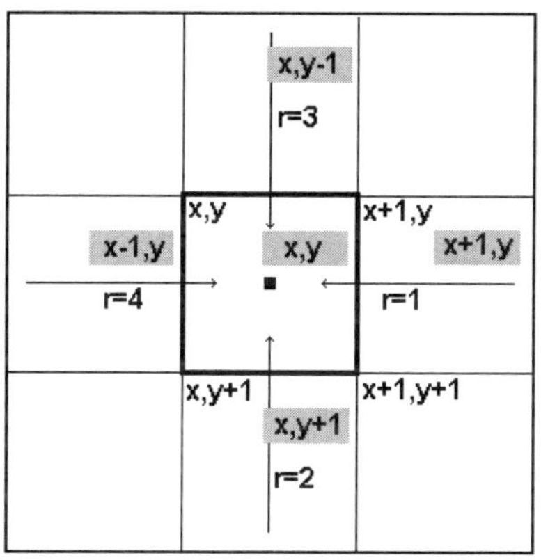


*Calculation of coordinates for path fields (gray shaded) and matrix points*

In all four directions the two corner points between which the path leads to the next field are checked. The path is correct when one of the two corner points belongs to the upper part and one belongs to the lower part of the labyrinth. Note that the new path cannot have the opposite direction of the last path segment; otherwise, you would return again.

Each field has four possible paths. Using the data related to how the labyrinth is stored, the program cannot recognize which walls block which paths. However, this isn't really necessary, because, in finding the path, the program only gets its bearings from the *n(x,y)* variables, which contain the connection to the upper or lower border.

The four possibilities are checked in the order of their probability, to avoid as many fruitless searches as possible and to enable the program to run quickly.

```
if (n(x+1,y)<>n(x+1,y+1))and(r<>1) then x2=x+1:y2=y:r=4:goto path
if (n(x+1,y+1)<>n(x,y+1))and(r<>2) then x2=x:y2=y+1:r=3:goto path
if (n(x,y)<>n(x+1,y))and(r<>3) then x2=x:y2=y-1:r=2:goto path
if (n(x,y)<>n(x,y+1))and(r<>4) then x2=x-1:y2=y:r=1:goto path
```

Most frequently a path will go to the right, then down, up, and infrequently, to the left. An optimum path would run 19 matrix fields to the right and 15 fields down. For each matrix field to the left, an additional field to the right must be traversed; for each field up an additional one, down must be traversed. Each of the queries performs two queries, both of which must be logical and simultaneously fulfilled:

- The two matrix points in the direction of the two path must have different *n()* values.
- The last path segment must not come from this direction.

If both of these criteria are fulfilled, the correct direction has been found and three variables are assigned:

- **x2** – x-coordinate of the new path field.
- **y2** - y-coordinate of the new path field.
- **r** - new direction.

Thereafter, the program continues running at the *path:* branch mark.

```
path:
draw x*8-4,y*8+12,x2*8-4,y2*8+12,2
x=x2:y=y2
```

The line is drawn from the last path point to the new one. The pixel coordinates result from the matrix width of 8 minus one half field of 4 pixels, because the path always runs over the middle of the fields. You won't use the 16 pixels at the upper border.

In this way one path segment after the other is drawn, until the path has reached the goal in the lower right corner.

The program finds a path using additional information that is carried along during the creation of the graphic in the form of another array. This array contains data about whether a wall point is connected to the upper or lower border. From this the program draws the separation line between the two parts of the graphic, which then also represents the solution path.

## 4.4 And now in color: Color for the Palm IIIc

Until now, the Palm IIIc was the only Palm with a color display of 256 colors. These colors are predefined in a palette but can also be addressed by their rgb values. In yBasic you can set one of these colors as the current color. After that all drawing functions are executed with this color, until another color is set as the current color.

The example shows that you can execute any graphic functions you want with every available color. In programs (except for purely artistic graphic programs, which are of minor importance on the Palm), color fulfills two important functions:

- **Signal effect** - Important elements are highlighted through signal colors (red, yellow) so that you perceive them immediately.
- **Distinguishability** - The human eye has a much easier time distinguishing colors than gray scales or line patterns.

The following simple example shows any color on the screen when you enter a color number.

```
#color1.bas
t1$="Color "
t2$="Select new color value"
f=0
while (f<256)
  f=val(input$(t1$+str$(f),t2$))
  draw color f,-1,0,1
  draw 0,16,160,100,7
wend
```

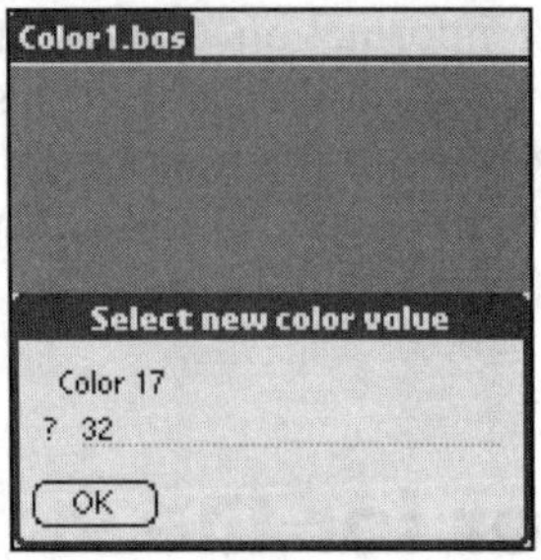


*Displayed color by color number*

**CD**

**Program on the companion CD**

You can also find this program on the companion CD to this book as *0424.bas.*

If you enter a color number that is greater than 255, the program terminates. The program consists of a single *while...wend* loop, in which a color number is queried using the *input$()* function. This has to be converted from the string into a number using *val()*.

The new *draw color* function sets the selected color number as the current color.

### *draw color <Color>, -1,0,<Mode>*

The color number between 0 and 255 is in the *Color* parameter. This color is defined as the current draw color for the following *draw* functions.

The following *1* and *0* parameters are fixed values that must appear in the function in this form. The last parameter, *Mode,* can accept different values:

| Mode | Meaning |
|---|---|
| 1 | Draw color or foreground color |
| 2 | Background color |
| 3 | Color for texts |

## Selecting colors through rgb

You cannot always get a good idea of what a color looks like from the palette color numbers. As you know from your familiarity with most of the better graphic programs, rgb values are more clear cut.

**Tip**

### rgb Color system

Every color on a computer monitor is composed of three color components: **R**ed, **G**reen, and **B**lue. Therefore, you can write every color as a combination of three numerical values that specify the percentages of the components. The higher a value, the stronger the component is represented in the color. Each of the values can range between 0 and 255. For example, rgb 255/0/0 yields pure red, rgb 255/128/0 results in orange, and rgb 255/255/255 results in clear white. Theoretically over 16.5 million colors are possible, all of which can be displayed on a TrueColor screen. Only the Palm IIIc uses a selected default palette of 256 colors, with some of the black shades being almost indistinguishable. On page 159 of this chapter, you can find a program that displays the complete palette.

In the following program, enter the values for r, g, and b. The program shows the color and the matching color number from the palette. The program always displays a color that corresponds as closely as possible to the rgb value, because not every rgb value can be exactly displayed on the Palm IIIc.

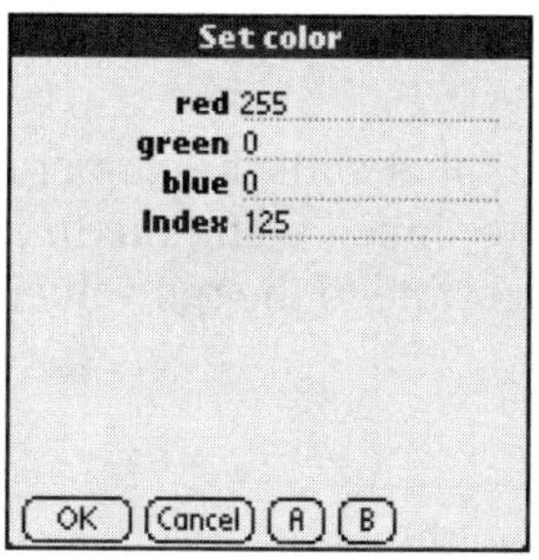


*Input form*

*Display of the color*

At program startup the form in which you enter the three rgb values appears. When you tap *OK*, a colored surface appears in the selected color. The number of the palette color is specified as text. This number also appears in the form when you return to it with a simple tap the screen.

```
#color2.bas
for i=0 to 7:s$(i)="":next i
s$(0)="red"
s$(2)="green"
s$(4)="blue"
s$(6)="Index"
```

```
draw color 255,-1,0,3
start:
f=form(9,4,"Set color")
if (f=0) then end
r=val(s$(1))
g=val(s$(3))
b=val(s$(5))
s$(7)=fn rgb2i(r,g,b)
draw color r,g,b,2
draw -1
draw "Color "+s$(7), 10,50
fn pen(0)
goto start
```

**CD**

**Program on the companion CD**

You can also find this program on the companion CD to this book as *0425.bas.*

Prior to the actual program startup, text fields are initialized and the text color is set to black by the *draw color* function using palette number 255. Mode 3 at the end of this function stands for the text color.

In the form the three variables *r*, *g*, and *b* are filled with the numerical values of the form input and then a palette color is determined using the *fn rgb2i()* function. This color corresponds as precisely as possible to the rgb value.

```
s$(7)=fn rgb2i(r,g,b)
```

This value is written to the lowest form field on the right.

### fn rgb2i(<r>, <g>, <b>)

This function searches the palette for a color that corresponds as precisely as possible to the specified rgb value. The r, g, and b are specified as numerical values between 0 and 255. The return value of the function is the number of the corresponding palette color.

A variant of the *draw color* function sets the background color for the graphic mode to the selected rgb value.

```
draw color r,g,b,2
```

### *draw color <r>, <g>, <b>, <Mode>*

If you use the *draw color* function in this form, you can specify rgb values directly. The function selects a color that corresponds as precisely as possible to the specified rgb value. The *r*, *g*, and *b* are specified as numerical values between 0 and 255. As usual, the *Mode* parameter is used.

After that the screen in the graphic area is cleared in our program with *draw -1*. On the Palm IIIc it is automatically filled in with the set background color.

Now a *draw* function writes the color number to this colored background in the set text color of black.

```
draw "Color "+s$(7), 10,50
```

### *draw <Text>, <x>, <y>*

If you specify one string and two coordinates after each other as parameters in the *draw* function, the text is written to the corresponding position on the screen.

At this point the program waits for a touch of the screen and then displays the input form in which the color number can now be seen.

```
fn pen(0)
goto start
```

## The Color palette

The next program example displays the complete color palette of the Palm IIIc on the screen.

```
#color3.bas
i=0
draw -1
for y=0 to 120 step 8
  for x=0 to 150 step 10
    draw color i,-1,0,1
    draw x,y+16,9,7,7
    i=i+1
  next x
next y
w=fn pen(0)
```

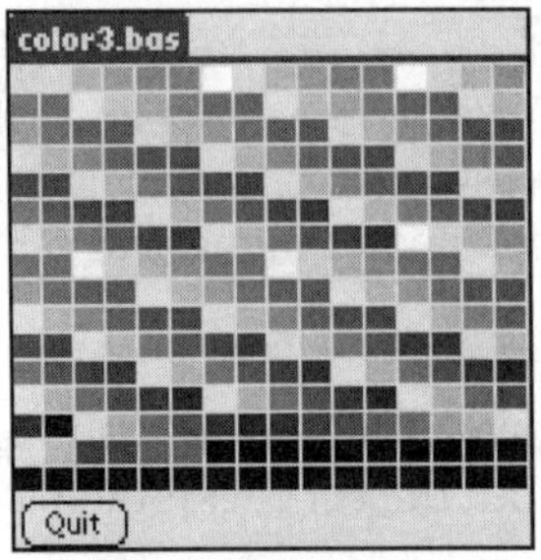


*The color palette of the Palm IIIc*

**CD**

**Program on the companion CD**

You can also find this program on the companion CD to this book as *0426.bas*.

The program consists of two loops nested within each other, which draw individual rectangles in the matrix. With each loop cycle the value *i* is increased by 1, regardless of the loop counters. This specifies the color number that is set as the current color prior to drawing a rectangle. Thereby each rectangle gets a different color, from 0 to 255.

## Charts in color

Presentation graphics are significantly easier to read when they are in color, for example, it's much easier to distinguish curves or bars when they are drawn in different colors.

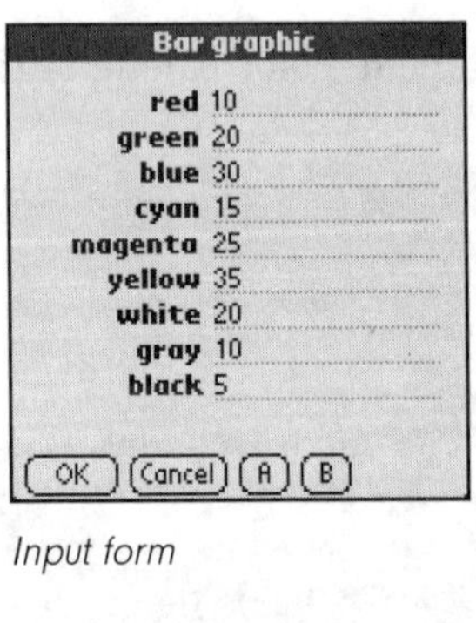


*Input form*

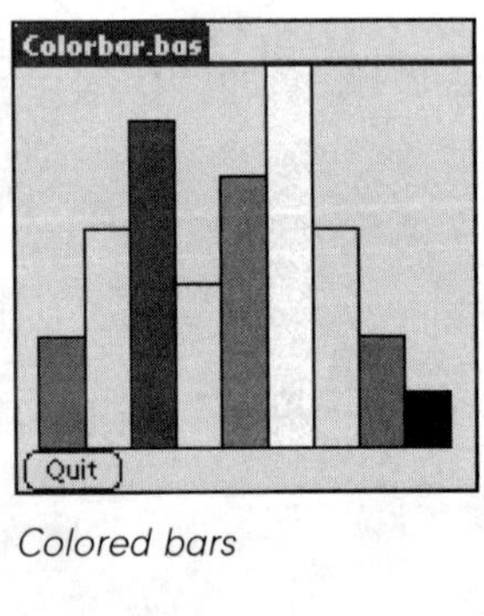


*Colored bars*

The next program is a variant of the previously described program for drawing bar charts. Each bar has a different color.

The program shows a new variant for inputting fixed defined data into variables. It inputs the field labels with the color names and the palette numbers of the bar colors from a *data* field.

```
#Colorbar.bas
dim f%(8)
data "red",125,"green",210,"blue",95
data "cyan",90,"magenta",5,"yellow",120
data "white",0,"gray",220,"black",255
for i=1 to 17 step 2:s$(i)="":next i
for i=0 to 16 step 2
  read s$(i):read f%(i/2)
next i
start:
j=form(9,9,"Bar chart")
if (j=0) then end
draw -1
m=val(s$(1))
for i=3 to 17 step 2
  if val(s$(i))>m then m=val(s$(i))
next i
for i=0 to 8
  y=int(val(s$(2*i+1))/m*130)
  draw color 255,-1,0,1
  draw i*16+8, 145-y, 15, y, 4
  draw color f%(i),-1,0,1
  draw i*16+8, 145-y, 15, y, 7
next i
w=fn pen(0)
goto start
```

**CD**

**Program on the companion CD**

You can also find this program on the companion CD to this book as *0427.bas*.

## *data <Value>, [<Value> ...]*

Use the *data* statement to define data in the program source code that is to be input into variables later with the *read* statement. The individual values are separated by commas and must correspond in type (number or string) to the type that the *read* statement expects.

> **Note**
>
> **Pay attention to line length**
>
> Keep in mind that the maximum line length of 80 characters also applies for *data* lines. However, you can easily write several *data* lines one after the other. It's only a matter of the sequence of all the data fields, not how many are in which line.

### *read <Variable>, [<Variable> ...]*

This inputs values from *data* lines to variables. You can also specify several variables, one after the other. With each *read* statement in the program an internal counter is increased by one, so that all the *data* fields are input, one after the other.

In the program nine color descriptions and their palette numbers are specified in *data* fields. In a loop, one string is input to the *s$()* form field and one number is input to the *f%()* variable field.

```
for i=0 to 16 step 2
read s$(i):read f%(i/2)
next i
```

Because only the even number form fields are input, the loop counts in increments of 2. The *f%()* field for the color numbers contains only nine variables (0 ... 8), whose index number therefore corresponds to half of the incrementation.

The form and the scaling of the values proceeds as in the original black and white program. No difference occurs until the bars are drawn. In the first step the draw color is set to black (255) and a normal bar is drawn.

```
draw color 255,-1,0,1
draw i*16+8, 145-y, 15, y, 4
```

After that the draw color is set to the color value from f%(i) and a filled rectangle is drawn with the same coordinates.

```
draw color f%(i),-1,0,1
draw i*16+8, 145-y, 15, y, 7
```

These two steps are performed for each of the nine bars.

**Tip**

**Coordinates for rectangles**

If you want to draw a colored rectangle with a boundary line, specify the same coordinates twice in the *draw* function. The boundary line *draw x1,y1,x2,y2,4* is automatically one pixel larger all the way around than the filled rectangle *draw x1,y1,x2,y2,7*.

## Curves in Color

Earlier in this chapter a program that displays number series in the form of function curves was described. If you want to compare several number series, you must restart the program each time. Placing the curves directly over each other in different colors makes the data more accessible. For example, you could compare stock prices of different companies with each other.

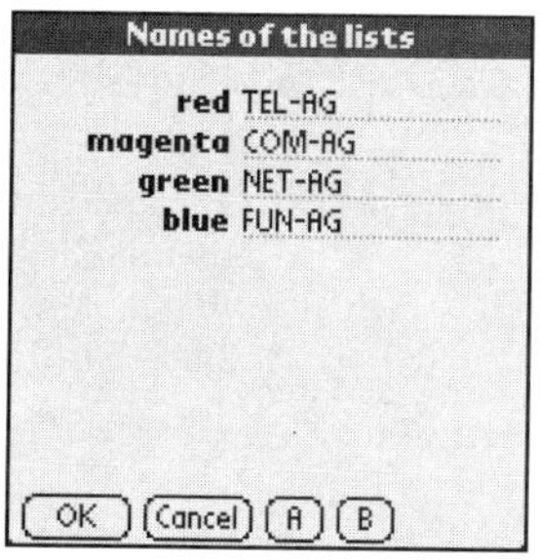


*Inputting the memo names ...*

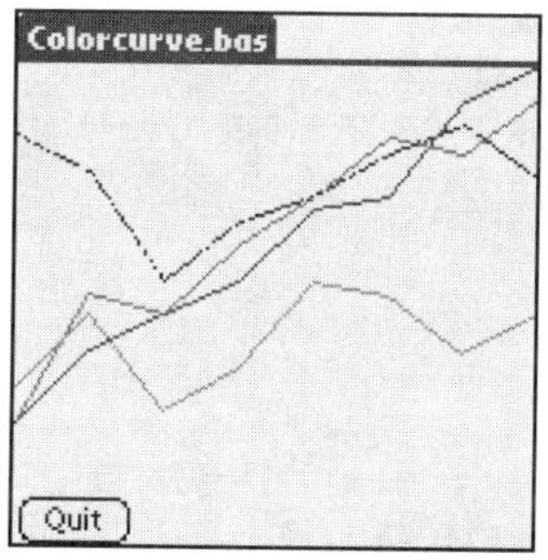


*... and the display of the curves*

Each number series is saved on a separate memo. The names of the memos that were used are entered in a form.

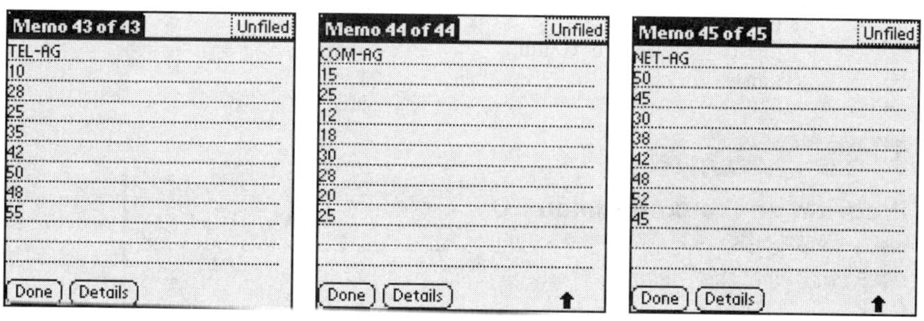


*Three of the memos used*

```
#Colorcurve.bas
dim d(160,3), f%(3)
data "red","magenta","green","blue"
data 125,5,210,95
for i=0 to 6 step 2
  read s$(i)
  s$(i+1)=""
next i
j=form(9,4,"Names of the lists")
if (j=0) then end
m=0
for i=0 to 3
  read f%(i)
  me=db.find("memo",s$(2*i+1))
  if (me<0) then goto error
  open "memo",me as #1
  input #1,x$
  n=0
  while (x$<>"")
    input #1,x$
    d(n,i)=val(x$)
    if d(n,i)>m then m=d(n,i)
    n=n+1
  wend
  close #1
next i
draw -1
n=n-2
for j=0 to 3
  draw color f%(j),-1,0,1
  moveto 0,145-(d(0,j)/m*130)
  for i=1 to n
    lineto i*160/n,145-(d(i,j)/m*130)
  next i
next j
w=fn pen(0)
end
error:
print "Memo not found"
end
```

**CD**

**Program on the companion CD**

You can also find this program on the companion CD to this book as *0428.bas,* with the memos used as *0429.txt, 0430.txt, 0431.txt* and *0432.txt.*

Basically, the program runs like the program described above for drawing a curve, with a couple of small, but important differences.

The *d()* data field is now two-dimensional. The second index value contains the number of the curve. This is counted off from 0 to 3 during inputting and again during drawing.

The additional *f%()* field contains the palette numbers of the curve colors. The names of the labels in the input form and the color palette numbers are input with *read*.

Now the input of the memo names occurs through a form. After that, the four memos are read one after the other in a loop, whereby the maximum of all values from all the memos is stored in the *m* variable, to scale all the curves accordingly later.

```
for j=0 to 3
  draw color f%(j),-1,0,1
  ...
next j
```

The drawing of the curves is repeated four times through a loop; each time the corresponding curve color is set to the current color from the *f%()* variable.

## Pie charts in color

yBasic offers a simplified function for displaying pie charts on the color Palm OS 3.5. It saves you the trouble of calculating the individual lines through trigonometric functions; moreover, it fills in segments in different colors.

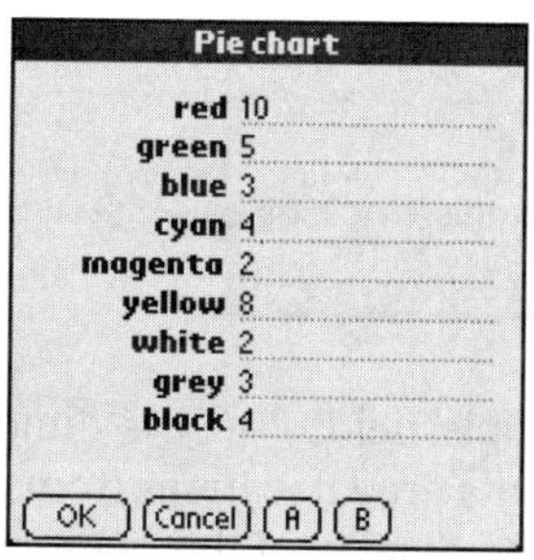


*Input form ...*

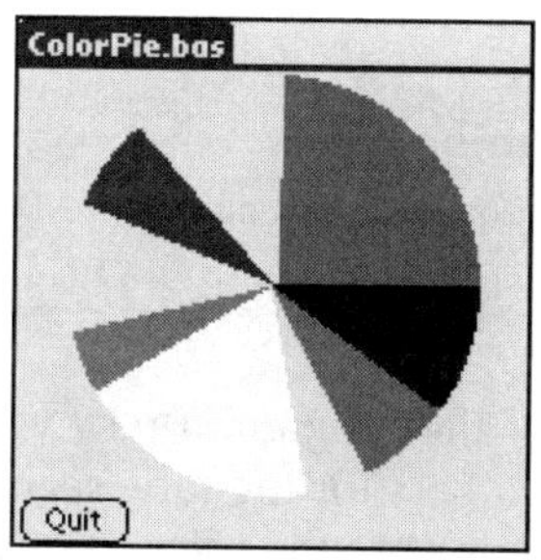


*...and pie chart*

The sample program is based on the program described above with some small changes.

```
#ColorPie.bas
dim f%(8)
data 125,210,95,90,5,120,0,220,255
for i=1 to 17 step 2:s$(i)="":next i
m=db.find("memo","Field labels")
if (m<0) then goto error
open "memo",m as #1
input #1,x$
for i=0 to 8
  input #1,s$(2*i)
  read f%(i)
next i
close #1
start:
j=form(9,9,"Pie chart")
if (j=0) then end
draw -1
s=0:pi=3.14159:y1=0
for i=1 to 17 step 2
  s=s+val(s$(i))
next i
for i=1 to 17 step 2
  y2=y1+val(s$(i))/s*2*pi
  draw color f%((i-1)/2),-1,0,1
  draw circle 80,80,64,y1,y2
  y1=y2
next i
w=fn pen(0)
goto start
error:
print "Field labels missing"
```

**CD**

**Program on the companion CD**

You can also find this program on the companion CD to this book as *0433.bas*.

At the beginning of the program a new variable field, *f%(8)* is dimensioned, in which the color numbers for the nine segments are later input from a *data* field. Nothing new happens until the calculation and display of the segments:

```
for i=1 to 17 step 2
  y2=y1+val(s$(i))/s*2*pi
  draw color f%((i-1)/2),-1,0,1
  draw circle 80,80,64,y1,y2
  y1=y2
next i
```

The fields of the input form are read out one after the other. The *y1* variable always contains the angle of the last segment line and thus the beginning angle of the new segment, *y2* the end angle of the segment.

The current draw color is set with *draw color*. Because the loop only counts the odd numbers in increments of 2, the loop counter has to be converted to determine the color from the *f%()* field.

The new *draw circle* function then draws the segment filled in color; therefore, drawing a circle at the beginning becomes unnecessary.

### *draw circle <x>, <y>, <r>, <w1>, <w2>*

This function draws a circle segment between two angles.

| Parameter | Meaning |
|---|---|
| x | x-coordinate of the center point |
| y | y-coordinate of the center point |
| r | Radius |
| w1 | Beginning angle |
| w2 | End angle |

When specifying the angle, keep in mind that this function behaves quite differently from other yBasic functions:

- Angles are specified in radian measure.
- The zero point is on the right (3 on the clock).
- Angles are counted in mathematically positive fashion, counter-clockwise – unlike normal practice in yBasic.
- Both angles can be in the range between 0 and 2*π only. No negative angles and no multiples of 2*π. are possible – unlike normal practice in yBasic.
- w2 must always be greater than w1. Thus angles can be measured in only one direction – unlike normal practice in yBasic.

To give you a clear idea of the function and avoid making the sample program more complicated through diverse conversion formulas, the segments have been arranged next to each other counterclockwise. The first segment begins on the right, not on the top.

# 4.5 Pictures and Logos in CASL

Graphic buttons and small logos help users run many programs. However, you shouldn't eliminate text information. Displaying texts as text rather than as ornate graphic fonts is always preferred.

CASL offers the option of displaying graphics on *button* or *label* objects. It uses a separate file format for this purpose, called *CBM* (= **C**ASL **Bit**m**ap). Files in this format can be drawn directly or taken from Windows BMP files with 1 bit color depth.

The next sample program is based on the drawing program described above. Here the buttons for selecting the form (line, rectangle, circle) are replaced by graphic buttons. Also, a logo appears in the upper right corner in the free area next to the *frame* name.

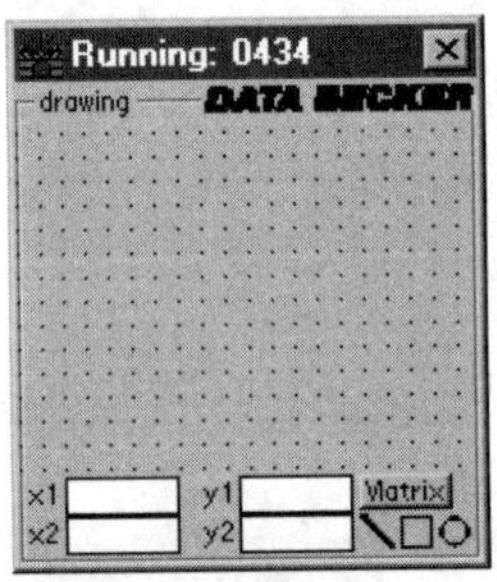


*Program in Windows ...*

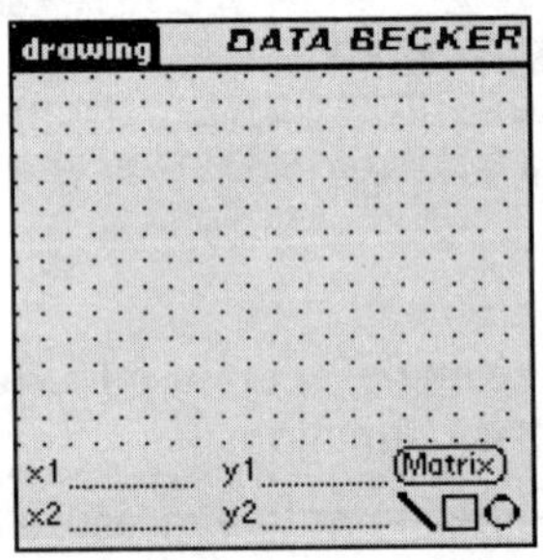


*... and on the Palm*

Before you can import such graphics into the program, you must create them.

Click the *New* icon in CASL. A dialog box appears, in which you can select a file type. Select *BitmapFile*.

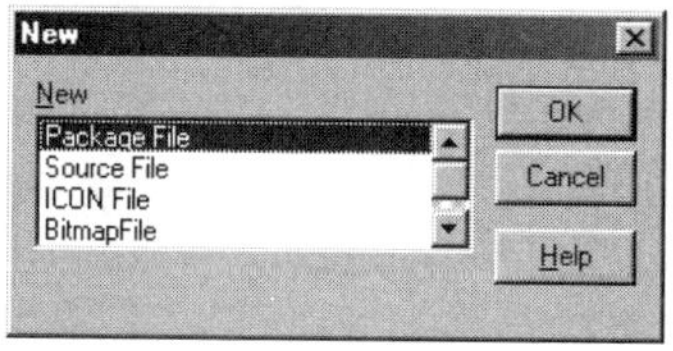


*Selecting a file format*

CASL opens a new window with a simple diamond matrix. Choose *Edit/Bitmap Properties*. Specify the size of this Raster. The new graphic is exactly as large as that specified here.

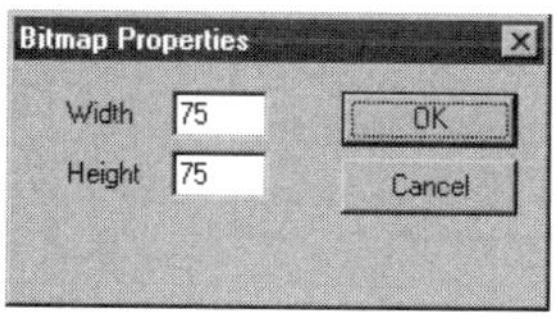


*Setting the bitmap size*

The size is specified in CASL coordinate units. The buttons for our example should be 75 x 75 units large.

*The blank matrix for a button*

Using the tools in the Image toolbar, draw the graphic on this matrix. If you cannot see the toolbar, turn it on with the *View/Image Toolbar* menu item.

*The Image Toolbar*

The icons make the functions of the individual tools almost self-explanatory:

- Pen for drawing individual pixels.
- Brush for wider lines. (You can change the size of this brush using key combinations Ctrl+2 through Ctrl+4.)

- Straight line.
- Rectangle.
- Filled-in rectangle.
- Circle or ellipsis.
- Filled-in circle or ellipsis.
- Filling an area.
- Selecting.

**Tip**

**White lines**

If you right-click the tools, you can draw white lines on black fields to erase objects.

Using these tools, draw the first button, a diagonal line.

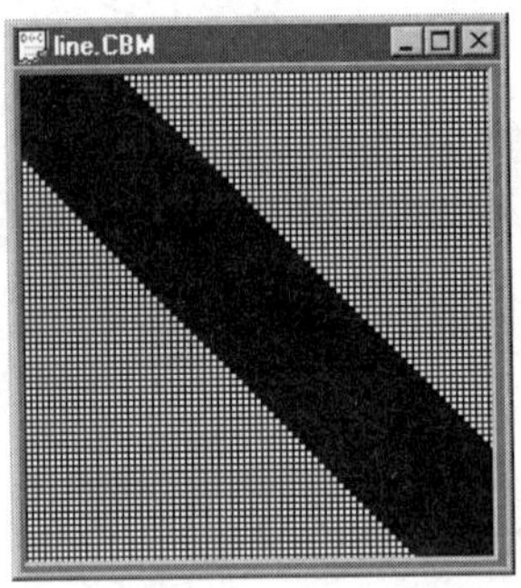


*Diagonal line as a graphic for a button*

The easiest way to create this graphic is out of two diagonal lines, which represent the lateral boundaries. Then fill in the area in between them.

Save the finished button as *Line.cbm.*

Use the same procedure to draw two new buttons in the same size with a square and a circle.

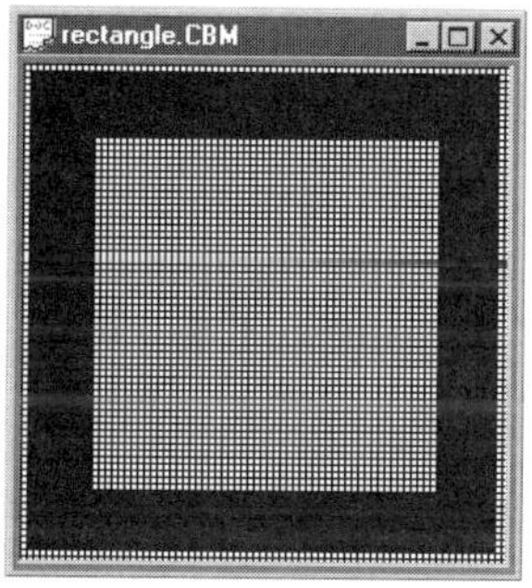


*Button for rectangle ...*

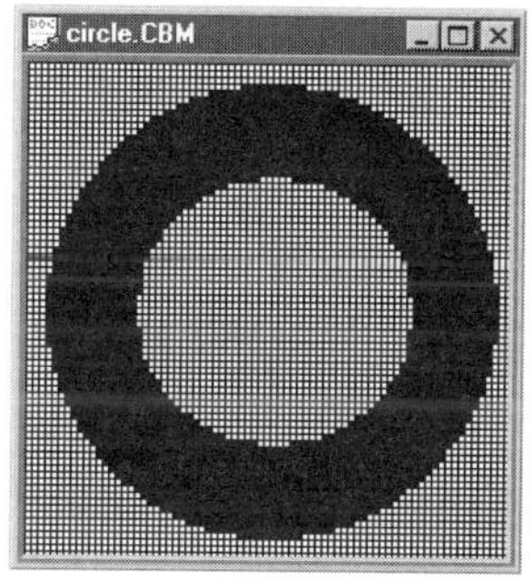


*... and circle*

Save these graphics as *Rectangle.cbm* and *Circle.cbm*.

The graphic for the logo in the upper right corner is already present as a graphic file in an optional file format. Use the paint program of your choice to convert such a graphic into black and white with 1 bit color depth; then save it in the BMP format. If you change the extension of this file to *.cbm*, you can use it in CASL.

To do this, choose *Project/Add Files*. A file selection box appears. Choose the *Bitmap Files (*.cbm)* option under File type. Then select the graphic file.

*The pictures in CASLide*

All of the pictures are displayed in separate windows in CASLide. You can find the names of all the pictures that belong to the current project in the *Images* folder in the left window.

If you have enabled the *Workbook Mode* option in the *View* menu, tabs appear at the lower border of the CASL main window. Use these tabs to bring the individual windows and graphics into the foreground.

After the graphics are all in the current project, integrate them into the program.

```
frame drawing;
  end;

label x1label, drawing;
  display "x1";
  position 20,820;
  end;

label y1label, drawing;
  display "y1";
  position 400,820;
  end;

label x2label, drawing;
  display "x2";
  position 20,900;
  end;

label y2label, drawing;
  display "y2";
  position 400,900;
  end;

text x1text, drawing;
  char_size 5,1;
  position 100,820;
  end;

text y1text, drawing;
  char_size 5,1;
  position 480,820;
  end;

text x2text, drawing;
  char_size 5,1;
  position 100,900;
  end;
```

```
text y2text, drawing;
  char_size 5,1;
  position 480,900;
  end;

button line, drawing;
  bitmap line;
  position 740,900;
  pixel_size 75,75;
  end;

button rectangle, drawing;
  bitmap rectangle;
  position 820,900;
  pixel_size 75,75;
  end;

button circle, drawing;
  bitmap circle;
  position 900,900;
  pixel_size 75,75;
  end;

button raster, drawing;
  display "Matrix";
  position 740,820;
  end;

label title, drawing;
  bitmap data;
  position 410,0;
  pixel_size 590,68;
  end;

variables;
  numeric x1;
  numeric y1;
  numeric x2;
  numeric y2;
  numeric i;
  numeric j;
  end;

function line;
  get x1text, x1;
  get y1text, y1;
  get x2text, x2;
  get y2text, y2;
  set drawing, pen, x1, y1;
```

```
  draw drawing, line, x2-x1, y2-y1;
  put x1text, x2;
  put y1text, y2;
  put x2text, "";
  put y2text, "";
  end;

function rectangle;
  get x1text, x1;
  get y1text, y1;
  get x2text, x2;
  get y2text, y2;
  set drawing, pen, x1, y1;
  draw drawing, rectangle, x2-x1, y2-y1;
  put x1text, x2;
  put y1text, y2;
  put x2text, "";
  put y2text, "";
  end;

function circle;
  get x1text, x1;
  get y1text, y1;
  get x2text, x2;
  get y2text, y2;
  set drawing, pen, x1, y1;
  draw drawing, circle, x2-x1, y2-y1;
  put x1text, x2;
  put y1text, y2;
  put x2text, "";
  put y2text, "";
  end;

function raster;
  for i=0, i<=1000;
    for j=100, j<=800;
      set drawing, pen, i, j;
      draw drawing, line, 0, 0;
    next j+50;
  next i+50;
  end;

function startup;
  raster;
  end;
```

CD

**Program on the companion CD**

You can also find this program on the companion CD to this book as *0434.csl*, along with the graphics used as *0435.cbm*, *0436.cbm*, *0437.cbm* and *0438.cbm*.

The program functions themselves are unchanged. Only the three buttons have been slightly modified.

```
button line, drawing;
  bitmap line;
  position 740,900;
  pixel_size 75,75;
  end;
```

In place of the *display* parameter, which specifies the text that is displayed on a button, use the *bitmap* parameter. Here the name of a graphic is specified. The *pixel_size* parameter contains the size of the graphic, and by extension, the size of the button.

Buttons with graphics are automatically displayed without the typical button border. If you want a border around this kind of button, you must draw it in the graphic.

The logo in the upper right corner is imported in similar fashion. The logo is defined as a new *label* object in the program.

```
label title, drawing;
  bitmap data;
  position 410,0;
  pixel_size 590,68;
  end;
```

The *bitmap* and *pixel_size* parameters are used in the same manner. The new *label* is set in an area in the upper right corner that the program does not otherwise use.

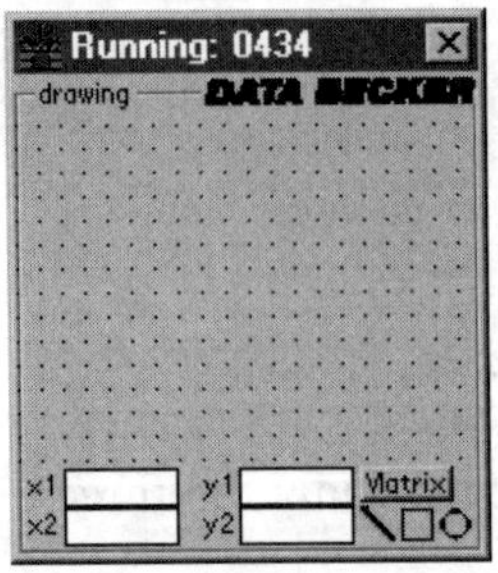


*The finished program in Windows ...*

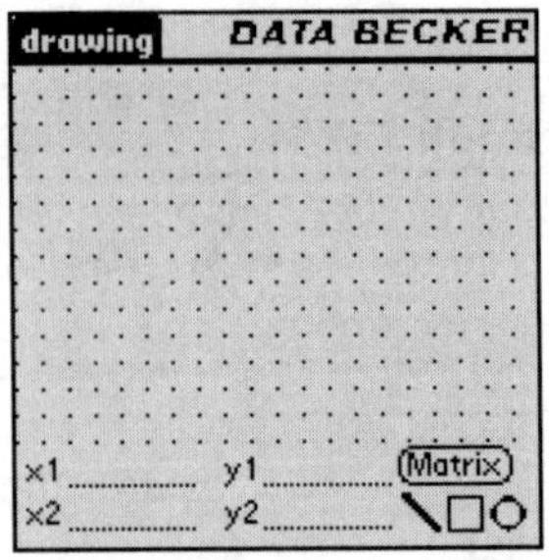


*... and on the Palm*

# 5. Designing interactive elements

In the early years of computer technology, programs prompted the user for different input and then output the results in number columns or as text. Today's programs have graphic interfaces with buttons. Program results are usually output interactively without noticeable delay. Palm programs follow this model.

## 5.1 Designing professional interfaces

Designing an efficient user interface requires not only technical knowledge about using the programming language but also knowledge of didactics and ergonomics to make operations as user-friendly as possible.

### Ergonomics

Program for human beings, not for the computer. Humans require user interfaces to be well organized and foolproof. Users should not need a manual for a function that is driven by dialog boxes. All the elements of the user interface should be self-explanatory and arranged in such a way that the whole results in a harmonious visual image.

The illustrations show a good user interface, one in which every conceivable mistake has been made. The example is a stopwatch.

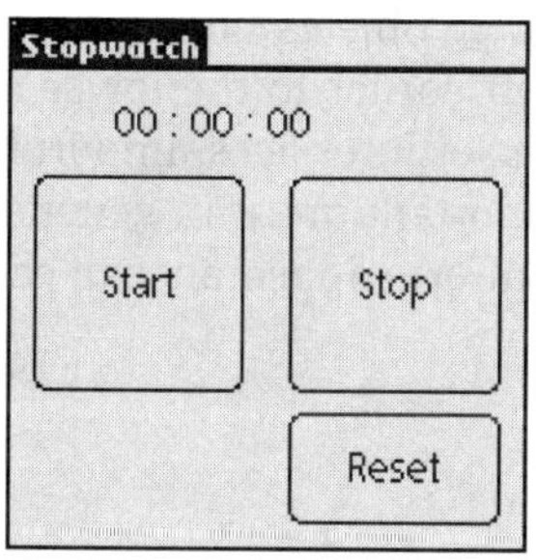


*Well-organized and functional stopwatch*

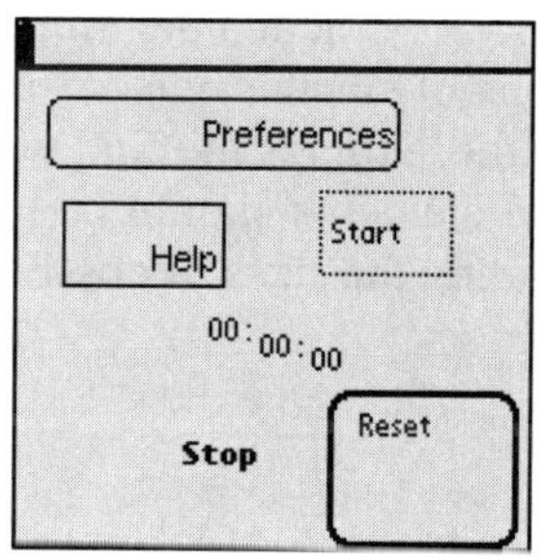


*Bad stopwatch*

The left picture employs a user interface that can be grasped at first glance. The buttons offer a uniform appearance and are designed for operation with a stylus or a finger. The hand does not cover up the time display (the most important part of a stopwatch). The program for actually making use of this stopwatch is available in chapter 6, on page 239.

The picture on the right could also be a user interface for a stopwatch. However, this one contains some serious errors in the design:

- The appearance is confusing.
- The title bar ordinarily found in Palm programs is missing.
- The buttons are very different in appearance, font, and size.
- Important buttons, like *Start* and *Stop*, are pushed into the background compared to unimportant functions.
- The *Stop* cannot be recognized readily because the typical border for a Palm button is missing.
- Functions such as *Settings* and *Help*, if they are at all necessary in such a simple program, belong either in the menu or on small buttons in the lower screen area.
- The time display is too small and in the wrong location on the screen. The slanted arrangement makes it difficult to read.
- Labels on buttons are usually centered in Palm programs. If they must be arranged differently for reasons of design, they should at least be uniform.
- Elements of a user interface should be arranged in vertical or horizontal rows for clarity. In the example, the buttons seem to be haphazardly placed on the screen. Buttons that logically belong together such as *Start* and *Stop* have no relationship whatsoever to each other here.

When you look at a picture, you notice the large objects first. You look over collections of smaller objects from the upper left corner to the lower right corner. Keep these things in mind when you design user interfaces. Important, often required elements should be larger than unimportant ones. In general, avoid manipulating the sizes. If possible, maintain a uniform appearance in each new program.

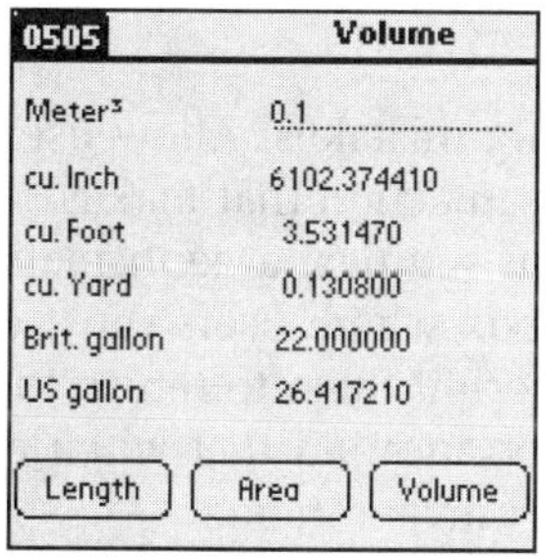


*Clear and functional user interface*

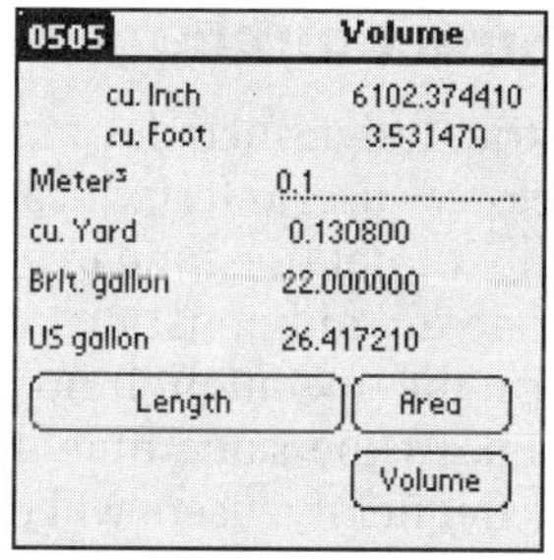


*Poor arrangement of the elements*

The example shows a program that converts an input value into various other units of measurement. The three buttons switch back and forth between different categories of units. You can find the program for the example on the left of page 206 in this chapter. While the user interface in the picture on the right is not awful, it is not consistent with the program:

- Humans process a picture from top to bottom, so it does not make sense to place an input field that is filled out prior to a calculation in the middle.
- The five calculated values are, from a logical standpoint, all equal. Therefore, they should also be arranged on a par below one another and not in two blocks or partially indented. The picture on the right suggests that the two upper values are a requirement for the value in the input field and that the ones below represent the results.
- The three buttons are equal alternatives and are logically placed next to one another. In the picture on the right, the *Length* button gains importance through its size, while the *Volumes* button is subordinate to the other buttons as a result of its location.

Remember that most users are accustomed to standard Palm OS interfaces. Adhere to their visual expectations as much as possible. The easiest approach is to use the preset standard elements. The users know their appearance and behavior. For example, always place the buttons for *OK* and *Cancel* in the bottom row. Don't use special technical terminology. It wouldn't make your program seem more educated, just harder to comprehend. Use words the same way that the Palm OS does. In the user dialog boxes, consistency is absolute. Do not use one word one time and another word another time for the same thing. Conversely, don't use the same word for different things.

## Allowing incorrect input

Part of human-centric design includes making mistakes. Allow users to experiment. However, before a user interface calls an action that makes serious changes to large amounts of data or fundamental settings, a confirmation message should appear. Create an additional dialog box where users must confirm that they want to perform the operation. If not, permit them to return to the original place in the program. At the same time, keep in mind that when confirmation messages occur too frequently, users will circumvent them.

Necessary warning

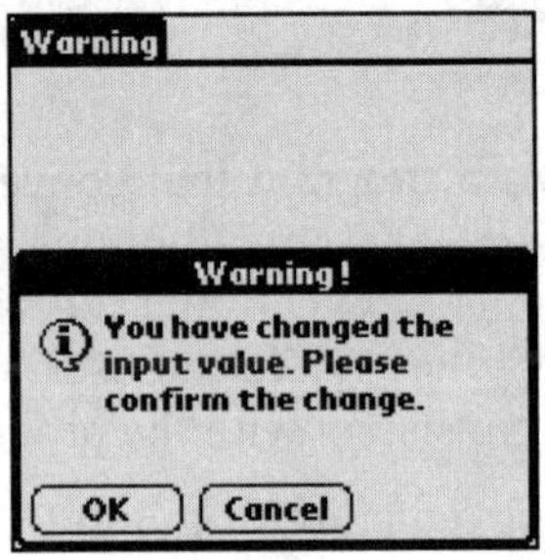


Unnecessary warning

With fatal changes, as in the figure on the left, a warning message is justified. Nevertheless, decide exactly what should appear in the window header and what type of icon should appear in the message box.

The message on the right only disrupts workflow. Design input fields in such a way that you can change the values again at any time.

Practical warning

This warning doesn't help

When you display a meaningful, critical warning, the user should have the opportunity to prevent the damage. The example on the right offers only one selection, which makes this warning impractical.

*Practical buttons*

*Another practical solution*

*Confusing!*

- The solution on the far left is clear to every user who can relate the buttons to the message text.
- While the solution in the middle uses less common button texts, the message is comprehensible. Based on your target user group and the texts used elsewhere in your program, choose which variant you prefer.
- The variant on the right is confusing. The message text complicates which button brings about which action. Furthermore, only two logical responses are possible to the posed question, not three.

Users require all relevant information in front of them. If an action causes a change in the values displayed in the user interface, these values should be evaluated immediately. This also applies when a button hides the current dialog box to show something on the screen - again, the result of this query should be visible somewhere in the new dialog box afterwards. A user interface should not expect the user to enter values or keywords that must be memorized. A direct selection from a list is much easier. Avoid programming situations where a text or value must be entered immediately. However, in cases where this becomes necessary, specify a reasonable default value that will work even when the user doesn't type in anything significant. Every user interface should also supply a practical result or at least a meaningful message with just *OK*, even without user input. After exiting the user interface, save the input to use it as a default the next time you call the program. Doing so will save the user time and effort when similar input is repeated.

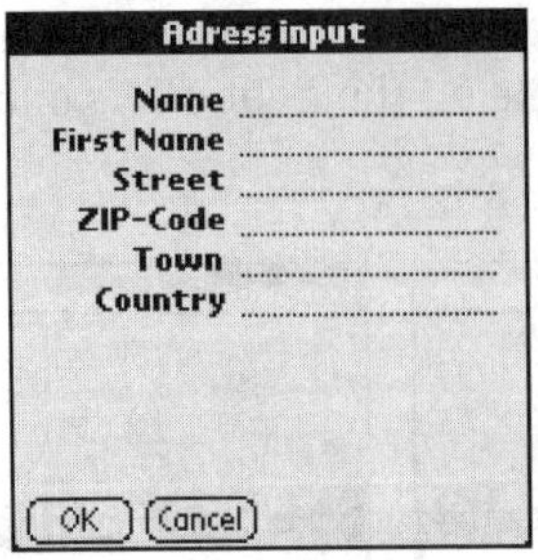


Practical input form

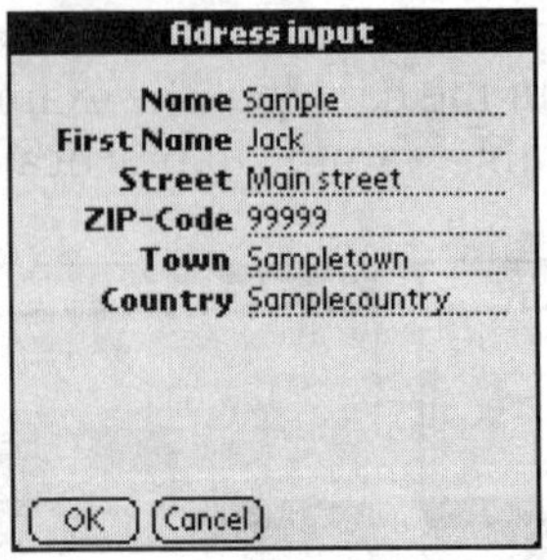


Superfluous default values

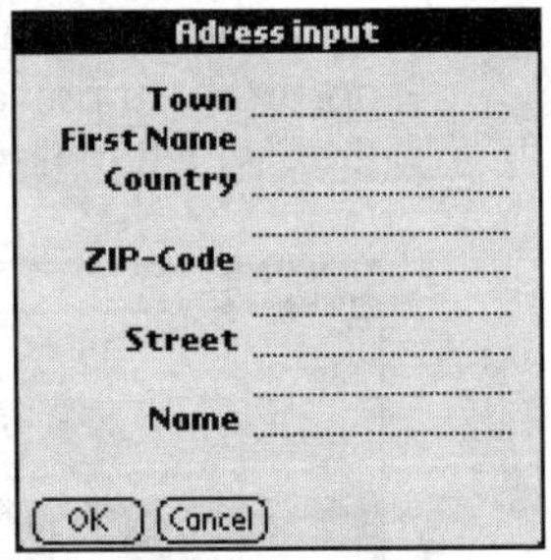


Confusing!

The figures show different input forms for an address.

- The first form is the best. The same order is used for the input fields as in the original Palm Address Book.
- In the second form the default values are meaningless, cumbersome, and annoying because they must be manually deleted every time. No default values are necessary for such simple input. The user understands the field labels without them.
- The third example is confusing because of the unusual order of the fields. Also, the blank lines suggest two-line input would be possible. In fact, when you enter very long texts in an input field in the original Palm Address Book, a second line already appears.

If several elements of the dialog box logically belong together, they should be physically connected and arranged in a column. If there is a logical order, it should be taken into consideration in the placement, for example, with coordinates that don't first ask for the y-value. Important and frequently used buttons should attract the eye. If options are mutually exclusive, they should disable one another in the user interface. Users will notice and won't enter information there.

## 5.2 Developing controls for custom programs

Every current computer platform, be it Palm OS, Windows, or another system, offers predefined control elements for user interfaces, such as buttons, menus, or input fields. Modern programming languages offer functions that can be used easily to create these standard control elements for respective platforms.

You saw *label, button, frame,* and *text* objects in the CASL sample programs in the preceding chapter. In this section, you learn about some additional control elements available in CASL.

As a foundation we use a program that displays a curve based on a value table. The program functions similarly to the yBasic program described above, only converted to CASL. The control elements used in the program correspond to the CASL sample program for displaying pie charts.

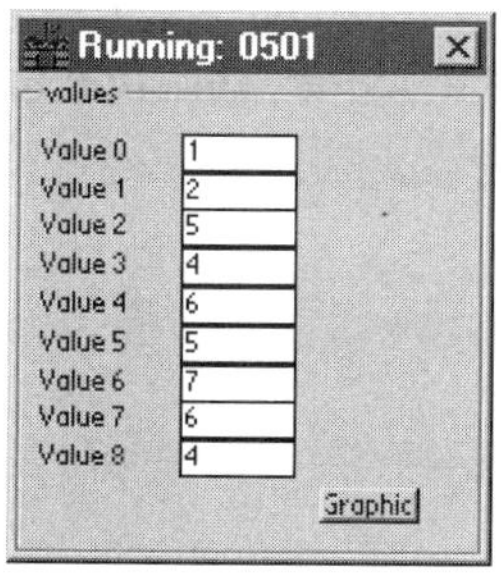


*Input form under Windows ...*

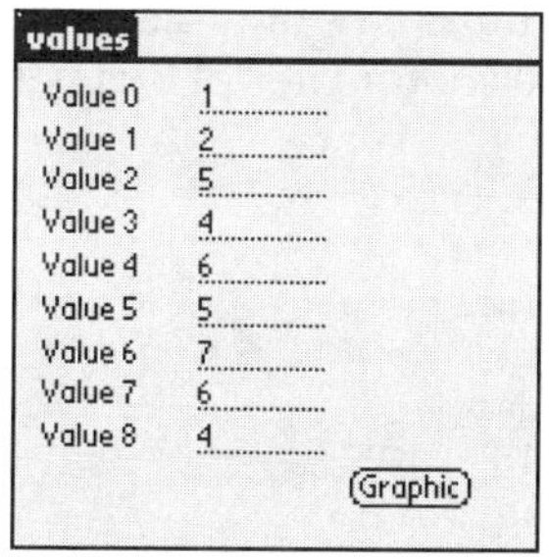


*... and on the Palm*

The data is input in a table and displayed in a curve when you tap the *Graphic* button.

Tapping the *Table* button displays the table again.

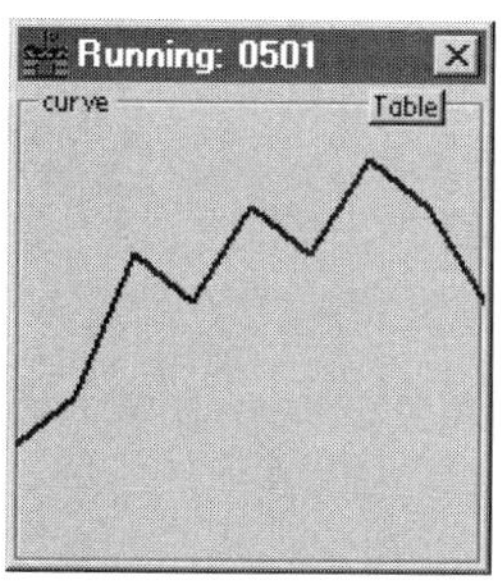


*Graphic under Windows ...*

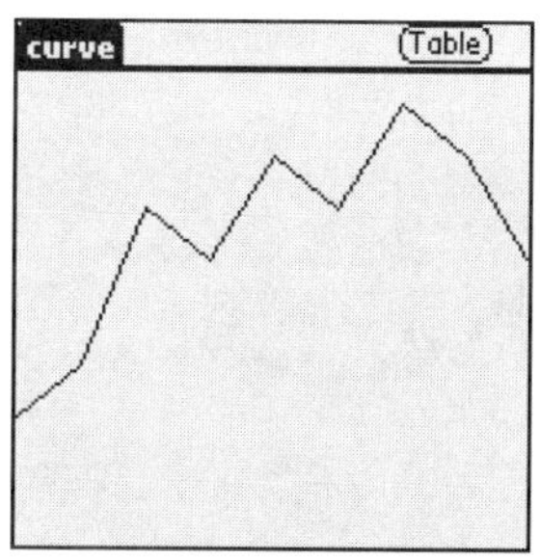


*... and on the Palm*

## Differences in the conversion to CASL

Take note of some important differences in the conversion of the yBasic program to CASL:

- In the dimensioning of arrays, the number of fields is specified in the array in CASL, not the highest possible index number (that is, 1 less than in yBasic).
- The index numbers in arrays are specified in brackets in CASL; in yBasic they are specified in parentheses.
- The *if* statement in CASL always requires an *end_if*.
- The *draw* function uses the offset vector to the next point as coordinates, not the absolute coordinates of this point as the *lineto* function in yBasic.

```
frame values;
  end;
label b[9], values;
  end;
text w[9], values;
  char_size 5,1;
  invokes calc;
  end;
button graphic, values;
  position 650,860;
  display "Graphic";
  end;

frame curve;
  end;
button table, curve;
  position 750,10;
  display "Table";
  end;

variables;
  numeric i;
  numeric m;
  numeric w1[9];
  string format="##";
  end;

function calc;
  m=0;
  for i=0, i<9;
    get w[i], w1[i];
    if w1[i]>m;
      m=w1[i];
```

```
    end_if;
  next i+1;
  end;

function graphic;
  hide values;
  show curve;
  set curve, pen, 0, 850-(w1[0]/m*700);
  for i=1, i<9;
    draw curve, line, 125, (w1[i-1]/m*700)-(w1[i]/m*700);
    set curve, pen, i*125, 850-w1[i]/m*700;
  next i+1;
  end;

function table;
  hide curve;
  show values;
  end;

function startup;
  hide curve;
  show values;
  for i=0, i<9;
    move b[i], 50, 120+i*80;
    move w[i], 350, 120+i*80;
    put b[i], "Value"+ string(i, format);
  next i+1;
  end;
```

**CD**

**Program on the companion CD**

You can also find this program on the companion CD to this book as *0501.csl.*

To enhance this program to make it possible to enter three different curves, display them individually or in combinations.

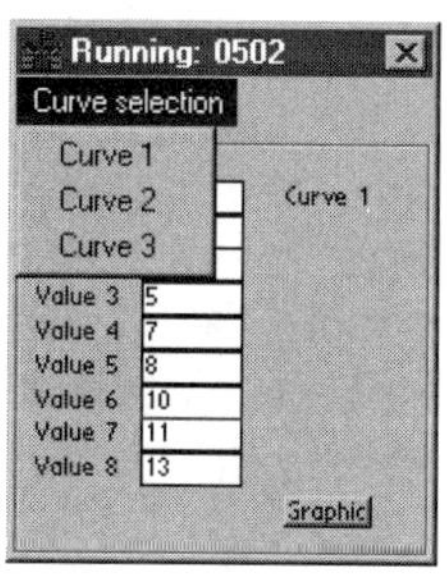


*Menu under Windows ...*

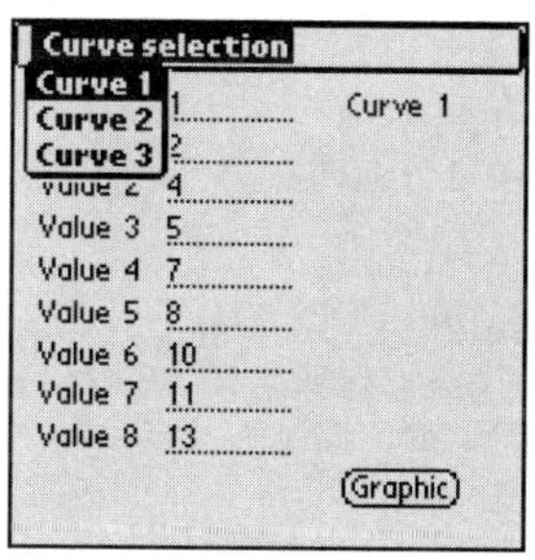


*... and on the Palm*

The new program contains a selection menu as a control. You can choose from three curves to enter three independent data series in the same form. The *label* object on the right displays which data series is currently visible in the form.

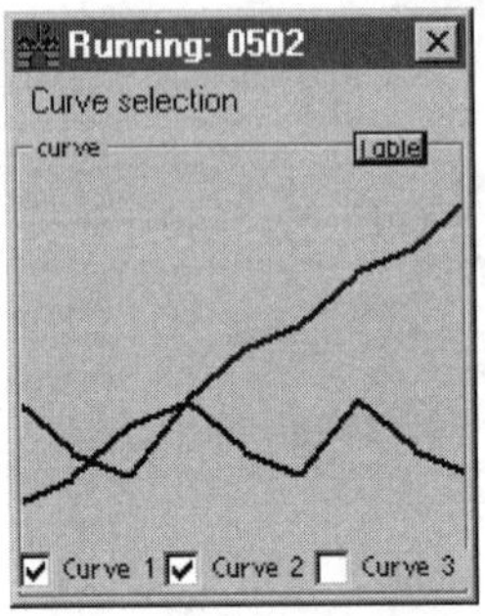


*Curves under Windows ...*

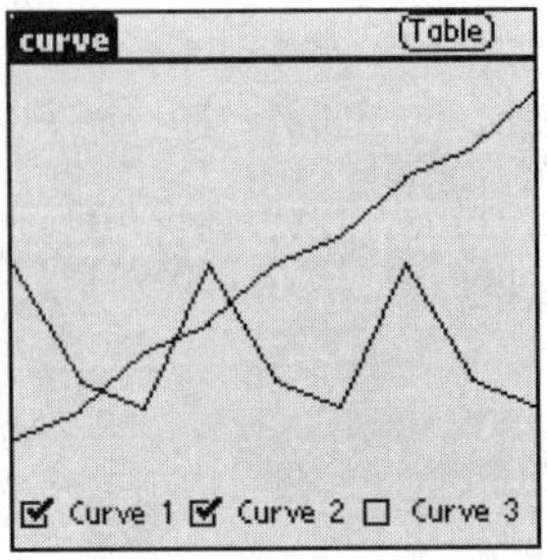


*... and on the Palm*

In the curve display, three checkboxes appear at the bottom to specify which of the three curves will be visible. This allows you to display single curves or any combination of more than one curve.

```
frame values;
  end;
label b[9], values;
  end;
text w[9], values;
  char_size 5,1;
  invokes calc;
  end;
button graphic, values;
  position 650,860;
  display "Graphic";
  end;
menu_top a;
  display "Curve selection";
  end;
menu_item Curvel, a;
  display "Curve 1";
  end;
menu_item curve2, a;
  display "Curve 2";
  end;
menu_item curve3, a;
  display "Curve 3";
  end;
label n, values;
```

```
  position 650,120;
  char_size 5,1;
  end;

frame curve;
  end;
button table, curve;
  position 750,10;
  display "Table";
  end;
button c[3], curve;
  char_size 6,1;
  checkbox;
  invokes graphic;
  end;

variables;
  numeric c;
  numeric i;
  numeric j;
  numeric k;
  numeric m;
  numeric m1[3];
  numeric w1[27];
  string format="##";
  end;

function curveno;
  put n, "Curve "+string(k+1,format);
  for i=0, i<9;
    put w[i], w1[i+9*k];
  next i+1;
  end;

function curve1;
  k=0;
  curveno;
  end;

function curve2;
  k=1;
  curveno;
  end;

function curve3;
  k=2;
  curveno;
  end;
```

```
function max;
  m=0;
  for i=0, i<3;
    if m1[i]>m;
      m=m1[i];
    end_if;
  next i+1;
  end;

function calc;
  m1[k]=0;
  for i=0, i<9;
    get w[i], w1[i+9*k];
    if w1[i+9*k]>m1[k];
      m1[k]=w1[i+9*k];
    end_if;
  next i+1;
  max;
  end;

function graphic;
  clear curve, rectangle,0,0;
  hide values;
  show curve;
  for j=0, j<3;
    get c[j], c;
    if c=1;
      set curve, pen, 0, 850-(w1[9*j]/m*700);
      for i=1, i<9;
        draw curve, line, 125, (w1[i-1+9*j]/m*700)-(w1[i+9*j]/m*700);
        set curve, pen, i*125, 850-w1[i+9*j]/m*700;
      next i+1;
    end_if;
  next j+1;
  end;

function table;
  hide curve;
  show values;
  end;

function startup;
  hide curve;
  show values;
  for i=0, i<9;
    move b[i], 50, 120+i*80;
    move w[i], 300, 120+i*80;
    put b[i], "Value "+ string(i, format);
    w1[i]=0;
```

```
    w1[i+9]=0;
    w1[i+18]=0;
  next i+1;
  m=0;
  for i-0, i<3;
    m[i]=0;
    put c[i], 1;
    put c[i], "Curve "+string(i+1,format);
    move c[i], i*330,900;
  next i+1;
  k=0;
  put n, "Curve "+string(k+1,format);
  end;
```

**CD**

**Program on the companion CD**

You can also find this program on the companion CD to this book as *0502.csl.*

The new control elements are defined at the beginning of the program. As the first control, you find the new menu there:

```
menu_top a;
  display "Curve selection";
  end;
menu_item curve1, a;
  display "Curve 1";
  end;
menu_item curve2, a;
  display "Curve 2";
  end;
menu_item curve3, a;
  display "Curve 3";
  end;
```

### *menu_top <Name>;*

*menu_top* defines a menu that opens when the user taps the *Menu* button on the Graffiti field. Each *menu_top* object needs a name that can be used later for assigning the individual menu items to this menu. Along with this comes another parameter:

| Parameter | Values | Meaning |
|---|---|---|
| display | String | Text that is to be displayed in the menu title line |

For each *menu_top* object, one or more *menu_item* objects appear, each of which represents a menu item.

### *menu_item <Name>, <Menu>;*

In addition to the name, the name of the menu in which the menu item is to be located must also be specified for each *menu_item*. Two optional parameters are also included:

| Parameter | Values | Meaning |
|---|---|---|
| display | String | Text that is to be displayed in the menu line |
| invokes | Function name | Name of the function that is to be called |

Every menu item calls a function. The name of this function is specified with the *invokes* parameter. If this parameter is missing, a function whose name is identical to the name of the *menu_item* is called.

In the example the name of the menu is simply *a*, while the three *menu_items* are called *curve1, curve2* and *curve3*. Because no *invokes* parameters are specified, the *curve1, curve2* and *curve3* functions are called, which have the same name.

An additional new object on the *values frame*, where the numerical values are input, is the *n label*, which displays the number of the currently selected curve.

```
label n, values;
  position 650,120;
  char_size 5,1;
  end;
```

Up until now, this *label* has had no value assigned. The program sets this value.

The curves display on a second *curve frame*. Three new checkboxes appear on this *frame*, defined as *button* objects with an additional *checkbox* parameter.

```
button c[3], curve;
  char_size 6,1;
  checkbox;
  invokes graphic;
  end;
```

If the *checkbox* parameter exists in a *button* definition, the *button* does not display as a button but rather as a checkbox. Consequently, some of the parameters have a slightly different function:

| Parameter | Values | Meaning |
|---|---|---|
| display | String | The text is displayed next to the checkbox as an explanation. |
| invokes | Function name | Name of the function that is to be called when the status of the checkbox changes. |
| char_size | Two integers | Width and height of the descriptive text field next to the checkbox. |

In the example, an array of three such control elements appears. If the user enables or disables one of them in the program, the program uses the *invokes* parameter to call the *graphic* function, which redraws the curves. The new functions of the program are explained on the basis of a typical program run, beginning with the *startup* function, which is called at each program startup.

```
function startup;
  hide curve;
  show values;
  for i=0, i<9;
    move b[i], 50, 120+i*80;
    move w[i], 300, 120+i*80;
    put b[i], "Value "+ string(i, format);
    w1[i]=0;
    w1[i+9]=0;
    w1[i+18]=0;
  next i+1;
  m=0;
  for i=0, i<3;
    m[i]=0;
    put c[i], 1;
    put c[i], "Curve "+string(i+1,format);
    move c[i], i*330,900;
  next i+1;
  k=0;
  put n, "Curve "+string(k+1,format);
  end;
```

Here, as in the previous program, the control elements that are defined through arrays are moved to their correct positions. The *w1[]*array, which later receives the input values, is filled with zeros. This array is now dimensioned to 27 because it has to receive the number series of all three curves.

**Tip**

**CASL knows only one-dimensional arrays**

In CASL it is not possible to define arrays that have several dimensions. However, you can manage by dimensioning the array so that all the necessary values can be received. To address a value, calculate the *i* index in accordance with the formula i = x + mx * y, whereby x and y are the coordinates in the imaginary/mathematical two-dimensional array and mx is the maximum defined value in x direction.

In the example, the first curve occupies the *w1[0]...w1[8]* variables, the second curve uses the *w1[9]...w1[17]* variables, and the third curve occupies the *w1[18]...w1[26]* variables.

This first loop accomplishes all of the tasks that are to be done for each value of a curve. A second new loop runs three times, once for each curve.

```
m[i]=0;
```

The maximum values of the individual curves are first set to 0.

```
put c[i], 1;
```

This *put* statement enables all three checkboxes. If you use a *put* statement to set a *button* object with *checkbox* to 1, the checkbox is enabled, although on 0 it is disabled.

```
put c[i], "Curve "+string(i+1,format);
```

A similar *put* statement defines the text next to the checkbox. The only difference is that *put* passes a string here, not a numerical value. Strings are always set as text next to the checkbox, although numerical values are used for enabling and disabling.

The text consists of the word *"Curve "* and a number. Numbers can only be appended to strings if they have been converted into a string beforehand using the *string()*. Every *string()* function also requires a formatting specification.

Finally, the *startup* function sets the *k* variable to 0. This variable always contains the number of the current curve in table view, from 0 to 2. Accordingly, *Curve 1* is then displayed in *label n*. (For a better visual effect, the labels *"Curve 1"* ... *"Curve 3"* appear here instead of 0 ... 2.)

After the *startup* function is finished, the user can enter numerical values in the table for Curve 1. With each change of a value, the *invokes* parameter of the *w[]text* field calls the *calc* function:

```
function calc;
  m1[k]=0;
  for i=0, i<9;
    get w[i], w1[i+9*k];
    if w1[i+9*k]>m1[k];
      m1[k]=w1[i+9*k];
    end_if;
  next i+1;
  max;
  end;
```

This function inputs all the input fields into the variables of the *w1[]*array corresponding to this curve and at the same time determines the current maximum of this curve *m1[k]*.

The maximum of each curve must always be kept up to date because it is required for scaling the graphic. It doesn't matter which table the user calls the graphic function from because all three curves must be drawn correctly.

When all the values of the table have been processed, the *max* function is also called.

**Note**

**Defining functions beforehand**

If a function is to call another function in a CASL program, the called function must be defined in the source text prior to the calling function. Otherwise, an error message stating that the called function is not known appears.

```
function max;
  m=0;
  for i=0, i<3;
    if m1[i]>m;
      m=m1[i];
    end_if;
  next i+1;
  end;
```

To scale the graphic, the *max* function calculates the maximum of all three curves.

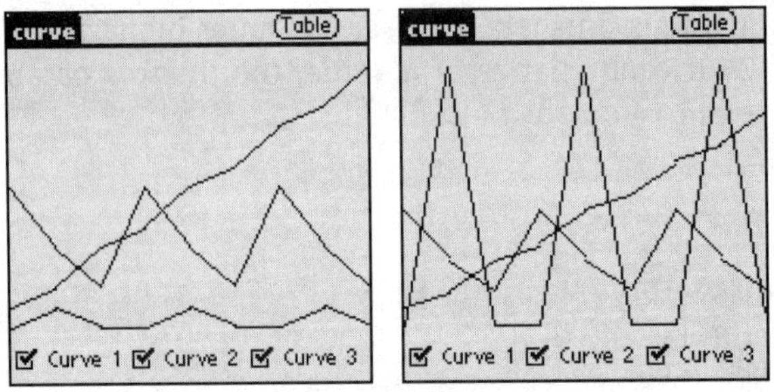


*The effects of changing one curve on the overall picture*

After you have entered all of the values of a curve, choose one of the other curves in the menu. Every menu item calls a function that sets the curve number in the *k* variable to the new value.

```
function curve2;
  k=1;
  curveno;
  end;
```

Then the *curve no* function is called each time. This function writes the new curve number to the *label n* and sets the input fields to the value of the corresponding curve. At the beginning these values are all still 0, but if you switch between two curves later, the correct values should always appear in the table.

**Tip**

**Update the values**

The user automatically expects a program with a graphical user interface to have all of its displayed values current. If this is not possible from a programming standpoint, you need to build in a button that can be used to update the display.

```
function curveno;
  put n, "Curve "+string(k+1,format);
  for i=0, i<9;
    put w[i], w1[i+9*k];
  next i+1;
  end;
```

With this method you need to define a single input form only because the form of the values to be displayed in all three curves is identical.

Once users have entered all the values for the three curves, they tap the *Graphic* button. This button calls the *graphic* function, which draws the curves.

```
function graphic;
  clear curve, rectangle,0,0;
  hide values;
  show curve;
  for j=0, j<3;
    get c[j], c;
    if c=1;
      set curve, pen, 0, 850-(w1[9*j]/m*700);
      for i=1, i<9;
        draw curve, line, 125, (w1[i-1+9*j]/m*700)-(w1[i+9*j]/m*700);
        set curve, pen, i*125, 850-w1[i+9*j]/m*700;
      next i+1;
    end_if;
  next j+1;
  end;
```

In this function the Redraw list is first deleted with *clear* to draw the curves on a blank *frame.*

### *clear <Frame>, <Form>, <xOffset>, <yOffset>;*

The *clear* function is used for drawing lines, rectangles, or circles in the background color. This allows you to delete individually drawn objects. The parameters are used in exactly the same manner as for drawing with the *draw* function. If you set *xOffset* and *yOffset* to 0, the Redraw list and thus the entire *frame* clear.

**Tip**

**The Redraw list**

CASL stores each drawn object in a Redraw list. When a *frame* is hidden and then redisplayed later, the entire drawing is redrawn using this Redraw list. If you delete objects using *clear*, this deletion is stored so that a drawing with multiple changes increases the size of the Redraw list considerably. Each drawing and clearing step is repeated in the reconstruction of a drawing. Thus if a graphic can be reproduced by means of stored values, delete the Redraw list by setting the last two parameters to 0 in the *clear* function at suitable times. A reconstruction of the drawing will then proceed faster than a repetition of all the modification steps.

In the next lines, the function places the *curve frame* in the foreground, and a loop checks whether the checkbox in question is checked for all three curves.

```
get c[j], c;
if c=1;
```

If checked, the program draws the curve. For this purpose the values are read out again through calculation from the curve number and the index of the value *w1[i+9*j]* in question from the one-dimensional array. For the scaling of the curve, the values are divided by the global maximum of all curves (*m* variable) and multiplied by 700. The area occupied by the curves is 700 y-coordinates high, because 150 coordinate units above and below are reserved for control elements.

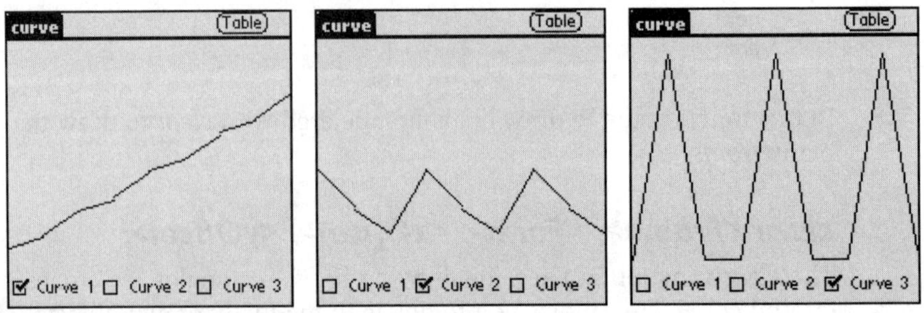


*The three individual curves from the last figure, scaled to the maximum of all three curves*

The same function is also executed when the user enables or disables one of the checkboxes. A redrawing of all the displayed curves is faster than deleting and redisplaying individual curves because the Redraw list would then become larger and larger.

If the user taps *Table*, the table of the last entered curve displays again because the displaying of the curve does not change the *k* variable. If the user now changes values in a curve, the maximum will be recalculated over and over again because it affects the scaling of all three curves.

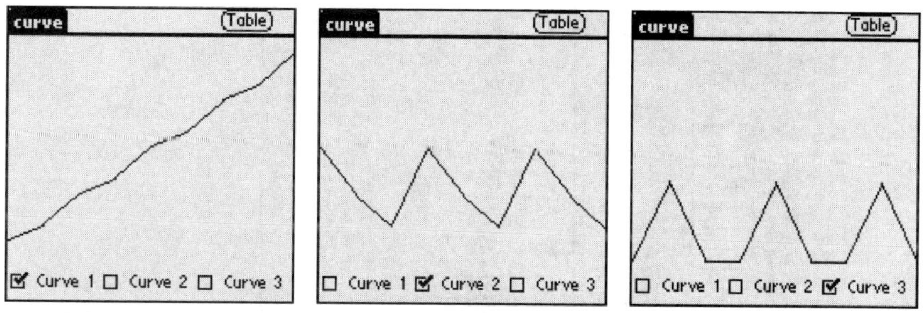


*Compared to the previous figures, only the values of the third curve have been changed*

# Error messages and Warnings

In almost all programs, situations occur whereby users should be warned or notified. In Windows a message displays in the middle of a screen in a small window. This message has to be confirmed by clicking the *OK* button before the program continues to run.

For example, the last program does not display negative values in the tables in the curve correctly. In this case, it would even be possible to adapt the program accordingly. However, in the program an appropriate warning should appear.

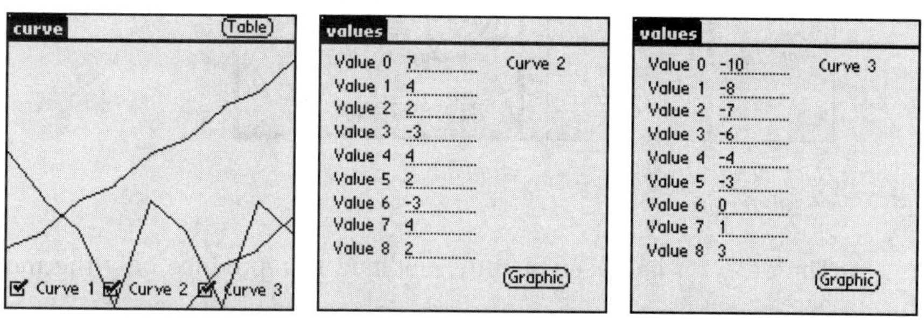


*Two curves with negative values*

If the program immediately brought the message on screen with each entered negative number, users would feel annoyed because it is sometimes possible that the negative numbers are supposed to be in the table. For this reason, the message does not appear until the program finds a negative number while drawing the curves.

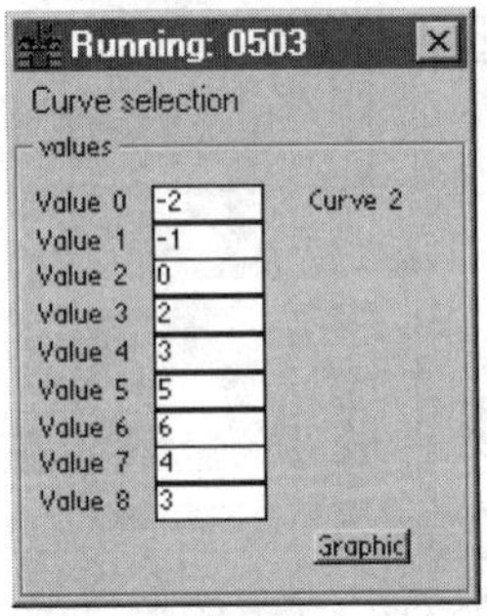


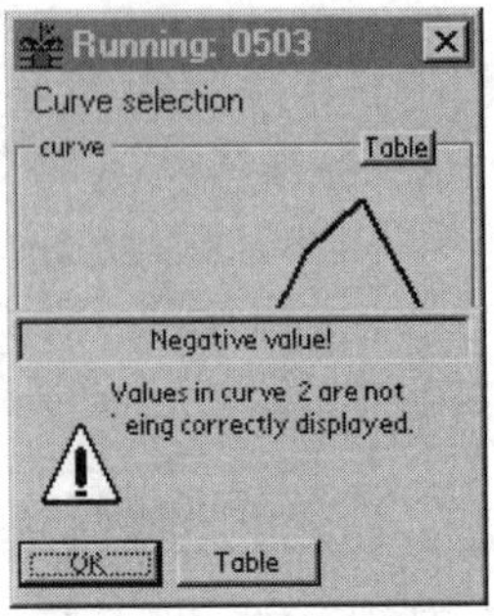


*Number series with negative values* *Warning*

The warning contains two buttons:

- **OK** – closes the warning and displays the graphic.
- **Table** – closes the warning and goes to the table with the defective curve.

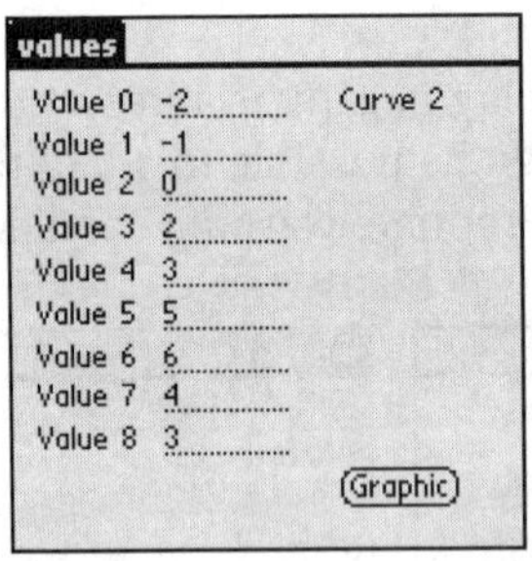


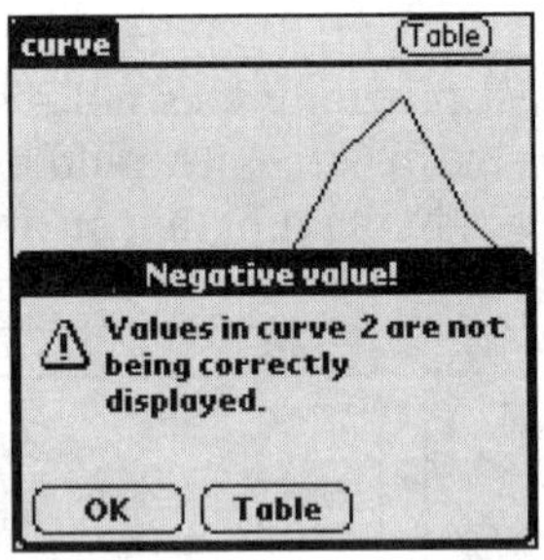


*Number series with negative values* *Warning*

The program has been slightly modified to reproduce only the modified parts here.

**CD**

**Program on the companion CD**

You can also find this program on the companion CD to this book as *0503.csl*.

```
variables;
  numeric c;
  numeric f;
  numeric i;
  numeric j;
  numeric k;
  numeric m;
  numeric m1[3];
  numeric w1[27];
  string t;
  string format="##";
  end;
...
function graphic;
  clear curve, rectangle,0,0;
  hide values;
  show curve;
  f=-1;
  for j=0, j<3;
    get c[j], c;
    if c=1;
      set curve, pen, 0, 850-(w1[9*j]/m*700);
      for i=1, i<9;
        draw curve, line, 125, (w1[i-1+9*j]/m*700)-(w1[i+9*j]/m*700);
        set curve, pen, i*125, 850-w1[i+9*j]/m*700;
        if w1[i+9*j]<0;
          f=j;
        end_if;
      next i+1;
    end_if;
  next j+1;
  j=0;
  if f>-1;
    t="Values in curve "+string(f+1,format)+" are   --not being
    ➥correctly displayed.";
    j=message_box(2,"Negative value!",t,"OK","Table","");
  end_if;
  if j=1;
    k=f;
    curveno;
    table;
  end_if;
  end;
```

In the *variables* part, two new variables are defined, *numeric f*, in which the number of the defective curve is stored, and *string t* for the text of the error message. This variable is used only because a line of the *graphic* function would otherwise be so long that it could no longer be reproduced in one line.

In the *graphic* function, the program checks each drawn value to determine if it is negative.

```
if w1[i+9*j]<0;
  f=j;
end_if;
```

If it is, the *f* variable is set to the number of the defective curve. To determine for the subsequent check that errors in curve 0 are also correctly gathered, *f* is set to -1 at the beginning of the function. If it has the value 0 or greater at the end, it means a negative value occurs somewhere.

```
  t="Values in curve "+string(f+1,format)+" are   --not being correctly
  ➥displayed.";
  j=message_box(2,"Negative value!",t,"OK","Table","");
end_if;
```

In this case the *message_box* function displays a message. Up to three buttons can be defined in this message. The return value of the function is the number of the tapped button: 0, 1, or 2.

If the value is 1, the user tapped the *Table* button. In this case the *k* variable is set to the number of the defective table, the *curveno* function then sets this to the current number, and finally the *table* function displays it.

```
if j=1;
  k=f;
  curveno;
  table;
end_if;
```

### *message_box (<Type>, <Title>, <Text>, <B0>, <B1>, <B2>;*

The *message_box* function can output messages of four different types (0 ... 3). The title and text of the message are freely selectable. Each message can contain up to three buttons. The return value of the function is the number of the tapped button.

If you want only one or two buttons to appear, enter blank strings "" in the remaining parameters.

The following program shows the different types of messages, which differ only in the displayed icon. The functionality of the different types is otherwise identical.

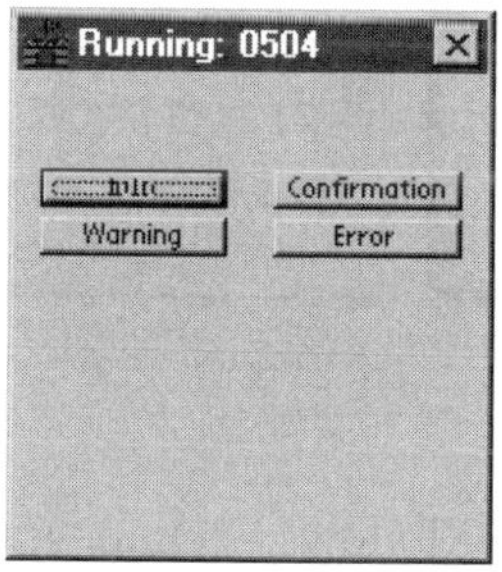


*Program at startup*

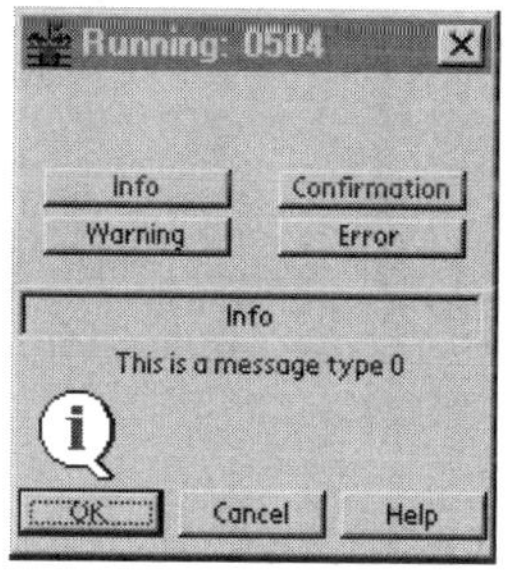


*Message Type 0*

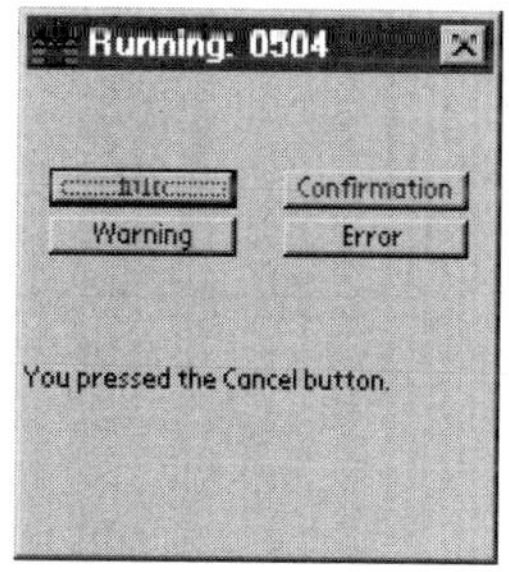


*Display of the tapped button*

The program shows four buttons. When you select one, a message of the corresponding type appears. To exit this message, tap a button. The program then displays which of the buttons has been pressed.

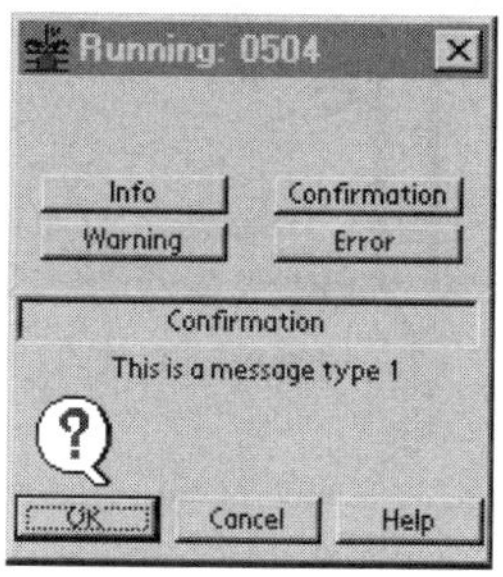


*Message Type 1*

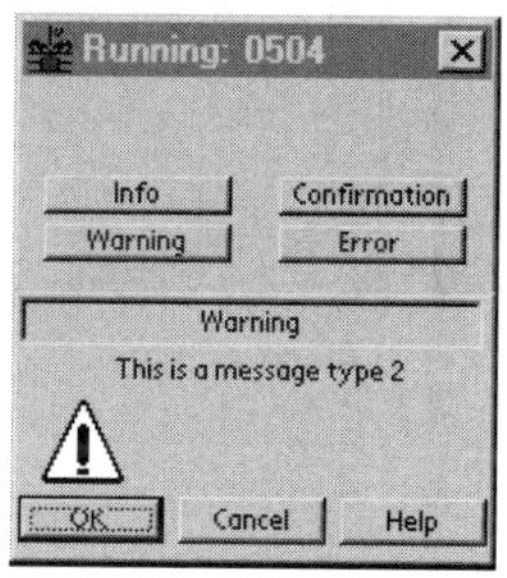


*Message Type 2*

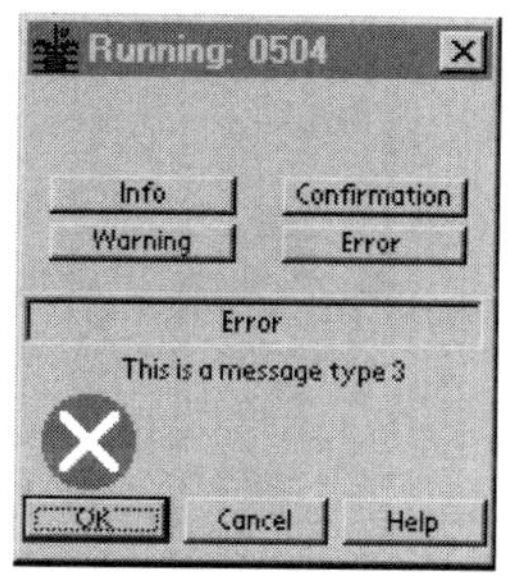


*Message Type 3*

| **Meaning of the messages** | | |
|---|---|---|
| 0 | Info | Informs the user (use sparingly). |
| 1 | Confirmation | Prompts that the user has to answer. |
| 2 | Warning | Warnings about critical actions, where there is danger of data loss or defective displays are to be expected. |
| 3 | Error | Use only in case of true defective functions or incorrect input. |

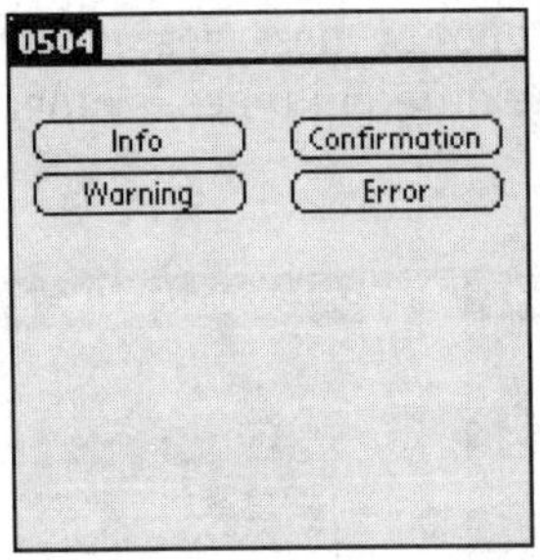


*Program at startup*

*Message Type 0*

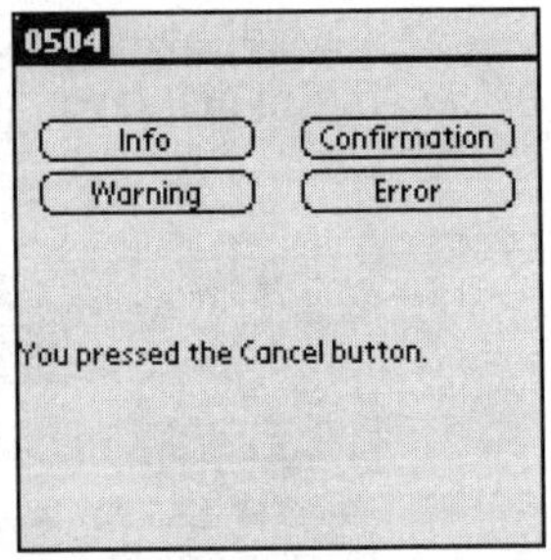


*Display of the pressed button*

The Palm font is somewhat wider than that of Windows, so line wrapping must occur earlier in the message texts. The texts can also be larger. Line wrapping happens automatically, so you cannot influence it.

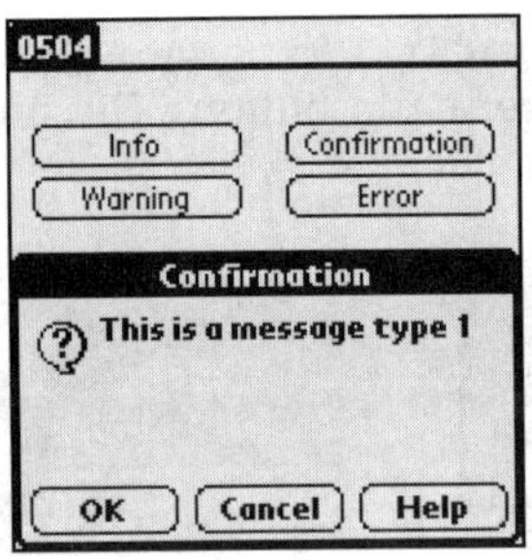


*Message Type 1*

*Message Type 2*

*Message Type 3*

```
button info;
  position 50,200;
  char_size 8,1;
  display "Info";
  end;

button confirm;
  position 550,200;
  char_size 8,1;
  display "Confirmation";
  end;

button warning;
  position 50,300;
  char_size 8,1;
  display "Warning";
  end;
```

```
button error;
  position 550,300;
  char_size 8,1;
  display "Error";
  end;

label message;
  position 0,600;
  char_size 20,1;
  end;

variables;
  numeric a;
  string b[3];
  string t="This is a message type ";
  end;

function info;
  a=message_box(0,"Info",t+"0",b[0],b[1],b[2]);
  put message, "You pressed the "+b[a]+" button.";
  end;

function confirm;
  a=message_box(1,"Confirmation",t+"1",b[0],b[1],b[2]);
  put message, "You pressed the "+b[a]+" button.";
  end;

function warning;
  a=message_box(2,"Warning",t+"2",b[0],b[1],b[2]);
  put message, "You pressed the "+b[a]+" button.";
  end;

function error;
  a=message_box(3,"Error",t+"3",b[0],b[1],b[2]);
  put message, "You pressed the "+b[a]+" button.";
  end;

function startup;
  b[0]="OK";
  b[1]="Cancel";
  b[2]="Help";
  end;
```

**CD**

**Program on the companion CD**

You can also find this program on the companion CD to this book as *0504.csl.*

Four *button* objects and one *label* object are defined at the beginning of the program. Later the *label* displays which button was tapped.

At the beginning, the *startup* function stores the *OK*, *Cancel*, and *Help* button texts in the *b[0]...b[2]* variables.

Each button calls a function of the same name, which displays the message. They differ only in type and in the texts that are displayed in the message title, as well as a number that is appended to the standardized message text.

By means of the return value of the *message_box* function, one of the button texts is selected. This button text is displayed in the *label* together with a ready-made text passage by a *put* function.

**Tip**

**Appropriate use of messages**

Use the messages sparingly and carefully decide which type you use. Excessive use of error messages and warnings hardens users and causes them to ignore the really important messages or look for a different program. Give the buttons meaningful names. As much as possible, use names like *OK* or *Cancel*, which the user is familiar with from the standard Palm OS messages, and consistently repeat the sequence.

## Creating forms easily with the CASL Form Editor

You can save yourself the trouble of calculating the coordinates for the individual elements when creating a user interface for a CASL program, and you can picture the future appearance of the program on the basis of the source text. How? CASL offers a graphically oriented form editor with which you can draw a user interface for a program and then transfer it to the program.

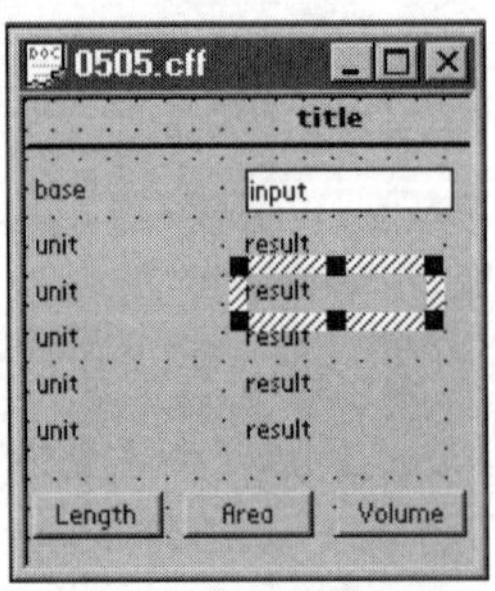


*Input form in the CASL Form Editor*

The forms are stored in a separate file format called CFF and automatically linked during compiling; thus the control elements no longer appear in the program code.

Enable *Add new form file to project* in the *Tools/IDE Settings* dialog box. This causes newly created forms to be automatically integrated into the current project when you save.

**Tip**

**More than one form for a program**

You can also insert several forms in a program that uses different *frames*. When several forms occur in a project, each form must have a *frame* defined on it. To create a new form, click the *New* button and then choose *Form File* in the list. You can also use the *Project/Add files* menu item to add existing forms to the current project. In this way you can use a form in several programs, as long as the control elements are identical in all of the programs.

All the forms in a project are displayed in the left window when you double-click the *Forms* folder icon. Each form appears within the CASLide in a separate window.

**Tip**

**Do not change form files**

The CFF files of the forms are stored in a special ASCII format. Do not attempt to edit these files with a text editor. CASL must have precisely the format used in these files. Otherwise, the form file can no longer be correctly inserted during compiling.

The Form Editor uses two custom toolbars that become active when you activate a form window. If you cannot see these toolbars, turn them on using the *View/Form Layout Toolbar* and *View/Form Controls Toolbar* menu items.

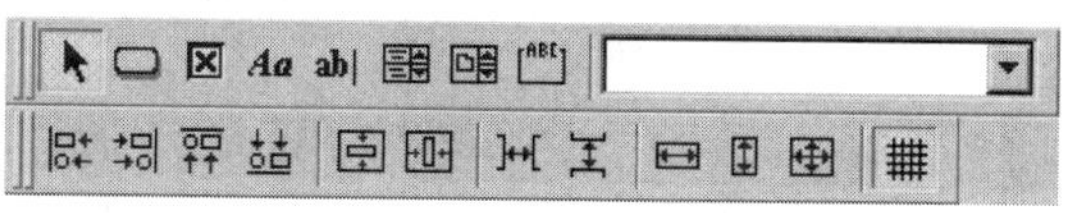

*The toolbars of the CASL Form Editor*

# Enhanced conversion program

Our next sample program converts metric units of measurement into British measurements. An input value is automatically converted into several other units. Use three buttons to toggle the table from measurements of length to areas and volumes.

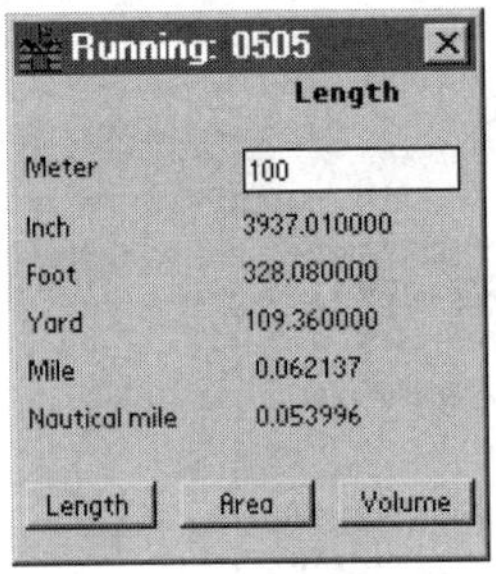


Conversion of lengths, ...

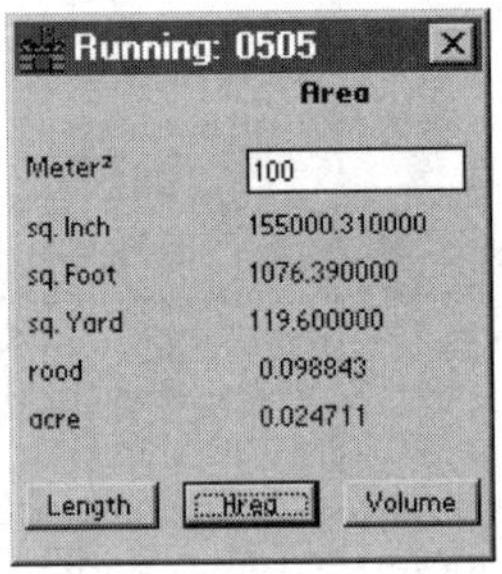


... areas ...

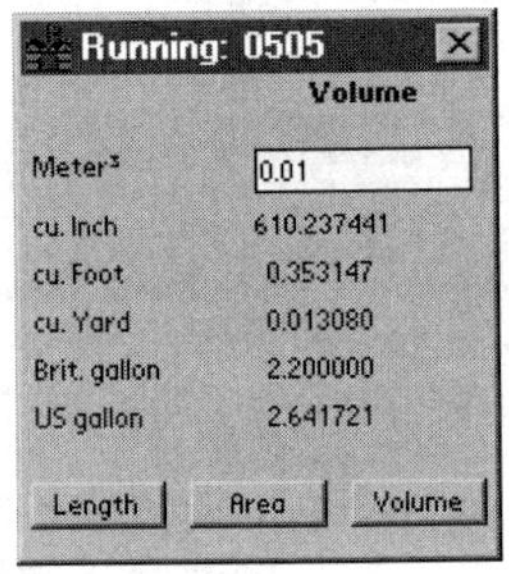


... and volumes

This program requires the following control elements, which we will create using the CASL Form Editor:

- One *label* to display the category currently being used in the upper right corner.
- One *label* to display the base unit in the upper left corner.
- One *text* to input the value to be converted.
- Five *labels* to display the other units of measurement in the left column.
- Five *labels* to display the converted values in the right column.
- Three *buttons* to toggle between the categories.

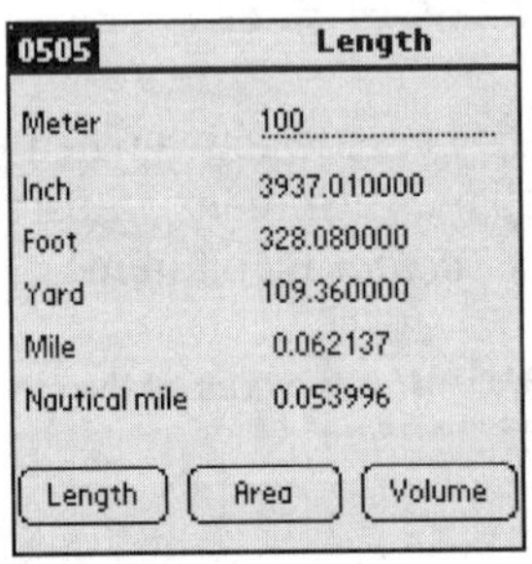


Conversion of lengths, ...

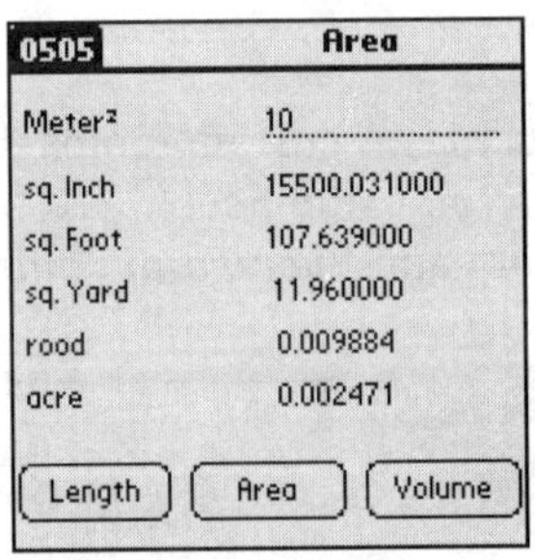


... areas ...

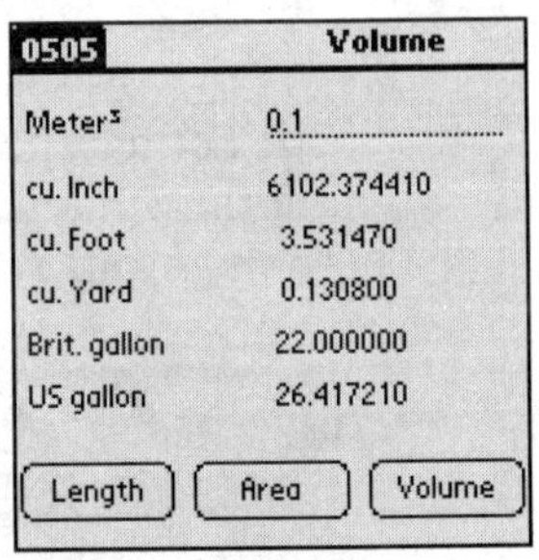


... and volumes

First, under *Project/Project Settings*, switch the two values for *Physical Screen Size* to 160 so that the form corresponds exactly to the Palm display in size.

When you create a new project, a new form file is also automatically created. If you cannot see the form file, double-click the *Forms* folder icon in the left window. Choose the only existing form file there. An empty gray window appears.

Click the icon (shown in the right margin) and a grid appears. Use it to get your bearings. The horizontal line indicates how much of the screen is covered by the program title line.

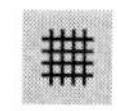

*Blank form without a grid ...*

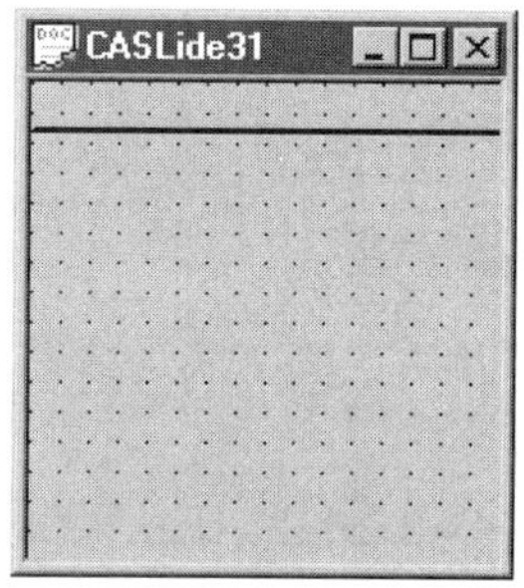


*... with a grid*

First, create the *label* for displaying the category currently being used in the upper right corner.

To do this, click the icon (shown in the right margin). When you move the mouse pointer over the form window, it turns into a small cross hair. Hold down the mouse button and use this cross hair to drag a rectangle in the upper right corner. When you release the mouse button, a name *label* followed by a two-digit number appears in this rectangle. When you create the objects with the CASL Form Editor, they are automatically numbered in sequence.

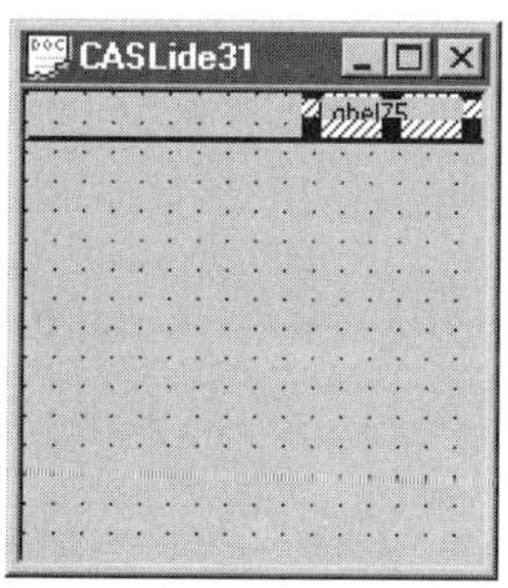


*The new label*

The mouse pointer now turns into a double arrow so that you can move this *label* anywhere on the form. When you double-click it, you have access to all the parameters of this object.

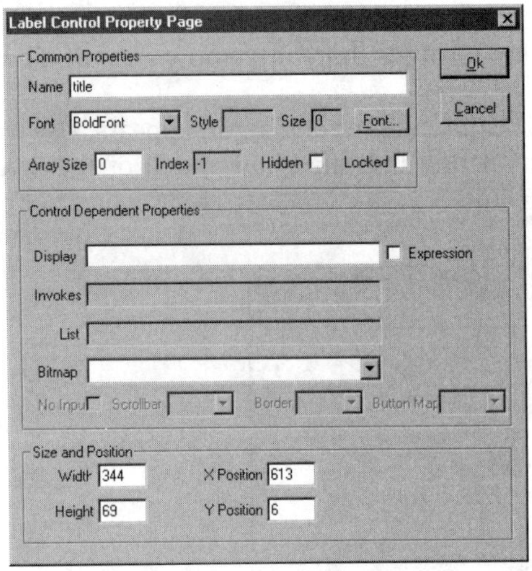


*Parameters for the label*

Change the default name in *title*. You will address the *label* in our program by this name. Then change the *Font* in *BoldFont*. You want to display the *label* in noticeable boldface type.

You could make adjustments to the coordinates in the lower fields, but in the example this is not necessary.

Create the *label* named *basis* in the same manner in the upper left corner. Use the normal *StdFont* as a font, as with all the other objects.

Next, create a *text* field, in which the values for conversion will be entered later. Give this the name *input*.

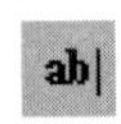


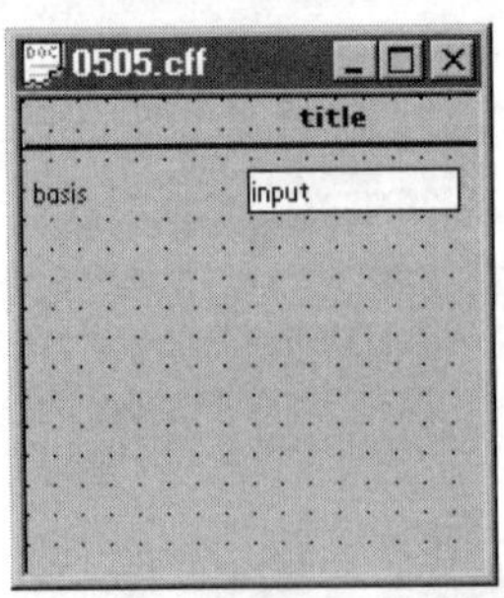


*The text object in the upper right corner*

The new *text* object and the *label* next to it on the left should fit exactly on one line.

Select both of them by dragging a rectangle around both elements. For this purpose, this control must be active. One element is marked by a dashed line, and the other is marked by a wide border of slanted lines.

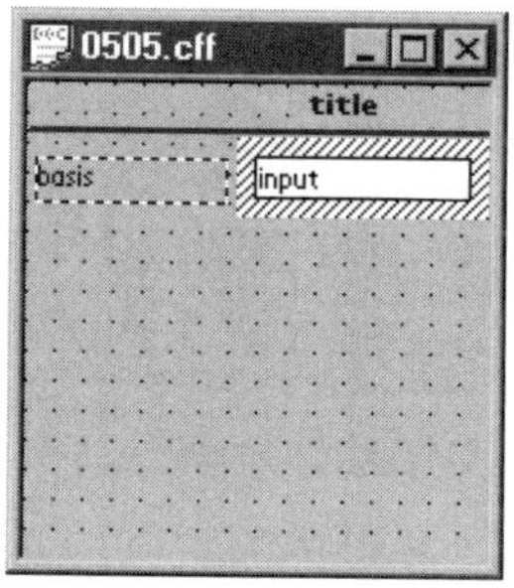


The two selected elements

Now click the icon (shown in the right margin) to align the selected objects at the base line of the object with the wide border of slanted lines.

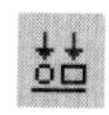

Next, create another *label* named *unit* underneath the *basis label*. Five *labels* in which the other units of measurement display should appear. These five labels combine in an array to be automatically filled by the program. To do this, double-click the new *label* and enter a 5 in the *Array Size* field.

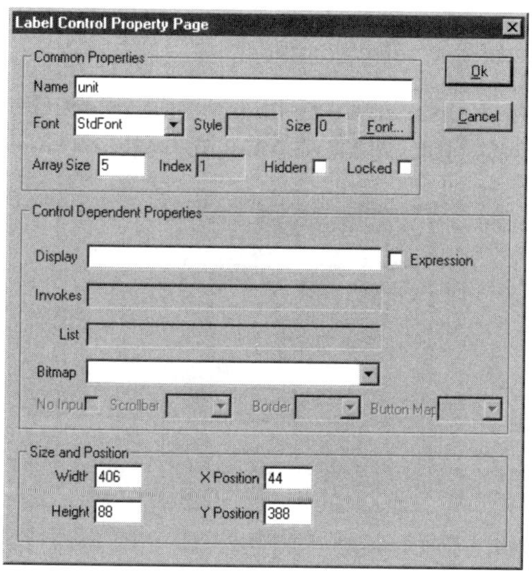


Parameters for the new label array

All five *labels* are arranged on top of one another in the same position. The one with the highest number is all the way at the top.

Move a *label* to the bottom position, then to the second position from the bottom and so on, until the last one is in its original position.

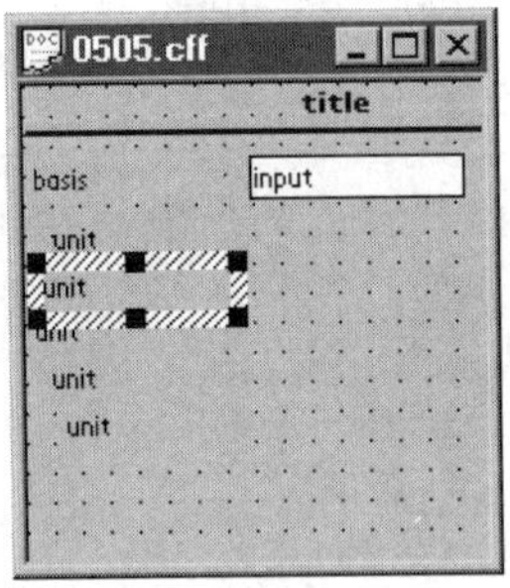


*The five labels of the array*

When you move the labels, they will not land in a neat row nor will the distance between the individual label objects be the same. Neither the placement nor the distance will appear entirely professional in the finished program.

Select all five *labels* with a rectangle.

Click the icon (shown in the right margin) to arrange all of the selected objects vertically.

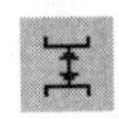

Press the Ctrl key while all the objects are still selected and click the *label basis* while holding down the key. This selects *label basis* and provides it with the slanted striped highlight as the last selected object.

Click the icon (shown in the right margin) to align all the selected objects horizontally at the left border of the object with the highlight.

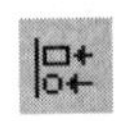

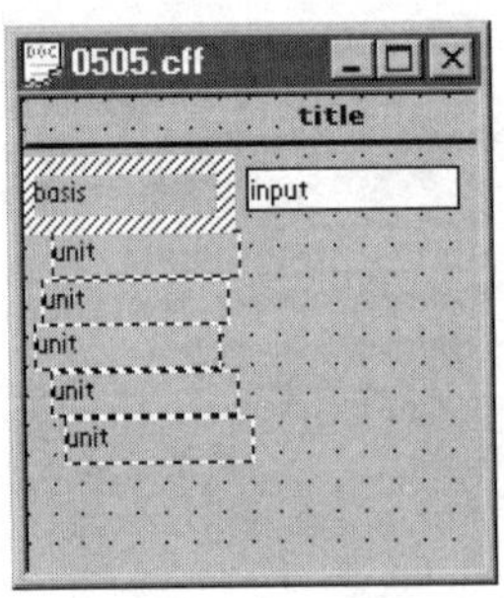


*The new labels before alignment ...*

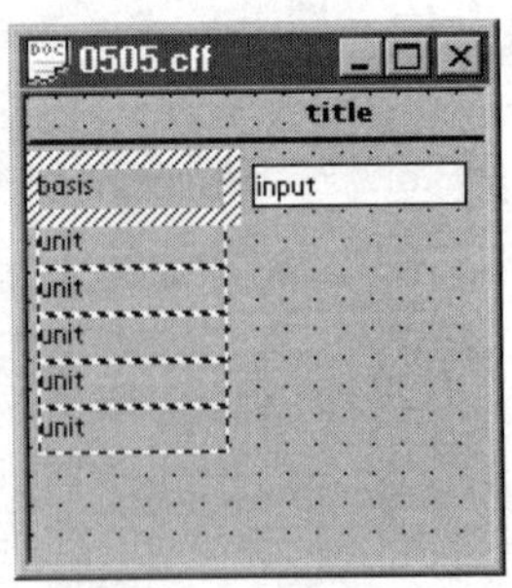


*The aligned labels*

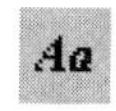


Using the same method, create an additional array under the *input text* object with five *label* objects and name this array *result.*

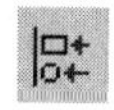

Align all of these under the *text* object. Even though they are all underneath one another, they still aren't at the same heights as the corresponding *labels* in the left column.

In this case it is not sufficient to give all the objects the same distance; instead, they must also lie on the same horizontal lines as the *labels* on the left. To do so, select the uppermost of the five new *labels* and click the *label* to the left while holding down the [Ctrl] key.

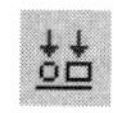

Next, click the icon (shown in the right margin) to align the right *label* on the horizontal base line of the left *label.* Do the same with the other four new *label* objects.

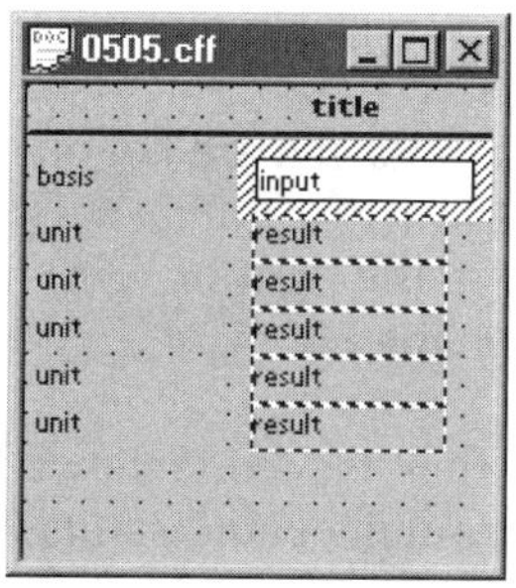


The new labels before alignment

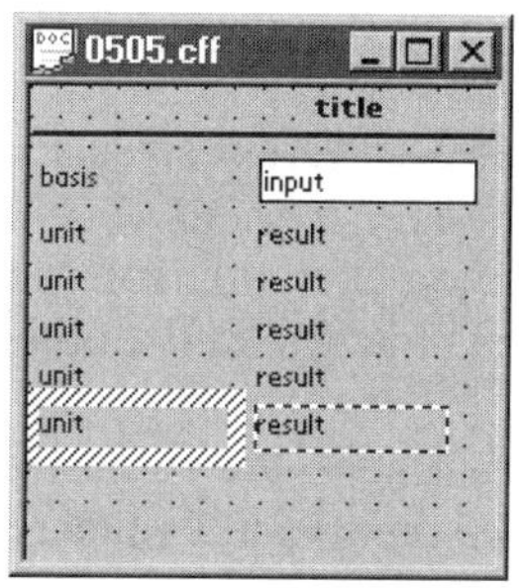


The aligned labels

Finally, you must create the three buttons on the lower border.

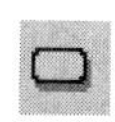

With the icon (shown in the right margin), you can place a rectangular *button* object in the form window. Name the first button *length* and enter the word *Length* in the *Display* field. It appears on the button.

Create two additional button objects named *area* and *volume* in exactly the same manner. Enter the names *Area* and *Volume* in the *Display* field.

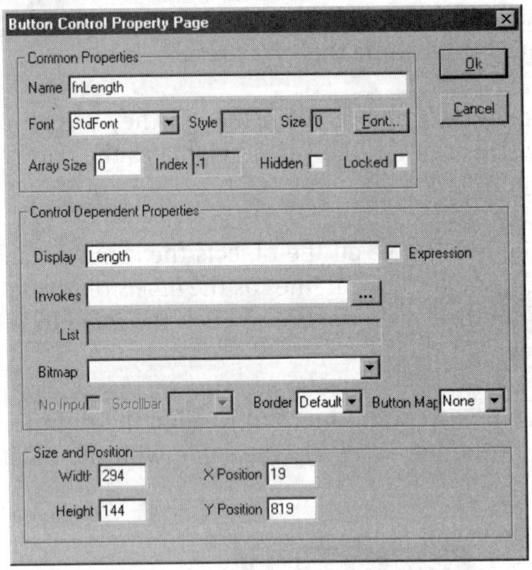


*Parameters for the first button*

The three buttons are of different sizes and distances and are not on one line.

Select all three and then click the icon (shown in the right margin) to give all the selected objects the size of the object with the highlight.

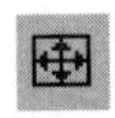

Then, while the three objects are still selected, click the icon (shown in the right margin) to make the selected objects horizontally equidistant.

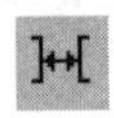

Finally, align the three buttons on a common horizontal line. With this the user interface for the new program is finished.

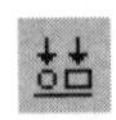

**Tip**

### Snap to grid

Instead of aligning the individual objects to each other horizontally and vertically and setting the distances, you can define a grid and then automatically align the objects to it. To do this, define a grid space using the *Layout/Grid/Grid Spacing* menu item. You specify this in Palm coordinates, not in CASL coordinates. Then enable the *Layout/Grid/Snap to Grid* menu item. This way the objects automatically snap into place on the grid points when they are moved. The size of the objects is also defined by the grid space.

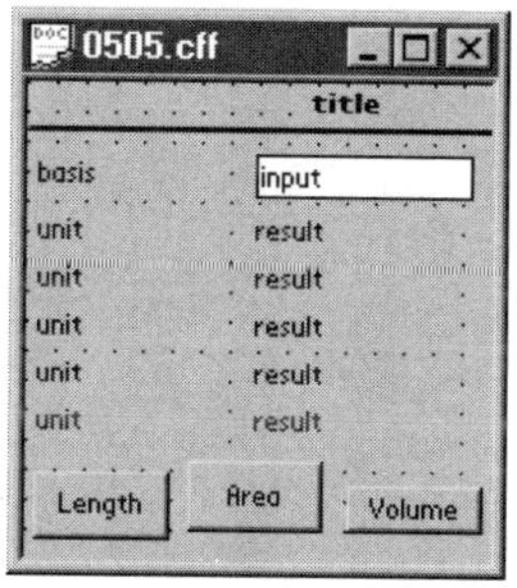

The three button objects before alignment

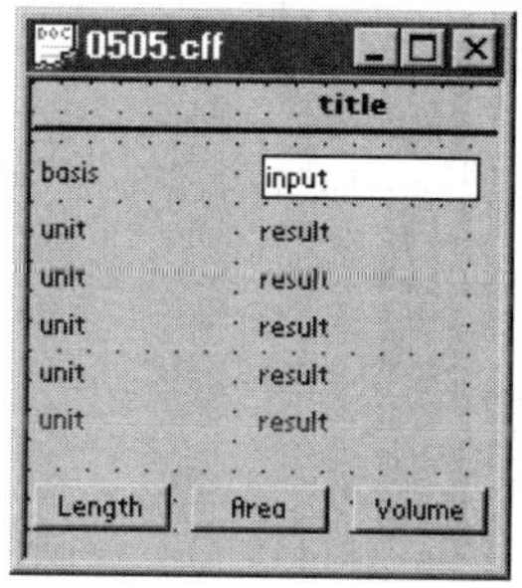

The adjusted and aligned button objects

CD

**Program on the companion CD**

You can also find the finished form file on the companion CD to this book as *0505.cff.*

However, the user interface alone does not make a functioning program. You must write one similar to this:

```
variables;
  numeric e;
  numeric i;
  numeric  f[5];
  string  le[5];
  numeric lf[5];
  string  fe[5];
  numeric ff[5];
  string  ve[5];
  numeric vf[5];
  string format="###.######";
  end;

function input;
  get input, e;
  for i=0, i<5;
    put result[i], string(e*f[i],format);
  next i+1;
  end;

function fnLength;
  for i=0, i<5;
    f[i]=lf[i];
```

```
    put unit[i], le[i];
  next i+1;
  put basis, "Meter";
  put title, "Length";
  input;
  end;

function area;
  for i=0, i<5;
    f[i]=ff[i];
    put unit[i], fe[i];
  next i+1;
  put basis, "Meter²";
  put title, "Area";
  input;
  end;

function volume;
  for i=0, i<5;
    f[i]=vf[i];
    put unit[i], ve[i];
  next i+1;
  put basis, "Meter³";
  put title, "Volume";
  input;
  end;

function startup;
  le[0]="Inch";
  lf[0]=39.3701;
  le[1]="Foot";
  lf[1]=3.2808;
  le[2]="Yard";
  lf[2]=1.0936;
  le[3]="Mile";
  lf[3]=6.2137E-4;
  le[4]="Nautical mile";
  lf[4]=5.3996E-4;
  fe[0]="sq. Inch";
  ff[0]=1550.0031;
  fe[1]="sq. Foot";
  ff[1]=10.7639;
  fe[2]="sq. Yard";
  ff[2]=1.1960;
  fe[3]="rood";
  ff[3]=9.8843E-4;
  fe[4]="acre";
  ff[4]=2.4711E-4;
  ve[0]="cu. Inch";
```

```
vf[0]=61023.7441;
ve[1]="cu. Foot";
vf[1]=35.3147;
ve[2]="cu. Yard";
vf[2]=1.3080;
ve[3]="Brit. gallon";
vf[3]=220;
ve[4]="US gallon";
vf[4]=264.1721;
fnLength;
end;
```

**CD**

**Program on the companion CD**

You can also find this program on the companion CD to this book as *0505.csl*.

This program no longer needs a part in which the objects of the user interface are defined. Thus it starts directly with the variable declaration. The following table explains the use of the variables.

| Variable name | Use |
|---|---|
| e | Numerical value of the input value |
| i | Loop counter |
| f[5] | Factors of the table currently being used |
| le[5] | Length units |
| lf[5] | Length conversion factors |
| fe[5] | Area units |
| ff[5] | Area conversion factors |
| ve[5] | Volume units |
| vf[5] | Volume conversion factors |
| format | Formatting specification for the output of the results |

The *startup* function defines the different units and the respective conversion factors. In the end, the *fnLength* function is called, causing the conversion table for length units to appear at the beginning. If no function was called, a completely blank table appears.

The *input text* object calls the function of the same name when the numerical value is changed or re-entered. This function calculates the results, based on the factors in the current table, and writes them to the *result label* objects in the right column.

```
function input;
  get input, e;
  for i=0, i<5;
    put result[i], string(e*f[i],format);
  next i+1;
  end;
```

Each of the three *button* objects calls a function of the same name.

```
function fnLength;
  for i=0, i<5;
    f[i]=lf[i];
    put unit[i], le[i];
  next i+1;
  put basis, "Meter";
  put title, "Length";
  input;
  end;
```

All of these functions operate according to the same system. The respective conversion factors are stored in the *f[5]* variable array, from where they are used for the calculation. The labels of the units appear in the left column of the table, the base unit appears to the left next to the input field, and the category (*Length*, *Area* or *Volume*) appears in the *label* in the upper right corner.

After the program has adjusted the user interface for the selected category, it performs a new calculation of all results using the now-current factors.

## Graphical user interfaces in HotPaw Basic

In the HotPaw Basic programs of the preceding chapters, you always used the standard *form()* function or the *input* and *print* functions of HotPaw Basic for input and output. However, you can only create typical input forms or very simple messages with these functions.

HotPaw Basic offers significantly more options for designing your own interactive user interface. You can use familiar elements from the Palm OS or from CASL: buttons, text input fields, checkboxes, or pick lists.

These elements are drawn in the graphic area and also use the same coordinates as graphic elements. As always, the zero point of the coordinate system is in the upper left corner. There are 160 coordinate units to the right and to the bottom.

### Defining form elements

Due to the interpreter structure of yBasic (programs are not compiled but read and processed step by step), you must observe the following rules when defining form elements such as buttons, text input fields, checkboxes, or pick lists:

- Form elements must be defined at the beginning of a program after a *draw -1*.
- The buttons must be defined first, then the other form elements.
- A total of 32 form elements may be used in a program, with no more than 15 buttons and 2 pick lists. The total number of selection options in all the lists may be no greater than 63.

## Counter

You know the problem: You are in the middle of counting something when someone suddenly distracts you, so you must start over. Mechanical counting devices that operate at the press of a button save time, especially if operations involve very large numbers such as traffic counts and inventories. If you have one of these devices in each hand, you can even count two values independently of each other.

The next program displays such a counting device on the Palm, three counters that run independently from each other. It should be possible to operate these counters using buttons large enough to control the three counters using three fingers next to each other on the Palm display.

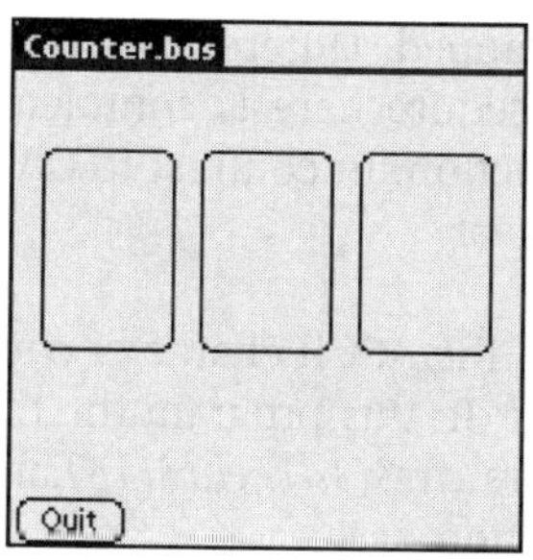


*Here's what the program will look like*

In this first version, the program contains only three buttons and three number fields in which the counters are incremented.

```
#counter.bas
draw -1
form btn 10,40,40,60," ",1
form btn 60,40,40,60,"",1
form btn 110,40,40,60,"",1
dim n%(2)
start:
c=asc(input$(1))-14
if ((c>=0) and (c<=2))
  n%(c)=n%(c)+1
  draw str$(n%(c),5),10+c*50,20,2
endif
goto start
```

CD

**Program on the companion CD**

You can also find this program on the companion CD to this book as *0506.bas*.

At the beginning, after clearing the graphic area with *draw -1*, the three buttons are defined with the *form btn* statement.

### *form btn <x>, <y>, <Width>, <Height>, <Text>, 1*

This statement draws a button. The upper left corner of the button lies at the x, y coordinates. *Width* and *Height* specify the width and height of the button in pixels. *Text* is a string that is displayed on the button. The *1* parameter is unchangeable and must be included in the specification.

Each button returns a character when it is tapped. Differentiate the buttons on the basis of these characters. Thus the procedure here is completely different from in CASL, where every button calls a function. In contrast to CASL, a yBasic program does not run object-oriented, but linear.

The first button defined in a program returns the ASCII character *chr$(14)*. Each additional button returns one number higher. In this program the three buttons from the left to the right return the characters *chr$(14)*, *chr$(15)*,and *chr$(16)*. This input is queried with the *input$(1)* function.

### *input$(1)*

This function is a general query function in yBasic. It waits until a Graffiti character is input, a previously defined button is tapped, or one of the following three keys is pressed: Address Book, ToDo List, or Memo Pad. After that the function returns the appropriate character.

| Character | Trigger |
|---|---|
| 5 | Address Book key |
| 6 | ToDo List key |
| 7 | Memo Pad key |
| 14 ... 28 | Buttons in order of their definition in the program |
| all others | Graffiti characters |

The Calendar key is used in yBasic to cancel every program and therefore cannot be evaluated separately.

In this program, the returned character is evaluated by the *asc()* function with 14 subtracted from it; therefore, the result in the variable *c* is a number between 0 and 2.

```
c=asc(input$(1))-14
```

### *asc( <Characters> )*

Returns the ASCII value of a character as a decimal numerical value. If the *Characters* parameter consists of a string of several characters, only the first one will be evaluated. If the *Characters* parameter is a blank string "", the function returns 0.

In this program, input will only be evaluated if the result lies between 0 and 2, thus with the return value of the *input$(1)* function between *chr$(14)* and *chr$(16)*. Only in these cases has one of the three buttons been tapped.

```
if ((c>=0) and (c<=2))
n%(c)=n%(c)+1
draw str$(n%(c),5),10+c*50,20,2
endif
```

The three counter values are stored in the *n%(2)* variable field. Depending on which button has been tapped, the appropriate counter is incremented by 1.

The *draw* function now writes the new number through the respective button. In contrast to CASL, it is not necessary to define any form elements in yBasic for outputting text. Write the texts directly at any coordinate position.

### *draw <Text>, <x>, <y> [, <Font>]*

The first parameter must be a string. For this reason, in the example the numerical value is converted into a string with the *str$()* function. After that the x, y-coordinates where the text is to be written are specified. The optional *Font* variable specifies the font.

| Font No. | Font |
|---|---|
| 0 | Normal |
| 1 | Bold |
| 2 | Large |

The sample program demonstrates the large font, which is particularly noticeable.

After the number has been written, the program returns to the *start* branch mark and waits for a button to be tapped again. Thus it runs in a continuous loop until the user presses the *Quit* button, which is specified by yBasic to stop the program.

## Input fields

As in CASL, in yBasic you can define input fields on the screen, where the user can enter characters using Graffiti. yBasic stores this input in the *s$()* variables, which are also used by the standard forms.

Next, enhance the last program so that the counters can be set to an adjustable value at any time. For example, if you continue counting at a specific spot where there was already an intermediate result/subtotal, you no longer need to add the numbers manually.

*Counter with number input fields*

Each of the three counters receives its own input field, where you can enter a value. The counter is set to this value when you tap the *Set* button.

```
#counter2.bas
draw -1
form btn 10,40,40,60," ",1
form btn 60,40,40,60,"",1
form btn 110,40,40,60,"",1
form btn 10,125,40,15,"Set ",1
form btn 60,125,40,15," Set",1
form btn 110,125,40,15," Set",1
form fld 10,110,40,12,"0",1
form fld 60,110,40,12,"0",1
form fld 110,110,40,12,"0",1
dim n%(2)
start:
c=asc(input$(1))-14
if ((c>=0) and (c<=2))
  n%(c)=n%(c)+1
  draw str$(n%(c),5),10+c*50,20,2
endif
if ((c>=3) and (c<=5))
  c=c-3
  n%(c)=val(s$(c))
  draw str$(n%(c),5),10+c*50,20,2
endif
goto start
```

**CD**

**Program on the companion CD**

You can also find this program on the companion CD to this book as *0507.bas.*

In addition to the three existing buttons, three new buttons are defined. Remember that button definitions must come before all other definitions and program lines.

Input fields are defined similarly to buttons; just use *form fld* here instead of *form btn.*

### *form fld <x>, <y>, <Width>, 12, <Text>, 1*

The coordinates of the upper left corner position a text input field. The width is variable and is specified in pixels, not in letters. The height is preset at 12 pixels but must still be specified in the *form fld* statement.

In the *Text* parameter, you can specify a text to be displayed by default in this field. If the field is blank, specify a blank string "" here.

The last parameter *1* is unchangeable and must be included in the specification of the function call.

The values that a user enters in such text fields are automatically stored in the *s$()* variables and can be retrieved at any time. The first input field defined in the program stores its contents in the *s$(0)* variable, the second stores its contents in *s$(1)*, and so on.

Two queries are now executed in the program one after the other. If the return value of the pressed button is 14, 15, or 16, the corresponding counter in the last version is incremented.

```
c=asc(input$(1))-14
if ((c>=0) and (c<=2))
n%(c)=n%(c)+1
draw str$(n%(c),5),10+c*50,20,2
endif
```

If the return value is 17, 18, or 19, in other words if one of the three new buttons has been pressed, the corresponding *s$()* variable is retrieved and the counter is set to this value.

```
if ((c>=3) and (c<=5))
c=c-3
n%(c)=val(s$(c))
draw str$(n%(c),5),10+c*50,20,2
endif
```

The new value is written to the corresponding number field in any case, regardless of whether a count button or a *Set* button has been pressed.

## Checkboxes

yBasic also uses checkboxes typical of the Palm OS, allowing users to enable or disable an option on the user interface. In contrast to Windows programs, you must directly touch a Palm OS checkbox to switch it. It's not enough to click the text next to it.

In the next version of the program, use such a checkbox to select whether the buttons of the Palm should be used for counting. In unfavorable environmental conditions, it can be easier to press the buttons (for example, in the cold with gloves on). The clicking noise serves as a confirmation.

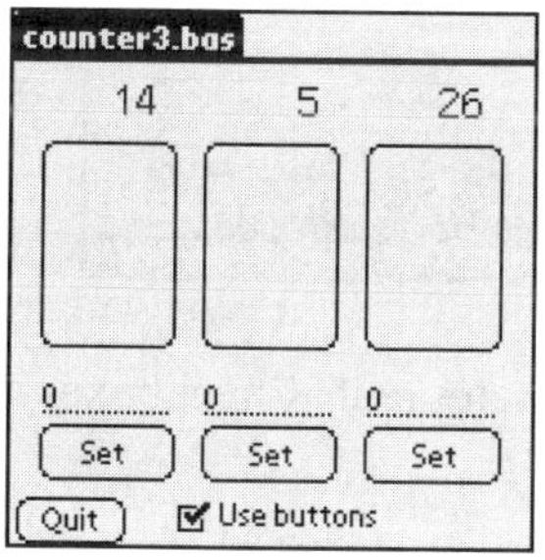


*The new version with a checkbox for using the buttons*

The program uses the three buttons for the Address Book, ToDo List, and Memo Pad in accordance with their arrangement for the left, middle, and right counters.

```
#counter3.bas
draw -1
form btn 10,40,40,60," ",1
form btn 60,40,40,60,"",1
form btn 110,40,40,60,"",1
form btn 10,125,40,15,"Set ",1
form btn 60,125,40,15," Set",1
form btn 110,125,40,15," Set",1
form fld 10,110,40,12,"0",1
form fld 60,110,40,12,"0",1
form fld 110,110,40,12,"0",1
form cbx 50,145,14,14,"",1
draw "Use buttons", 65,145
dim n%(2)
start:
c=asc(input$(1))
if ((c>=14) and (c<=16))
  c=c-14
  n%(c)=n%(c)+1
  draw str$(n%(c),5),10+c*50,20,2
endif
if ((c>=17) and (c<=19))
  c=c-17
  n%(c)=val(s$(c))
  draw str$(n%(c),5),10+c*50,20,2
endit
if((c>=5) and (c<=7) and (val(s$(3))>0))
```

```
    c=c-5
    n%(c)=n%(c)+1
    draw str$(n%(c),5),10+c*50,20,2
  endif
  goto start
```

**CD**

**Program on the companion CD**

You can also find this program on the companion CD to this book as *0508.bas.*

The checkbox is defined by the *form cbx* statement. Checkboxes must be defined in the program after the buttons.

### *form cbx <x>, <y>, 14, 14, "", 1*

With checkboxes, you must specify the x, y-coordinates only. All other parameters are predefined. You must specify them, but they cannot be changed.

Such a field is always 14 x 14 pixels in size. Specify a descriptive text next to it using the *draw* statement.

```
form cbx 50,145,14,14,"",1
draw "Use buttons", 65,145
```

The program now contains a third query. Aside from the two previous events (a number button is pressed or a new initial value is set), there is a new event: a button is pressed. This event may only be evaluated when you activate the new checkbox.

```
if((c>=5) and (c<=7) and (val(s$(3))>0))
c=c-5
n%(c)=n%(c)+1
draw str$(n%(c),5),10+c*50,20,2
endif
```

A checkbox writes in enabled state the *"1"* string in the next free *s$()* variable. If the field is disabled, it writes the *"0"* string in the same variable.

In the example, the *s$(0)* through *s$(2)* variables occupy the three input fields. The checkbox, which is defined by this, is assigned the *s$(3)* variable. The condition:

```
val(s$(3))>0)
```

queries whether this field is enabled. If it is and simultaneously a value between *chr$(5)* and *chr$(7)* is returned, meaning that one of the buttons has been pressed, the corresponding counter is also incremented.

**Note**

**Evaluating checkboxes**

Checkboxes in yBasic always write their current state in the *s$()* variable, when a button is tapped. In contrast, in CASL the value is changed even by the enabling or disabling of the checkbox. In the sample program that means: After you have toggled the checkbox on or off, you must first press one of the buttons before you can use the Palm buttons for further counting.

# Customized pocket calculator

You have used the *form(9...)* form several times for data input and output with calculations. In addition to this form, yBasic also offers two other standard forms with which you can create simple calculation programs without having to define every button and every number field yourself.

## Improved loan calculator

Use one of these forms to improve the loan calculator from page 49 of Chapter 3 so that users can enter numbers the way they would on any pocket calculator, without using Graffiti characters.

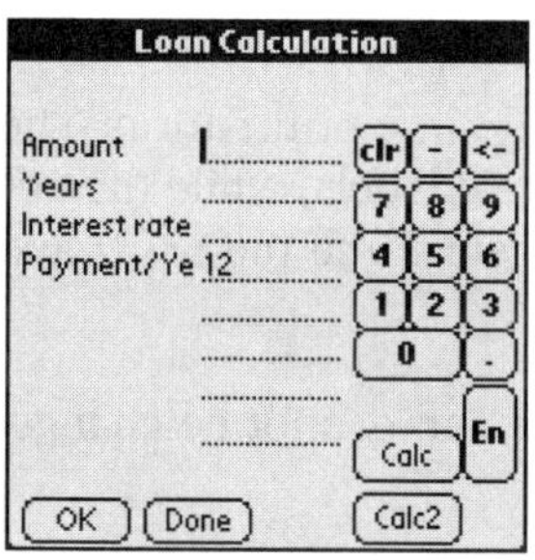


*Loan calculator with numeric keyboard*

```
#Loan2.bas
for i=0 to 11:s$(i)="":next i
s$(2)="Amount"
s$(4)="Years"
s$(6)="Interest rate"
```

```
s$(8)="Paymt./Year"
s$(9)=12
start:
j=form(12,0,"Loan calculation")
if (j=0) then end
r=(val(s$(7))/100)/val(s$(9))
p=val(s$(3))
n=val(s$(9))*val(s$(5))
a=fn pmt(p,r,n)
s$(10)="Payment"
s$(11)=str$(a,8,2)
goto start
```

**CD**

**Program on the companion CD**

You can also find this program on the companion CD to this book as *0510.bas.*

The calculation of the loan payment rates runs exactly as in the original program. Compared to the previous version, the program has only been decisively changed in two points:

- Variables beginning with *s$(2)* and higher are used for the form fields.
- The form is now no longer displayed with *form(9, ...)*, but rather with *form(12, ...)*.

This last change causes the display of the numeric keyboard:

### *form(12,0, <Title>)*

The *Title* variable specifies the text in the title line of the form. The even-numbered variables *s$(2) ... s$(16)* contain the field labels, while the odd-numbered variables *s$(3) ... s$(17)* contain the input fields. Use the *s$(0)* and *s$(1)* variables for static texts.

The buttons on the digit field are predefined and cannot be changed. They can be used for entering the numbers in all fields.

| Button | Function |
|---|---|
| 0 ... 9 | Digits. |
| . | Decimal point. |
| clr | Clears the current input field. |

| Button | Function |
|---|---|
| - | Negative sign for entering negative numbers. |
| <- | Deletes the last input character (Backspace). |
| En | Puts the cursor in the next input field. |

The *form(12, ...)* function, like the *form(9, ...)* function, has a return value that depends on which of the four buttons in the lower area has been tapped:

| Button | Return value |
|---|---|
| OK | 1 |
| Done | 0 |
| Calc | 2 |
| Calc2 | 3 |

In our program only the *Done* button is queried. This causes the program to terminate. All other buttons calculate the result and have the program return to the *start* branch mark for a further calculation.

## Adding machine

Old mechanical adding machines recorded each calculation step on a paper strip. The result of a calculation always appeared in the line following the calculation so that the result could be used for the next calculation.

The next program simulates this type of adding machine on the Palm; the difference is that you can also enter formulas with more than one operand in a line. Clicking *OK* determines the result of the line and writes it to the next line, where it can immediately continue being used.

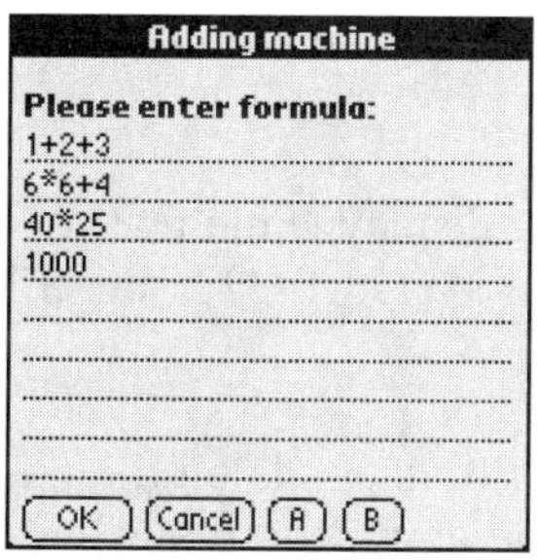


Inputting formulas

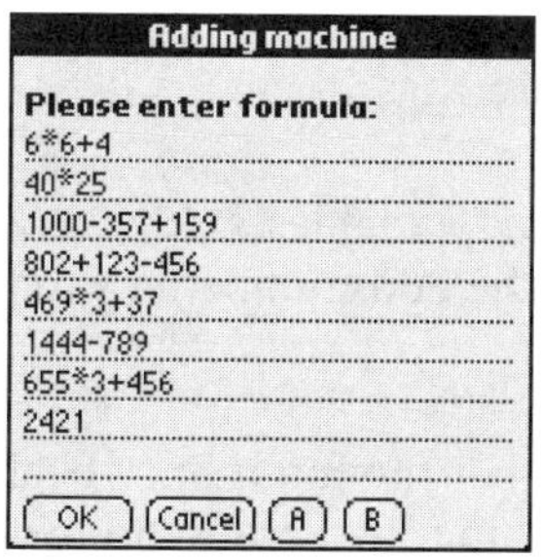


Automatic scrolling to the bottom line

At the end of the screen, the program has to perform automatic scrolling. Each line must be moved up by one line to perform a new calculation at the bottom.

```
#Calculator.bas
s$(0)="Please enter formula:"
i=3
start:
j=form(10,10,"Calculator")
if (j=0) then end
s$(i+2)=str$(eval(s$(i)))
i=i+2
if (i>17) then gosub scroll
goto start
scroll:
for i=3 to 19 step 2
  s$(i-2)=s$(i)
next i
s$(19)=""
i=17
return
```

**CD**

**Program on the companion CD**

You can also find this program on the companion CD to this book as *0511.bas.*

The form for inputting is another form predefined in yBasic, which is displayed as the *form(10, ...)* function. This form is especially well suited for inputting longer texts or for when a description for each input line is unnecessary.

### *form(10, <Lines>, <Title>)*

The *Lines* variable specifies the number of lines for input. *Title* is the text that appears in the title line.

The even-numbered variables *s$(0), s$(2) ...* display static texts at the top border of the form. The odd-numbered variables *s$(1), s$(3) ...* describe the input fields.

Which index number the input lines begin with depends on the number of text lines at the beginning. If there is no text line at all, the input lines begin with *s$(1)*. In the example with a text line, the first input line is *s$(3)* and so on.

As is usual in yBasic forms, all input fields always contain strings, not numerical values.

In the program the *i* variable specifies the index number of the current input field. At the beginning this is set to 3, because the first input line corresponds to the variable *s$(3)*.

The formula that the user enters in the current line s$(i) is evaluated with the *eval()* function, and the result is written to the next line *s$(i+2)*. The input fields all have odd index numbers.

```
s$(i+2)=str$(eval(s$(i)))
```

### *eval( <Text> )*

This function mathematically evaluates a formula that is in a string and returns the result.

After the calculated result is entered in the new line, the *i* counter is incremented by 2, and the form waits for the next formula. The valid variables for the input fields go to *s$(19)* only.

```
if (i>17) then gosub scroll
```

The entire screen contents must be moved up one line so that the program can continue calculating. For this purpose, the *scroll* subroutine is called.

```
scroll:
for i=3 to 19 step 2
s$(i-2)=s$(i)
next i
s$(19)=""
i=17
return
```

From top to bottom, each input line is read out in order, and the contents are entered in a line further up again. The *s$(19)* field, which contained the last result, is emptied and the line counter is set to line 17 again, which now contains the last result. Then the program can continue running normally.

Hereafter the program shifts by one line only; therefore, this subroutine is called with each new line after the line counter has reached the bottom border of the screen.

# 6. Time functions for all purposes

Like any other computer, every Palm has an integrated clock. However, with the exception of the Palm m100, the Palm OS standard functions limit your use of the clock. Even though the current time displays in the upper left corner on the Program startup interface and even though appointments are accurate within five minutes, without add-on software you wouldn't notice that the clock performs at split-second precision.

In this chapter you learn how to make practical use of the integrated clock, with the help of small programs.

## 6.1 Stopwatch: The Palm as a measuring instrument

The occasion doesn't have to be a track meet. Plenty of other opportunities occur to use a stopwatch for measuring short periods of time. Although many contemporary wristwatches offer stopwatch function, their small size makes them awkward to use.

The next program shows a stopwatch with big buttons, allowing you to operate the stopwatch using your fingers instead of the stylus.

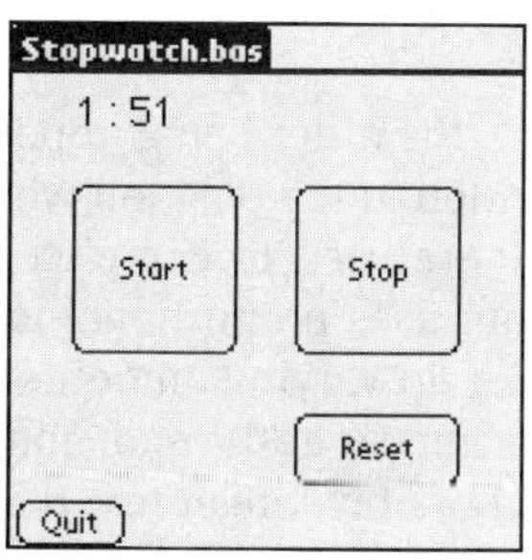


*A stopwatch on the Palm*

The user interface of this clock is self-explanatory. It consists of only three buttons: *Start* starts the clock, *Stop* stops it, and *Reset* sets it back to 0. If you tap *Start* following a *Stop* without resetting the time, the clock continues running at the place where it was stopped.

```
#Stopwatch.bas
draw -1
form btn 20,50,50,50,"Start",1
form btn 90,50,50,50,"Stop",1
form btn 90,120,50,20,"Reset",1
reset:
draw "0 : 00  ",20,20,2
while (asc(input$(1))<>14)
wend
a%=timer
start:
m$=str$(int((timer-a%)/60))
s$=str$(int((timer-a%)mod 60))
if (len(s$)=1) then s$="0"+s$
draw m$+" : "+s$+"  ",20,20,2
if (asc(inkey$)=15) then goto stop
goto start
stop:
b=asc(input$(1))-13
on b goto 110, 120, 130
110 a%=timer-60*val(m$)-val(s$)
goto start
120 goto stop
130 goto reset
end
```

CD

**Program on the companion CD**

You can also find this program on the companion CD to this book as *0601.bas.*

At the beginning the three buttons are defined, the order being important for the later queries. After that the text *"0: 00  "* is written to the position where the time is to appear later. The spaces after the last 0 are used to completely overwrite any existing and longer text. Because the Palm uses proportional font, depending on the contained digits, the times can take up varying amounts of space on the screen. To make certain that no half digits appear at the end, add a couple of spaces to the end of a new text to overwrite a possibly longer text that was in the same place earlier. The same line can be called after a reset, when there could be longer numbers here.

```
draw "0 : 00  ",20,20,2
```

Next comes a *while...wend* loop, which waits until the user taps the *Start* button. As the first button in the program, this button has the return value of *chr$(14)*. The return values of buttons in HotPaw Basic depend on the order of their definition in the program. The first button always returns the value *chr$(14)*, the second one returns *chr$(15)* and so on.

```
while (asc(input$(1))<>14)
wend
```

When this button has been tapped, the *a%* variable is set to the *timer* value, which is the current timing mark at the start of the clock.

```
a%=timer
```

### *timer*

This function returns an integral numerical value that is based on the system clock of the Palm. This number is incremented by 1 for every second, making it possible to measure times with the precision of a second.

Now the clock is running visibly on the screen. The time is constantly being retrieved, written to the screen and then retrieved again. The hours and minutes are calculated from the *timer* value and stored in two string variables.

```
m$=str$(int((timer-a%)/60))
```

If you subtract the initial value of *a%* from the current *timer* value, the result is the number of seconds that have passed since the start with the *Start* button. If you divide the result by 60 and take only the integral part, the result is the minutes.

```
s$=str$(int((timer-a%)mod 60))
```

The seconds are calculated in similar fashion, only don't use the integral part of the quotient, but the indivisible remainder instead. Both results must be converted to strings for display.

```
if (len(s$)=1) then s$="0"+s$
```

The first ten seconds of every minute are single-digit numbers. However, on every digital clock the seconds are always displayed using two digits. This line adds an additional 0 in front of the single-digit number specifications so that the seconds are always two-digit. The *len* function is used for this purpose.

### *len( <Text> )*

This function determines the number of characters in a string.

```
draw m$+" : "+s$+"  ",20,20,2
```

In this line the minutes and seconds are written to the display. For this purpose, a string that includes the two variables, a colon, and two spaces at the end is formed. These spaces ensure that any text that is longer is completely overwritten. If the *Stop* button was tapped sometime while the last four program lines were running, the program now branches to a special program section that evaluates this button. Otherwise, it continues at the *start:* branch mark. Thus the time is retrieved again and written to the screen.

```
if (asc(inkey$)=15) then goto stop
goto start
```

The *inkey$* function checks whether the *Stop* button has been pressed.

### *inkey$*

This function returns the character of the last pressed button. Unlike *input$*, this function does not wait for a button to be pressed but returns the character of the last pressed button that has not yet been evaluated.

In the sample program the *Stop* button has, as the second button defined in the program, the return value of *chr$(15)*. If the ASCII value of this button is *15*, the program branches to the *stop:* branch mark.

The *goto* loop, which continuously updates the time in the display, no longer runs here. The display stops so that you can read it.

```
b=asc(input$(1))-13
```

The program waits for the user to tap a button. When the stopwatch stops, it is reset to 00:00 with *Reset* at 00:00, or it is restarted with *Start*. The user may also tap *Stop*, although doing so serves no purpose. The program does not offer any other options. The number 13 is deducted from the return value of the button with a number between 1 and 3 left over. The three buttons in the program return the values *chr$(14)*, *chr$(15)* and *chr$(16)*.

```
on b goto 110, 120, 130
```

You can use the *on...goto* statement to go to a specified line number in the program depending on a numerical value. The numerical value for the query must be integral and at least 1.

**Note**

**Specification of line numbers**

In a HotPaw Basic program, you can use line numbers for individual lines; the entire program does not need line numbers. The specified line numbers must always be at least as great as the actual number of the line in the program but can also be greater. All line numbers must be specified in ascending order, but with spaces in between that are as large as you want.

Three line numbers appear here: 110, 120, 130.

```
110 a%=timer-60*val(m$)-val(s$)
goto start
120 goto stop
130 goto reset
```

For the three possible buttons, the three ways the program can continue running are:

- **Start** – The clock should continue running from the displayed time. Thus two stop times are added. In this case the current *timer* value is retrieved and the stop time is subtracted from the display. This results in a new zero point, from which the clock can continue running and displays the time.
- **Stop** – Even though pressing on the *Stop* button a second time doesn't make sense, it still has to be evaluated somehow. The program returns to the place where it waits for the tap. The displayed time is not changed.
- **Reset** – The program returns to the beginning and displays the time *"0: 00"*. Now the program waits for a tap on the *Start* button and for the clock to begin running again with a new zero value.

## Precision of clocks

The precision of a clock depends decisively on which source the corresponding clock program gets its time signals from. After the *Start* button was pressed, the last sample program displayed a new time each instance the internal system clock counted one second further. When someone pressed the *Stop* button, the time specifications were no longer changed.

So this program has the precision of a second, measured on the Palm system clock. The stopwatch does not record the range between the actual tapping of the Start button and the moment where the system clock outputs the next second. This time period can last between 1 and 99 hundredths of a second without making a difference in the display.

This precision is constant on all Palm devices and on the emulator, because the very precisely running system clock is read out every second.

Another possibility is to output a time cycle by calculating multiples of the processor clock/cycle. This time cycle is not only regular but also specifies small fractions of a second. However, it requires an identical processor clock/cycle on all the used devices, which is no longer the case on current devices.

**Note**

**Clock frequencies of current Palms**

All devices of the Palm-III series, the classic Palm III, Palm IIIx, Palm IIIe, Palm IIIxe, and also the Palm V run at 16 MHz. The Palm Vx and the Palm IIIc as well as the Handspring Visor and the Visor deluxe run at 20 MHz clock frequency. The new devices Visor Platinum, Visor Edge, and Visor Prism use the latest Motorola Dragonball processor with 33 MHz.

If you want to program a stopwatch that can display tenths and hundredths of seconds, the *timer* function won't help because the system clock only outputs a new value once per second.

### *fn 17*

HotPaw Basic uses an internal counter that is incremented one hundred times per second. Thus you can use it to measure hundredths of a second. This counter runs on the basis of the processor cycle/clock but detects the processor type and therefore runs on every Palm and Visor exactly in the hundredth second cycle. The *fn 17* function returns an integer that is incremented by 1 every hundredth second. The initial value is set with the start of the yBasic interpreter so that it cannot be evaluated as an absolute value. Only the differences between several calls of the *fn 17* function are important.

**Tip**

**fn 17 on the emulator**

If HotPaw Basic is running on the Palm OS Emulator, it cannot detect a Dragonball processor type from which a clock frequency could be determined. For this reason incorrect information in the *fn 17* function occurs. This counter runs on the Emulator about three times as fast as on a Palm.

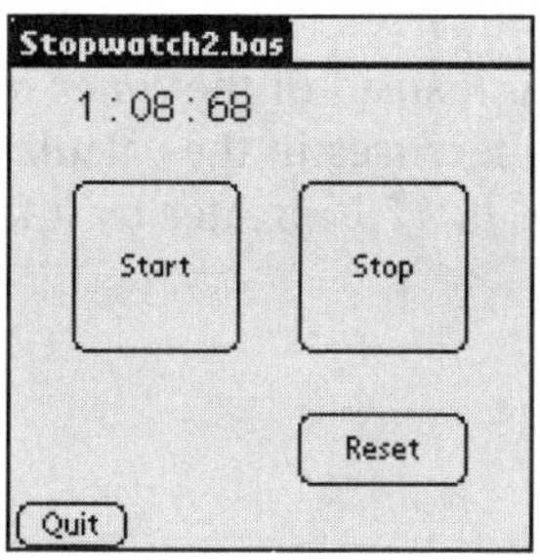


*Stopwatch with hundredths of a second*

Using this function, change the stopwatch to display hundredths of a second.

```
#Stopwatch2.bas
draw -1
form btn 20,50,50,50,"Start",1
form btn 90,50,50,50,"Stop",1
form btn 90,120,50,20,"Reset",1
reset:
draw "0 : 00 : 00  ",20,20,2
while (asc(input$(1))<>14)
wend
a%=fn 17
start:
m$=str$(int(((fn 17)-a%)/6000))
s$=str$(int((((fn 17)-a%)mod 6000)/100))
if (len(s$)=1) then s$="0"+s$
h$=str$(int(((fn 17)-a%)mod 100))
if (len(h$)=1) then h$="0"+h$
draw m$+" : "+s$+" : "+h$+"  ",20,20,2
```

```
if (asc(inkey$)=15) then goto stop
goto start
stop:
b=asc(input$(1))-13
on b goto 110, 120, 130
110 a%=(fn 17) -6000*val(m$)-100*val(s$)-val(h$)
goto start
120 goto stop
130 goto reset
end
```

**CD**

**Program on the companion CD**

You can also find this program on the companion CD to this book as *0602.bas.*

The program has only been slightly changed. Instead of the *timer* function, the *fn 17* function is now read out. Additional differences in the calculation of minutes and seconds occur because the result of *fn 17* is greater by a factor of 100 than the result of *timer.*

```
m$=str$(int(((fn 17)-a%)/6000))
s$=str$(int((((fn 17)-a%)mod 6000)/100))
```

An additional *h$* variable is introduced, which stores the hundredths of a second.

```
h$=str$(int(((fn 17)-a%)mod 100))
if (len(h$)=1) then h$="0"+h$
```

This value is always brought to two places for the output. If the time is restarted after a stop, the hundredths must be considered for the new initial value.

```
110 a%=(fn 17) -6000*val(m$)-100*val(s$)-val(h$)
```

The new program is identical in operation to its predecessor. The buttons and output of the result run in the same manner.

This stopwatch is precise on all Palms and Visors; however, you cannot run it on the Emulator.

## Stopwatch in CASL

CASL offers various functions for measuring time. You use some of them in the following section on programming stopwatches.

CASL has an integrated *timer*. Here you specify a number of thousandths of a second, after which an event is triggered. This then starts a specified function.

The first sample program uses the *timer* to control a stopwatch that runs precisely to hundredths of a second.

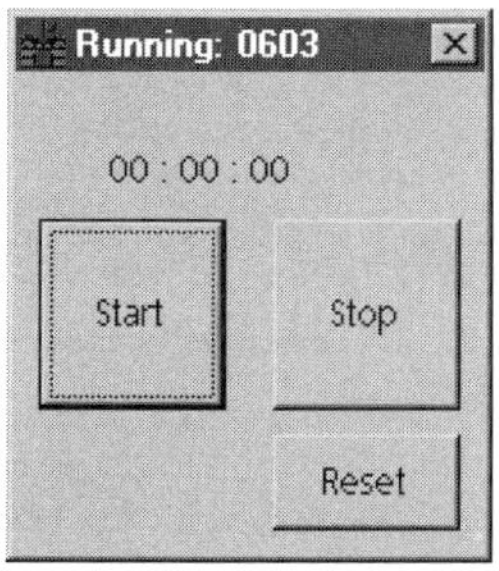


*Stopwatch in Windows ...*

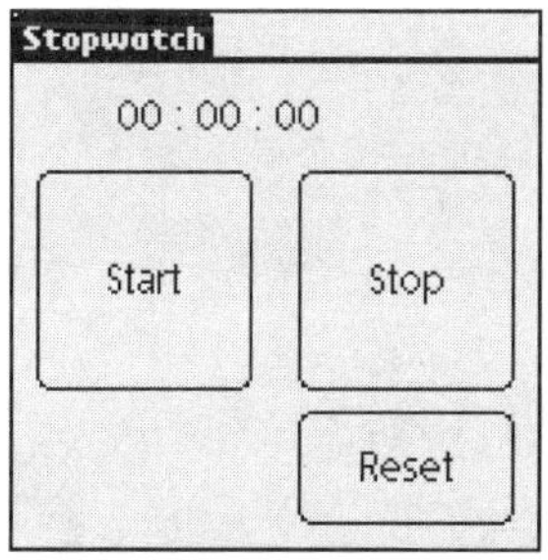


*... and on the Palm*

The user interface of the stopwatch and the functions of the three buttons correspond to the HotPaw Basic program from the last example. However, the program functions completely differently. It does not access the system time; it runs with the CASL *time* instead.

```
label time;
  font "largefont";
  position 200,150;
  end;

button start;
  font "largefont";
  position 50,300;
  pixel_size 400,400;
  display "Start";
  end;

button stop;
  font "largefont";
  position 550,300;
  pixel_size 400,400;
  display "Stop";
  end;
```

```
button reset;
  font "largefont";
  position 550,750;
  pixel_size 400,200;
  display "Reset";
  end;

variables;
  numeric m;
  numeric s;
  numeric h;
  numeric st;
  end;

function time;
  if st=0;
    h=h+1;
    if h>=100;
      h=0;
      s=s+1;
      if s>=60;
        s=0;
        m=m+1;
      end_if;
    end_if;
    put time, string(m,"0#")+" : "+string(s,"0#")+" :"+string(h,"0#");
    timer time, 10;
  end_if;
  end;

function start;
  st=0;
  timer time, 10;
  end;

function stop;
  st=1;
  end;

function reset;
  h=0;
  s=0;
  m=0;
  put time, string(m,"0#")+" : "+string(s,"0#")+" : "+string(h,"0#");
  end;

function startup;
  reset;
  end;
```

**CD**

**Program on the companion CD**

You can also find this program on the companion CD to this book as *0603.csl.*

At the start of the program, one *label* for the output of the time and the three *buttons* are defined, each of which call a function of the same name. For all displays, use the large font from the Palm OS.

```
font "largefont";
```

Such a *font* specification must always be the first parameter in the definition of a CASL object.

The *Start* button sets the *st* variable to 0, which the program later evaluates as "Clock running", and then calls a *timer*.

```
function start;
  st=0;
  timer time, 10;
  end;
```

### *timer <Function>, <Time>;*

*timer* starts a CASL-internal counter, which, when the specified time has elapsed, executes the function that is specified in the *Function* parameter. The *Time* parameter is specified in milliseconds. CASL programs do not run linear, but as object-oriented so that the program does not have to wait for the *timer*. Instead, the *timer* runs independently and triggers the event after the specified time.

The most important part of the program is the *time* function, which is started when the *Stop* button is tapped and regularly updates the time display. This function is always called after the expiration of ten milliseconds, because it is supposed to update the displayed time one hundred times a second.

```
function time;
  if st=0;
    h=h+1;
    if h>=100;
      h=0;
      s=s+1;
```

```
      if s>=60;
        s=0;
        m=m+1;
      end_if;
    end_if;
    put time, string(m,"0#")+" : "+string(s,"0#")+" : "+string(h,"0#");
    timer time, 10;
  end_if;
  end;
```

This function first queries whether the variable is *st = 0*, which means that the *Start* button has been pressed and the clock is running.

If this is the case, the *h* variable, which contains the hundredths of a second, is incremented by 1. In precisely the same manner, the *m* variable is incremented after 60 seconds. This variable counts the minutes and sets the seconds back to 0 for this purpose.

Now the program forms a string of the minutes, seconds, and hundredths and displays it in the *time label*. Use the *"0#"* formatting specification for the display of the three numerical values. The 0 stands for a digit that is always displayed. If the number is only single-digit, it appears as a leading zero.

After this calculation completes, the *timer* restarts to exactly ten milliseconds after the *time* function restarts.

```
function stop;
  st=1;
  end;
```

The *Stop* button sets the *st* variable to 1. This means that the next time the *timer* calls the *time* function, additional time does not display; therefore, the *timer* won't start again and the clock stops. When the user taps *Start* again, the clock can continue running without reinitialization because it is independent from the current system time.

```
function reset;
  h=0;
  s=0;
  m=0;
  put time, string(m,"0#")+" : "+string(s,"0#")+" : "+string(h,"0#");
  end;
```

The *Reset* button sets the three variables that store the time specifications to 0 and writes this 0 to the *time label* on the screen. This resets the clock.

```
function startup;
  reset;
  end;
```

At the start of the program, the time is set to 0, which corresponds exactly to tapping the *Reset* button. In the program, the *startup* function simply calls the *reset* function.

## Clock runs too slowly

Test this stopwatch and compare the displayed times with a different clock that runs accurately. Notice that the CASL stopwatch is running too slowly. How can that happen when you can prove the CASL-*timer* is running very precisely?

After exactly ten milliseconds, a function is called that calculates the new string for displaying the time. The time is not really determined from a clock. The last displayed time is simply incremented by ten milliseconds. This step is repeated after another ten milliseconds, and so on.

The entire process would be absolutely correct if the Palm, like any other computer, didn't require some time for computing. Thus, some time passed during the calculation and the display runs before the *timer* restarts. Consequently, between two displays, not only did the time period of ten milliseconds pass from the *timer* but also the calculation time period. However, the displayed time is only incremented by ten milliseconds, although more time passed. For this reason the display runs more slowly than a real clock.

One way to solve the problem would be to update the time less often. That way the calculation time wouldn't count as much in comparison to the time period that the *timer* specifies. Every computer-controlled clock has this problem. For this reason, later this chapter demonstrates yet another solution for programming an accurate stopwatch by synchronizing the time with the very precise system clock of the Palm.

To do this, change the *time* and *start* functions slightly.

```
function time;
  if st=0;
    h=h+10;
```

```
    if h>=100;
      h=0;
      s=s+1;
      if s>=60;
        s=0;
        m=m+1;
      end_if;
    end_if;
    put_time, string(m,"0#")+" : "+string(s,"0#")+" : "+string(h,"0#");
    timer time, 100;
  end_if;
  end;

function start;
  st=0;
  timer time, 100;
  end;
```

In this example the *timer* runs 100 milliseconds each time before the *time* function is recalled. Accordingly, this function increments the displayed time each time by ten hundredths of a second.

If you completely do without the display of hundredths of a second, the *timer* can run for a full second and then switch the display by 100 additional hundredths of a second, which makes the clock even more accurate.

```
function time;
  if st=0;
    h=h+100;
    if h>=100;
      h=0;
      s=s+1;
      if s>=60;
        s=0;
        m=m+1;
      end_if;
    end_if;
    put_time, string(m,"0#")+" : "+string(s,"0#")+" : "+string(h,"0#");
    timer time, 1000;
  end_if;
  end;

function start;
  st=0;
  timer time, 1000;
  end;
```

**CD**

**Program on the companion CD**

You can also find these programs in their entirety on the companion CD to this book as *0604.csl* and *0605.csl*.

The CASLwin Runtime, the Emulator, and a genuine Palm all compute at different speeds, causing the time loss to come into play by varying degrees as a result of the calculation. The table shows measured values for a minute with program versions that have different *timer* values.

| 1 Min. | 1/100 Sec. | 1/10 Sec. | Sec. |
|---|---|---|---|
| Palm | 00 : 11 : 98 | 00 : 43 : 00 | 00 : 58 : 00 |
| Emulator | 00 : 21 : 34 | 00 : 48 : 80 | 01 : 00 : 00 |
| CASLwin-Runtime | 00 : 43 : 87 | 00 : 59 : 50 | 01 : 00 : 00 |

The values in the table are not accurate to the last decimal place, indicating a certain inaccuracy because of reaction time and slowness of the mouse buttons due to the manual measurement. However, the table shows that sufficient accuracies are not achieved until a *timer* interval of one second, especially because the error increases the longer the measured time is.

## Optimizing the program

One way to optimize the program would be to restart the *timer* right at the beginning of the *time* function. This would eliminate the time loss for the calculation and the displaying of the new time. Remember that the *timer* runs completely independently of the running program. Thus it can be restarted right at the start of the *time* function.

```
function time;
  if st=0;
    timer time, 10;
    h=h+1;
    if h>=100;
      h=0;
      s=s+1;
      if s>=60;
        s=0;
        m=m+1;
      end_if;
    end_if;
    put time, string(m,"0#")+" : "+string(s,"0#")+" : "+string(h,"0#");
  end_if;
end;
```

**CD**

**Program on the companion CD**

You can also find this program in its entirety on the companion CD to this book as *0606.csl*.

With a refresh rate of one hundredth of a second, the clock runs somewhat faster than in the original program version but still not fast enough. Not until you lower the refresh rate to ten hundredths of a second does the program run at sufficient speed.

| 1 Min. | 1/100 Sec. | 1/10 Sec. | Sec. |
|---|---|---|---|
| Palm | 00 : 16 : 11 | 00 : 54 : 40 | 01 : 00 : 00 |
| Emulator | 00 : 35 : 74 | 01 : 00 : 00 | 01 : 00 : 00 |
| CASLwin-Runtime | 00 : 59 : 89 | 01 : 00 : 00 | 01 : 00 : 00 |

This table shows that the calculation and display of the new time takes longer than one hundredth of a second but less than a tenth of a second; otherwise, the conversion of the *timer* in the source code wouldn't make itself so conspicuous.

Either way, the *timer* is not well suited to stopwatch programming because the inaccuracies add up over longer periods of time. You need a function that regularly synchronizes the measured time on the basis of the system clock.

## Synchronization with the system time

The next stopwatch is supposed to synchronize its time at regular intervals with the system time. This prevents inaccuracies from adding up over longer periods of time. CASL uses a *timevalue()* function for this purpose.

### *timevalue()*

This function returns the time in milliseconds that have passed since the start of the program. This time is calculated from the system time, not by a counter that can be interrupted by other events, thereby producing a precisely running stopwatch, similar to our last HotPaw Basic sample program.

```
label time;
  font "largefont";
  position 200,150;
  end;

button start;
  font "largefont";
  position 50,300;
  pixel_size 400,400;
  display "Start";
  end;

button stop;
  font "largefont";
  position 550,300;
  pixel_size 400,400;
  display "Stop";
  end;

button reset;
  font "largefont";
  position 550,750;
  pixel_size 400,200;
  display "Reset";
  end;

variables;
  numeric m;
  numeric s;
  numeric h;
  numeric st;
  numeric z;
  numeric a;
  end;

function time;
  if st=0;
    a=timevalue()-z;
    m=int(a/60000);
    s=int(a%60000/1000);
    h=int(a%1000/10);
    put time, string(m,"0#")+" : "+string(s,"0#")+" : "+string(h,"0#");
  end_if;
  timer time, 10;
  end;

function start;
  st=0;
  z=timevalue()-a;
```

```
    timer time, 10;
    end;

  function stop;
    st=1;
    end;

  function reset;
    m=0;
    s=0;
    h=0;
    a=0;
    put time, string(m,"0#")+" : "+string(s,"0#")+" : "+string(h,"0#");
    end;

  function startup;
    reset;
    end;
```

> **CD**
>
> **Program on the companion CD**
>
> You can also find this program on the companion CD to this book as *0607.csl.*

The user interface, *label,* and *button* objects are the same as the ones in the last program version. Therefore, the new program looks identical on screen to the last one.

If you tap the *Start* button in this version, the time is retrieved from the system clock by the *timevalue()* function and stored in the *z* variable. Prior to this, an *a* value is subtracted, which is still 0 at the beginning but later contains the last stopped time so that the clock continues running with the correct starting time. After that a *timer* starts, which calls the *time* function after ten milliseconds.

This function calculates the current run-time of the stopwatch from the time that *timevalue()* reads out from the system clock, minus the start time. The result is stored in the *a* variable and then reduced by division and modulo into minutes, seconds, and hundredths. As in the last program version, a string is formed of this and displayed in the *time label.*

**Tip**

**Modulo operator in CASL**

The Modulo operator is represented in CASL with the percentage sign. You can learn more about how modulo works on page 41 of Chapter 3.

After that a *timer* is restarted, which recalls the *time* function after ten milliseconds. Because this function uses *timevalue()* to calculate the true run-time of the clock each time from the system time, no inaccuracies add up over time.

Between the calls of the *time* function only the *timer* runs, but no function is directly active. During this interval, you can trigger new events by pressing the buttons. If the user taps the *Stop* button during this interval, the *st* variable is set to 1.

If the *timer* calls the *time* function again, the displayed time no longer changes. The clock stops. A delay of as much as nine milliseconds can pass between the tapping of the button and the next call of the *time* function by the *timer*. However, this time period is below the display accuracy of our clock and can thus be ignored.

On a *Reset* in this program version, not only must the displayed time be reset but also the initial value of *a*. The clock has to read a new initial value from the system time on the next *Start*.

This stopwatch is sufficiently accurate for practical use. Inaccuracies cannot add up. The measuring errors of the clock are, with a maximum of nine milliseconds, in any event smaller than the inaccuracy that results from manual operation.

# 6.2 Universal time clock: Calculating the time zones

Time zones, measured in increments of a full hour and based on degrees of latitude, were introduced to avoid inconvenience and chaos. Every $15^{th}$ degree of latitude corresponds to one hour (15 * 24 = 360).

0° runs exactly through the observatory of Greenwich, England, a borough of London, and sets the universal time (UT or UTC = **U**niversal **T**ime **C**oordinated), commonly known as GMT (= **G**reenwich **M**ean **T**ime).

Each small country lies completely within a time zone to simplify the calculation. Thus the time zones run along political boundaries, not precisely along the degrees of latitude.

A small number of countries use individual time zones with a 30-minute time shift relative to the neighboring zone. India, Nepal, Iran, and parts of Australia are among these. Canada and the USA stretch over five time zones, while Russia, the largest country in the world, extends across ten time zones. Greenland has four time zones, whereas Brazil, Mexico, and Australia each have three.

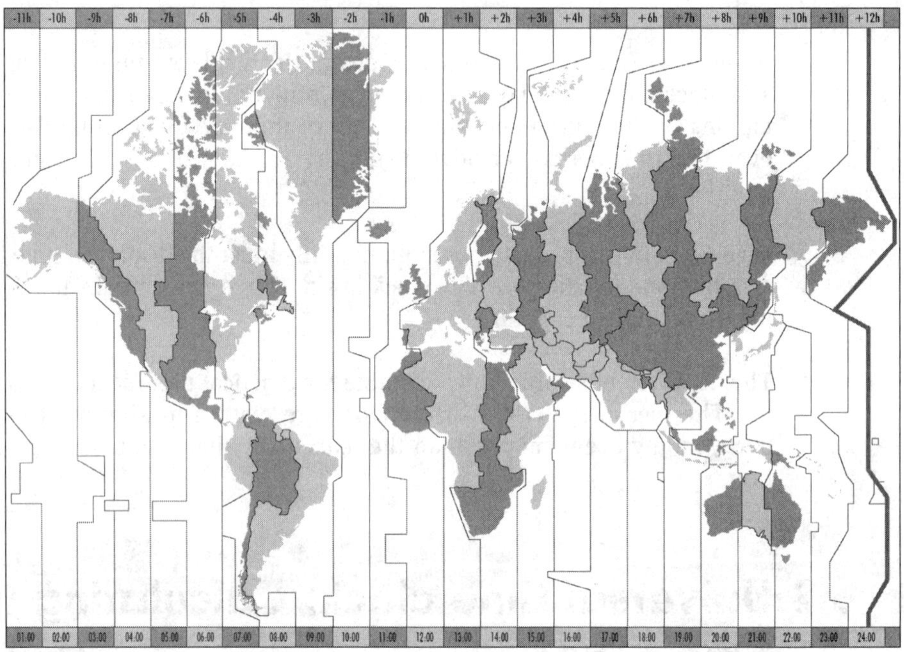


*Time zones of the earth*

The time shift complicates the coordination of transportation and telecommunications. In Russia all trains travel on Moscow time. In Canada they operate on Toronto time. In the United States, everything operates on universal time, so it might be 10 A.M. in Boston but 8 A.M. in Denver.

The table shows the global time zones and their relative shifts compared to UTC.

The next Palm program displays a universal time clock in HotPaw Basic. The clock displays the current Central European Time (MEZ = CET) as well as UTC and two other selectable time zones. However, it does not consider daylight saving time because the date for switching the time varies in many countries and would therefore require more extensive data.

*The universal time clock on the Palm*

The display in the upper left corner (MEZ) is taken from the system clock of the Palm. The program calculates the UTC based on the system clock and displays it in the upper right corner. UTC is an hour behind MEZ.

You can select the two other time zones from list boxes. The contents of the lists and the respective time shifts are on a memo.

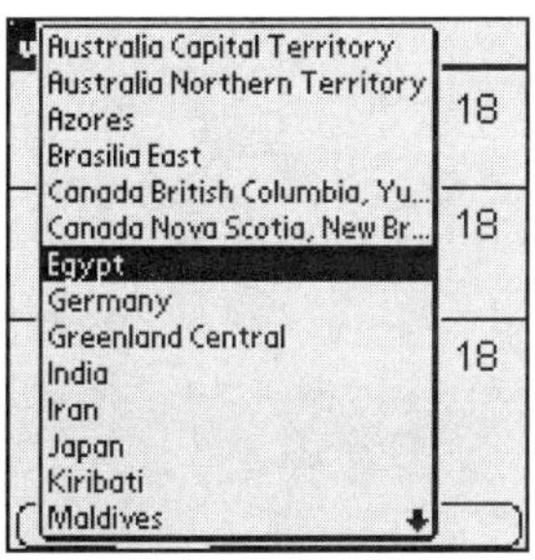


*Selection list of the time zones*

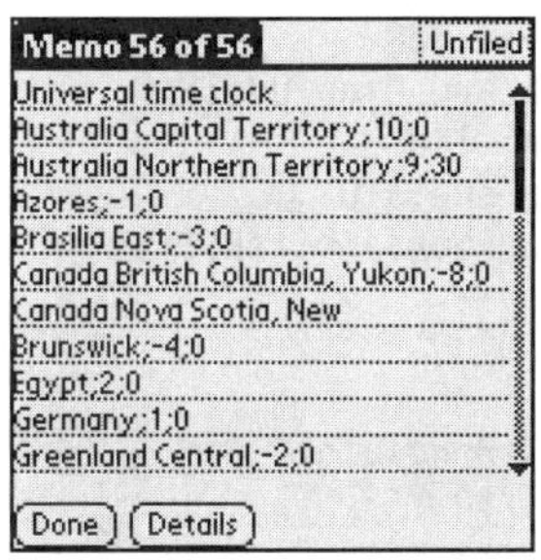


*Memo with time zones and time shifts*

The memo contains 30 lines with different time zones. Theoretically it could be longer, but HotPaw Basic processes only a maximum of 30 entries in a selection list.

**Tip**

**Longer lists**

If you need more selections in a program than a list appears to accommodate, build a preselection into the user interface through checkboxes or buttons, with which the user can reasonably restrict the number of possible options. Then have the program generate a corresponding list with a maximum of 30 entries, depending on which preselection the user has chosen.

```
Egypt;2;0
Australia Capital Territory;10;0
Australia Northern Territory;9;30
Azores;-1;0
Brazil Ost;-3;0
Germany;1;0
Greenland Central;-2;0
Great Britain;0;0
India;5;30
Iran;3;30
Japan;9;0
Canada British Columbia, Yukon;-8;0
Canada Nova Scotia, New Brunswick;-4;0
Kiribati;13;0
Maldive Islands;5;0
Mexico Mexico City;-6;0
Nepal;5;45
New Zealand;12;0
Norfolk Island;11;30
Russia Irkutsk and Ulan Ude;8;0
Russia Magadan;11;0
Russia Moscow Zone;3;0
Russia Omsk and Novosibirsk;6;0
Thailand;7;0
USA Alaska;-9;0
USA East;-5;0
USA Hawaii and Honolulu;-10;0
USA Mountain;-7;0
United Arab Emirates;4;0
West Samoa;-11;0
```

**CD**

**Program on the companion CD**

You can also find this file in the companion CD to this book as *0608.csv*.

The memo is written in CSV format in order to import and export the file from all spreadsheets. In this way you can easily exchange data from spreadsheets with the Palm. The individual columns of the table are separated from each other by semicolons.

|  | A | B | C | D |
|---|---|---|---|---|
| 1 | Universal time clock |  |  |  |
| 2 | Australia Capital Territory | 10 | 0 |  |
| 3 | Australia Northern Territory | 9 | 30 |  |
| 4 | Azores | -1 | 0 |  |
| 5 | Brasilia East | -3 | 0 |  |
| 6 | Canada British Columbia, Yukon | -8 | 0 |  |
| 7 | Canada Nova Scotia, New Brunswick | -4 | 0 |  |
| 8 | Egypt | 2 | 0 |  |
| 9 | Germany | 1 | 0 |  |
| 10 | Greenland Central | -2 | 0 |  |
| 11 | India | 5 | 30 |  |
| 12 | Iran | 3 | 30 |  |
| 13 | Japan | 9 | 0 |  |
| 14 | Kiribati | 13 | 0 |  |
| 15 | Maldives | 5 | 0 |  |
| 16 | Mexico Mexico City | -6 | 0 |  |
| 17 | Nepal | 5 | 45 |  |

*The time zone table in a spreadsheet*

You can change the list at any time. If the list is longer, the program always inputs the first 30 lines. Only the format of the list is important:

- **1st** Column – Name of the country that appears in the selection list in the program.
- **2nd** Column – Time shift in hours compared to UTC.
- **3rd** Column – Additional time shift in minutes for countries that are outside of the normal time zones.

```
#worldclock.bas
draw -1
form btn 60,147,98,12,"Update",1
dim l$(30),z(30,1)
m=db.find("memo","Universal time clock")
if (m<0) then goto error
open "memo",m as #1
input #1,x$
for i=1 to 30
  input #1,x$
  j=instr(x$,";")
  l$(i)=left$(x$,j-1)
  z$=right$(x$,len(x$)-j)
  j=instr(z$,";")
  z(i,0)=val(left$(z$,j-1))
  z(i,1)=val(right$(z$,len(z$)-j))
next i
```

```
close #1
form lst 10,70,30,8,l$,1
form lst 10,110,30,8,l$,1
draw 0,50,160,50,1
draw 0,90,160,90,1
draw "MEZ",10,33,1
draw "UTC",90,33,1
start:
t$=fn time$(1)
draw left$(t$,2)+" : "+mid$(t$,3,2)+" : "+right$(t$,2)+"  ",10,20,2
h=val(left$(t$,2))-1
m=val(mid$(t$,3,2))
s$=right$(t$,2)
y=20
hx=0
mx=0
gosub displaytime
y=55
hx=h3
mx=m3
gosub displaytime
y=95
hx=h4
mx=m4
gosub displaytime
if (asc(inkey$)<13) then goto start
h3=z(val(s$(0)),0)
m3=z(val(s$(0)),1)
h4=z(val(s$(1)),0)
m4=z(val(s$(1)),1)
goto start
displaytime:
h2=h+hx
if (h2<0) then h2=h2+24
if (h2>23) then h2=h2-24
m2=m+mx
if (m2>59) then m2=m2-60:h2=h2+1
h$=str$(h2)
if (len(h$)=1) then h$="0"+h$
m$=str$(m2)
if (len(m$)=1) then m$="0"+m$
draw h$+" : "+m$+" : "+s$+"  ",90,y,2
return
error:
print "Memo Universal time clock not found"
```

**CD**

**Program on the companion CD**

You can also find this program on the companion CD to this book as *0609.bas*.

At the beginning a button is defined for updating. Button definitions must always be at the very beginning of the program. This button is necessary because HotPaw Basic does not update a value selected from a selection list until a button is tapped. HotPaw Basic does not run in object-oriented mode, as does CASL. This means that the selection of a list item does not trigger an action independently, although it must be explicitly queried. However, HotPaw Basic takes care of this automatically when any button is tapped. If the user selects a time zone from the list in the program, the selected option is visible on the screen even though the variables aren't rewritten until the *Update* button is tapped.

```
form btn 60,147,98,12,"Update",1
dim l$(30),z(30,1)
```

The *l$(30)* array contains the strings that are displayed in the selection list. Only fields *1 ... 30* are used, field *0* stays blank because the selection lists do not use this field.

In the *z(30,1)* array, the hour specifications of the respective time shift for the individual list entries are stored in the *z(n,0)* fields, while the minute specifications are stored in the *z(n,1)* fields. Here too, fields *z(0,0)* and *z(0,1)* remain blank.

```
m=db.find("memo","Universal time clock")
if (m<0) then goto error
open "memo",m as #1
```

Now the program looks for a memo named *"Universal time clock"*. If the program does not find a memo with this name, it goes to the *error* branch mark, outputs a message there, and then ends.

```
input #1,x$
for i=1 to 30
input #1,x$
```

Normally, however, the program first inputs the *"Universal time clock"* title line and then discards it. After that a loop inputs the 30 lines and evaluates them immediately with different string functions.

**Tip**

**Line lengths**

An input line can be longer than a screen line on a memo. A logical line always runs until the next Return character, not until the optical end of the line on the screen.

```
j=instr(x$,";")
l$(i)=left$(x$,j-1)
z$=right$(x$,len(x$)-j)
j=instr(z$,";")
z(i,0)=val(left$(z$,j-1))
z(i,1)=val(right$(z$,len(z$)-j))
```

In the first line the position of the first semicolon in the input string is determined in the *j* variable.

### *instr(<String1>, <String2>)*

The *instr()* function looks for *String2* in *String1*. *String2* can consist of one or more characters. The function returns the position where *String2*appears for the first time.

### *left$(<String>, <Number>)*

The *left$()* function forms a new string that consists of the specified number of characters. The program begins counting this number from the left, that is, from the beginning of the first string.

### *right$(<String>, <Number>)*

The *right$()* function forms a new string that consists of the specified number of characters. The program begins counting this number from the right, that is, from the end of the first string.

### *len( <String> )*

This function determines the number of characters in a string.

The *l$(i)* field variable then contains the description of the country, namely all characters that are in front of the first semicolon in the input line.

The remainder of the input line, after the first semicolon, is stored in the *z$* variable. This variable only serves as a butter memory and is overwritten with each new line. Once again the program searches for a semicolon within the *z$* string.

The *z(i,0)* field variable contains the part before the semicolon, converted into a numerical value. This value specifies the time shift in hours compared to UTC.

The *z(i,1)* field variable contains the part after the semicolon, converted into a numerical value. This value specifies the additional time shift in minutes compared to UTC. Such an additional value occurs only in countries where time zones are unusual.

```
form lst 10,70,30,8,l$,1
form lst 10,110,30,8,l$,1
```

Two selection lists are created with the *l$(30)* array. Use these selection lists to select different time zones for the two time displays in the lower area. In both selection lists the eight value is preselected. This is the value for Great Britain, which lies in the UTC time zone without a time shift. Thus these displays show the correct time even before you have selected a time zone in the lists.

```
start:
t$=fn time$(1)
```

The actual program for time display starts with the *start:* branch mark.

## *fn time$(1)*

This function, based on the current system time, returns a string that displays this time in six figures. For example, *"175823"* means 5:58 PM and 23 seconds.

The *left$()*, *mid$()*, and *right$()* functions insert colons into this string and then display the time in this form in the upper left area, the MEZ field.

## *mid$(<String>, <Position>, <Length>)*

This function reads individual characters or character strings from a string. Three parameters are specified for this purpose:

- **String** - The string that is to be read.
- **Position** - Position of the first read character. The first character in the string gets the number 1, not 0, as is the case with the arrays.
- **Length** - Length of the string that is to be read.

The string with the time specification, which the *fn time$(1)* function has returned, is stored in the *t$* variable, in order to access it for the other displays. In this way the same system time is used for all of the display fields so that no differences in the second display occur.

For further evaluation, the individual parts of the time display are stored separately:

- **h** - Hours as a numerical value. Compared to the current system time, an hour is deducted to get to UTC.
- **m** - Minutes as a numerical value.
- **s$** - Seconds as a string. This value is identical in all time zones and can thus be displayed unchanged everywhere.

The calculation of the three time specifications in the right part of the screen runs identically every time. Only three variable factors are required:

- **y** - y-coordinate of the display field.
- **hx** - Time shift in hours compared to UTC.
- **mx** - Additional time shift in minutes.

These three values are set differently and then the *display:* subroutine is called.

```
display:
h2=h+hx
if (h2<0) then h2=h2+24
if (h2>23) then h2=h2-24
m2=m+mx
if (m2>59) then m2=m2-60:h2=h2+1
h$=str$(h2)
if (len(h$)=1) then h$="0"+h$
m$=str$(m2)
if (len(m$)=1) then m$="0"+m$
draw h$+" : "+m$+" : "+s$+"  ",90,y,2
return
```

The *h2* value is the time of the corresponding time zone plus the respective time shift. If the conversion results in a value smaller than 0, 24 hours are added to it. With a value greater than 23, 24 hours are deducted.

Similarly, the minute display is calculated from the additional time shift in minutes. If a value greater than 59 is achieved here, 60 minutes are deducted for the display and an hour is added to the hour display. You cannot get negative values here because all countries that use special time zones are to the east of Greenwich and therefore have a positive time shift.

The string is created from the numerical values of the hours and minutes. Single-figure values have a 0 placed in front of them, causing all times to display in two figures. The resulting string is written to the corresponding display field.

This operation is repeated for all three universal times. After that the loop restarts and outputs the current time again. The entire operation runs continuously until the user taps the *Quit* button, which is specified by HotPaw Basic.

If the user selects a different time zone for one of the displayed universal times, HotPaw Basic does not automatically detect this. A change of selection in a list field is not registered until a button has been tapped. This is why the program has the *Update* button in the lower right area. This button is queried once in each loop cycle at the end.

```
if (asc(inkey$)<13) then goto start
h3=z(val(s$(0)),0)
m3=z(val(s$(0)),1)
h4=z(val(s$(1)),0)
m4=z(val(s$(1)),1)
goto start
```

The *inkey$* function always returns the value of the last pressed button that hasn't yet been evaluated. Thus if no button was pressed during a loop cycle, the program returns to the *start:* branch mark right away.

If the *Update* button has been pressed and not yet evaluated, *inkey$* returns the *chr$(14)* value. This is the first defined button in the program.

In this case the time shifts for both list fields are read out from the *z()* array. The numbers of the selected list elements are in the *s$(0)* and *s$(1)* variables as strings. The values for the time shift are stored in the *h3, m3, h4, m4* variables and, to display the time, are evaluated from there in the second and third call of the *Display* subroutine in each loop cycle.

## 6.3 Analog clock: Combining graphics with the clock

The digital time display, today's standard, became fashionable about 25 years ago. Prior to that, for centuries, time was displayed analogously using pointers on a dial or clock face. Digital watch popularity has subsided somewhat in the past few years because people have recognized that analog clocks are faster and can be read more clearly in bad weather conditions and at great distances, for example at airports. The human eye comprehends a graphic faster than numbers or letters. The image of an analog clock imprints itself on the short-term memory so that you can correctly convert it, even if it was blurred or you didn't see all of it. On the other hand, if you don't get a good look at a digital clock, you cannot draw any reliable conclusions from the displayed time.

The following example is meant not only to show how to program a clock but also to illustrate basic principles on the representation of analog displays, as they can be used not just for clocks, stopwatches, and alarm clocks but also for displaying different measured values or statistical data.

The next HotPaw Basic program shows an analog clock on the Palm.

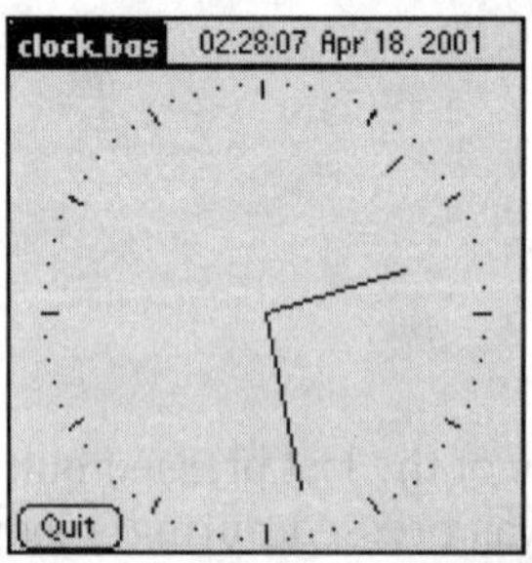


*The analog clock on the Palm*

Three hands revolve around the common center of the round dial, displaying the hour, minute, and second. Additionally, a digital time display runs in the upper right corner.

```
#clock.bas
pi=3.1415926
draw -1
for i=0 to 59 step 5
  x1=80+65*cos(pi/30*i)
  y1=88+65*sin(pi/30*i)
```

```
  x2=80+70*cos(pi/30*i)
  y2=88+70*sin(pi/30*i)
  draw x1,y1,x2,y2,1
next i
for i=0 to 59
  x1=80+69*cos(pi/30*i)
  y1=88+69*sin(pi/30*i)
  draw x1,y1,x1,y1,1
next i
start:
t$=fn time$(0)
h=val(mid$(t$,1,2))
m=val(mid$(t$,3,2))
s=val(mid$(t$,5,2))
if (m<>m1)
  h2=pi/6*(h1-3+m1/60)
  draw 80,88,80+45*cos(h2),88+45*sin(h2),-1
  h2=pi/6*(h-3+m/60)
  draw 80,88,80+45*cos(h2),88+45*sin(h2),1
  m2=pi/30*(m1-15)
  draw 80,88,80+55*cos(m2),88+55*sin(m2),-1
  m2=pi/30*(m-15)
  draw 80,88,80+55*cos(m2),88+55*sin(m2),1
endif
if (s<>s1)
  s2=pi/30*(s1-15)
  draw 80+57*cos(s2),88+57*sin(s2),80+63*cos(s2),88+63*sin(s2),-1
  s2=pi/30*(s-15)
  draw 80+57*cos(s2),88+57*sin(s2),80+63*cos(s2),88+63*sin(s2),1
  d$=fn date$(0,1)
  draw mid$(t$,1,2)+":"+mid$(t$,3,2)+":"+mid$(t$,5,2)+"  "+d$,60,1
endif
h1=h : m1=m : s1=s
goto start
```

**CD**

**Program on the companion CD**

You can also find this program on the companion CD to this book as *0610.bas.*

The display of an analog clock is based on the *sine* and *cosine* trigonometric functions. You use them to determine the coordinates from the angle of the clock hand in the right-angled coordinate system. HotPaw Basic, like most programming languages, calculates trigonometric functions in radian measure.

Therefore, a *pi* variable is defined in the program first. This variable represents the number $\pi$.

One minute on the clock corresponds to an angle of *pi/30*. The first program loop calculates the scale lines for five minutes for the big hand or one hour for the little hand.

```
for i=0 to 59 step 5
  x1=80+65*cos(pi/30*i)
  y1=88+65*sin(pi/30*i)
  x2=80+70*cos(pi/30*i)
  y2=88+70*sin(pi/30*i)
  draw x1,y1,x2,y2,1
next i
```

The center of the clock lies at the coordinates 80,88. The clock lies somewhat asymmetrically on the screen, because space is lost on top for the title line. Make full use of the bottom of the screen because the *Quit* button takes up space only on the left border.

The x1,y1 coordinates represent the inner point of a scale line, x2,y2 are the coordinates of the outer point. The inner points lie on a radius of 65 pixels around the center, while the outer points on a radius of 70 pixels.

A similar loop, but with an incrementation of 1, calculates the scale lines for the individual minutes.

```
for i=0 to 59
  x1=80+69*cos(pi/30*i)
  y1=88+69*sin(pi/30*i)
  draw x1,y1,x1,y1,1
next i
```

Here only one point is calculated each time.

**Tip**

**Drawing individual points**

If you specify the same coordinates in the *draw* function for the starting point and the end point of the line, a single pixel is drawn at this place.

After creating the dial in this manner, the actual clock program begins at the *start:* branch mark.

```
start:
t$=fn time$(0)
h=val(mid$(t$,1,2))
m=val(mid$(t$,3,2))
s=val(mid$(t$,5,2))
```

Similar to the last example, the program uses the *fn time$(1)* function to read out the time as a string and to store the hours, minutes, and seconds as three numerical values in the *h*, *m* and *s* variables.

Depending on the mechanism that is used, two different displays appear on analog clocks. On some clocks the minute hand performs a regular circular motion, while on others it jumps one minute further at the full minute. The latter procedure has the advantage that the time can be better read to the minute at a glance. Fractions of minutes are ordinarily not important in everyday life. Use this procedure for the clock program as well.

Nevertheless, the hour hand has to perform a regular circular motion and would be less useful if it jumped ahead by one full hour on each full hour.

If the minute has changed in the regular query cycle of the system clock, both hands must be moved. A true movement is not possible on the screen, so you must delete the existing hand and draw a new one.

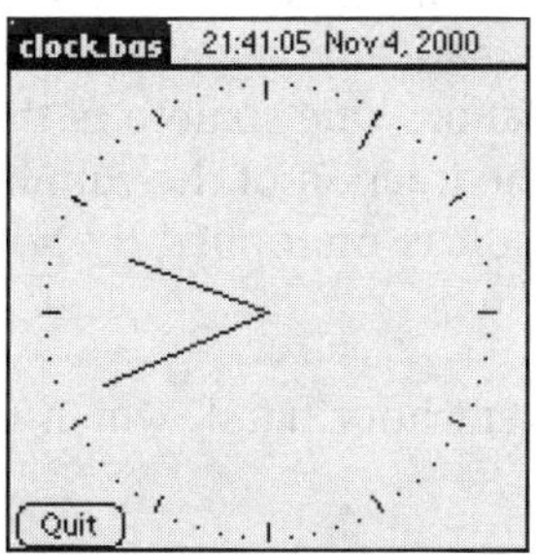


*"Normal" clock display*

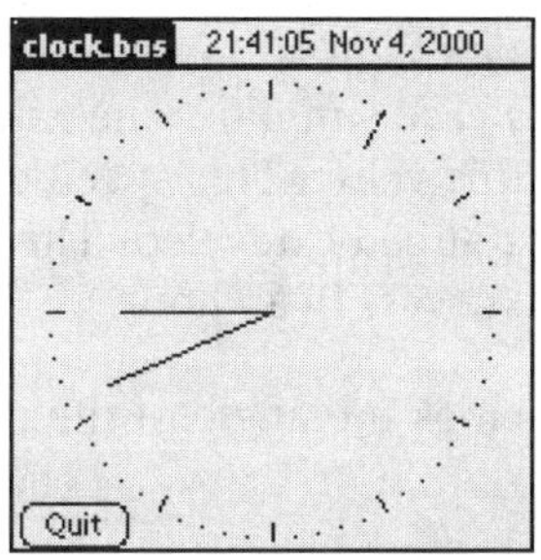


*Here's what it would look like if the hour hand moved forward only once an hour*

**Tip**

**Movement of the hands on the clock**

The minute hand of an analog clock moves pi/30 per minute, while the hour hand moves pi/6 per hour or (1/60)*(pi/6) per minute.

These calculations are performed at each new minute:

```
if (m<>m1)
h2=pi/6*(h1-3+m1/60)
draw 80,88,80+45*cos(h2),88+45*sin(h2),-1
h2=pi/6*(h-3+m/60)
draw 80,88,80+45*cos(h2),88+45*sin(h2),1
m2=pi/30*(m1-15)
draw 80,88,80+55*cos(m2),88+55*sin(m2),-1
m2=pi/30*(m-15)
draw 80,88,80+55*cos(m2),88+55*sin(m2),1
endif
```

The *m* variable contains the current minute specification. At the end of the cycle the *m1* variable is set to the minute specification that is being used. If the next *fn time$(1)* query results in a different minute value, a new minute has started. The hour can change at the same time in the jump from minute 59 to minute 00.

First the program calculates the current position of the hour hand. Here you have the same problem you had with some of the examples from the graphics chapter: The position of the clock hand cannot be "read" from the screen.

```
h2=pi/6*(h1-3+m1/60)
```

The exact angle of the existing hand is calculated from the last used hour *h1*-3, because the zero point of the angular scale is at 03:00, not at 12:00. Keep in mind: HotPaw Basic calculates angles mathematically negatively, that is, clockwise, which in this case simplifies the calculation. One sixtieth of the *m1*minute value is added to this value. This specifies the fraction of the running hour that the hour hand has already traveled. The result is multiplied by *pi/6,* the angle that the hour hand covers in an hour.

This *h2* value specifies the angle of the current hour hand, which must first be deleted.

```
draw 80,88,80+45*cos(h2),88+45*sin(h2),-1
```

The hour hand is a line from the center of the clock to a radius of 4 pixels.

**Tip**

**Deleting lines**

To delete a line, use the same *draw* function that you use to draw a line; however, the last parameter must be -1.

The program uses the same formula to calculate the new position of the hour hand from the current hour *h* and the current minute *m*.

```
h2=pi/6*(h-3+m/60)
draw 80,88,80+45*cos(h2),88+45*sin(h2),1
```

To calculate the position of the minute hand, you subtract 15 minutes from the minute specification to compensate the zero point of the angular scale. The zero point is at 15 minutes on the clock, not at 00 minutes. The result is multiplied by pi/30, the angle that the minute hand covers in a minute.

```
m2=pi/30*(m1-15)
draw 80,88,80+55*cos(m2),88+55*sin(m2),-1
```

Here again the clock hand is first deleted at its last position and then redrawn in the current position.

```
m2=pi/30*(m-15)
draw 80,88,80+55*cos(m2),88+55*sin(m2),1
```

The minute hand ranges from the center of the clock to a radius of 55 pixels.

Aside from this query, which updates every minute of the minute and hour hands, another query runs that, in accordance with the same principle, updates every second of the second hand and the digital display in the upper right corner.

```
if (s<>s1)
  s2=pi/30*(s1-15)
  draw 80+57*cos(s2),88+57*sin(s2),80+63*cos(s2),88+63*sin(s2),-1
  s2=pi/30*(s-15)
  draw 80+57*cos(s2),88+57*sin(s2),80+63*cos(s2),88+63*sin(s2),1
  d$=fn date$(0,1)
  draw mid$(t$,1,2)+":"+mid$(t$,3,2)+":"+mid$(t$,5.2)+"  "+d$,60,1
endif
```

The second hand has no influence on the other two hands of the clock, and they have no influence on the second hand. Therefore, the position of the second hand can be calculated from the last used second, the clock hand can be deleted and redrawn on the basis of the current second.

The second hand does not start from the center; instead, it is only a division mark that moves on a circular path. It covers only the area between the radii 57 and 63, thereby running exactly between the minute hand with a radius of 55 and the hour division marks of the dial, which start at 65 pixels from the center.

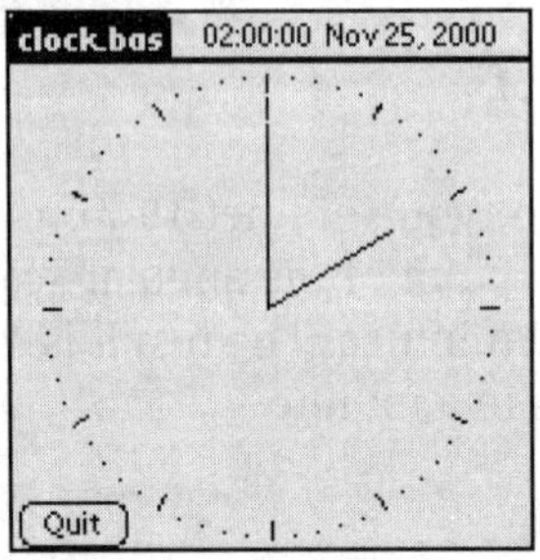


*The second hand between the minute hand and the dial*

With this method the second hand cannot overwrite any other parts of the graphic. If it started from the center, it would cover the minute and hour hands at specific times and delete them so that the program would have to regenerate them.

The digital display in the upper right corner is very easy to program in comparison to the analog display.

```
d$=fn date$(0,1)
   draw mid$(t$,1,2)+":"+mid$(t$,3,2)+":"+mid$(t$,5,2)+"  "+d$,60,1
```

Here the system date is read out first, and then a string is formed from the current values for hour, minute and second along with the date. This string is then written on the screen in the upper right corner.

### fn date$(0,1)

This function generates a string from the current system date in the format of *"Nov 4, 2000"*.

### fn date$(0)

This function generates a string from the current system date in the format of *"20001104"*.

After the loop has completed one cycle, the values used for hour, minute, and second are stored.

```
h1=h : m1=m : s1=s
goto start
```

This happens regardless of whether the position of one of the clock hands has changed or not. After that the program goes back to the *start:* branch mark and begins anew.

## The clock at the Europa Center in Berlin

In addition to the known methods of displaying the time, the analog clock and the digital clock, some unusual methods with certain advantages are also available.

This example doesn't just deal with an interesting, exotic type of clock and the evaluation of time functions in HotPaw Basic, it also discusses making logical decisions (light on/off) on the basis of specified sequences (time) using simple mathematical functions like division and modulo. The problem of converting analog data into digital data and finding appropriate formulas for doing this comes up over and over again in programming.

You learn different display options for the same problem and their different effects on the viewer: Black and white, color, and bitmap graphics.

*The clock in front of the Europa Center in Berlin - it's 5:39 PM (Foto: Jens Dengler http://me.in-berlin.de/~jd)*

For example, in 1975 D. Binninger invented a clock that displays the time using 23 geometrically arranged lamps and set it up at the Kurfürstendamm in Berlin at the Uhlandstrasse subway station. This clock combines digital precision with the simple readability of an analog clock (after a certain period of acclimatization).

In 1996 the clock was taken down from the Kurfürstendamm and assembled again at the Europa Center, where it can still be seen today. For more information, point your browser at http://www.europa-center-berlin.de.

*Different times*

**Tip**

### Operation of the clock

The display of the clock is based on the 5 system. In this system, instead of using the second place of a number to continue counting after nine units, you do this after four units. In the top row each lamp stands for five hours. The lamps in the second row display individual hours until five lamps are full again. When all four lamps in this row are lit up, they are turned off again in the next hour and an additional lamp in the top row is turned on.

The two lower lamp rows display the minutes. Here the upper row contains eleven lamps for five minutes each, while the lower four lamps are for one minute each. In a row of four lamps you can tell at first glance how many are turned on. In a row of eleven lamps, this is no longer possible. For this reason, the third, the sixth, and the ninth lamps give off a red light instead of yellow so the viewer can make out the quarter hours.

The round lamp, shown on the original clock, flashes in a cycle of two seconds. It has been omitted from the program because it wastes too much space on the small Palm display.

The next program simulates this clock on the Palm.

```
#berlin-clock.bas
draw -1
start:
t$=fn time$(0)
d$=fn date$(0,1)
h=val(mid$(t$,1,2))
m=val(mid$(t$,3,2))
s=val(mid$(t$,5,2))
if (h<>h1)
  for i=0 to 3
    if (h/((i+1)*5))>=1 then c=7 else c=-7
    draw i*40,16,37,30,c
```

```
    next i
    for i=0 to 3
      if (h mod 5)>i then c=7 else c=-7
      draw i*40,48,37,30,c
    next i
  endif
  if (m<>m1)
    for i=0 to 10
      if (m/((i+1)*5))>=1 then c=7 else c=-7
      draw i*14,80,11,30,c
    next i
    for i=0 to 3
      if (m mod 5)>i then c=7 else c=-7
      draw i*40,112,37,30,c
    next i
  endif
  if (s<>s1)
    draw mid$(t$,1,2)+":"+mid$(t$,3,2)+":"+mid$(t$,5,2)+"  "+d$,70,147
  endif
  h1=h : m1=m : s1=s
  goto start
```

**CD**

**Program on the companion CD**

You can also find this program on the companion CD to this book as *0611.bas.*

The time in this program is updated in a manner similar to the program for the analog clock. In a loop, the system time is read out permanently with the function:

```
t$=fn time$(0)
h=val(mid$(t$,1,2))
m=val(mid$(t$,3,2))
s=val(mid$(t$,5,2))
```

The graphic is updated each time the hour, minute, or second has changed compared to the last loop cycle. For this purpose, at the end of each cycle the currently used values are copied to the *h1*, *m1* and *s1*variables.

The upper two rows of lamps (black rectangles on the Palm) must be updated on a new hour.

```
if (h<>h1)
for i=0 to 3
  if (h/((i+1)*5))>=1 then c=7 else c=-7
  draw i*40,16,37,30,c
next i
for i=0 to 3
  if (h mod 5)>i then c=7 else c=-7
  draw i*40,48,37,30,c
next i
endif
```

The first loop calculates from left to right whether the lamp is switched on or off, while the second does the same for the lower lamp row. The modulo function is ideal for this sawtooth-shaped course. The table shows how many lamps in each row must be turned on for the corresponding hour display.

| Time | 0 | 1 | 2 | 3 | 4 | 5 | 6 | 7 | 8 | 9 | 10 | 11 | 12 | 13 | 14 | 15 | 16 | 17 | 18 | 19 | 20 | 21 | 22 | 23 |
|---|---|---|---|---|---|---|---|---|---|---|---|---|---|---|---|---|---|---|---|---|---|---|---|---|
| top | 0 | 0 | 0 | 0 | 0 | 1 | 1 | 1 | 1 | 1 | 2 | 2 | 2 | 2 | 2 | 3 | 3 | 3 | 3 | 3 | 4 | 4 | 4 | 4 |
| bottom | 0 | 1 | 2 | 3 | 4 | 0 | 1 | 2 | 3 | 4 | 0 | 1 | 2 | 3 | 4 | 0 | 1 | 2 | 3 | 4 | 0 | 1 | 2 | 3 |

Depending on whether a lamp is to be enabled or disabled, the last parameter for the *draw* function is set to 7 or -7. In each case all the rectangles of a row are redrawn, because in some cases black rectangles must be overwritten in white.

The second query, which displays the minutes, runs according to a similar system. This query redraws the rectangles whenever the current minute is different from the last used minute.

```
if (m<>m1)
  for i=0 to 10
    if (m/((i+1)*5))>=1 then c=7 else c=-7
    draw i*14,80,11,30,c
  next i
  for i=0 to 3
    if (m mod 5)>i then c=7 else c=-7
    draw i*40,112,37,30,c
  next i
endif
```

The only difference is that the first loop runs from 0 to 10, not just to 3, because eleven lamps appear for five minutes each.

Only the digital display at the bottom right is updated for each new second. Other than this, the clock has no second hand.

One drawback to this version is that the five-minute display is difficult to make out. In the Berlin original, every third lamp differs in color. However, HotPaw Basic doesn't offer any option for automatically filling a rectangle with a gray scale or a fill pattern. You must write your own function to fill the area line by line or display a graphic. The next program shows a different alternative.

## The clock in original colors on the Palm IIIc

On the Palm IIIc you can display the clock in its original colors, which makes it much easier to read.

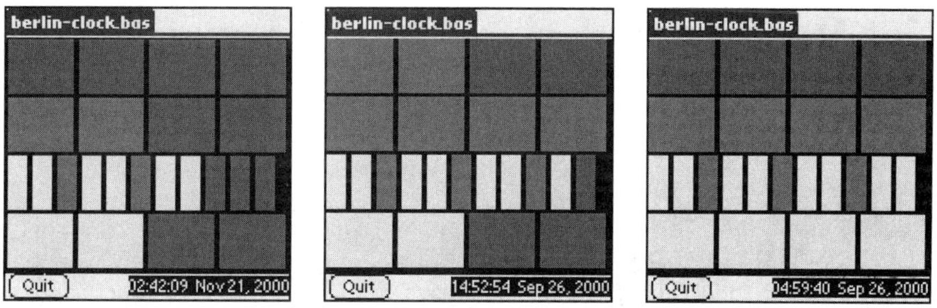


*Different times in color*

```
#berlin-clock.bas
dim f%(2)
f%(0)=120:f%(1)=120:f%(2)=125
draw color 255,-1,0,2
draw color 0,-1,0,3
draw -1
start:
t$=fn time$(0)
d$=fn date$(0,1)
h=val(mid$(t$,1,2))
m=val(mid$(t$,3,2))
s=val(mid$(t$,5,2))
if (h<>h1)
  for i=0 to 3
    if (h/((i+1)*5))>=1 then c=125 else c=165
    draw color c,-1,0,1
    draw i*40+1,17,37,30,7
  next i
  for i=0 to 3
    if (h mod 5)>i then c=125 else c=165
    draw color c,-1,0,1
    draw i*40+1,49,37,30,7
  next i
```

```
endif
if (m<>m1)
  for i=0 to 10
    if (m/((i+1)*5))>=1 then c=f%(i mod 3) else c=165
    draw color c,-1,0,1
    draw i*14+1,81,11,30,7
  next i
  for i=0 to 3
    if (m mod 5)>i then c=120 else c=165
    draw color c,-1,0,1
    draw i*40+1,113,37,30,7
  next i
endif
if (s<>s1)
  draw mid$(t$,1,2)+":"+mid$(t$,3,2)+":"+mid$(t$,5,2)+"  "+d$,70,147
endif
h1=h : m1=m : s1=s
goto start
```

**CD**

**Program on the companion CD**

You can also find this program on the companion CD to this book as *0612.bas.*

The calculation of the times and the enable states of the different lamps run precisely as in the black and white version. The only differences are in the display.

```
dim f%(2)
f%(0)=120:f%(1)=120:f%(2)=125
```

At the beginning an array is defined with three color numbers. It contains the color yellow 120 twice and the color red 125 once. The rhythm of the color change in the five-minute lamps results from this.

```
draw color 255,-1,0,2
draw color 0,-1,0,3
```

The background color is set to black 255 and the text color is set to white 0. Because the background color always affects the entire graphic area on the screen, the text color must be set to white for the digital clock display to achieve the highest possible contrast.

The first parameter of the *draw color* statement specifies the palette number of the color, while the last parameter determines what this color is to be used for: 1 = Foreground color, 2 = Background color, 3 = Text color.

The four loops that draw the lamps now look a bit different:

```
for i=0 to 3
  if (h/((i+1)*5))>=1 then c=125 else c=165
  draw color c,-1,0,1
  draw i*40+1,17,37,30,7
next i
```

Depending on whether the lamp is to be enabled or disabled, the color red 125 or gray 165 is used. *draw color* sets this as a foreground color and uses it to draw a filled rectangle. Thus the last parameter in the *draw* statement is no longer changed.

```
if (m/((i+1)*5))>=1 then c=f%(i mod 3) else c=165
```

The third row with the eleven lamps for five minutes each is an exception. Here the color is supposed to change with each third lamp. You can achieve such a rhythm with the modulo function. This always results in a value between 0 and 2, which is used as an index in the *f%()* field variable. This variable, in turn, contains the color red 125 for the index value of 2 and the color yellow 120 for 0 and 1.

## Bitmap graphics in HotPaw Basic

Not everyone has a Palm IIIc. However, even as the owner of a black and white Palm, you don't have to forfeit clarity. HotPaw Basic offers the option of displaying bitmap graphics to display the different colored lamps through different patterns.

*Different times with bitmap patterns*

Before you change the program, you should take a small excursion into the theory of binary coded bitmaps.

## Binary coded Bitmaps

This bitmap graphic consists of black and white dots in a grid. The program does not draw single lines and rectangles but a grid of specified size that is filled with black and white dots to display a graphic.

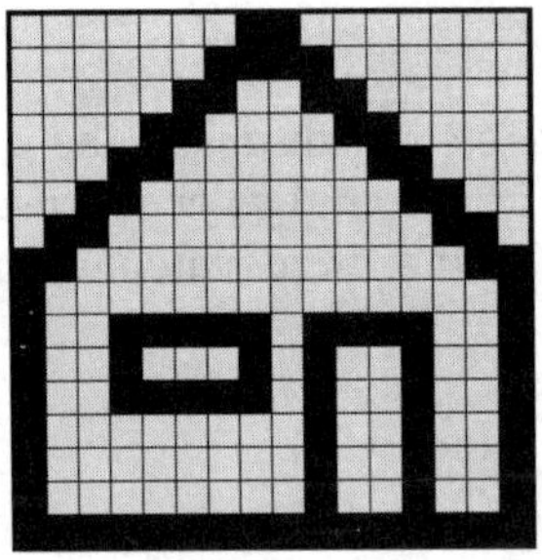

*Example of a bitmap graphic*

The figure shows such a bitmap highly enlarged with 16 pixels in width and height.

> **Note**
>
> **Bitmap sizes in HotPaw Basic**
>
> Due to the method with which bitmap graphics are stored in HotPaw Basic, they can be a maximum size of 32 x 32 pixels. The width has to be an integral multiple of 8, that is 8, 16, 24 or 32 pixels. Eight bits, here eight pixels, correspond to one byte. HotPaw Basic addresses Palm memory in bytes just as other programming languages on other hardware platforms do. However, with whole bytes it is only possible to express bit numbers in multiples of 8.

Black and white pixels can be represented as numbers 1 and 0. You can form a hexadecimal number between 0 and 5 from four of these binary numbers. The following table shows the 16 different hexadecimal numbers and their bit coding.

| 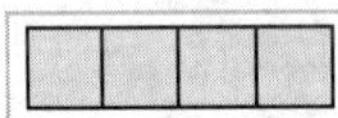 | 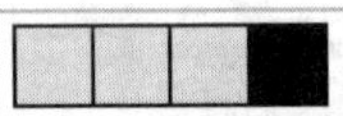 |  | 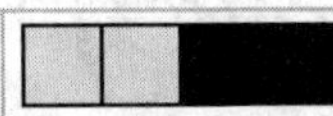 |
|---|---|---|---|
| 0000 = 0 | 0000 = 1 | 0000 = 2 | 0000 = 3 |
|  | 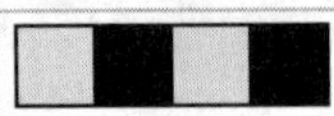 |  |  |
| 0000 = 4 | 0000 = 5 | 0000 = 6 | 0000 = 7 |

| 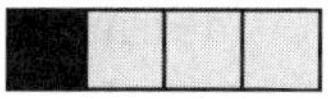 | 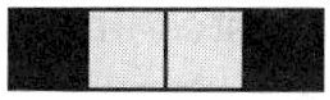 |  |  |
|---|---|---|---|
| 0000 = 8 | 0000 = 9 | 0000 = A | 0000 = B |
|  |  |  |  |
| 0000 = C | 0000 = D | 0000 = E | 0000 = F |

In this way it is possible to display an entire bitmap graphic bit coded in the hexadecimal system by dividing it up into blocks of four pixels each and then converting them to hexadecimal numbers.

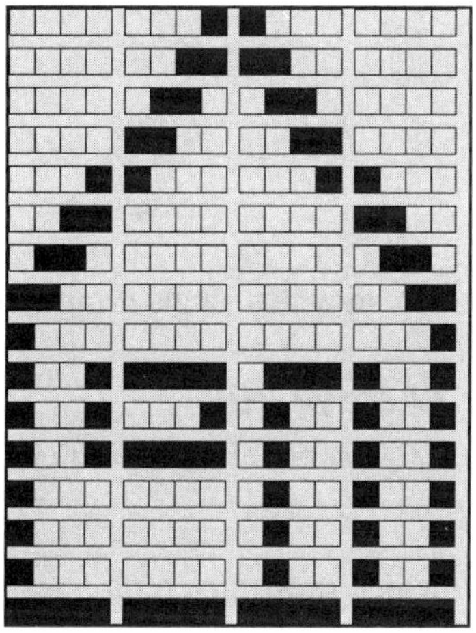

*The example image divided into 4 pixel blocks*

In hexadecimal display the image would then look like this:

```
0180
03C0
0660
0C30
1818
300C
6006
C003
8001
9F79
9149
9F49
8049
8049
8049
FFFF
```

In HotPaw Basic, bitmaps like this are stored line by line in string arrays.

```
dim b$(15)
b$(0)="0180"
b$(1)="03C0"
b$(2)="0660"
b$(3)="0C30"
b$(4)="1818"
b$(5)="300C"
b$(6)="6006"
b$(7)="C003"
b$(8)="8001"
b$(9)="9F79"
b$(10)="9149"
b$(11)="9F49"
b$(12)="8049"
b$(13)="8049"
b$(14)="8049"
b$(15)="FFFF"
```

This bitmap can draw anywhere on the screen with a single *draw* command.

### *draw <x>, <y>, <b>, <h>, 100, <Array>$(0)*

With this form of the *draw* command, you specify the x,y-coordinates of the upper left corner of the bitmap first.

Next specify the width and the height, which must match the measurements of the stored bitmap.

The parameter 100 is fixed. This display form is defined for the *draw* command using it.

The name of the array in which the bitmap data is stored is specified as the last parameter. You must include the index number 0 in the specification to differentiate the array from an individual variable of the same name that may be present.

```
#Bitmap.bas
dim b$(15)
b$(0)="0180"
b$(1)="03C0"
b$(2)="0660"
b$(3)="0C30"
b$(4)="1818"
b$(5)="300C"
b$(6)="6006"
```

```
b$(7)="C003"
b$(8)="8001"
b$(9)="9F79"
b$(10)="9149"
b$(11)="9F49"
b$(12)="8049"
b$(13)="8049"
b$(14)="8049"
b$(15)="FFFF"
draw -1
draw 72,72,16,16,100,b$(0)
j=fn pen(0)
```

**CD**

**Program on the companion CD**

You can also find this program on the companion CD to this book as *0613.bas.*

This program uses the *draw* command to draw the graphic shown earlier in the illustration. The last line waits for a tap on the display to prevent the program from terminating immediately after drawing the graphic.

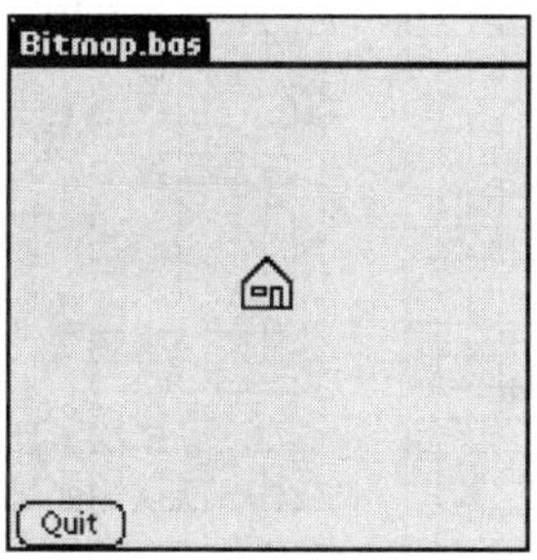


*The bitmap graphic on the Palm*

**Tip**

**Bitmap editor**

In chapter 10 you can also find a graphic editor for creating and editing bitmaps for HotPaw Basic.

## Bitmap graphics for displaying the clock

Returning to the clock, you should note three states per lamp: “red”, “yellow”, and “off”, each displayed by different bitmaps. Each lamp has two different sizes. Accordingly, you need six different bitmaps.

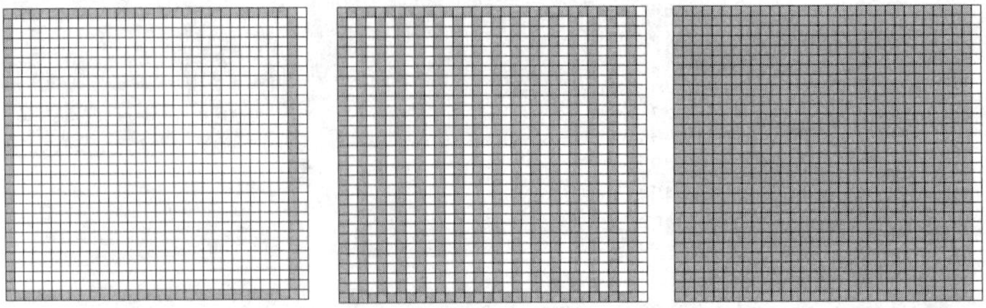

*Larg lamp off - w1$()* *Large lamp yellow - g1$()* *Large lamp red - r1$()*

These bitmaps are 32 pixels in width, corresponding to eight hexadecimal numbers, and are 30 lines in height.

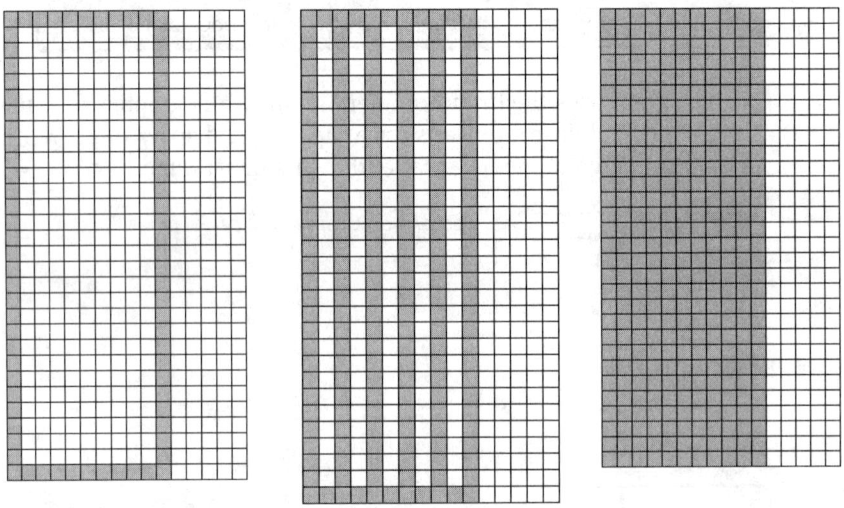

*Small lamp off - w2$()* *Small lamp yellow - g2$()* *Small lamp red - r2$()*

These bitmaps are 16 pixels in width, corresponding to four hexadecimal numbers, and are 30 lines in height.

You can even create bitmaps with such a simple structure in the program using simple loops.

```
#berlin-clock.bas
draw -1
dim w1$(29), r1$(29),g1$(29)
dim w2$(29),r2$(29),g2$(29)
```

```
w1$(0)="FFFFFFFE"
w1$(29)="FFFFFFFE"
g1$(0)="FFFFFFFE"
g1$(29)="FFFFFFFE"
w2$(0)="FFE0"
w2$(29)="FFE0"
g2$(0)="FFE0"
g2$(29)="FFE0"
for i=1 to 28
  w1$(i)="80000002"
  w2$(i)="8020"
  g1$(i)="AAAAAAAA"
  g2$(i)="AAA0"
next i
for i=0 to 29
  r1$(i)="FFFFFFFE"
  r2$(i)="FFE0"
next i
start:
t$=fn time$(0)
d$=fn date$(0,1)
h=val(mid$(t$,1,2))
m=val(mid$(t$,3,2))
s=val(mid$(t$,5,2))
if (h<>h1)
  for i=0 to 3
    if (h/((i+1)*5))>=1
      draw i*36,16,32,30,100,r1$(0)
    else
      draw i*36,16,32,30,100,w1$(0)
    endif
  next i
  for i=0 to 3
    if (h mod 5)>i
      draw i*36,48,32,30,100,r1$(0)
    else
      draw i*36,48,32,30,100,w1$(0)
    endif
  next i
endif
if (m<>m1)
  for i=0 to 10
    if (m/((i+1)*5))>=1
      if (i mod 3=2)
        draw i*14,80,16,30,100,r2$(0)
      else
        draw i*14,80,16,30,100,g2$(0)
      endif
    else
```

```
        draw i*14,80,16,30,100,w2$(0)
      endif
    next i
    for i=0 to 3
      if (m mod 5)>i
        draw i*36,112,32,30,100,g1$(0)
      else
        draw i*36,112,32,30,100,w1$(0)
      endif
    next i
  endif
  if (s<>s1)
    draw mid$(t$,1,2)+":"+mid$(t$,3,2)+":"+mid$(t$,5.2)+"  "+d$,70,147
  endif
  h1=h : m1=m : s1=s
  goto start
```

**CD**

**Program on the companion CD**

You can also find this program on the companion CD to this book as *0614.bas*.

At the beginning, the program dimensions the six string arrays that are to receive the bitmap graphics:

```
dim w1$(29), r1$(29),g1$(29)
dim w2$(29),r2$(29),g2$(29)
```

All the arrays have 30 lines from 0 to 29. The first and last lines look different for the white and yellow lamps and are manually allocated in the following program lines.

```
w1$(0)="FFFFFFFE"
w1$(29)="FFFFFFFE"
g1$(0)="FFFFFFFE"
g1$(29)="FFFFFFFE"
w2$(0)="FFE0"
w2$(29)="FFE0"
g2$(0)="FFE0"
g2$(29)="FFE0"
```

In HotPaw Basic the width of a bitmap must always be an even number of hexadecimal numbers. However, the yellow lamps *g1$()* and *g2$()* require an odd number of pixels for the pattern you are using. The narrow lamps *w2$()*, *g2$()*

and *r2$()* can be only eleven pixels wide, so that eleven pieces fit on the display with spacing in between. For this reason, leave the last five pixels white here and arrange the bitmaps to be somewhat overlapping later.

```
for i=1 to 28
  w1$(i)="80000002"
  w2$(i)="8020"
  g1$(i)="AAAAAAAA"
  g2$(i)="AAA0"
next i
```

Lines 1 to 28 of each bitmap are all identical. These are automatically created using a loop for the white *w1$(), w2$()* and yellow *g1$(), g2$()* lamps.

All the lines of the bitmap are identical for the red lamps *r1$(), r2$()* so that they can be created in a separate loop.

```
for i=0 to 29
  r1$(i)="FFFFFFFE"
  r2$(i)="FFE0"
next i
```

After that the program starts the time calculation, as in the preceding version. There won't be any differences until the display. The following routine runs on each new hour:

```
if (h<>h1)
  for i=0 to 3
    if (h/((i+1)*5))>=1
      draw i*36,16,32,30,100,r1$(0)
    else
      draw i*36,16,32,30,100,w1$(0)
    endif
  next i
  for i=0 to 3
    if (h mod 5)>i
      draw i*36,48,32,30,100,r1$(0)
    else
      draw i*36,48,32,30,100,w1$(0)
    endif
  next i
endif
```

The indenting, which is only possible with restrictions on a memo, makes the structure clearer.

Two loops run one after the other for the five-hour lamps and for the one-hour lamps. Depending on whether the lamp has to be enabled or disabled, the program uses an *if...else...endif* query for each of the four lamps per row to decide whether to draw the *r1$()* bitmap or *w1$()* bitmap. The bitmap sizes and the y-coordinate are preset, whereas the loop counter indents the x-coordinate by 36 pixels to the right each time.

A similar routine runs on each new minute:

```
if (m<>m1)
  for i=0 to 10
    if (m/((i+1)*5))>=1
      if (i mod 3=2)
        draw i*14,80,16,30,100,r2$(0)
      else
        draw i*14,80,16,30,100,g2$(0)
      endif
      else
        draw i*14,80,16,30,100,w2$(0)
    endif
  next i
  for i=0 to 3
    if (m mod 5)>i
      draw i*36,112,32,30,100,g1$(0)
    else
      draw i*36,112,32,30,100,w1$(0)
    endif
  next i
endif
```

Here too the indenting illustrates the structure. The routine has two differences compared to the hour counter:

- The first loop runs from 0 to 10 for the eleven five-minute lamps. These lamps are drawn at a horizontal distance of 14 pixels, although they are 16 pixels wide. The five pixels at the right border are only caused by bit coding but are not really necessary for the graphic. Because the individual bitmaps are drawn from left to right, they can overlay the free area of the bitmap drawn beforehand without problems.
- If an enabled five-minute lamp is to be drawn in the first loop, a second query runs, which uses the modulo function to determine whether the new lamp is the third, the sixth, or the ninth in the row. In this case the lamp is displayed in "red" (filled out) instead of in "yellow" (striped).

*Times at a distance of five minutes*

The program version runs on any Palm because it requires neither color nor gray scales for the display.

# 7. Automating appointments and tasks

A Palm is every bit as functional as a PC. As shown in the preceding chapters, you can program numerous variants. However, first and foremost, people like to you use the Palm as an organizer or PDA (= **P**ersonal **D**igital **A**ssistant).

A PDA helps to organize the personal and professional life of its owner. This includes the management of appointments and addresses, lists with tasks that are due, and note sheets for collecting different information.

These four important tasks are instantly available on the Palm through four buttons in the lower area of the case. Pressing one of these buttons turns the device on.

In this chapter you learn how to use small programs to improve the functionality of the four standard applications.

**Note**

**Tasks and addresses in CASL**

The processing of tasks, appointments, and addresses is not directly contained within the language range of CASL. However, add-on libraries with functions for addresses and tasks do exist, which are based on the general CASL database format and can process the Palm-internal databases. These libraries are covered in Chapter 10.

## 7.1 Access to the Palm Date Book

The most frequently used Palm application is the Date Book. Just enter your appointments and automatically synchronize them with the PC.

The Date Book data is stored in an internal database on the Palm, which can be processed by programming interfaces in addition to the standard Date Book applications. This means that other programs can also access this data.

**Tip**

**Date Book+ on the Visor**

The Visor has a Date Book with significantly enhanced functionality, called Date Book+. It uses the same Date Book database as the normal Palm Date Book. This means that you can run all the programs that work with the Palm Date Book database on the Visor without making any special adjustments.

Date Book

HotPaw Basic has different functions for date calculation, as well as functions for reading entries from the Palm Date Book or writing new entries.

You can see the data structure of such a Date Book entry using a very simple program. It reads the first Date Book entry of the current day and shows its data structure. In this form the program has little practical use, because you can see all the data of an appointment much more clearly in the Date Book itself. This is only meant to show how you output data from the Date Book.

*Appointment in the Date Book*

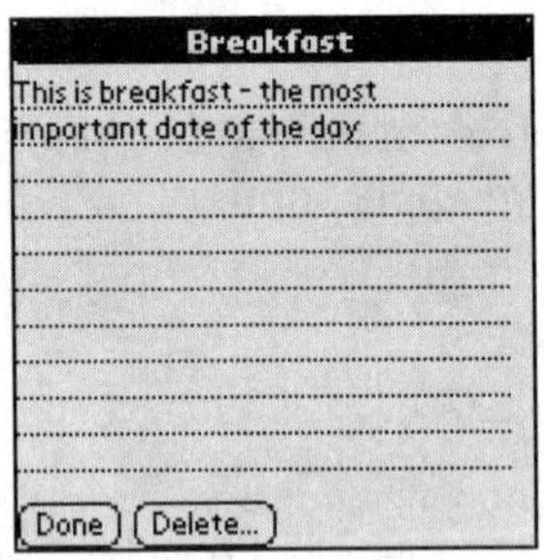


*Note about this appointment*

These appointments are entered in one day. The program finds the first appointment and displays it.

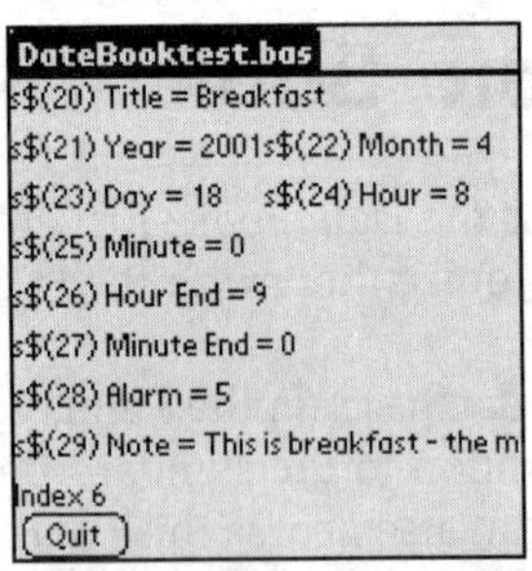


*Display of the appointment data*

While reading out the Date Book, HotPaw Basic stores the data in the *s$(20) ... s$(29)* variables.

```
#DateBooktest.bas
t=find("date",0,val(fn date$(0)))
get$("date",t,10)
draw -1
draw "Index "+str$(t),0,135
draw "s$(20) Title = "+s$(20),0,15
draw "s$(21) Year = "+s$(21),0,30
draw "s$(22) Month = "+s$(22),80,30
draw "s$(23) Day = "+s$(23),0,45
draw "s$(24) Hour = "+s$(24),80,45
draw "s$(25) Minute = "+s$(25),0,60
draw "s$(26) Hour End = "+s$(26),0,75
draw "s$(27) Minute End = "+s$(27),0,90
draw "s$(28) Alarm = "+s$(28),0,105
draw "s$(29) Note = "+s$(29),0,120
w=fn pen(0)
```

CD

**Program on the companion CD**

You can also find this program on the companion CD to this book as *0701.bas.*

The program looks for the first appointment of the current day.

```
t=find("date",0,val(fn date$(0)))
```

Two functions are used for this purpose:

### *fn date$(0)*

Returns a string with an eight-figure number that specifies the current date in the format of YYYYMMDD, for example, *20001224* for December 24, 2000. The format of this date number is always the same. To display the date in a program, you must generate the format typical for the country from this date number. (In the United States the dates displays month/day/year, whereas in Europe, they display in the format of day.month.year.)

### *find("date",0, <Date number>)*

This function returns the index number of the first appointment on the specified day. The day must be specified as an eight-figure numerical value in the format of YYYYMMDD. Each appointment has an index number in the Date Book. The program counts off these index numbers from the oldest appointment, beginning at 0, to the latest appointment.

In the example the program uses the *val()* function from the string that *fn date$(0)* returns to determine a numerical value, which can then be passed to the *find("date",0, ...)* function.

```
get$("date",t,10)
```

Using the index number determined in this manner, the program then retrieves the data of the appointment.

## get$("date", <Index> ,10)

This function retrieves the data of an appointment and writes it to the variables *s$(20) ... s$(29)* in accordance with the following pattern. The previous contents of these variables are automatically overwritten. All the variables contain strings.

| Variable | Contents |
|---|---|
| s$(20) | Title |
| s$(21) | Year |
| s$(22) | Month |
| s$(23) | Day |
| s$(24) | Hour |
| s$(25) | Minute |
| s$(26) | Hour End |
| s$(27) | Minute End |
| s$(28) | Alarm Minutes (0 if no alarm) |
| s$(29) | The first 63 characters of a note about this appointment |

```
draw "Index "+str$(t),0,135
```

The program writes the index number of the appointment in the bottom screen line. In the example, the number is 2, which references the third appointment in the Date Book in chronological order. Thus on the days prior to this, a total of two appointments are entered.

```
draw "s$(20) Title = "+s$(20),0,15
draw "s$(21) Year = "+s$(21),0,30
draw "s$(22) Month = "+s$(22),80,30
```

```
draw "s$(23) Day = "+s$(23),0,45
draw "s$(24) Hour = "+s$(24),80,45
draw "s$(25) Minute = "+s$(25),0,60
draw "s$(26) Hour End = "+s$(26),0,75
draw "s$(27) Minute End = "+s$(27),0,90
draw "s$(28) Alarm = "+s$(28),0,105
draw "s$(29) Note = "+s$(29),0,120
```

The following program lines write the variable names, their meanings, and the contents of the variables to specific positions on the screen.

```
w=fn pen(0)
```

Only the last line waits for the user to tap the display. Otherwise, the program would terminate immediately, without your being able to see the display.

The next program example shows you how to create appointments in the Date Book with HotPaw Basic. You would not write a program to create a single appointment because you can use the normal Date Book functions more efficiently. However, when it comes to generating lots of appointments automatically based on a specific scheme, using a program is a good idea.

## Lawnmower Date Book (irregularly repeating appointments)

You can use the Palm Date Book to create appointments that are automatically repeated. This repetition can occur after a specified number of days, weeks, months, or years, or even on a regular basis on specific weekdays.

However, you cannot create appointments that are repeated on an irregular basis. Even though HotPaw Basic cannot change the structure of the internal Date Book database so that irregularly repeating appointments would be possible, it can create an appointment at any time.

The following program shows you how to create appointments that do not fit into the standard repetition paterns of the Palm Date Books.

Most homeowners mow their lawns on Saturdays. It's different at public parks and swimming pools, where the mowing occurs during the week. You could make an appointment with a simple weekly repetition if it really had to appear in the Date Book each Saturday. However, mowing the lawn is, like many other agricultural tasks, dependent on the season. For example, the lawn is mowed more often in the summer than in the spring or fall. In the winter it is not mowed at all. You could also create schedules for orchards, farming, or breeding cattle.

You cannot represent such irregularities with the normal Palm Date Book.

*Input form*

*Message, after which the appointments were created*

The program shows an input form, in which you specify how many weeks in the respective months an appointment is to be created. Four weeks are set by default for the months in the springtime (March, April) and in the fall (September, October), while two weeks are set for the summer months (May through August). The winter months (December through February) do not appear.

You can also set different repetition rates for each month. Click *OK* to create the appointments in the Date Book and an appropriate message appears.

*Here's what the appointments that the program creates look like*

The appointments are created without time, repetition, and alarm. They always appear right at the top on the respective days.

To find all such appointments at once, simply use the Find function of the Palm OS.

*Search query for "Mow the lawn"*

All appointments with this keyword are listed in order.

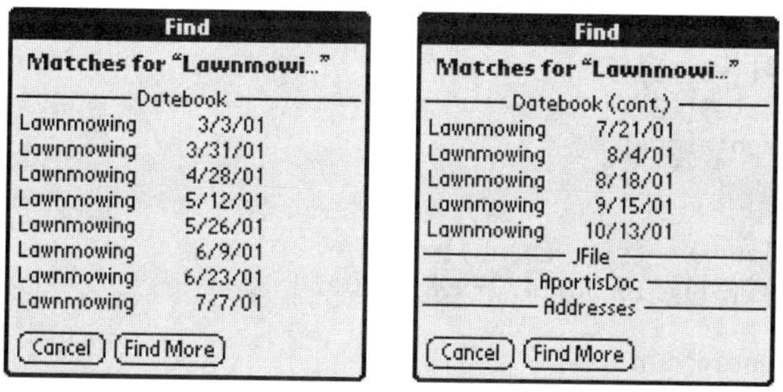


*Listing of the appointments by the search query*

Compare this list with the input reproduced in the input form from earlier. You can recognize the patterns: every four weeks in spring and fall and every two weeks in the summer months.

```
#Lawnmowing.bas
s$(20)="Lawnmowing"
s$(0)="March"
s$(1)="4"
s$(2)="April"
s$(3)="4"
s$(4)="May"
s$(5)="2"
s$(6)="June"
s$(7)="2"
s$(8)="July"
s$(9)="2"
s$(10)="August"
s$(11)="2"
s$(12)="September"
```

```
s$(13)="4"
s$(14)="October"
s$(15)="4"
s$(16)="November"
s$(17)=""

start:
f=form(9,9,"Lawnmowing calendar")
if (f=0) then end
s$(21)=left$(fn date$(0),4)
for i=22 to 29
  s$(i)=""
next i
t1=val(s$(21))*10000+301
gosub first
gosub appointment
for i=1 to 17 step 2
  if (val(s$(i))>0)
    for j=1 to int(4/val(s$(i)))
      t2=t2+val(s$(i))*7
      t1$=fn date$(t2)
      gosub appointment
    next j
  else
    if ((i<17)and(val(s$(i+2))>0))
      t1=val(s$(21))*10000+(i/2+3.5)*100+1
      gosub first
      gosub appointment
    endif
  endif
next i
print "Appointments for "+s$(20)+" created"
end

appointment:
s$(22)=mid$(t1$,5,2)
s$(23)=right$(t1$,2)
put "date",new,10
return

first:
while (fn dayow(t1)<>7)
  t1=t1+1
wend
t1$=str$(t1)
t2=fn days(t1)
return
```

**CD**

**Program on the companion CD**

You can also find this program on the companion CD to this book as *0702.bas*. The indentation is only for readability and is not included in the original program on the CD, because it is difficult to display on memos.

The program uses the even-numbered variables *s$(0) ... s$(16)* for the texts in the input form and uses the odd-numbered variables *s$(1) ... s$(17)* for the input fields. The data for the new appointments to be created, like data from read appointments, must appear in the variables *s$(20) ... s$(29)*.

| Variable | Contents |
|---|---|
| s$(20) | Lawnmowing |
| s$(21) | Current year |
| s$(22) | Calculated month |
| s$(23) | Calculated day |
| s$(24) | "" |
| s$(25) | "" |
| s$(26) | "" |
| s$(27) | "" |
| s$(28) | "" |
| s$(29) | "" |

In the first program lines, the default values are initialized and then the form is created.

```
...
f=form(9,9,"Lawnmowing calendar")
if (f=0) then end
```

If the user taps *Cancel* in the form, the *form()* function returns the value 0, and the program terminates.

```
s$(21)=left$(fn date$(0),4)
```

The *s$(21)* variable contains the year number for writing an appointment to the Date Book. This is set to the current year. The first four places of the string that *fn date$(0)* returns specify the year number.

```
for i=22 to 29
  s$(i)=""
next i
```

The remaining variables *s$(22) ... s$(29)* are deleted to prevent the program from writing incorrect values, which could still appear, to the new appointments.

The calculation of the appointments begins in March. For this purpose a *t1* variable is defined, which contains as a numerical value the date of March 1 in the current year. The current year is already stored in the *s$(20)* variables. If you multiply this number by 10,000, the result is the first four places of an eight-figure number. If you add 301 to it, you also get the fifth and sixth place of 03 for the month and the seventh and eighth place of 01 for the day.

In this place now the *first:* subroutine is called, which calculates the date of the first Saturday after the date stored in *t1*.

```
first:
while (fn dayow(t1)<>7)
  t1=t1+1
wend
t1$=str$(t1)
t2=fn days(t1)
return
```

### *fn dayow( <Date number> )*

This function calculates the day of the week from an eight-figure date number. The days of the week are specified as numbers, as shown in the following table.

| Weekday | Numeral |
|---|---|
| Sunday | 1 |
| Monday | 2 |
| Tuesday | 3 |
| Wednesday | 4 |
| Thursday | 5 |
| Friday | 6 |
| Saturday | 7 |

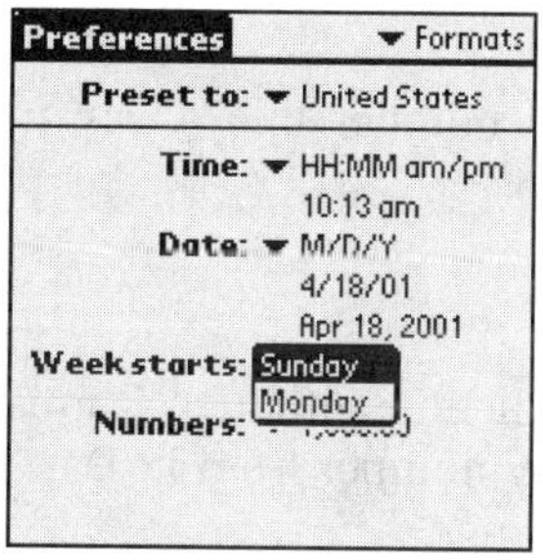


*Setting the beginning of the week for the standard Palm Date Book*

This setting has no influence on the day numbering of HotPaw Basic. If it did, programs would not run correctly on all Palms.

In the example, the program uses a *while...wend* loop to check whether the day in the *t1* variable is a Saturday. If not, the date number in *t1* is incremented by one day. This continues until the first Saturday after March 1 is located.

**Note**

**Different date formats in HotPaw Basic**

HotPaw Basic knows three different formats in which date specifications appear. The different functions for date calculation use different formats:

- **Date number** – Eight-figure number whose first four digits specify the year, the fifth and sixth digits specify the month, and the last two digits specify the day.
- **String** – Some of the functions work with the date number formatted as a string. In this case, filter out parts of the date specification using the *left$()*, *mid$()*, and *right$()* string functions.
- **Day number** – Number that specifies the number of days since January 1, 1904. The Palm Date Book begins with this day. Here, in contrast to the normal PC date book, you can process significantly older data. The absolute value of this day number is usually not important. However, with the day number, you can specify time periods of any desired length much more easily than with a date specification. If you add a specified time period in days to a date number, you can only get the correct date if it is still in the same month as the original date. You can add or subtract any value you want to/from a day number and then convert the result back to a valid date.

When the program has found the date of the first Saturday in March, it is stored as a string in the *t1$* variable and as a day number in the *t2* variable. The appointments are then calculated from the *t2* variable.

### *fn days ( <Date number> )*

This function converts an eight-figure date number into a day number since January 1, 1904.

### *fn days ( <String> )*

You can also specify a string in the same function, although it must contain an eight-figure number. You can calculate a day number from it. Day numbers are always output as numerical values, not as strings.

The first Saturday in March should also be the date for the first appointment. The program now starts the *appointment:* subroutine, which writes the appointments to the Date Book.

```
appointment:
s$(22)=mid$(t1$,5,2)
s$(23)=right$(t1$,2)
put "date",new,10
return
```

This subroutine determines the month and the day of the first appointment from the *t1$* string. The values are stored in the *s$(22)* and *s$(23)* variables. Then the *put "date",new,10* function creates a new appointment.

### *put "date"new,10*

This function writes a new appointment to the Date Book. The values for this are taken from the *s$(20) ... s$(29)* variables. The function itself does not have any variable parameters. It must appear in the program in the exact wording shown.

After this first appointment has been entered, a loop starts, which evaluates the input form:

```
for i=1 to 17 step 2
  if (val(s$(i))>0)
    for j=1 to int(4/val(s$(i)))
      t2=t2+val(s$(i))*7
      t1$=fn date$(t2)
      gosub appointment
    next j
  else
    if ((i<17)and(val(s$(i+2))>0))
      t1=val(s$(21))*10000+(i/2+3.5)*100+1
      gosub first
```

```
        gosub appointment
      endif
    endif
  next I
```

The indention makes the structure clearer.

The loop queries all the values from the input form, thus running once for each month.

First the loop queries whether the numerical value in the corresponding input field is greater than 0. This always means that a number of weeks for the appointment repetition has been entered.

If this is the case, an additional loop starts up. This loop runs as many times as the appointment is to be repeated in the month. The *int(4/val(s$(i)))* formula calculates this. With a four-week repetition, the result is 1; with a two-week repetition, the result is 2; with a one-week repetition, the result is 4. Even a three-week repetition can cause, at the most, one additional appointment in the same month, aside from the current appointment.

The date of the next appointment is precisely the number of weeks specified for this month after the last appointment and is stored again in the *t2* variable.

```
t2=t2+val(s$(i))*7
t1$=fn date$(t2)
```

The corresponding string format is determined from the calculated date and a new appointment is created with the *appointment:* subroutine.

If a 0 or nothing at all has been entered for a month, there should be no appointment in this month. The next appointment is therefore the first Saturday of the following month.

```
if ((i<17)and(val(s$(i+2))>0))
```

This query verifies that the currently calculated month is not November and that an appointment repetition is specified in the following month. If it were November or if no appointment was scheduled for the next month, then no appointment can be calculated for the first Saturday of the next month. In this case, the loop counter is merely incremented and after that the net month is checked.

```
t1=val(s$(21))*10000+(i/2+3.5)*100+1
```

This formula calculates the number of the next subsequent month and thus the day number of the first day of this month from the current loop counter, which specifies the index of the *s$()* variable.

After that the *first:* subroutine starts up again, calculating the date of the first Saturday. The *appointment:* subroutine creates an appointment on this day.

In the next picture, for example, the user is on vacation for all of August, and for this reason has not scheduled any appointments. The next appointment is automatically placed on the first Saturday in September and repeated from there in the normal manner. As a result, different data for September and October occur than in the earlier example, where appointments in August appeared.

*A month without an appointment*

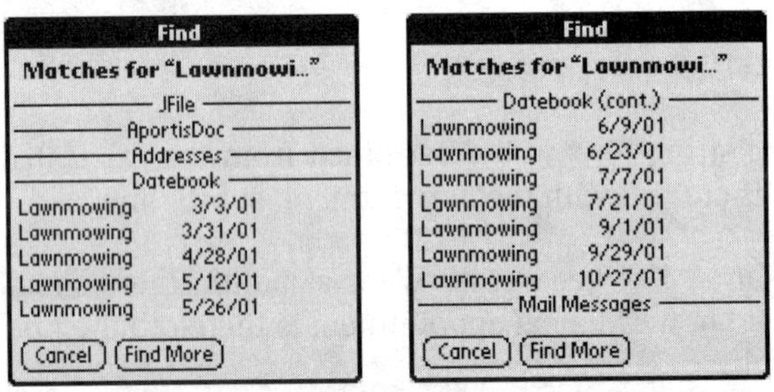


*Listing of the new appointments*

After all the appointments are created, the program displays a corresponding message and then terminates.

```
print "Appointments for "+s$(20)+" created"
end
```

You can also have the program create totally different appointments by making a small modification. To do this, change the text that is assigned to the *s$(20)* variable in the first program line.

## Overview of the date functions in HotPaw Basic

| Function | Conversion from ... | ... to |
|---|---|---|
| fn date$(0) | Current system date | String |
| fn date$(0,1) | Current system date | Date in clear text (American format) |
| fn date$( <Day number> ) | Day number | String |
| fn date$(-1) | Select date | String |
| fn days( <Date number> ) | Date number | Day number |
| fn days( <String> ) | Date number | String |
| fn dayow( <Date number> ) | Date number | Weekday |

You can convert strings to date numbers and vice versa at any time using the *val()* and *str$()* functions.

The *fn date$(-1)* function is an unusual feature among the date functions. Here the date selection appears that the Palm Date Book uses when you tap the *Go To* button for a specified date.

*Current date*

*Selection of a random date*

The date selection displays the current date in inverse video and enclosed in brackets. If you want to select a new date, select the year and the month first. When you tap a day, the date is immediately input and the date selection ends. You can always return to the current date by pressing the *Today* button.

You can see the operation of *fn date$(-1)* in the following simple program.

The program displays a date selection and then displays the date number and day number of the selected date.

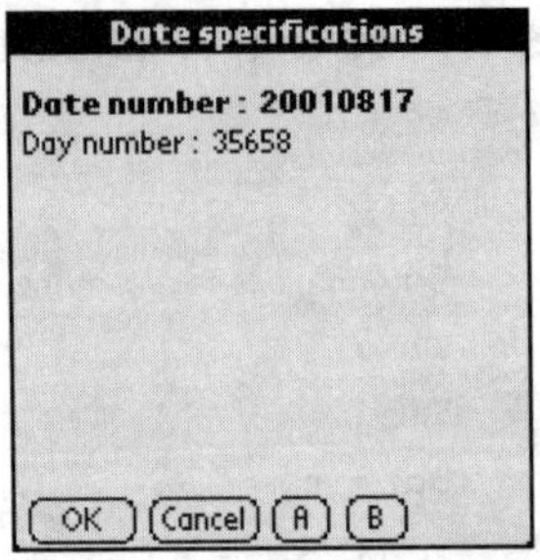


Display of the program

```
#Dateselection.bas
d$=fn date$(-1)
s$(0)="Date number :  "+d$
if (d$<>"       0")
  s$(2)="Day number :  "+str$(fn days(d$))
endif
f=form(10,2,"Date specifications")
```

**CD**

**Program on the companion CD**

You can also find this program on the companion CD to this book as *0703.bas*.

The selected date is stored as a string in the *d$* variable. If the user taps *Cancel* in the date selection, the *fn date$(-1)* function returns the “       *0*” string (seven spaces and a zero). This cannot be evaluated with *fn days()*. For this reason a query is built into the program that does not call *fn days()* in such a case.

Canceling the date selection

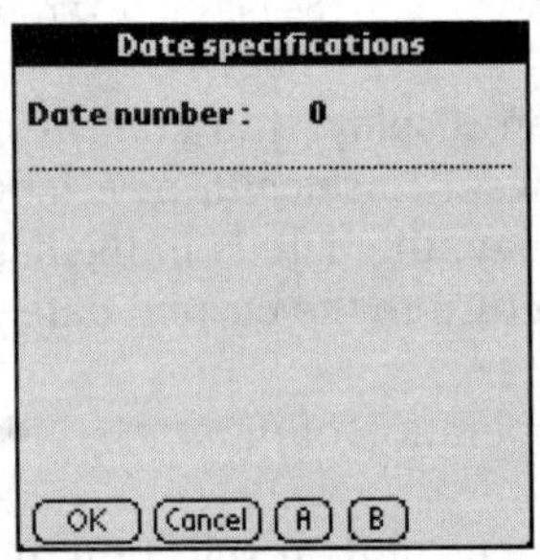


Displayed result

## Calculating Easter and other flexible holidays

The Council of Niceae (325 AD) decided that Easter would always fall on the Sunday after the first full moon of the spring. Because the number of days in a year are not an integral multiple of the duration of a revolution of the moon around the earth, Easter can occur between March 22 and April 25.

On this foundation, the mathematician Carl Friedrich Gauss developed a calculation method that is known as the Gaussian Easter formula and with which the date of Easter Sunday can be calculated until the year 2199.

Using the Gaussian formula, the next program calculates Easter Sunday in a random year between 1904 and 2031 and enters it into the Date Book as an appointment. Theoretically a calculation would also be possible for earlier or later years, but the Palm Date Book only functions in this time period.

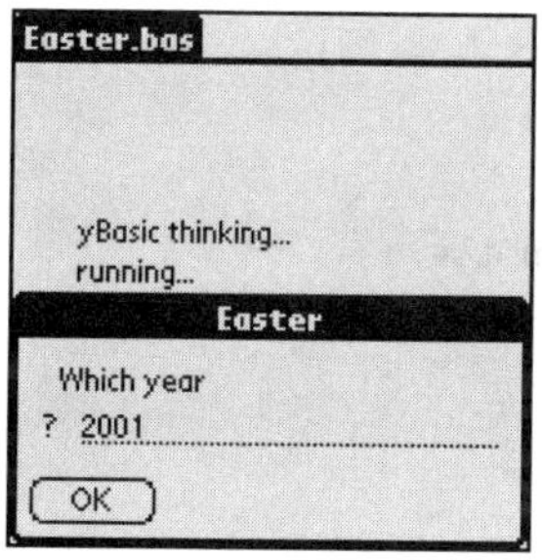


*Inputting a year number*

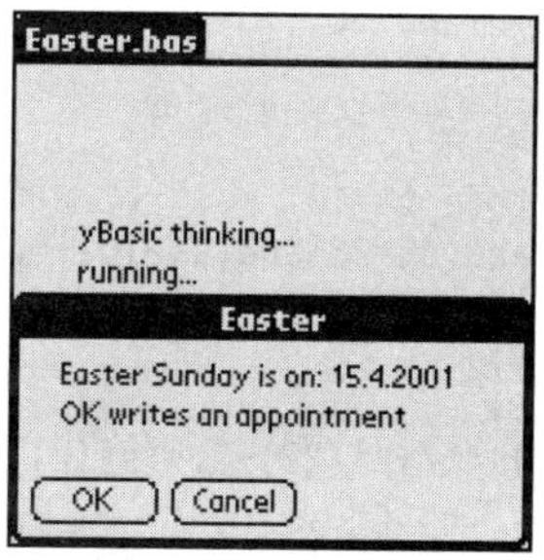


*Calculating Easter*

The user enters a year number and the program calculates the date of Easter Sunday for this year. If you tap the *OK* button, the program writes an appointment in the Date Book; if you tap *Cancel*, it won't.

*The new appointment in the Date Book*

```
#Easter.bas
t1$="Which year"
t2$="Easter Sunday is on: "
t4$=chr$(10)+"OK writes an appointment"
s$(20)="Easter Sunday"
for i=24 to 29
  s$(i)=""
next i
start:
j%=val(input$(t1$,"Easter",1))
if ((j%<1904)or(j%>2031))
  print "Year number invalid"
  goto start
endif
a%=j% mod 19
b%=j% mod 4
c%=j% mod 7
d%=(19*a%+24) mod 30
e%=(2*b%+4*c%+6*d%+5) mod 7
s$(22)="3"
t%=d%+e%+22
if (t%>31)
  t%=t%-31
  s$(22)="4"
  if (t%=26) then t%=19
  if ((t%=25)and(d%=28)and(a%>10)) then t%=18
endif
s$(23)=str$(t%)
s$(21)=str$(j%)
t3$=t2$+s$(23)+"."+s$(22)+"."+s$(21)+t4$
x%=msgbox(t3$,"Easter",2)
if (x%=1) then put "date",new,10
```

**CD**

**Program on the companion CD**

You can also find this program on the companion CD to this book as *0704.bas*. The indentation is only for readability and is not included in the original program on the CD, because it is difficult to display on memos.

At the beginning some strings for the dialog boxes are defined and the *s$(24)* ... *s$(29)* fields with the unused appointment specifications are cleared.

**Tip**

**Wordwrapping in dialog boxes**

Dialog boxes that are displayed with the *msgbox()* function can contain up to three lines of text. The individual lines are separated with the *chr$(10)* character.

```
start:
j%=val(input$(t1$,"Easter",1))
if ((j%<1904)or(j%>2031))
  print "Year number invalid"
  goto start
endif
```

The input year number is stored in the *j%* variable. If this number lies outside of the Palm Date Book's time period, a message appears and the program goes back to the input form.

With a valid year number the program calculates the date of Easter Sunday using the Gaussian Easter formula and stores it directly in the *s$(21) ... s$(23)* variables, which are later used to write the appointment.

```
t3$=t2$+s$(23)+"."+s$(22)+"."+s$(21)+t4$
x%=msgbox(t3$,"Easter",2)
if (x%=1) then put "date",new,10
```

A message is created from the date specifications, and a ready-made text displays the calculated date in a *msgbox()*. If the user taps *OK*, the *msgbox()* function returns the value 1; if the user taps *Cancel*, the function returns the value 0. If the user tapped OK, the *put "date",new,10* statement creates the appointment.

## Enhancing the program with other flexible holidays

Some of the other flexible holidays are directly dependent on Easter Sunday, while some are also calculated in a totally different manner.

| Holiday | Calculation | Possible time period |
|---|---|---|
| Easter Sunday | Gaussian Easter formula | March 22 - April 25 |
| Easter Monday | 1 day after Easter Sunday | March 23 - April 26 |
| Good Friday | 2 days before Easter Sunday | March 20 - April 23 |
| Shrove Monday | 48 days before Easter Sunday | February 3 - March 8 |

| Holiday | Calculation | Possible time period |
|---|---|---|
| Ash Wednesday | 46 days before Easter Sunday | February 5 - March 10 |
| The Ascension | 39 days after Easter Sunday | April 30 - June 3 |
| Pentecost | 49 days after Easter Sunday | May 10 - June 13 |
| Whitmonday | 50 days after Easter Sunday | May 11 - June 14 |
| Corpus Christi | 60 days after Easter Sunday | May 21 - June 24 |
| Mother's Day | Second Sunday in May | May 8 - May 14 |
| Thanksgiving | First Sunday in October | October 1 - October 7 |
| First.Advent | Sunday after November 26 (the fourth Advent falls no later than December 24) | November 27 - December 3 |
| Day of Prayer and Repentance | 11 days before First Advent | November 16 - November 22 |

In rare cases Mother's Day and Pentecost can fall on the same day. For example, this happened in 1967, 1978, and 1989, and will happen again in 2008.

| Further information about calendar and holiday calculation | |
|---|---|
| www.computus.de | The best page on the Date Book |
| www.uni-bamberg.de/~ba1lw1/fkal.html | Gaussian Easter formula and Date Book tables |
| www.salesianer.de/util/kalender.html | Date Book program for PCs and FAQ on calculations |
| members.aol.com/teuchi/news/anlass.html | Online computer for flexible holidays |

The next program example calculates different holidays and enters them into the Date Book as appointments. A further interesting aspect is the user interface, which consists of texts and control elements and does not use a ready-made HotPaw Basic form this time. This user interface can also be used for similar programs after some small adjustments.

*Holidays calculated for different years*

Enter a year number in the input field at the top and then tap the *Calculate* button. The program calculates all the holidays from the list for the specified year.

Enable the checkbox in the left column for the holidays that you want to accept as appointments in the Date Book. Now when you tap the *Enter appointments* button, the corresponding appointments are written to the Date Book.

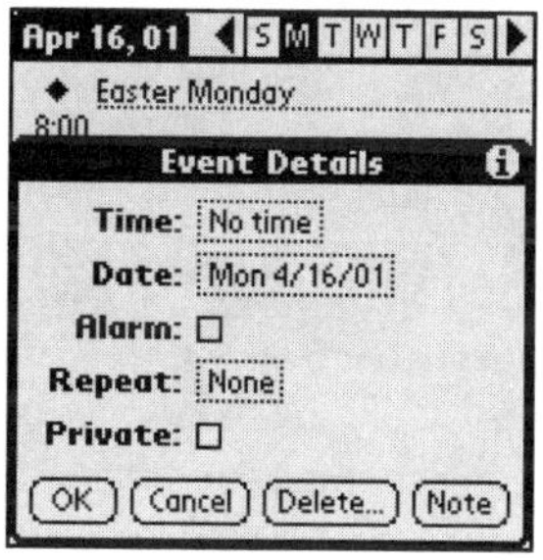


New appointment

Entered appointments in different years

```
#Holidays.bas
draw -1
form btn 100,17,55,12,"Calculate",1
form btn 60,147,95,12,"Enter appointments",1
form fld 30,15,45,12,"",1
for i=2 to 9
  form cbx 0,i*14,14,14,"",1
next i
dim f$(7),t$(7),m$(7),v%(5)
data "Easter Sunday","Easter Monday"
data "Good Friday","Ash Wednesday"
data "The Ascension","Pentecost"
data "Mother's Day","1. Advent"
data 1,-2,-46,39,49
for i=0 to 7
  read f$(i)
  draw f$(i),20,(i+2)*14+2
next i
for i=1 to 5
  read v%(i)
next i
draw "Year",0,15
for i=24 to 29
  s$(i)=""
next i

start:
x%=asc(input$(1))
```

```
if (x%=14) then gosub calculate
if (x%=15) then gosub appointments
goto start:

calculate:
j%=val(s$(0))
if ((j%<1904)or(j%>2031))
  print "Year number invalid"
  return
endif
a%=j% mod 19
b%=j% mod 4
c%=j% mod 7
d%=(19*a%+24) mod 30
e%=(2*b%+4*c%+6*d%+5) mod 7
m$(0)="03"
t%=d%+e%+22
if (t%>31)
  t%=t%-31
  m$(0)="04"
  if (t%=26) then t%=19
  if ((t%=25)and(d%=28)and(a%>10)) then t%=18
endif
t$(0)=str$(t%)
if (len(t$(0))=1) then t$(0)="0"+t$(0)
o%=fn days(s$(0)+m$(0)+t$(0))
draw t$(0)+"."+m$(0)+"."+s$(0)+"   ",110,30
for i=1 to 5
  a$=fn date$(o%+v%(i))
  t$(i)=right$(a$,2)
  m$(i)=mid$(a$,5,2)
  draw t$(i)+"."+m$(i)+"."+s$(0)+"   ",110,30+i*14
next i
z%=val(s$(0))*10000+0508
while (fn dayow(z%)<>1)
  z%=z%+1
wend
a$=str$(z%)
t$(6)=right$(a$,2)
m$(6)=mid$(a$,5,2)
draw t$(6)+"."+m$(6)+"."+s$(0)+"   ",110,114
z%=val(s$(0))*10000+1127
while (fn dayow(z%)<>1)
  z%=val(fn date$(fn days(z%)+1))
wend
a$=str$(z%)
t$(7)=right$(a$,2)
m$(7)=mid$(a$,5,2)
draw t$(7)+"."+m$(7)+"."+s$(0)+"   ",110,128
return
```

```
appointments:
for i=0 to 7
  if (s$(i+1)="1")
    s$(20)=f$(i)
    s$(21)=s$(0)
    s$(22)=m$(i)
    s$(23)=t$(i)
    put "date",new,10
  endif
next i
return
```

**CD**

**Program on the companion CD**

You can also find this program on the companion CD to this book as *0705.bas*. The indentation is only for readability and is not included in the original program on the CD, because it is difficult to display on memos.

The program is organized into four important parts:

- Initializations and construction of the user interface at the beginning.
- Main program with evaluation of the buttons, beginning at the *start:* branch mark.
- Subroutine for calculating the holidays, beginning at the *calculate:* branch mark.
- Subroutine for entering the appointments in the Date Book, beginning at the *appointments:* branch mark.

In HotPaw Basic the button definitions must always appear at the beginning of a program with a graphic user interface.

```
form btn 100,17,55,12,"Calculate",1
form btn 60,147,95,12,"Enter appointments",1
```

The first button in a program, the *Calculate* button, always returns the value *chr$(14)*, with each additional button returning one number higher. Thus the *Enter appointments* button has the return value of *chr$(15)*. These return values do not have to be specified in the button definitions.

```
form fld 30,15,45,12,"",1
for i=2 to 9
  form cbx 0,i*14,14,14,"",1
next i
```

After the buttons, the input field and the seven checkboxes are defined. The input field stores its value in the *s$(0)* variable; the checkboxes store it in the following *s$(1) ... s$(7)* variables. The allocation of these variables also occurs automatically through the order of the definitions in the program and does not need to be separately specified.

In the next step, variable fields are dimensioned and texts are input for the eight holidays to be calculated. The loop, which reads the texts from the *data* lines, also immediately writes them to the screen. These texts can be used later for the appointments.

The following variable list helps in the overview:

| Variable | Contents |
|---|---|
| a$ | String with date for intermediate calculations |
| a%, b%, c%, d%, e% | Temporary values for intermediate calculations in the Gaussian Easter formula |
| f$(0) ... f$(7) | Names of the holidays |
| i | Loop counter |
| j% | Input year number as numerical value |
| m$(0) ... m$(7) | Strings with the months of the holidays |
| o% | Day number of Easter Sunday |
| s$(0) | Input year number |
| s$(1) ... s$(8) | Return values of the checkboxes |
| s$(20) ... s$(23) | Values for writing of appointments |
| s$(24) ... s$(29) | Non-used variables for writing of appointments |
| t$(0) ... t$(7) | Strings with the days of the holidays |
| t% | Calculated day as numerical value |
| v%(0) ... v%(5) | Shift toward Easter for five holidays |
| x% | Return value of the last pressed button |
| z% | Numerical value with date for intermediate calculations |

After all the texts and form elements have been written to the screen and the variables of the *s$()* field that are not required are set to a blank string, the initialization phase is terminated and the short main program starts up.

```
start:
x%=asc(input$(1))
if (x%=14) then gosub calculate
if (x%=15) then gosub appointments
goto start:
```

This program part waits for the user to press one of the two buttons and then starts the respective subroutine. If the return value of *input$(1)* is neither *14* nor *15*, that is, neither of the two buttons, the user has written a Graffiti character or pressed a key, both of which are not supposed to have any effect on the program. The program then returns to the branch mark and waits for the next input.

If the user taps *Calculate*, a subroutine starts, which first checks the input year number to determine whether it lies within the range of validity for the Palm Date Book.

```
calculate:
j%=val(s$(0))
if ((j%<1904)or(j%>2031))
  print "Year number invalid"
  return
endif
```

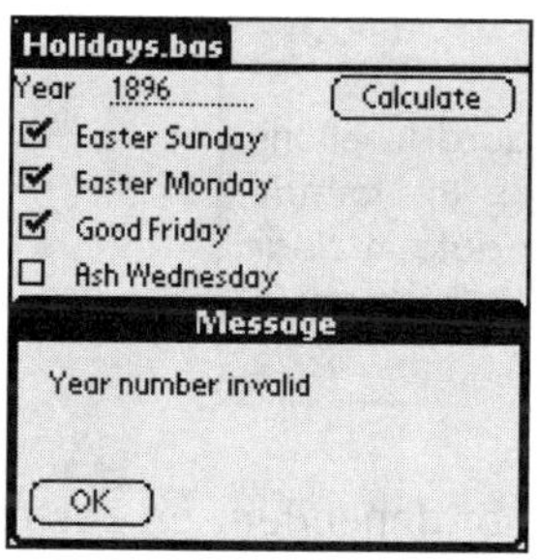


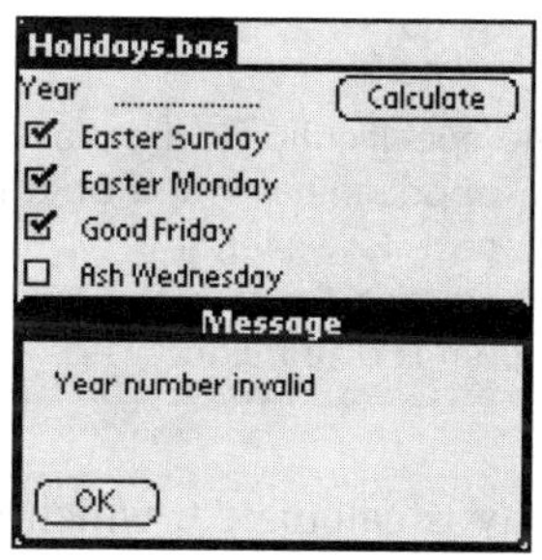


*Invalid year numbers*

If the user does not enter any year number at all, the *val()* function returns *0*, which is less than 1904; therefore, the program also recognizes this case as invalid. With an invalid input, the program outputs a message and the subroutine returns to the main program with *return*.

If the year is acknowledged as valid, the Gaussian Easter formula runs as in the last program example and determines the date of Easter Sunday.

```
o%=fn days(s$(0)+m$(0)+t$(0))
```

For the additional calculations, the *fn days()* function determines a day number from this result and stores it in the *o%* variable.

Five of the holidays to be calculated, Easter Monday, Good Friday, Ash Wednesday, The Ascension, and Pentecost, are directly dependent on Easter Sunday. Therefore, numerical values were already stored in the *v%()* variables during initialization. These values specify how many days are to be added or deducted.

The program needs the day number of Easter Sunday. The date number doesn't always give the correct result because Easter can fall on two different months.

```
for i=1 to 5
  a$=fn date$(o%+v%(i))
  t$(i)=right$(a$,2)
  m$(i)=mid$(a$,5,2)
  draw t$(i)+"."+m$(i)+"."+s$(0)+"    ",110,30+i*14
next i
```

This loop adds the corresponding values from *v%()* to the day number of Easter Sunday and then determines the date of the respective holiday with *fn date$()*.

**Tip**

**Country-specific date formats**

As long as you display date specifications with the standard functions of the Palm OS, such as an appointment in the Date Book, the formatting of the date is of no concern. However, if you write a date in clear text as a string, as you do here, use the formatting that is customary in the country where your program is distributed.

Next, Mother's Day is calculated, which is not dependent on Easter, but rather always falls on the second Sunday in May. Thus May 8 is the earliest date Mother's Day can occur.

```
z%=val(s$(0))*10000+0508
```

This line determines the date number of May 8 from the input year.

```
while (fn dayow(z%)<>1)
  z%=z%+1
wend
```

As long as *fn dayow()* does not return a value of 1, the date being used is not a Sunday. The date number is incremented by 1 until the program reaches a Sunday. This must be the second Sunday in May, which is Mother's Day.

## Adaptation to the American date format

If you want to distribute this program in America, you must assume that users will enter the birthdays in the Address Book in the American format. This concerns functionality, not just visual effects. The program must write as well as read birthdays in the correct format.

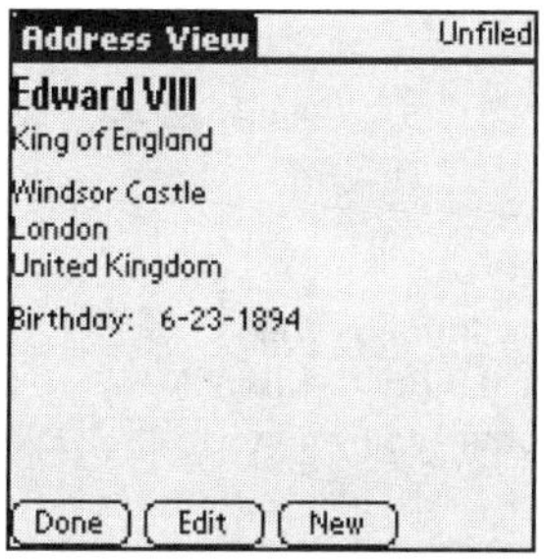


*Address with birthday in the American date format*

```
# Birthday2US.bas
while (get$("addr",n%,20)<>"error")
  if (s$(37)<>"")
    z%=instr(s$(37),"-")
    s$(22)=str$(int(val(s$(37))))
    s$(23)=str$(int(val(mid$(s$(37),z%+1))))
    s$(20)="Birthday "+s$(21)+" "+s$(20)
    s$(21)=left$(fn date$(0),4)
    for i=24 to 29
      s$(i)=""
    next i
    put "date",new,10
  endif
  n%=n%+1
wend
print "Appointments created"
```

**CD**

**Program on the companion CD**

You can also find this program on the companion CD to this book as *0710us.bas*. The indentation is only for clarity and is not included in the original program on the CD, because it is difficult to display on memos.

A total of three lines are changed:

```
z%=instr(s$(37),"-")
```

This line finds the separator between Month and Day. In American format this is a hyphen, not a period as in the German format.

```
s$(22)=str$(int(val(s$(37))))
s$(23)=str$(int(val(mid$(s$(37),z%+1))))
```

Because of the switched order of Day and Month, switch the variable numbers. Other than that, the formulas remain the same.

**Tip**

**Computing with date numbers and day numbers**

You can add and subtract days to/from date numbers as long as the result is in the same month. However, if the possibility exists that addition or subtraction can result in a date in a different month, you must use a day number for the calculation.

The date number of Mother's Day is evaluated, day and month are stored in the *t$(6)* and *m$(6)* variables, and the date is written to the screen.

```
a$=str$(z%)
t$(6)=right$(a$,2)
m$(6)=mid$(a$,5,2)
draw t$(6)+"."+m$(6)+"."+s$(0)+"    ",110,114
```

Finally, the date for the first Sunday in Advent is calculated using a similar procedure. This holiday is always on the Sunday following November 26, so the earliest possible date is November 27.

```
z%=val(s$(0))*10000+1127
```

This line determines the date number of November 27 from the input year.

A maximum of six days must be added to this November 27, something that is not possible with a date number, because the new date could be in November or in December. Therefore, this time the loop converts the date number to a day number, increments it by 1, and then converts the result back to a date number.

```
while (fn dayow(z%)<>1)
  z%=val(fn date$(fn days(z%)+1))
wend
```

After that the variables are stored according to the same scheme, as with the other holidays, and the date is written to the screen.

```
a$=str$(z%)
t$(7)=right$(a$,2)
m$(7)=mid$(a$,5,2)
draw t$(7)+"."+m$(7)+"."+s$(0)+"    ",110,128
```

This concludes the calculation of the holidays. The subroutine returns to the main program with *return* and waits for the user to tap the *Enter appointments* button or specify a new year number for calculation.

If the user taps *Enter appointments,* the other subroutine is started.

```
appointments:
for i=0 to 7
  if (s$(i+1)="1")
    s$(20)=f$(i)
    s$(21)=s$(0)
    s$(22)=m$(i)
    s$(23)=t$(i)
    put "date",new,10
  endif
next i
return
```

A loop runs through the eight holidays and verifies whether the respective checkbox is enabled. The checkboxes use the *s$(1) ... s$(8)* variables, because the *s$(0)* variable is already allocated for the input field with the year number.

If a checkbox is enabled, the *s$(20) ... s$(23)* variables are created from those of the appointment, filled with the corresponding values, and the appointment is written.

## Automatically deleting appointments

If you want to try out this program, create the appointments in a year from the past. The Palm Date Book offers an easy option for automatically deleting older appointments.

Entry/Delete in the Date Book menu

*Time frame of the entries to be deleted*

Select *Entry/Delete* in the menu of the Date Book and then create settings determining the time when all entries are to be removed from the Date Book. Unfortunately, no option is offered for setting the limit to longer than one month in the Palm Date Book.

Visor users are at an advantage. In *Date Book+* on the Visor you can specify any date. All entries prior to this date can then be deleted.

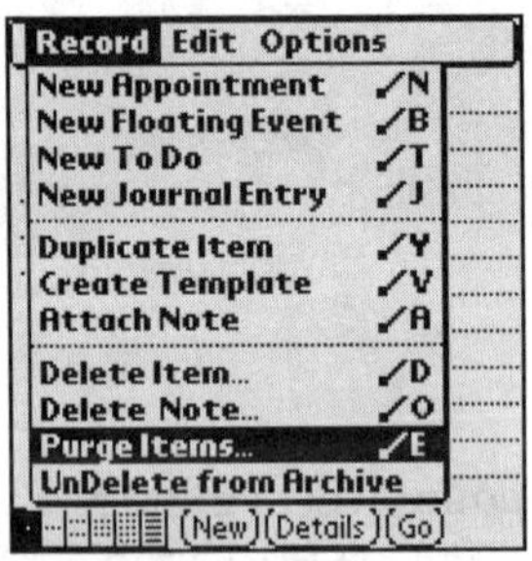


*Entry/Delete entries in the Date Book menu on the Visor*

*Setting the entries to be deleted - specify the date in the upper right corner*

In this way you can try out holidays in years in which you definitely have not entered any other appointments.

## Customizing the program for international use

When you write a program that is intended for use beyond the borders of your country, be sure to customize the date and time specifications to the formats typical of the respective target countries.

The Palm OS offers seven different date formats in the *Preferences* program alone:

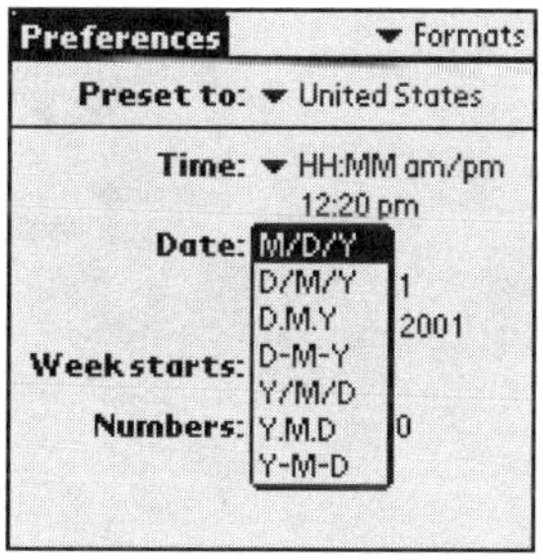


*Preferences for the date format*

Unfortunately, you cannot directly retrieve these formats from HotPaw Basic and incorporate them into your own programs. The programs must be specially programmed for the appropriate date format.

The following listing shows the program described earlier in a version for the American date format. The specifications appear in the order of month, day, year with hyphens in between.

```
# Holidays_US.bas
draw -1
form btn 100,17,55,12,"Calculate",1
form btn 60,147,95,12,"Enter appointments",1
form fld 30,15,45,12,"",1
for i=2 to 9
  form cbx 0,i*14,14,14,"",1
next i
dim f$(7),t$(7),m$(7),v%(5)
data "Easter Sunday","Easter Monday"
data "Good Friday","Ash Wednesday"
data "The Ascension","Pentecost"
data "Mother's Day","Advent"
data 1,-2,-46,39,49
for i=0 to 7
  read f$(i)
  draw f$(i),20,(i+2)*14+2
next i
for i=1 to 5
  read v%(i)
next i
draw "Year",0,15
for i=24 to 29
  s$(i)=""
next i
```

```
start:
x%=asc(input$(1))
if (x%=14) then gosub calculate
if (x%=15) then gosub appointments
goto start:

calculate:
j%=val(s$(0))
if ((j%<1904)or(j%>2031))
  print "Year number invalid"
  return
endif
a%=j% mod 19
b%=j% mod 4
c%=j% mod 7
d%=(19*a%+24) mod 30
e%=(2*b%+4*c%+6*d%+5) mod 7
m$(0)="03"
t%=d%+e%+22
if (t%>31)
  t%=t%-31
  m$(0)="04"
  if (t%=26) then t%=19
  if ((t%=25)and(d%=28)and(a%>10)) then t%=18
endif
t$(0)=str$(t%)
if (len(t$(0))=1) then t$(0)="0"+t$(0)
o%=fn days(s$(0)+m$(0)+t$(0))
draw m$(0)+"-"+t$(0)+"-"+s$(0)+"   ",110,30
for i=1 to 5
  a$=fn date$(o%+v%(i))
  t$(i)=right$(a$,2)
  m$(i)=mid$(a$,5,2)
  draw m$(i)+"-"+t$(i)+"-"+s$(0)+"   ",110,30+i*14
next i
z%=val(s$(0))*10000+0508
while (fn dayow(z%)<>1)
  z%=z%+1
wend
a$=str$(z%)
t$(6)=right$(a$,2)
m$(6)=mid$(a$,5,2)
draw m$(6)+"-"+t$(6)+"-"+s$(0)+"   ",110,114
z%=val(s$(0))*10000+1127
while (fn dayow(z%)<>1)
  z%=val(fn date$(fn days(z%)+1))
wend
a$=str$(z%)
t$(7)=right$(a$,2)
```

```
m$(7)=mid$(a$,5,2)
draw m$(7)+"-"+t$(7)+"-"+s$(0)+"   ",110,128
return

appointments:
for i=0 to 7
  if (s$(i+1)="1")
    s$(20)=f$(i)
    s$(21)=s$(0)
    s$(22)=m$(i)
    s$(23)=t$(i)
    put "date",new,10
  endif
next i
return
```

**CD**

**Program on the companion CD**

You can also find this program on the companion CD to this book as *0705us.bas*. The indentation is only for readability and is not included in the original program on the CD, because it is difficult to display on memos.

The differences are in the places where a calculated date is written to the screen. For example:

```
draw m$(i)+"-"+t$(i)+"-"+s$(0)+"   ",110,30+i*14
```

The order of the variables is switched so that the month comes before the day. In addition, hyphens are used between the variables instead of periods.

*Calculating holidays with the American date format*

# Outputting birthdays from the Date Book to a memo

Many people store birthdays in the Date Book, which is really quite practical. There's one drawback: Usually you don't see the birthdays until right before they occur. An overview page would be more practical. The only thing is, you don't want to go to the trouble of entering all the birthdays on a memo a second time.

The next program reads birthdays from the Date Book and writes them to a memo. In addition, the program shows you how to find appointments in the Date Book and how to write memos, which up to now you have been reading.

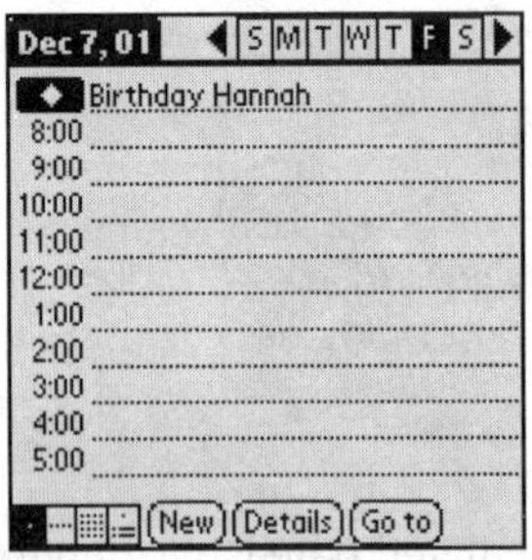


*Birthday entry in the Date Book*

The program assumes that birthdays are entered as appointments, as shown in the figure. The word "Birthday" comes first, followed by the person's name. If you have entered the birthdays in a different format in your Date Book, you can easily make the necessary modifications to the program.

If you use the Find function to search for the word *Birthday,* it displays all the birthday appointments. However, exporting this list can be difficult.

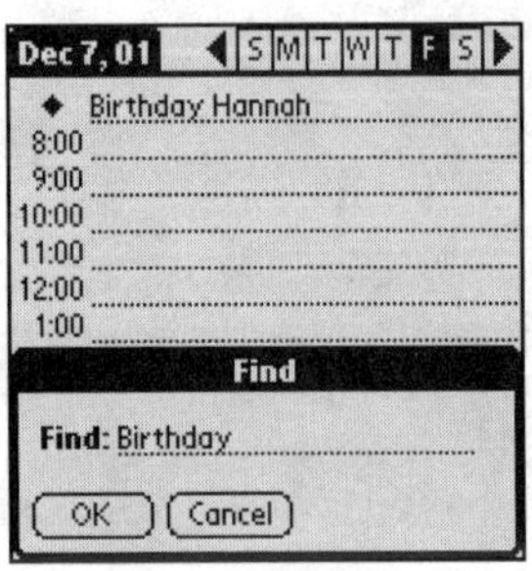


*Searching for "Birthday"*

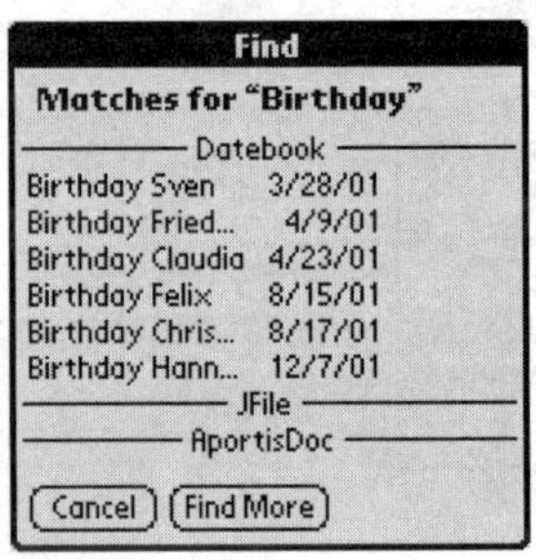


*Search results*

The program proceeds in a similar manner. It finds all the appointments that start with the word "Birthday" and then writes them to a memo, where they are permanently available.

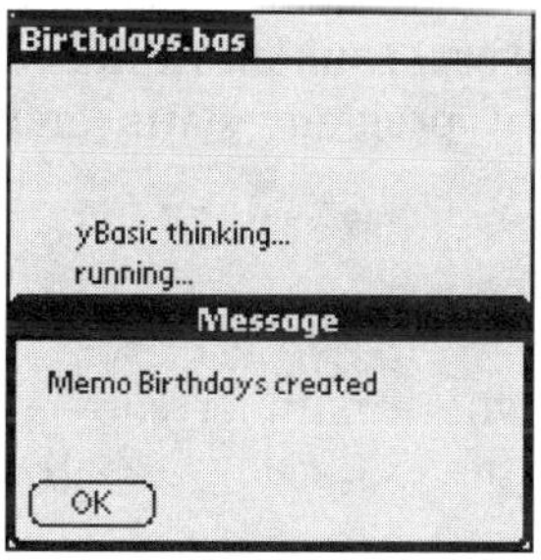


*Message at the end of the program*

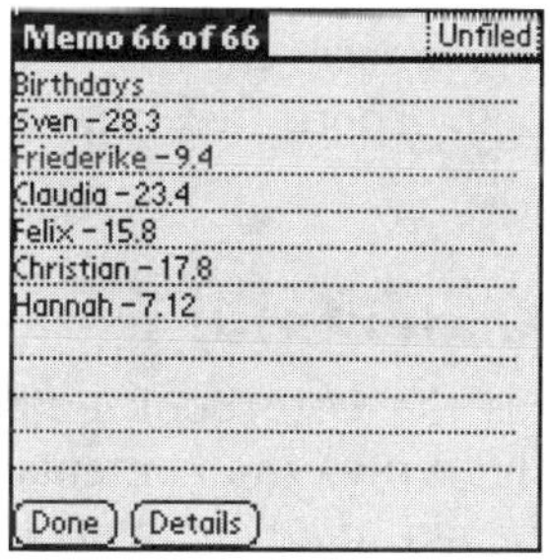


*The new memo*

The program does not need a user interface. When you start it up, it automatically searches the Date Book for birthdays and creates the memo. After that a message appears, stating that the work is completed.

```
#Birthdays.bas
open new "memo","Birthdays" as #4
n%=0
while (get$("date",n%,10)<>"error")
  if (left$(s$(20),8)="Birthday")
    print #4,mid$(s$(20),10)+" - "+s$(23)+"."+s$(22)
  endif
  n%=n%+1
wend
close #4
print "Memo Birthdays created"
```

**CD**

**Program on the companion CD**

You can also find this program on the companion CD to this book as *0706.bas*. The indentation is only for readability and is not included in the original program on the CD, because it is difficult to display on memos.

First the program has to create a new memo and open it for write access.

### *open new "memo", <Title> as #4*

The title line of the new memo must be specified in the *Title* parameter.

The appointments in the Date Book are numbered in chronological order, starting with 0. The program uses the *n%* variable as a counter. At the beginning this counter is set to 0. Thereafter, the actual program starts and runs in a *while...wend* loop.

### *get$("date", <Index>, 10)*

This function reads the Date Book entry, whose number corresponds to the specified index, and writes the contents to the *s$(20) ... s$(29)* variables, as they are used by the *put "date"* statement.

If this function does not find an appointment with the corresponding index number, it returns the *"error"* string. This terminates the *while...wend* loop in the program.

```
if (left$(s$(20),10)="Birthday")
```

The program checks the read appointment to determine whether the title begins with the word "Birthday". If this is the case, a new line is written to the

```
print #4,mid$(s$(20),12)+" - "+s$(23)+"."+s$(22)
```

This line contains the name of the person from the title of the appointment without the word "Birthday" as well as the day and month from the *s$(23)* and *s$(22)* variables.

**Tip**

**String processing with mid$()**

Usually you use the *mid$()* function to read a specific part of a string, whereby you specify the position of the first character and the length of the part to be read - *mid$(<String>,<Position>,<Length>)*. If you omit the *<Length>* parameter, you can use it to read the entire remainder of a string beginning at the specified position - *mid$(<String>,<Position>)*. In contrast to the *right$()* function, you do not have to know the length of the string, nor do you have to know how many characters the remaining part contains.

### *print #4, <String>*

Writes a string as a new line to a memo opened for write access. Each *print* statement creates a new line, to avoid concern about the line breaks.

If the read appointment does not start with the word "Birthday", nothing is written to the memo.

In each case the *n%* index counter is incremented by 1. After that the loop verifies the next Date Book entry.

When the program reaches the end of the database containing the Date Book entries, the *get$("date"...)* statement returns the *"error"* string and the loop is terminated.

The program closes the memo and outputs a message to this effect.

### *close #4*

Closes an opened memo. Remember to close all the files you open. Otherwise, you would be wasting memory and other applications may not be able to access the corresponding files or memos properly.

**Tip**

**Adapting to the American Date format**

To adapt this program to the American date format, all you need to do is change a single line, namely the one in which the date is written to the memo:

```
print #4,mid$(s$(20),12)+" - "+s$(22)+"-"+s$(23)
```

# 7.2 Working with the To Do List

The To Do List is an important tool that can help you plan your time. That way important activities are not forgotten.

To Do List items are managed internally in a database similar to the one used for appointments. However, a few differences occur:

- To Do List items can have priorities and categories, which is not possible with Date Book. In addition, you can create To Do list items without a due date.
- Date Book entries always have an appointment and can also have a time, an alarm, and a repetition. This is not possible with To Do List items.

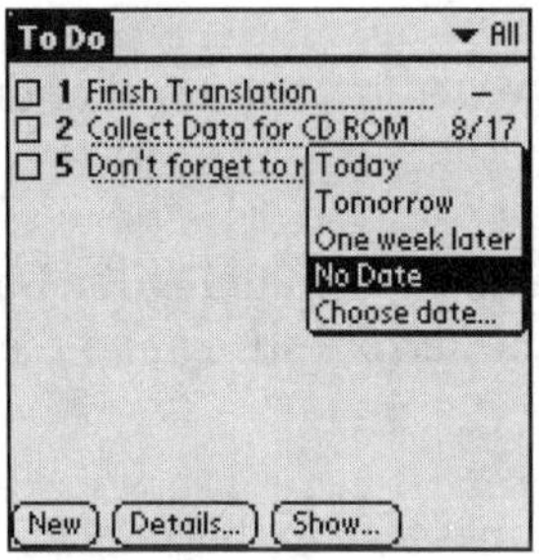


*To Do List with date selection*

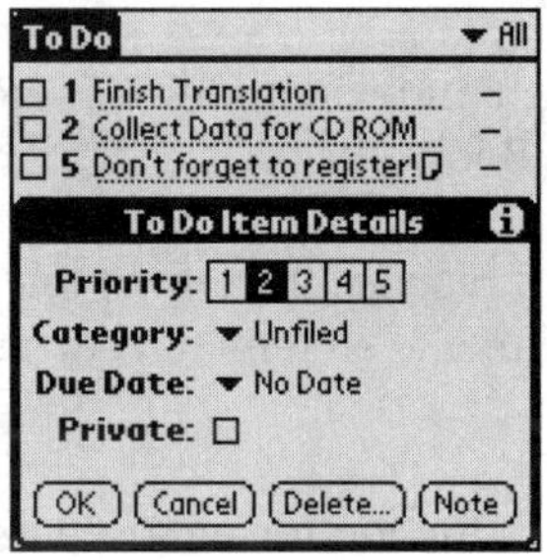


*To Do List item details*

One of the innovations in the Palm OS 3.5 is that the To Do List items display on a screen page together with the appointments of the current day.

*Displaying To Do List items in the Date Book of Palm OS 3.5*

**Tip**

### Date Book+ on the Visor

Date Book+ on the Visor manages To Do List items like appointments and offers five different types of appointments: *Running event, To Do List item, Day journal, Template* and *Appointment.* They all appear in the Date Book so that you can assign a different function to the To Do List button on the Visor.

HotPaw Basic offers various functions for accessing the To Do List to find, read, and create To Do List items. The following example programs show you how to work with the To Do List in HotPaw Basic.

## To Do List items for remembering holidays

Big holidays usually arrive unexpectedly. Even if they are familiar holidays such as Christmas or Easter, you often wind up preparing at the very last minute. It's even worse with birthdays, wedding days, and similar festive affairs that the advertising world does not bring to our attention.

The next program automatically creates To Do List items in the To Do List that come due a couple of days before such festive occasions. The program not only shows you how to create To Do List items but also the possibilities for combining the Date Book and To Do List.

The program uses a custom interface in which default values are also already entered, not a standard form from HotPaw Basic as a user interface.

*Start setting of the program*

*Changed specifications*

The program shows a form with three columns. Enter the name of a holiday in the large column on the right. In the column next to it on the left, enter how many days before you want to set the due date of the To Do List item. In the checkboxes all the way to the left, determine which of the listed holidays you want to create as To Do List items.

Set the priority for the new To Do List items in the list field in the upper right. The holidays can be entered manually as appointments in the Date Book or by using the holiday program described earlier in this chapter. The only deciding factor is that the appointment terminology read the same as specified in this program.

Three holidays are already entered by default. However, you can also change them whenever you want.

When you tap the *Enter To Do List items* button, wait a few seconds while the many appointments in the Date Book process. Then a message appears, stating that the new To Do List items have been created.

Message upon completion

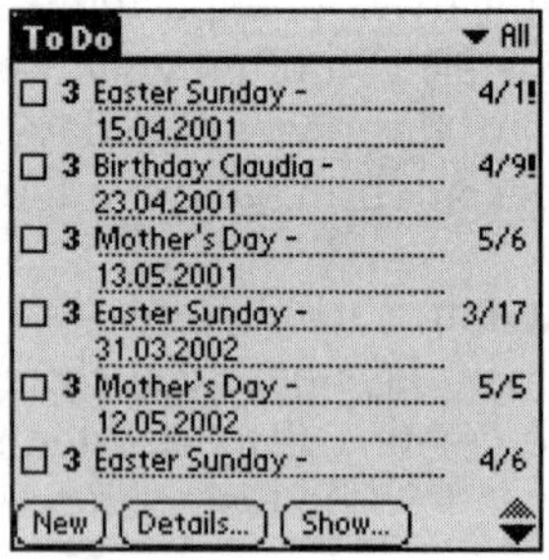


The new To Do List items

Use the *Display* button in the To Do List to switch on the *Show Due Date* option so that the due dates are included in the display.

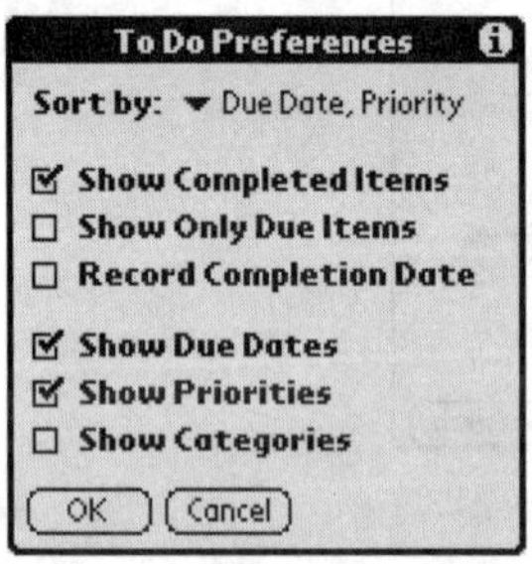


*To Do List settings*

Thereafter, To Do List items with an expired due date appear with an exclamation point after the date.

```
#Reminder.bas
draw -1
form btn 60,147,95,12,"Make To Do List items",1
data "14", "Christmas"
data "14","Easter Sunday"
data "7","Mother's Day"
data "","","","","",""
dim a$(5)
for i=0 to 5
```

```
.

  a$(i)=str$(i)
  read s$(3*i+1)
  read s$(3*i+2)
  form cbx 0,i*14+45,14,14,"",1
  form fld 15,i*14+45,20,12,s$(3*i+1),1
  form fld 38,i*14+45,120,12,s$(3*i+2),1
next i
form lst 130,30,5,3,a$,1
draw "Reminders about holidays",0,15
draw "Days   Holiday   Prio.:",15,30,1
for i=20 to 29
  s$(i)=""
next i

start:
x%=asc(input$(1))
if (x%=14) then gosub todolistitems
goto start

todolistitems:
draw "Please wait...",0,130
for i=2 to 17 step 3
  if (s$(i-2)="1")
    n=1
    while (get$("date",n,10)<>"error")
      if (s$(20)=s$(i))
        if (len(s$(22))=1) then s$(22)="0"+s$(22)
        if (len(s$(23))=1) then s$(23)="0"+s$(23)
        s$(20)=s$(20)+" - "+s$(23)+"."+s$(22)+"."+s$(21)
        d%=fn days(s$(21)+s$(22)+s$(23))
        d$=fn date$(d%-val(s$(i-1)))
        s$(21)=left$(d$,4)
        s$(22)=mid$(d$,5,2)
        s$(23)=right$(d$,2)
        s$(24)=s$(18)
        put "todo",new,10
      endif
      n=n+1
    wend
  endif
next i
draw "                                    ",0,130
print "To Do List items created"
return
```

CD

**Program on the companion CD**

You can also find this program on the companion CD to this book as *0707.bas*. The indentation is only for readability and is not included in the original program on the CD, because it is difficult to display on memos.

Because button definitions in HotPaw Basic programs must always appear at the beginning, the only button is defined at the beginning of the program.

After that a loop generates the checkboxes and text input fields line by line.

```
for i=0 to 5
  a$(i)=str$(i)
  read s$(3*i+1)
  read s$(3*i+2)
  form cbx 0,i*14+45,14,14,"",1
  form fld 15,i*14+45,20,12,s$(3*i+1),1
  form fld 38,i*14+45,120,12,s$(3*i+2),1
next i
```

The six checkboxes and twelve text input fields use the *s$(0) ... s$(17)* variables. In this order of object generation, a checkbox, a time specification, and a holiday label always follow each other. The entire operation repeats itself six times.

The loop also inputs the default values for the text input fields from the *data* lines.

| Use of the s$() variables in the program | |
|---|---|
| s$(0) | Return value 1st checkbox |
| s$(1) | 1st time specification (Default value 14) |
| s$(2) | 1st holiday label (Default value "Christmas") |
| s$(3) | Return value 2nd checkbox |
| s$(4) | 2nd time specification (Default value 14) |
| s$(5) | 2nd holiday label (Default value "Easter Sunday") |
| s$(6) | Return value 3rd checkbox |
| s$(7) | 3rd time specification (Default value 7) |
| s$(8) | 3rd holiday label (Default value "Mother's Day") |
| s$(9) | Return value 4th checkbox |

| Use of the s$() variables in the program | |
|---|---|
| s$(10) | 4th time specification |
| s$(11) | 4th holiday label |
| s$(12) | Return value 5th checkbox |
| s$(13) | 5th time specification |
| s$(14) | 5th holiday label |
| s$(15) | Return value 6th checkbox |
| s$(16) | 6th time specification |
| s$(17) | 6th holiday label |
| s$(18) | Return value of the Priority list field |
| s$(19) | - not used - |
| s$(20) | Title of appointment and To Do List item |
| s$(21) | Year |
| s$(22) | Month |
| s$(23) | Day |
| s$(24) | Priority |
| s$(25) | - not used - |
| s$(26) | - not used - |
| s$(27) | - not used - |
| s$(28) | - not used - |
| s$(29) | - not used - |

The *a$()* variable field is used for the list field with the five categories. Although it has nothing to do with the input fields, the program creates it to save an additional loop. At the end of the loop, the program generates this selection list.

```
form lst 130,30,5,3,a$,1
```

After that the texts must still be written to the screen, which cannot happen in HotPaw Basic until all of the form elements have been created. The *s$(20) ... s$(29)* variables are also deleted, to avoid writing incorrect values to the To Do List items, in case some data remains in the memory.

```
start:
x%=asc(input$(1))
if (x%=14) then gosub to do list items
goto start
```

This part of the program waits for the user to tap the *Enter To Do List items* button and then starts a subroutine. If the return value of *input$(1)* is not *14*, that is, not the button, the user has written a Graffiti character or pressed a key, neither of which has any effect on the program. Thus the program returns to the *start:* branch mark and waits for the next input.

The subroutine first displays a "Please wait ..." message in the lower screen area, because the calculation of the To Do List items can take some time when the volume of appointments is high.

```
draw "Please wait...",0,130
```

**Tip**

**Announce waiting times**

Users expect a response when they tap a button. If this triggers a calculation that takes a long time, you should display some kind of notice. Even a couple of seconds seem like a long wait to the user who doesn't know whether something is happening or whether the program didn't even register the button click.

A loop queries all the input fields with holiday labels, one after the other.

```
for i=2 to 17 step 3
...
next i
```

The loop counter was selected in such a way that it encounters precisely the index numbers of the holiday labels in the *s$()* variable field.

For such a holiday, the loop first queries whether its checkbox is enabled.

```
if (s$(i-2)="1")
...
endif
```

If not, the program doesn't need to do anything more and can continue immediately with the next holiday.

After that an *n* index value is set to 1 and a *while...wend* loop searches the entire Date Book database, whereby the index value is incremented by 1 every time.

```
n=1
while (get$("date",n,10)<>"error")
  ...
  n=n+1
wend
```

As long as the return value of *get$("date",n,10)* is not *"error"*, an appointment has been found The program checks whether the title of the appointment in *s$(20)* corresponds to the holiday in the respective input field *s$(i)*.

```
if (s$(20)=s$(i))
...
endif
```

If this is the case, an appointment has been found for which a To Do List item has to be created as a reminder.

Because date functions are used in the calculation on the basis of strings, the date must be in precise eight-figure display. If the values read from the appointment for month or day are only single figure, a *0* must be placed in front.

```
if (len(s$(22))=1) then s$(22)="0"+s$(22)
if (len(s$(23))=1) then s$(23)="0"+s$(23)
s$(20)=s$(20)+" - "+s$(23)+"."+s$(22)+"."+s$(21)
```

Then the title of the new To Do List item is generated in the *s$(20)* variable. It contains the label of the appointment and the date of this appointment as a reminder. The due date of the To Do List item is a few days earlier. This date must now be calculated.

```
d%=fn days(s$(21)+s$(22)+s$(23))
```

In the *d%* variable a day number is determined from the values of the input appointment. Using such day numbers the shifts can now be calculated by a specified number of days.

```
d$=fn date$(d%-val(s$(i-1)))
```

The numerical value of the corresponding input field is deducted from the calculated day number. This input field specifies the time duration of how long the To Do List item must be due. The *fn date$()* function calculates a string with the date.

String functions then determine the three variables in which the year, month, and day are passed to the To Do List item.

```
s$(21)=left$(d$,4)
s$(22)=mid$(d$,5,2)
s$(23)=right$(d$,2)
```

The priority is in the To Do List item definition in the *s$(24)* variable. It is read from the return value of the *s$(18)* selection list.

```
s$(24)=s$(18)
```

After that the *put* statement writes a new To Do List item.

```
put "todo",new,10
```

The writing of To Do List items proceeds in similar fashion to the writing of appointments. The necessary values must also appear in the *s$(20) ... s$(29)* variables.

### *put "todo",new,10*

This statement creates a new To Do List item. The contents of the *s$(20) ... s$(29)* variables are used in accordance with the table.

| Variable | Contents |
|---|---|
| s$(20) | Title |
| s$(21) | Year (blank if no due date) |
| s$(22) | Month |
| s$(23) | Day |
| s$(24) | Priority |
| s$(25) | Done |
| s$(26) | Category number |
| s$(27) | Category name |
| s$(28) | - not used - |
| s$(29) | The first 63 characters of a note about this To Do List item |

After all the To Do List items have been written, the program deletes the "Please wait ..." text by overwriting it with spaces and displays a "To Do List items created" message.

```
draw "                                  ",0,130
print "To Do List items created"
```

Then the subroutine returns to the main program.

If you run the program on Visor, the newly created To Do List items appear both in the To Do List and in the Date Book.

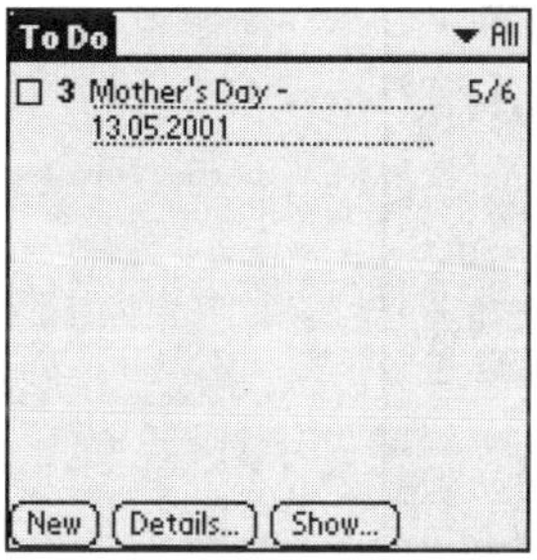


New To Do List item in the To Do List

New To Do List item in the Date Book+ on the Visor

**Tip**

**Adapting to the American date format**

If you want to use this program with the American date format, you can accept all of the calculations as they are. The allocation of the *s$(21) ... s$(23)* variables for Year, Month, and Day are independent from the date display. Only one line has to be changed, namely the one that writes the To Do List item text. At the end of this line a date specification appears in clear text.

```
s$(20)=s$(20)+" - "+s$(22)+"-"+s$(23)+"-"+s$(21)
```

## Checklist for regular To Do List items

The normal To Do List on the Palm does not have a feature for automatically repeating To Do List items or even for creating just a copy of a To Do List item. You must manually recreate regular To Do List items each time.

On the Visor, where To Do List items are treated like appointments, you won't have this problem. Thus Visor users could theoretically skip the following example. However, take a look at the next example anyway, because you can find methods for retrieving To Do List items and browsing the To Do List item database.

The next program retrieves the To Do List. Then you can specify for each To Do List item how often and in which intervals the To Do List item is to be automatically repeated. The program offers two input fields for each To Do List item, in which you can enter the duration until the next repetition, as well as the number of repetitions. Then check those To Do List items in the first column that are to be repeated.

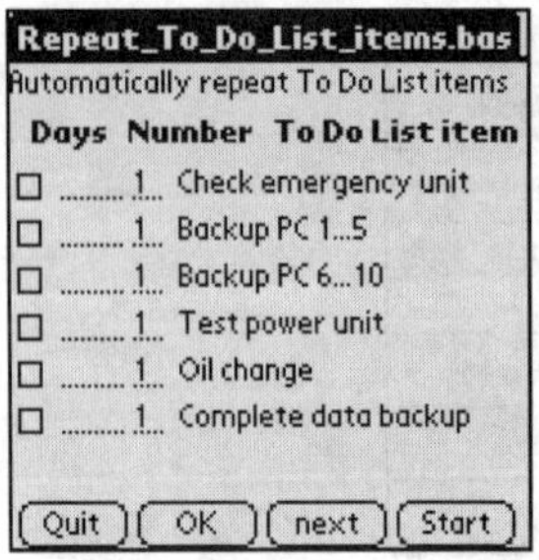


*The program retrieves the To Do List*

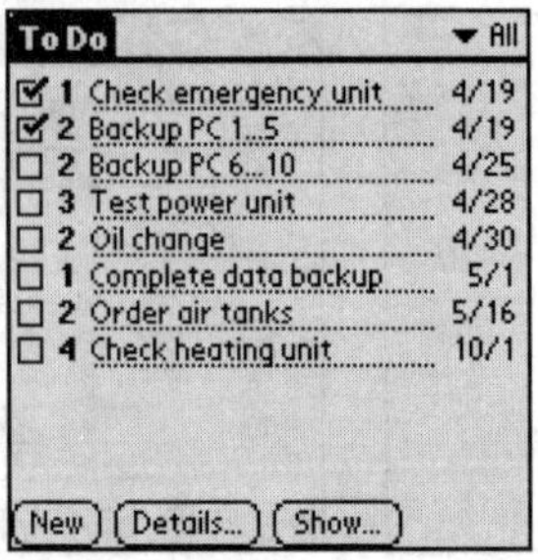


*Normal display of the To Do List prior to program startup*

Clicking *OK* creates a new To Do List item for each repetition.

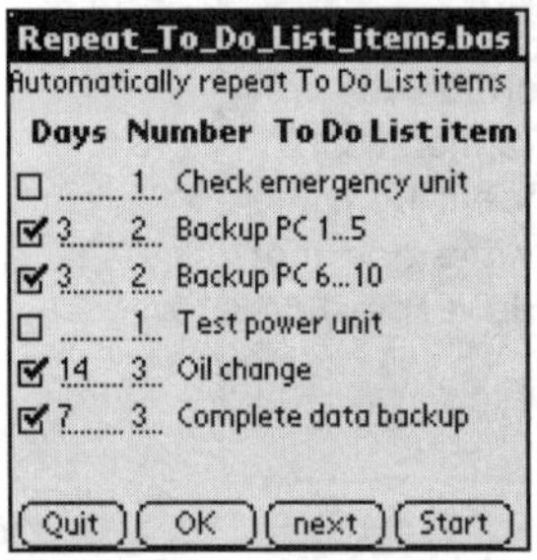


*Setting the repetitions*

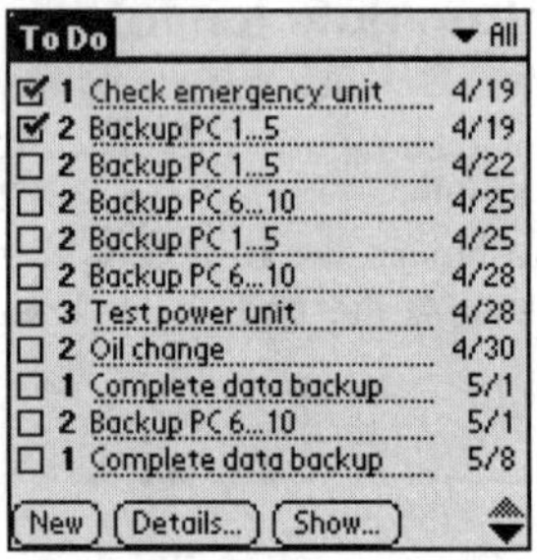


*The To Do List with the new To Do List items*

If the To Do List contains more than six displayed To Do List items, you can have an additional page with To Do List items displayed by using the *next* button. The *Start* button sets the display back to the beginning of the To Do List.

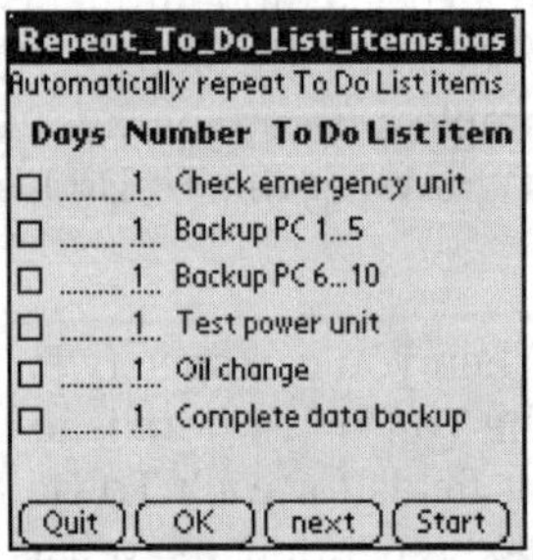


*First part of the To Do List*

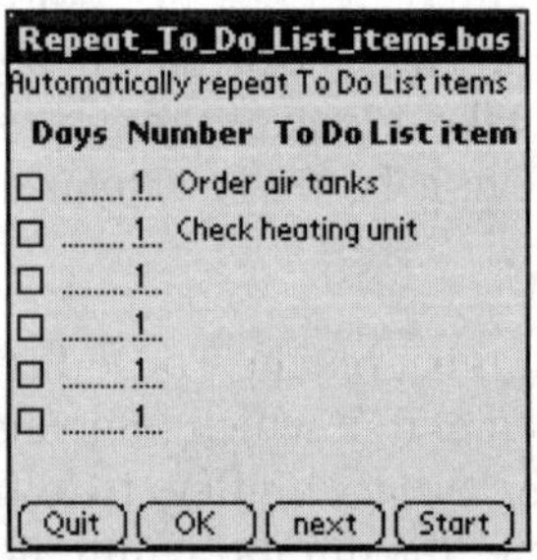


*Second part of the To Do List*

```
#Repeat_To_Do_List_items.bas
draw -1
form btn 40,147,35,12,"OK",1
form btn 80,147,35,12,"next",1
form btn 120,147,35,12,"Start",1
for i=0 to 5
  form cbx 0,i*14+45,14,14,"",1
  form fld 15,i*14+45,20,12,"",1
  form fld 38,i*14+45,10,12,"1",1
  s$(i+2)="1"
next i
dim t$(5)
draw "Automatically repeat To Do List items",0,15
draw "Days   Number   To Do List item",7,30,1
for i=20 to 29
  s$(i)=""
next i
n=0
gosub readIn

start:
x%=asc(input$(1))
if (x%=14) then gosub todolistitems
if (x%=15) then gosub readIn
if (x%=16) then n=0:gosub readIn
goto start

readIn:
for m=0 to 5
  draw "
",52,m*14+45
next m
m=0
while ((get$("todo",n,10)<>"error")and(m<6))
  t$(m)=s$(20)
  draw t$(m),52,m*14+45
  n=n+1:m=m+1
wend
return

todolistitems:
draw "Please wait...",0,130
for i=0 to 5
  if (s$(i*3)="1")
    a=find("todo",t$(i),0)
    get$("todo",a,10)
    if (len(s$(22))=1) then s$(22)="0"+s$(22)
    if (len(s$(23))=1) then s$(23)="0"+s$(23)
    d%=fn days(s$(21)+s$(22)+s$(23))
```

```
      for j=1 to val(s$(i*3+2))
        d$=fn date$(d%+j*val(s$(i*3+1)))
        s$(21)=left$(d$,4)
        s$(22)=mid$(d$,5,2)
        s$(23)=right$(d$,2)
        s$(25)="0"
        put "todo",new,10
      next j
    endif
  next i
  draw "                                    ",0,130
  print "To Do List items created"
  return
```

**CD**

**Program on the companion CD**

You can also find this program on the companion CD to this book as *0708.bas*. The indentation is only for readability and is not included in the original program on the CD, because it is difficult to display on memos.

At the beginning, the program defines the three buttons and then defines the checkboxes and input fields in a loop line by line. A default value of *1* is set in the input fields for the number of repetitions. This value must be written simultaneously to the corresponding *s$()* variables.

**Tip**

**Initializing the input fields**

The values of the *s$()* variable are not automatically assumed in the definition of an input field in HotPaw Basic. You must define the same value twice for the variable and the default value of the input field. Also, no possibility for entering a value in an input field occurs later in the program. They can only be retrieved.

Then a variable field is dimensioned, in which later the To Do List item texts are placed in temporary storage for display purposes.

```
dim t$(5)
```

After the texts are written to the screen and the *s$(20) ... s$(29)* variables are deleted, the program calls the *readIn* subroutine for the first time. It reads the first six To Do List items and displays them on the screen.

```
readIn:
for m=0 to 5
  draw "
",52,m*14+45
next m
m=0
while ((get$("todo",n,10)<>"error")and(m<6))
  t$(m)=s$(20)
  draw t$(m),52,m*14+45
  n=n+1:m=m+1
wend
return
```

The lines in which the To Do List items are displayed are first filled with a long sequence of spaces. This allows To Do List items with shorter texts to display without error in places where previous To Do List items appeared with longer texts. In the first cycle this is unimportant, because as yet no texts appear in the lines.

A *while...wend* loop now reads up to six To Do List items, but in any case runs only as long as the *get$ ("todo",n,10)* statement does not report an error, thus while To Do List items continue to appear in the list.

### get$("todo", <Index> ,10)

This statement reads the To Do List item with the *Index* number from the To Do List. All To Do List items are numbered consecutively. If *get$("todo"...)* does not find a To Do List item with the corresponding number, the *"error"* string is returned.

**Note**

**Numbering of To Do List items**

The To Do List items are numbered in consecutive order. If new To Do List items are inserted or if To Do List items are deleted, the number of all the To Do List items can change. You cannot permanently identify a To Do List item on the basis of its number. For this reason, always search for To Do List items by their label in the list.

The various data of the read To Do List item are written to the *s$(20) ... s$(29)* variables.

The program additionally stores the label/name of the read To Do List item in the *t$(m)* variable, because this would otherwise be lost when the next To Do List item is read. This label is also written to the corresponding line on the screen.

The *m* and *n* counters are incremented:

- **m** counts the lines with To Do List items on the screen, running from 0 to 6.
- **n** counts the current read To Do List item, running from 0 to the end of the To Do List.

When a screen page with six To Do List items has been read, the subroutine returns to the main program.

After this first screen display, the actual program starts with the *start:* branch mark. The program queries the buttons and calls the corresponding subroutines:

- **OK** (Return value: 14) - The *to do list items:* subroutine is started, which creates the new To Do List items.
- **next** (Return value: 15) - The *read:* subroutine is started again. Because the *n* counter is not changed, the following six To Do List items are read.
- **Start** (Return value: 16) - Takes you back to the beginning of the To Do List after a *next*. The *n* counter is set back to 0 and the *read:* subroutine is called again, which now reads the first six To Do List items.

The *to do list items:* subroutine creates the new To Do List items. At the beginning a "Please wait ..." text is displayed, because here, too, the browsing of the To Do List can take a few seconds.

The loop runs through the six displayed To Do List items and queries whether the respective checkbox is enabled, that is, whether the To Do List item is to be repeated.

```
for i=0 to 5
  if (s$(i*3)="1")
  ...
  endif
next i
```

If this is the case, the program finds a To Do List item with the corresponding label in the To Do List.

```
a=find("todo",t$(i),0)
```

These labels are stored in the *t$()* variables in the *readIn:* subroutine for this purpose, because HotPaw Basic cannot otherwise read the text written on the screen.

## *find("todo", <Title> , <Index>)*

This function finds a To Do List item in the list with the name specified in the *Title* parameter. The search begins with the To Do List item that has the specified index number. If the function finds a matching To Do List item, it returns the index number of the To Do List item. If it doesn't find a matching To Do List item, it returns *-1*.

```
get$("todo",a,10)
```

After that, *get$("todo",a,10)* reads out the data of the found To Do List item *get$("todo",a,10)* to the *s$(20) ... s$(29)* variables.

Because date functions on the basis of strings are used in the calculation of the due dates for the new To Do List items, the date must be in precise eight-figure display. If the values read from the existing To Do List item for Month or Day are only single digit, a *0* must be placed in front of them.

```
if (len(s$(22))=1) then s$(22)="0"+s$(22)
if (len(s$(23))=1) then s$(23)="0"+s$(23)
```

In the next step, a day number is determined from the due date and stored in the *d%* variable.

```
d%=fn days(s$(21)+s$(22)+s$(23))
```

Using such day numbers, the program can then calculate the shifts by a specified number of days. Therefore, a loop runs as often as repetitions have been specified for this To Do List item in the corresponding input field.

```
for j=1 to val(s$(i*3+2))
  ...
next j
```

For each repetition, the value of the left input field from the respective line is added to the day number. This specifies the time period until the next repetition of thc To Do List item.

```
d$=fn date$(d%+j*val(s$(i*3+1)))
```

The *fn date$()* function calculates a string with the date from the result.

String functions determine three variables, in which year, month, and day are passed to the To Do List item.

```
s$(21)=left$(d$,4)
s$(22)=mid$(d$,5,2)
s$(23)=right$(d$,2)
```

The priority and the category are to be added to the new To Do List item unchanged. The corresponding *s$(24)* and *s$(27)* variables are not changed but written out just as they were read in; so no actual program lines are necessary. The *put "todo",new,10* statement always automatically writes all *s$(20) ... s$(29)* variables to the new To Do List item.

If a To Do List item has already been taken care of, an *"1"* in the *s$(25)* variable occurs. However, you don't want the new To Do List items to be marked as taken care of. Thus the *s$(25)* variable has to be set to *"0"* before the new To Do List item is created.

```
s$(25)="0"
```

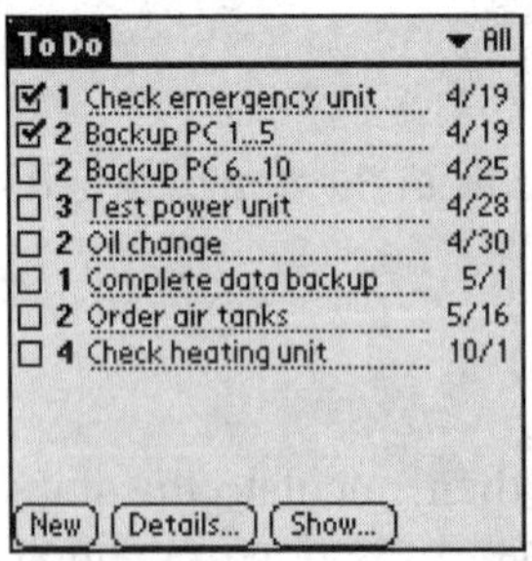


*The old To Do List*

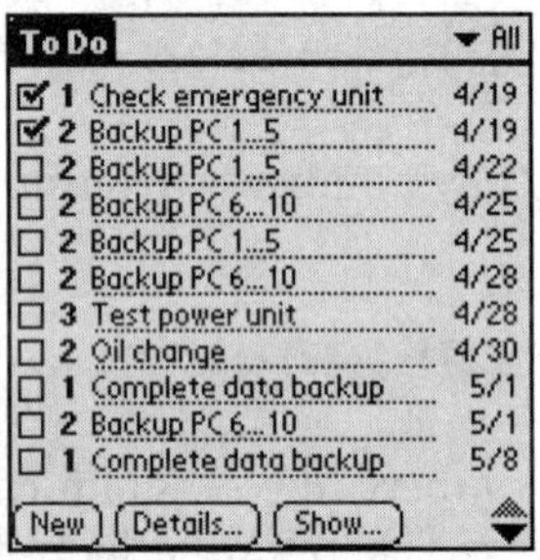


*The To Do List with the new To Do List items*

After that the *put* statement writes a new To Do List item.

```
put "todo",new,10
```

After all the To Do List items have been written, the program deletes the "Please wait ..." text by overwriting it with spaces and displays a "To Do List items created" message.

```
draw "                                    ",0,130
print "To Do List items created"
```

Then the subroutine returns to the main program. The main program waits for the user to set new repetitions or tap the button for browsing in the To Do List.

**Tip**

**Adaptation to the American date format**

This program doesn't write a date as a string anywhere but uses system functions from the Palm OS, such as reading and generating a To Do List item. You don't need to change anything in the program to display the date in American date format if this format is selected in the *Preferences* program.

**Tip**

**HotPaw Basic button layout**

Remember that HotPaw Basic can use the buttons for the Address Book, To Do List items, and Memo Pad for its own purposes. You cannot switch directly from the HotPaw Basic program to the To Do List using the To Do List button to view your new To Do List items. First tap the house to switch to the Program Startup interface or use SwitchHack, which is described on page 40 of Chapter 2.

## Additional functions for working with the To Do List

HotPaw Basic offers some other functions for finding or modifying To Do List items in the list.

### *find("todo",-11, <Date number> )*

Finds the first To Do List item that is due on the specified date.

### *find("todo",-12, <Date number> )*

Finds the next additional To Do List item that is due on the specified date.

### *find("todo",-13, <Date number> )*

Finds the first unaccomplished To Do List item that is due on the specified date or earlier.

### *find("todo",-14, <Date number> )*

Finds the next unaccomplished To Do List item that is due on the specified date or earlier.

### *find("todo",-16, <Index> )*

Finds a To Do List item that has been modified since the last HotSync, starting with the specified index number.

### *put "todo", <Index>, 10*

Modifies the To Do List item with the specified index number. The *s$(20) ... s$(29)* variables are used, which are not blank. If a variable contains only a blank string, the original value remains preserved in the To Do List item.

## 7.3 Importing addresses from the Address Book

HotPaw Basic also offers a function with which you can read data from the Address Book of the Palm.

### *get$("addr", <Index>, 20)*

Reads the Address Book entry with the specified index number to the *s$(20) ... s$(38)* variables. The addresses are numbered in consecutive order on the Palm.

The order of the fields does not correspond precisely to the order of the entries in the Address Book display.

| Variable | Contents |
|---|---|
| s$(20) | Last name |
| s$(21) | First name |
| s$(22) | Company |
| s$(23) | First number (Standard: Office) |
| s$(24) | Second number (Standard: Private) |
| s$(25) | Third number (Standard: Fax) |
| s$(26) | Fourth number (Standard: Others) |
| s$(27) | Fifth number (Standard: E-Mail) |

| Variable | Contents |
|---|---|
| s$(28) | Address |
| s$(29) | City |
| s$(30) | State |
| s$(31) | Zip code |
| s$(32) | Country |
| s$(33) | Title |
| s$(34) | Custom 1 |
| s$(35) | Custom 2 |
| s$(36) | Custom 3 |
| s$(37) | Custom 4 |
| s$(38) | The first 63 characters of the note |

First, note the example of how to read out data from an address. The following figures show the sample address used in the Palm Address Book.

*Sample address first page*

*Second page*

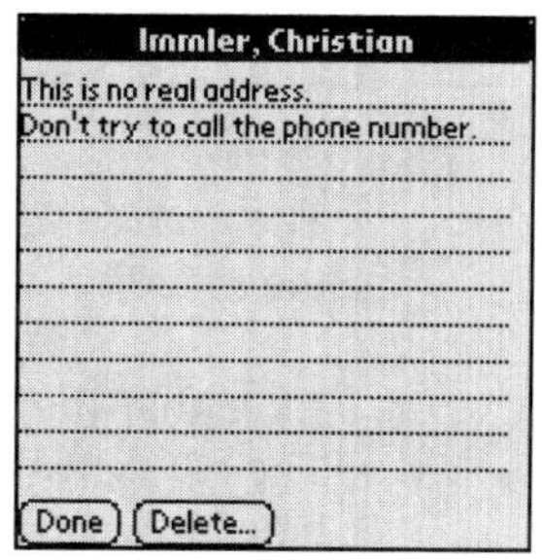


*Note on the address*

You can also save a note in the Palm Address Book on each address.

*Display of the address in the program*

The HotPaw Basic program reads out the address and displays the individual data fields together with the index number of the *s$()* variable.

```
#Addresses.bas
a$=get$("addr",0,20)
draw -1
for i=0 to 8
  draw str$(2*i+20)+" - "+s$(2*i+20),0,15+i*12
  draw str$(2*i+21)+" - "+s$(2*i+21),80,15+i*12
next i
draw "38 - ",0,123
draw left$(s$(38),32),18,123
draw mid$(s$(38),33),18,135
w=fn pen(0)
```

**CD**

**Program on the companion CD**

You can also find this program on the companion CD to this book as *0709.bas.*

The *get$("addr",0,20)* function reads the first address from the Address Book to the *s$(20) ... s$(38)* variables. This is the sample address from the figures.

After that the *s$(20) ... s$(37)* variables are displayed on the screen in a loop. The *s$(38)* variable contains the first 63 characters of the note. This string is divided into two parts and appears on the screen in two lines.

The program displays how to read out address data; however, it isn't otherwise effective.

## Entering birthdays from the Address book to the Date Book

The next HotPaw Basic program fulfills a practical function. The Palm Address Book offers four freely definable fields for each address. Many users store birthdays in one. By default these fields are named *Custom 1 ... Custom 4.*

**Tip**

**Renaming user-defined fields**

You can rename the *Custom 1 ... Custom 4* user-defined fields to any other name you choose. Select the *Options/User fields* option in the menu of the Address Book. The new names then apply for the corresponding field in all addresses.

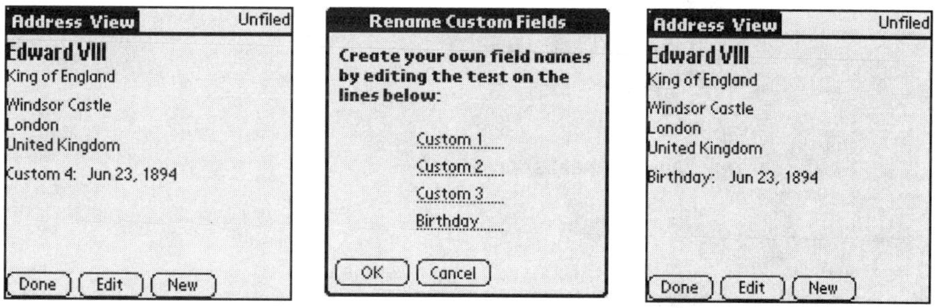


*Renaming user-defined fields*

The program assumes that in the *Custom 4* field the birth date is entered in the format of day, month, year. It doesn't matter whether the name of the field is *Custom 4* or renamed to *Birthday*, for example. In any event, it reads out to the *s$(37)* variable.

The program does not have a user interface. When you start it, it reads the entire Address Book in order. If an entry in the *Custom 4* field occurs, it is interpreted as a date and an appointment because it is created in the current year. The first and last names from the Address Book entry are written to the appointment along with the word “Birthday”.

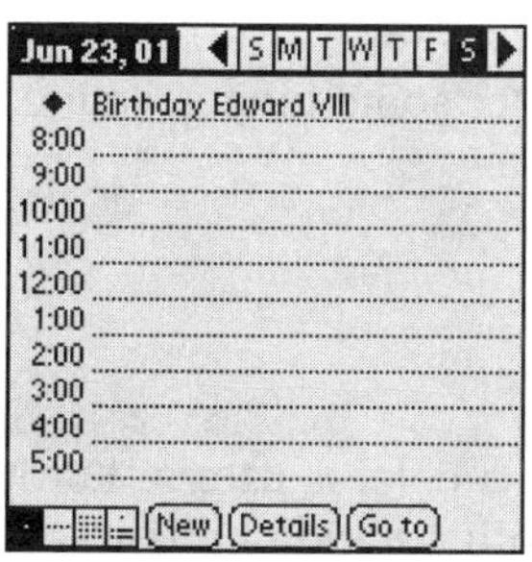


*Automatically created appointment*

```
#Birthday2.bas
while (get$("addr",n%,20)<>"error")
  if (s$(37)<>"")
    z%=instr(s$(37),".")
    s$(23)=str$(int(val(s$(37))))
    s$(22)=str$(int(val(mid$(s$(37),z%+1))))
    s$(20)="Birthday "+s$(21)+" "+s$(20)
    s$(21)=left$(fn date$(0),4)
    for i=24 to 29
      s$(i)=""
    next i
    put "date",new,10
  endif
  n%=n%+1
wend
print "Appointments created"
```

**CD**

**Program on the companion CD**

You can also find this program on the companion CD to this book as *0710.bas.* The indentation is only for readability and is not included in the original program on the CD, because it is difficult to display on memos.

The program reads one Address Book entry after the other, until it reaches the end of the Address Book. For this purpose, the return value of the *get("addr", <Index> ,20)* function is queried in a *while...wend* loop. This function returns the *"error"* string , if no address is found with the specified index number.

```
while (get$("addr",n%,20)<>"error")
  ...
wend
```

For each address the program checks whether something is entered in the *Custom 4* field.

```
if (s$(37)<>"")
  ...
endif
```

If this is the case, this entry is evaluated as a date. A date in Europe is usually written in the order of Day, Month, Year, with a period in between each one. A day and a month must be read from this format. At the end of the chapter you can find a customized version for America.

```
z%=instr(s$(37),".")
```

The *instr()* function determines the position of the first period in the string. This represents the separation between Day and Month.

```
s$(23)=str$(int(val(s$(37))))
```

If you determine the numerical value of the total string with *val()*, the result is a number with decimal places, whereby the integral part represents the day and the decimal places after the comma represent the month and the year.

```
s$(22)=str$(int(val(mid$(s$(37),z%+1))))
```

In the next step, everything up to and including the first comma is truncated and the numerical value of the new string is determined using the same method. This specifies the month.

Both values are written to the corresponding *s$(23)* and *s$(22)* variables, from which the appointment is later created.

**Tip**

**Using the s$() variables**

Remember that the *s$(20) ... s$(29)* variables are used for appointments, To Do List items, and addresses. They contain variable types of values. Read all the required values before you describe the variables again. Before you create an appointment or a To Do List item, delete all the variables containing variables with values from the last reading that are no longer required.

The values for telephone number and company, which were read from the address to these two variables, are not needed for the appointment and can therefore be overwritten without problems.

The text of the appointment is written to the *s$(20)* variable.

```
s$(20)="Birthday "+s$(21)+" "+s$(20)
```

This text consists of the word "Birthday", the first name and the last name. These were stored in the *s$(21)* and *s$(20)* variables during the reading of the address.

You also need a year number for an appointment. Don't take this number from the specified birth date, because the appointment is to be entered in the current year as a birthday, not in the person's birth year.

```
s$(21)=left$(fn date$(0),4)
```

The *fn date$(0)* function determines the current date as a string. The first four places specify the current year, stored in the *s$(21)* variable for creating the new appointment.

```
for i=24 to 29
  s$(i)=""
next i
put "date",new,10
```

Finally a loop deletes the *s$(24) ... s$(29)* variables. These contain values that were read out from the address and should not be used for the appointment. The *s$(30) ... s$(38)* variables also contain data from the read address. However, this data is not written to a new appointment. The program does not need to worry about deleting the data because it is overwritten by the data from the next address in the loop cycle.

At the end of a cycle the appointment is written. After that the *n%* index value is incremented by 1 to read the next address.

```
n%=n%+1
```

After all the addresses have been verified and the appointments have been created, the program displays a message and then terminates.

```
print "Appointments created"
```

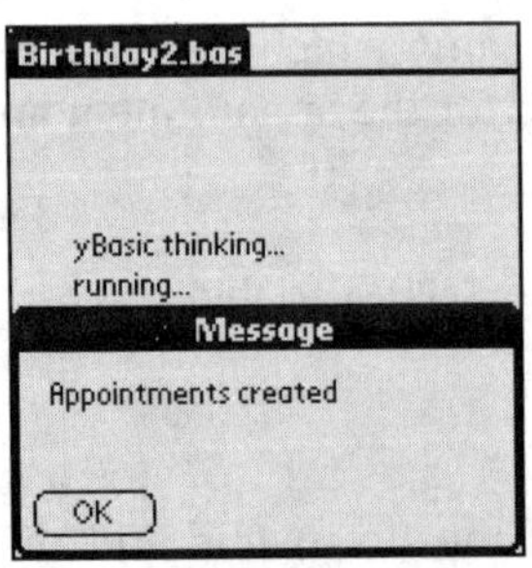


*Message at the end of the program*

# 8. Evaluations of databases

Databases store all different kinds of information. After all, you want to manage more than addresses and appointments on your Palm; you want data in other formats, statistics, inventory information, or finances. Several database systems exist for processing and displaying data of all kinds. The best known systems are JFile, MobileDB, HanDBase, ThinkDB, DB and List.

| Database | Download address |
|---|---|
| JFile | www.land-j.com |
| HanDBase | www.handbase.com |
| ThinkDB | www.thinkingbytes.com |
| MobileDB | www.mobilegeneration.com |
| List | www.magma.ca/~roo/list/list.html |

All of these systems are based on the same principle: A record consists of different fields that can be displayed in a row and column grid, similar to a table. Each row is a record, and the columns are the different data fields. When you tap a row, the record is displayed in an input form in which you can see all the fields and edit the data.

HotPaw Basic supports five different database formats: JFile, MobileDB, HanDBase, DB, and List. The full range of functions is not available for each of the database formats. By default CASL does not offer any option for accessing such databases. However, CASL can create databases in its own format and automatically synchronize them with the PC during a HotSync.

The combination of databases and HotPaw Basic programs results in various new possibilities:

- Databases can supply input data for programs or be used as a permanent memory for the results that a program supplies. This way the information is available later and can be distributed to other users.
- Conversely, you can create programs that access existing databases and evaluate them.

In this chapter you learn different examples of working with databases using the JFile, MobileDB, and DB database systems.

> **Tip**
>
> **Database converter**
>
> In Chapter 10 you can find descriptions of some programs for creating, editing, and converting databases of different Palm formats on the PC.

# 8.1 Accessing JFile databases with HotPaw Basic

JFile is probably the best known of the database systems for the Palm. It offers some additional features that are not part of the standard database repertoire: For example, using the infrared beam you can send single databases to another Palm or copy the structure of a databases to create a new one that contains the same field labels and formats but different data.

## Operating JFile

When you start the program, a list of all the installed JFile databases appears. When you click one of the names, the database opens for editing.

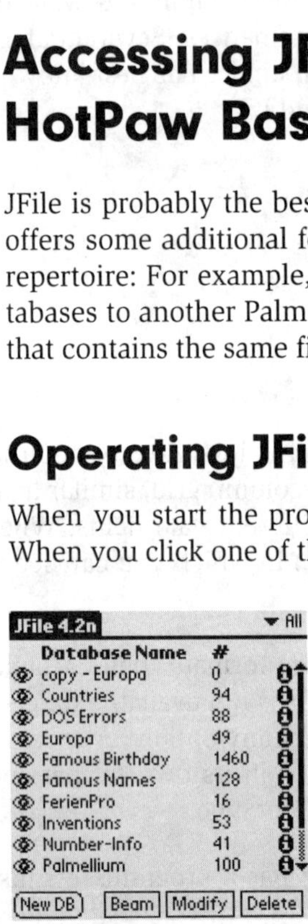


*List of the databases in JFile*

> **Note**
>
> **Limitations of the shareware version**
>
> In the unregistered shareware version, which you can find on the companion CD to this book, you can use only one database. Even if several Jfile databases are installed on the Palm, only one is displayed in the list.

Each database consists of numerous records that are displayed line by line. All the records are built from the same data fields. Each data field forms a column of the display. You can display various columns using the small arrows in the upper right area.

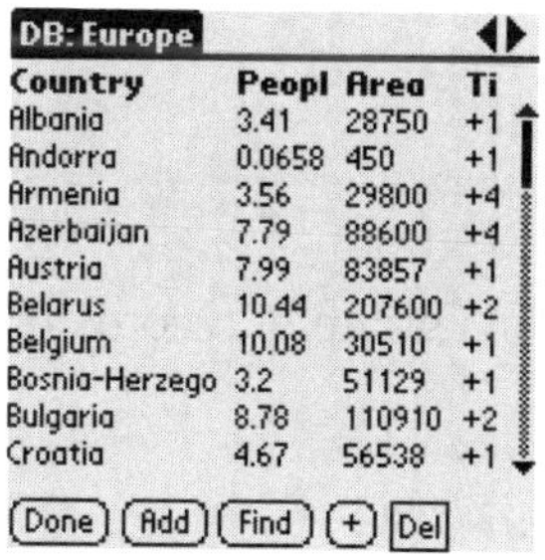


*Display of a database*

Identify a record in the database using the *Find* button. In the search you can specify whether to find the word in all data fields or only in a specified one.

*Input of a search word*

The + button continues the search with the same search text.

## Sorting

The database can be sorted by any column. By clicking the column heading, a small selection menu appears. You can sort the entire database by the contents of this data field either forward or backwards. In addition, the menu offers a display about the number of records and the option of changing the column width.

In this sorting only one criterion is considered. However, if an entry in a column appears more than once, all the records containing the same value remain in random arrangement. In such cases the *Tools/Sort Items* menu item or */S* provides help. Use them to sort the records by several criteria.

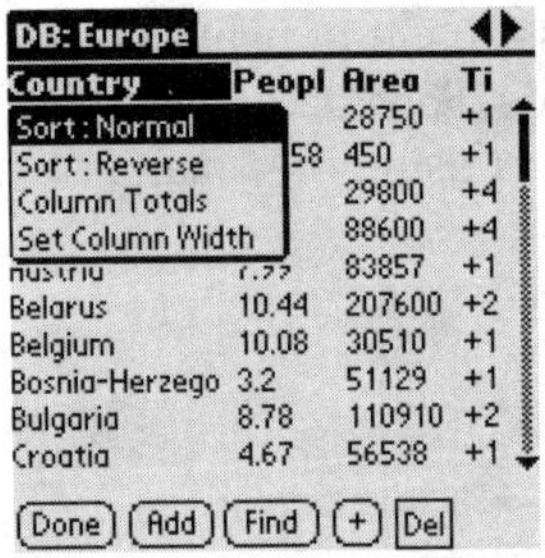


*Sorting by a single column*

The second sorting criterion is applied within a group of records that are identical after the first sorting criteria.

*Input of several sorting criteria*

Using the *Tools/Filter Records* menu item or */F*, you can restrict the display to those records that contain or do not contain a specific term in a field.

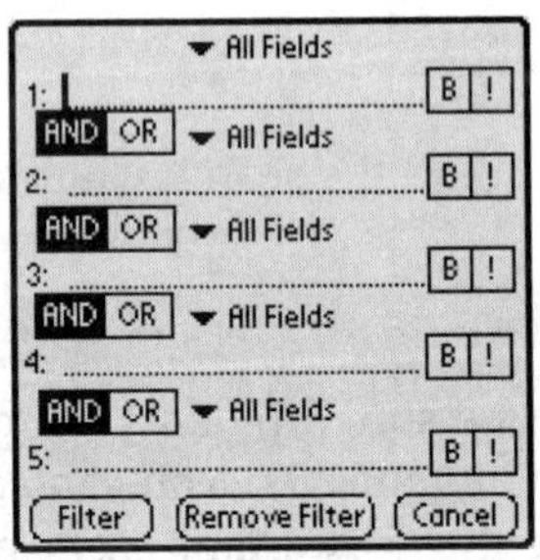


*Input of a filter criterion*

*Setting several filter criteria in Advanced Filter*

*Tools/Advanced Filter* or */V* allows you to input several filter criteria that are combined with one another through AND or OR.

*Tools/Show All Records* or */L* disables the filter and displays all the records again.

## Creating custom databases

In the list overview of all databases, you can create a new database using *New DB*. You must name all the occurring fields and define their type.

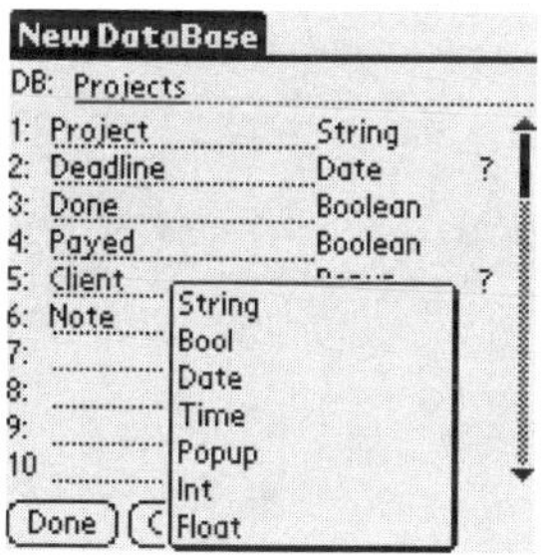


*Definition of a Database*

Each field can have one of the following types:

- **String** - Text
- **Bool** - Checkbox Yes/No
- **Date** - Date (When filling it out, a calendar appears, from which you can choose the date.)
- **Time** - Time
- **Popup** - When filling it out, a list appears of random definable keywords, of which one can be selected.
- **Int** - Integer
- **Float** - Floating point number

> **Note**
>
> **HotPaw Basic supports only string fields in some database functions**
>
> If you want to access the JFile Database using HotPaw Basic, you can only use data fields of the *String* type in some database functions. However, a simple readout of the data is possible with *Float* and *Integer* fields.

You can change the structure of a database later by tapping *Modify* in the list of databases and then selecting a database. You can change the name of the database in Jfile. This does not have to match the DOS file name of the file on the PC.

Open the database as you normally would after specifying the structure. Use *Add* to add new records to it. For this purpose, an input page appears, containing all the data fields in the defined order.

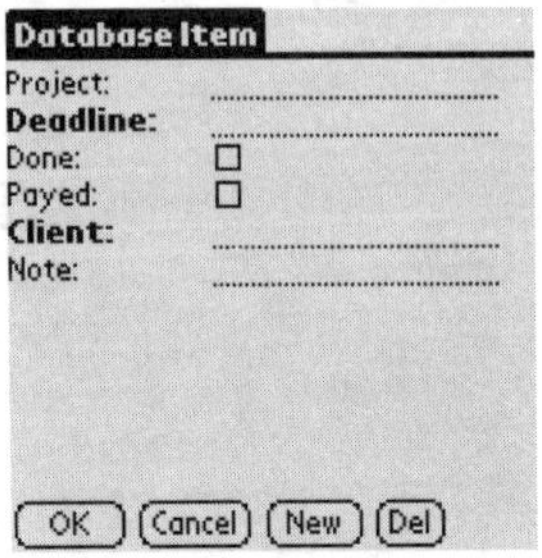


*Input screen for a new record*

The fields appear in bold. When you click a field name, a calendar or pick list opens up, from which you can select predefined entries. In the example, this list is still blank in the *Customer* field. When you click it, a *Modify Popup List* tab appears, with which you can create this list.

*Definition of a pick list*

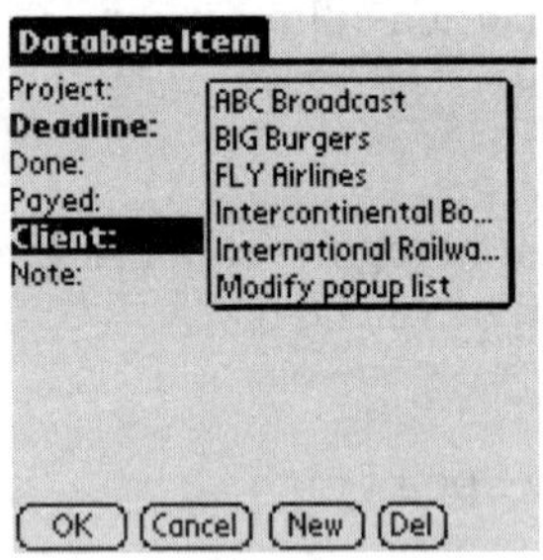


*Pick list for data input*

In the future, this list will appear when you tap the corresponding field in the input screen.

## Copying structure

Often users have several similar databases. You no longer have to recreate every database. JFile 4 makes it possible to copy the database structure of a database and make a new one out of it with the same filed definitions.

To do this, choose *Options/Copy database structure* or */C* in the database list, and then click a database. A new database is created from the structure of this one, which does not yet contain any records. Automatically the word *copy* appears in front of the name of this database.

JFile databases can be transferred to the PC during a HotSync. They can be protected with a password and even searched using the global *Find* function. Click the Info icon after a database name in the database list to make these settings.

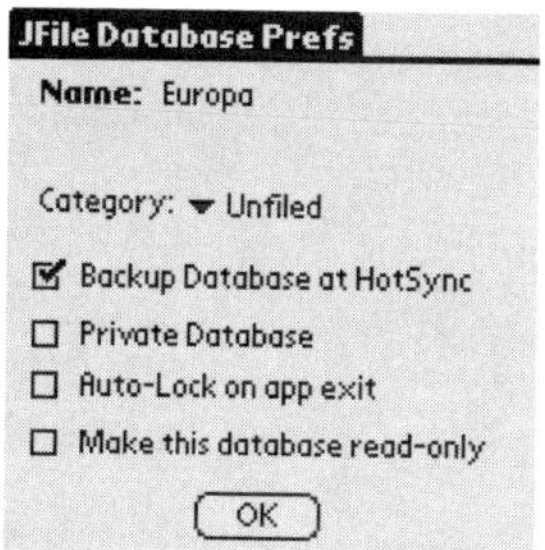


*Special properties of a database*

| JFile | 4.2n (4.1b Shareware version) |
|---|---|
| Software manufacturer or programmer | Land-J Technologies |
| Category | Database |
| Size | 107 KB |
| Hardware requirements | Any Palm |
| Software requirements | Palm OS 2.0 or higher |
| Language | English |
| Costs | Shareware fee US $ 24.95 |
| Download address | www.land-j.com |
| On CD | Yes |

# Calculations in databases

JFile cannot perform calculations within a database. The sample database from the last figures contains a list of all 49 countries of Europe, with the area and number of inhabitants specified for each country. The number of inhabitants doesn't really give us much to work with if it is not placed in relation to the area of the country. Our first HotPaw Basic program in this chapter is designed to display the number of inhabitants per $km^2$ for any country from the database.

**CD**

**Database on the companion CD**

You can also find this database on the companion CD to this book as *Europa_p.pdb.*

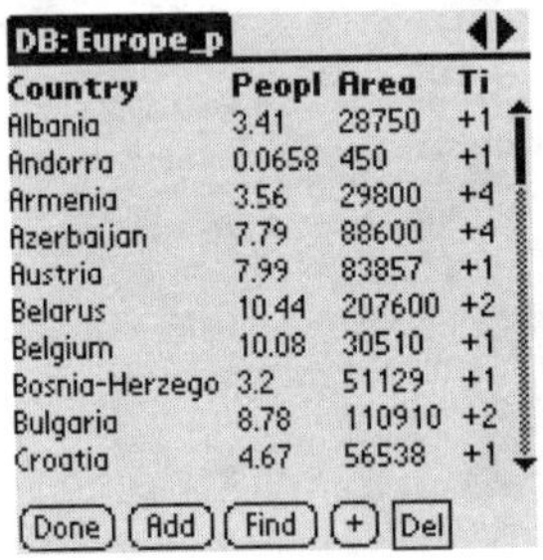


*The Europa_p database in JFile*

The program assumes that the JFile database *Europa_p* is installed. According to this scheme, you can evaluate measured results or economics, or anything else that can be displayed by numbers in a table.

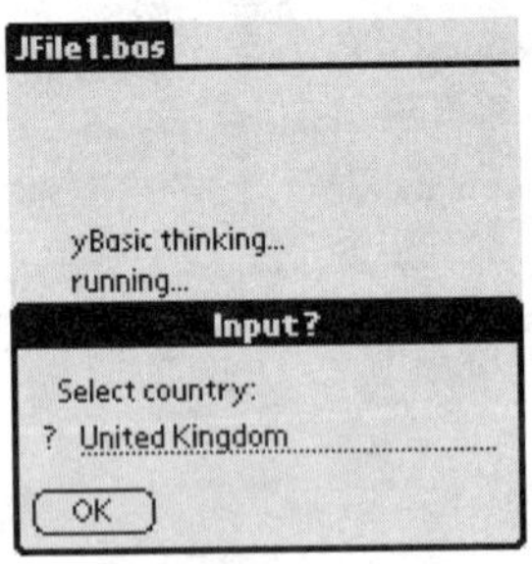


*Input of a country name*

*Display of the results*

```
#JFile1.bas
start:
l1$=input$("Select country:")
n%=0:l2$=""
while ((l2$<>l1$) and (l2$<>"error"))
  l2$=db$("Europe_p",n%,1)
  b=val(db$("Europe_p",n%,3))
  f=val(db$("Europe_p",n%,4))
  n%=n%+1
wend
if (l2$="error")
  print "Country not found"+chr$(10)+"or database not available"
```

```
else
  s$(0)=l2$
  s$(2)="Population: "+str$(b)+" Mio."
  s$(4)="Area: "+str$(f)+" km²"
  s$(6)="Pop/km²: "+str$(b*1000000/f)
  j=form(10,4,"Statistics")
  if j=0 then end
endif
goto start
```

**CD**

**Program on the companion CD**

You can also find this program on the companion CD to this book as *0801.bas.* The indentation is only for readability and is not included in the original program on the CD, because it is difficult to display on memos.

First the program queries the user for a country that is to be evaluated. This can be stored in the *l1$* variable.

```
l1$=input$("Select country:")
n%=0:l2$=""
```

After that two variables still must be reset. *n%* contains the index with which the records in the database are counted, and *l2$* contains the country readout from the database. Both variables are at *0* or *""* in the first program cycle; however, in further cycles they contain values that must first be deleted.

Next a *while...wend* loop runs through the database until either the country is found or the end of the database has been reached.

```
while ((l2$<>l1$) and (l2$<>"error"))
  l2$=db$("Europe_p",n%,1)
  b=val(db$("Europe_p",n%,3))
  f=val(db$("Europe_p",n%,4))
  n%=n%+1
wend
```

For this purpose, the *db$()* function reads out the first field of the record.

### *db$( <Database>, <Index>, <Field number>)*

This function reads a specified field from a database. HotPaw Basic does not have to open the database. The function uses three parameters:

- **Database** – String with the name of the database; this name does not have to match the name of the PDB file in Windows.
- **Index** – Number of the record that is to be read. The counting begins with the first record at 0.
- **Field number** – Number of the field that is to be read from the record. The counting begins with the first field at 1.

If no record with the specified index number is found, the *db$()* function returns the *"error"* string.

> **Tip**
>
> **Database functions use s$() variables**
>
> The database functions in HotPaw Basic use the *s$(20) ... s$(39)* variables for temporary storage. If you use these in the program, save the contents to other variables before you apply a database function.

The first field in the program, *Country*, is read to the *l2$* variable; the third field, *Population*, is read to the *b* variable; and the fourth field, *Area*, is read to the *f* variable. After that the index number *n%* is incremented by 1.

If the country output from the database of *l2$* is equal to the input country of *l1$* or if the *db$()* function returns the *"error"* error message, the *while...wend* loop terminates.

If the *db$()* function returns an error, two causes are possible:

- The specified database does not exist on the Palm.
- No record with the specified index number was found.

In the program the second case means that the loop ran through the entire database without finding the country.

```
if (l2$="error")
  print "Country not found"+chr$(10)+"or database not available"
else
```

In this case an error message is output and after the *endif,* the program returns to the *start:* branch mark, where a new prompt appears.

*Error message, when a country is not found*

If the desired country was found in the database, it is in the *l2$* variable. A HotPaw Basic standard form is used to output the results, which takes the values from the *s$(0) ... s$(6)* variables with even-numbered numbers. For this purpose, strings are formed from the values of the database with explanatory text.

```
s$(0)=l2$
s$(2)="Population: "+str$(b)+" Mio."
s$(4)="Area: "+str$(f)+" km²"
s$(6)="Ew/km²: "+str$(b*1000000/f)
```

To determine the number of inhabitants per square kilometer, the readout inhabitant number must be multiplied in the *b* variable times 1,000,000, because it is specified in millions in the database.

```
j=form(10,4,"Statistics")
if j=0 then end
```

This data is displayed in a standard form. If the user taps *Cancel* there, the *form()* function returns the value *0* and the program terminates. Otherwise, it continues running at the *start:* branch mark, so that you can select a new country.

## European program version

The last version of the program assumes that the numbers are in American format in the database, using the point as a decimal character. HotPaw Basic supports only this form for number specifications. In Jfile you can enter floating point numbers with the point or the comma as a decimal character. In Europe, ordinarily the comma is used as a decimal character.

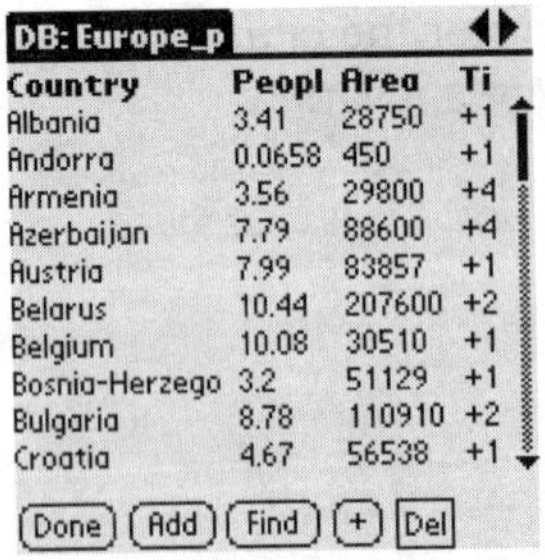


*Database in European format*

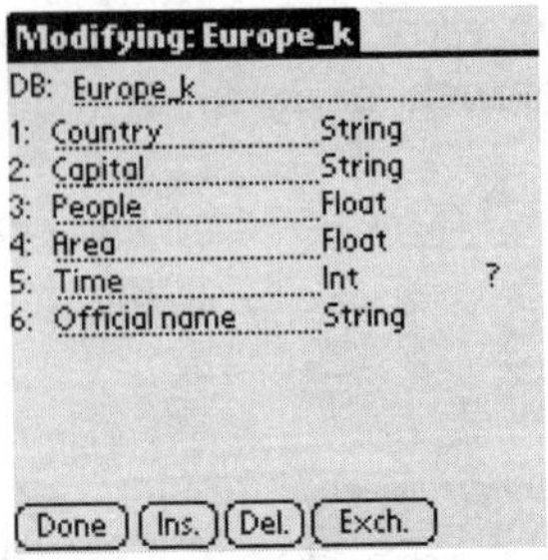


*Structure of the database*

**CD**

### Database on the companion CD

On the companion CD to this book, you can also find a second version of the database, this time with commas, under the name of *Europe_k.pdb.*

If the data is in this form, you cannot convert it into numerical values directly from the read strings using the *val()* function, because HotPaw Basic does not accept the comma as a decimal character.

To evaluate data with decimal numbers in the comma format, you must modify the program a bit.

```
#JFile2.bas
start:
11$=input$("Select country:")
n%=0:12$=""
while ((12$<>11$) and (12$<>"error"))
  12$=db$("Europe_k",n%,1)
  b$=db$("Europe_k",n%,3)
  f$=db$("Europe_k",n%,4)
  n%=n%+1
wend
if (12$="error")
  print "Country not found"+chr$(10)+"or database not available"
else
  s$(0)=12$
  z%=instr(b$,",")
  if (z%<>0)
    b=val(b$)+val("0."+mid$(b$,z%+1))
  else
    b=val(b$)
  endif
```

```
    z%=instr(f$,",")
    if (z%<>0)
      f=val(f$)+val("0."+mid$(f$,z%+1))
    else
      f=val(f$)
    endif
    s$(2)="Population: "+str$(b)+" Mio."
    s$(4)="Area: "+str$(f)+" km²"
    s$(6)="Pop/km²: "+str$(b*1000000/f)
    j=form(10,4,"Statistics")
    if j=0 then end
  endif
  goto start
```

CD

**Program on the companion CD**

You can also find this program on the companion CD to this book as *0802.bas*. The indentation is only for readability and is not included in the original program on the CD, because it is difficult to display on memos.

When inputting the records from the database, in this program version the floating point values for *Population* and *Area* are stored as strings.

```
b$=db$("Europe_k",n%,3)
f$=db$("Europe_k",n%,4)
```

For calculation in the form, the *instr()* function checks whether a comma occurs in the input strings.

```
z%=instr(b$,",")
```

If yes, *instr$()* returns the position of this character in the string.

```
b=val(b$)+val("0."+mid$(b$,z%+1))
```

In such a case the *val()*function can only evaluate the part of the string before the comma. This corresponds to the integral part of the value. The part after the comma is truncated at the comma by *mid$()*; the *"0"*character is placed in front of it in the string, and then it is evaluated by *val()* and added to the integral part.

```
else
  b=val(b$)
endif
```

In case the string read from the database does not contain a comma, it is an integer that can be directly evaluated by *val()*.

The further calculation proceeds precisely in this manner and yields the same result as in the program variant that used the point as the decimal character.

*Results of the program*

# Displaying the results of the calculation in the database

If you don't want to use the program only to display specified data but also to compare the results or pass them on to other users, it's a good idea to write the results of the calculation back to the database. If you get statistics on a given topic on the Palm and want to draw important conclusions from the statistics, you can, instead of performing the necessary calculations manually, write a simple program that immediately stores the results back in the database.

In the example, you could calculate the number of inhabitants per km² for each country and write it to the database. During the next HotSync, the database with the new values can be written back to the PC. Additionally, you can then beam the database to other users by way of the infrared port.

Unfortunately, HotPaw Basic does not let you modify the structure of a JFile database. However, you need an additional data field to display the results of the calculation. You must create this data field manually. Use the following procedure:

To avoid conversions, use the *Europa_p* database with the decimal points. Tap the *Modify* button in list view of Jfile and then select the *Europe_p* database. A form appears with the database structure.

List view in Jfile

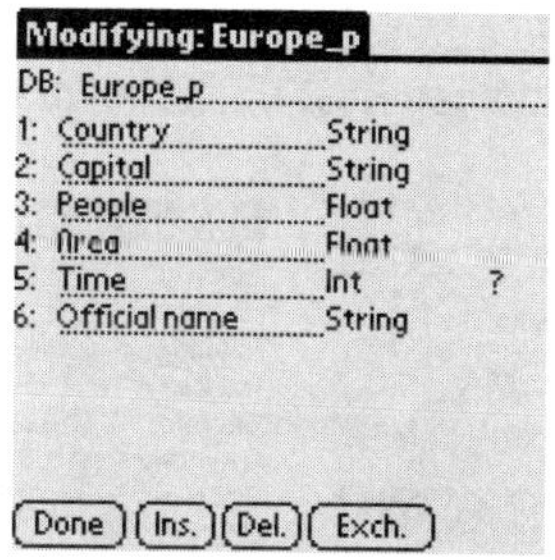


Structure of the database

Tap the *Ins* button. Use this to insert a new field called *Pop./km* after the *Area* field.

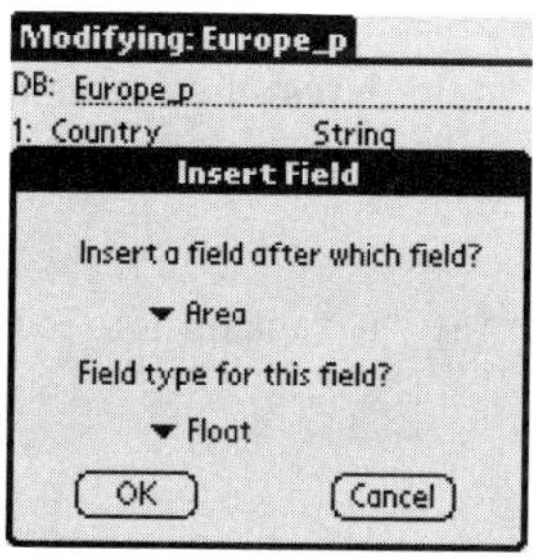


Inserting a new field

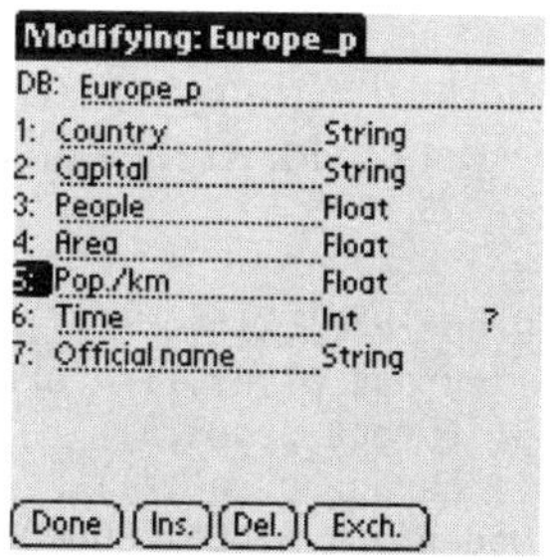


Naming the new field

To do this, select the *Area* field in the top list and select the *Float* type for the new field in the bottom list. Confirm with *OK*. In the display of the database structure a new field without a name appears between the *Area* and *Time Shift* fields. Write the name *Pop./km* in the name field.

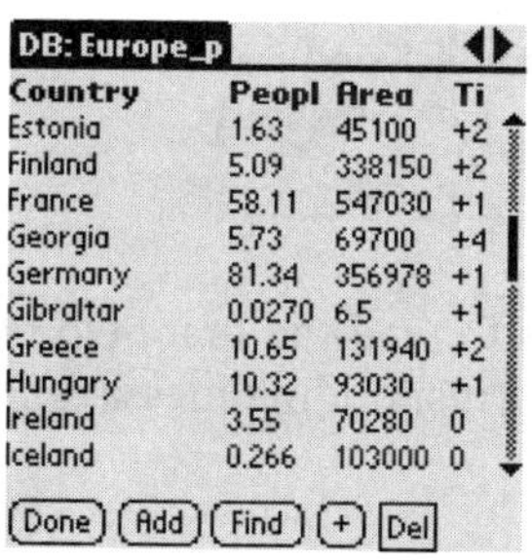


The new field in Database view

The new field in Record view

The new field is entered in the database, but it is still empty. Hit the *Done* button to close the database in JFile. Then start the HotPaw Basic program.

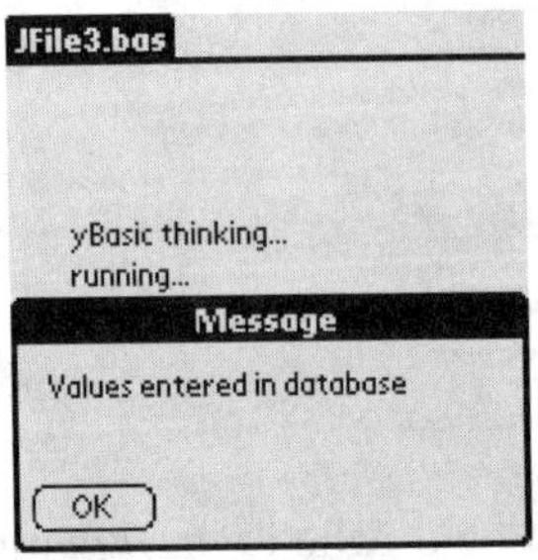


Message at the end of the program

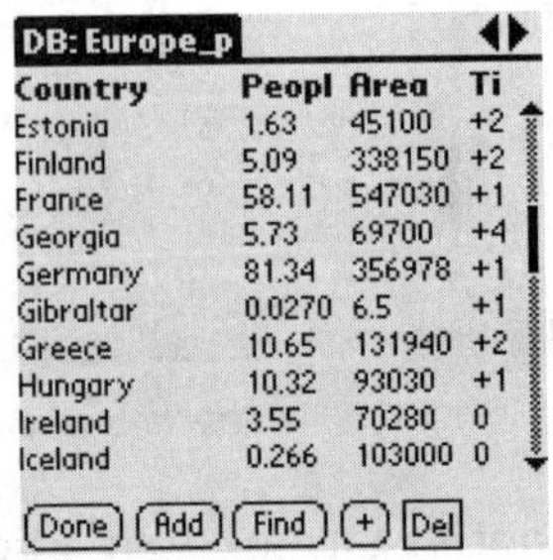


The new values in the database

The program finds the *Europe_p* database, calculates the values, and enters them in the new data field. At the end a confirmation message appears.

```
#JFile3.bas
if (db$("Europe_p",1,1)="error") then print "Database not found":end
while (db$("Europe_p",n%,1)<>"error")
  b=val(db$("Europe_p",n%,3))
  f=val(db$("Europe_p",n%,4))
  db$("Europe_p",n%,5)=b*1000000/f
  n%=n%+1
wend
print "Values entered in database"
```

**CD**

**Program on the companion CD**

You can also find this program on the companion CD to this book as *0803.bas*. The indentation is only for readability and is not included in the original program on the CD, because it is difficult to display on memos.

At the very beginning, the program attempts to read the first field of the first record of the database. If no error occurs, a corresponding message is output and the program terminates.

Then a *while...wend* loop runs through all the records. In the process, the *Inhabitants* and *Area* fields are read out of each record and the new value for Inhabitants per km² is calculated from them. This value is written back to the database using the same *db$()* function.

**Tip**

**Writing values to the database**

The reading and writing of values to a field of a JFile database functions with the same *db$( <Database>, <Record>, <Data field> )* function as the reading of a value. Only the placement of the equals sign is decisive (=):

- If the *db$()* function is after the equals sign, a value is read from the database and assigned to the variable before the equals sign.
- If the *db$()* function is before the equals sign, the value after the equals sign is written to the database.

# 8.2 Encryption of databases

Databases are ideal for storing passwords, PINs, and other secret information. You can easily forget such things because the amount of information to remember is increasing. Internet providers, telephone providers, and banks all assign their own user names and passwords. Added to these are the many customizable Web pages, newsletters, and online shops on the Internet, which require that you log on with a user ID.

You can store all such data in a database in such a way that it can be accessed at any time. However, if your Palm is lying around somewhere or if it's stolen, the danger that unauthorized persons might look at your data is worrisome. The same applies for your backup data on the PC, where this password database can be copied over local networks by other users and looked at even without the Palm by using suitable converters. In this book you learn about such converters for accessing JFile and other Palm databases in Chapter 10.

You must encrypt a database that contains secret information. Unfortunately, JFile and the other well-known database systems on the Palm don't have any features for encryption of databases. Our next HotPaw Basic program makes possible the encryption of a JFile database and shows a simple but effect encryption procedure that can be used for encrypting other types of data such as memos.

> **Note**
>
> **Important limitation**
>
> The program introduced is based on the exchange of single characters through their ASCII values and therefore functions only with strings and not with data fields of other types, such as *Float, Integer, Boolean, ...* HotPaw Basic does not offer an option for verifying field types in databases. For this reason, use this program only to encrypt databases that consist of data fields of the *String* type.

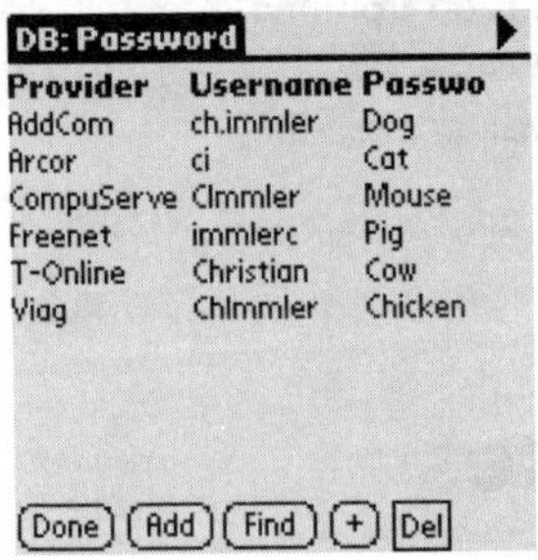


*Database with user data in JFile*

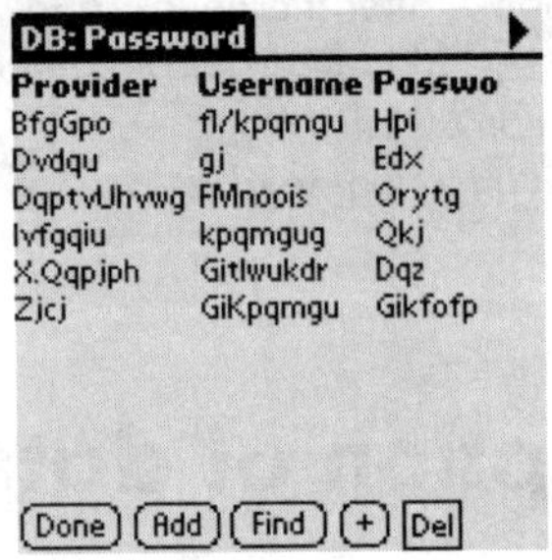


*The same database encrypted with the HotPaw Basic program*

The original database is changed during the encryption. Later the unencrypted data is no longer present. During the next HotSync, the database can be transferred to the PC in the encrypted form if the *Backup database at HotSync* option is enabled in the database settings, located in the JFile menu under *Options/ Database Prefs*.

*The encryption program*

*Message after encryption*

CD

**Database on the companion CD**

You can also find the database used on the companion CD to this book as *Password.pdb*

The same program is used for encrypting and decrypting. At the user interface, enter the name of the database to be edited plus a secret code. This code, which must consist of exactly four numbers, can be used for decrypting. Which Palm you use is unimportant. Use the infrared beam to transfer an encrypted database using the normal JFile functions to another Palm. Decrypt it there with the same HotPaw Basic program and the same code.

Theoretically you could have variable lengths and different characters in the code. To keep the explanation of the procedure simple, limit the code to a uniform length.

```
#Secret.bas
draw -1
form btn 10,80,140,20,"Encrypt database",1
form btn 10,110,140,20,"Decrypt database",1
form fld 80,25,75,12,"",1
form fld 100,45,55,12,"",1
draw "Database:",10,25
draw "Code (4 numbers):",10,45
dim k%(3)

start:
x%=asc(input$(1))
if (x%=14) then q=1:gosub encr
if (x%=15) then q=-1:gosub encr
goto start

encr:
d$=s$(0)
if (d$="") then print "Specify database":return
if (db$(d$,1,1)="error") then print "Database not found":return
if ((len(s$(1))<>4)or(not(val(s$(1))>0))) then print "Code
➥invalid":return
draw "Please wait ...",50,145
n=db.len(d$,-16)
k=0
for i=0 to 3
  k%(i)=val(mid$(s$(1),i+1,1))
next i
```

```
for i=0 to n-1
  j=1
  while (db$(d$,i,j)<>"error")
    y$=db$(d$,i,j)
    z$=""
    for m=1 to len(y$)
      z=asc(mid$(y$,m,1))
      z$=z$+chr$(z+k%(k)*q)
      k=k+1
      if k>3 then k=0
    next m
    db$(d$,i,j)=z$
    j=j+1
  wend
next i
draw "                                        ",50,145
if (q=1)
  print "Database encrypted"
else
  print "Database decrypted"
endif
return
```

**CD**

**Program on the companion CD**

You can also find this program on the companion CD to this book as *0805.bas*. The indentation is only for readability and is not included in the original program on the CD, because it is difficult to display on memos.

In the first part of the program the two buttons and input fields are defined and the texts are written to the screen.

The actual main program, which begins at the *start:* branch mark, waits for the user to tap one of the buttons and then calls the subroutine that performs the encryption. In the process a *q* variable is passed, which specifies the direction of the encryption.

The encrypting or decrypting begins at the *encr:* branch mark.

At the beginning three tests are performed to determine whether the input in the form is valid:

- A name for a database must be specified.
- This database must be found and contain at least one record.
- A four-figure code that has a numerical value must be specified.

If one of these three tests fails, the subroutine returns to the main program with an error message. The user can correct the input there. Up to this point, no changes have been made to the database.

```
d$=s$(0)
if (d$="") then print "Specify database":return
```

The first test is the easiest. The program only verifies whether the *d$* string, in which the name of the database was exported from the s$(0) input field, is not blank.

```
if (db$(d$,1,1)="error") then print "Database not found":return
```

The second test attempts to read the first field from the first record of the database. If a mistake occurs, it means that no valid database with this name exists.

```
if ((len(s$(1))<>4)or(not(val(s$(1))>0))) then print "Code invalid":
return
```

Two criteria are checked in the third test. The test fails if the length of the input code does not equal 4 or if the corresponding numerical value is not greater than 0. The "not greater" does not correspond to a "less than or equal to." If the string begins with a letter, the *val()* function returns neither a 0 nor a numerical value but the *NaN* (= Not a Number) error message instead. To include this case, note the *not()* function.

### *not( <Logical Expression> )*

If the logical expression is true, the result of the *not()* function is false. Conversely, if the logical expression is false, then the result of the *not()* function is true.

In the example, if the expression *(val(s$(1))>0)* returns a logical *false*, the numerical value of the code is either 0 or it is a code that begins with a letter and thus causes the error message *NaN* (= **N**ot **a** **N**umber). A code with the numerical value of 0 would not bring about any encryption and must therefore be ruled out.

Through the inversion with the *not()* function both invalid cases return a logical *true*, which in conjunction with the *or*-operator of the two test criteria is sufficient to display an error message and return to the main program.

After the three tests are finished and the database name and the code have been validated, a “Please wait ... " message appears on the screen.

Before the actual encryption begins, the program reads the number of records of the database.

### *db.len( <Database> ,-16)*

This function specifies the number of records in a JFile database. The *Database* parameter contains the name of the database.

## The encryption procedure

In the procedure for the encryption of a text, the numbers of the code digits are added to the ASCII values of the individual characters. The code is read always from front to back and repeated at the end. The following example shows the principle. The code used is: 3814.

| Original | D | a | s | g | r | o | s | s | e | B | u | c | h |
|---|---|---|---|---|---|---|---|---|---|---|---|---|---|
| Code | 3 | 8 | 1 | 4 | 3 | 8 | 1 | 4 | 3 | 8 | 1 | 4 | 3 |
| Encrypted | G | i | t | k | u | w | t | w | h | J | v | g | k |

Because the number added to the individual letters changes, the same letters are not encrypted into the same letters again. Otherwise, you could use the frequency distribution of letters typical for every language to attempt to decrypt a text.

The *k* variable contains a counter that increments from 0 to 3 and is then reset to 0. This way the four code numbers are applied in order.

```
k=0
for i=0 to 3
  k%(i)=val(mid$(s$(1),i+1,1))
next i
```

The code numbers are read out of the string in the *s$(1)* input field and stored in the *k%(0)* ... *k%(3)* variables.

After all of these initializations, the actual encryption algorithm starts. A loop runs through all the records of the database:

```
for i=0 to n-1
  ...
next i
```

*n-1* must be used as the end of the counting, although *n* specifies the number of records, because the numbering in the database starts at 0 with the first record.

**Tip**

**Counting of records and fields**

The records in a JFile database are counted from top to bottom starting at 0. The individual fields of a record are counted (in column view) from left to right beginning at 1.

A *while...wend* loop runs over all the data fields within a record, until an *"error"* is returned. In this way it is possible to encrypt databases without having to know prior to the encryption how many fields they contain.

```
j=1
while (db$(d$,i,j)<>"error")
  ...
  j=j+1
wend
```

With each field the *j* counter is incremented by 1. As long as a valid field is read from the database, its contents can be stored in the *y$* variable.

```
y$=db$(d$,i,j)
z$=""
```

The *z$* variable later contains the encrypted data field. At the beginning it is set to a blank string.

A loop now runs character by character over the entire *y$* string.

```
for m=1 to len(y$)
  ...
next m
```

The ASCII value of each character is determined, the numerical value of the corresponding code is added to it, and a character is made of it again with *chr$()*.

This character is appended to the *z$* string, causing the complete encrypted string to appear at the end of a cycle.

```
z=asc(mid$(y$,m,1))
z$=z$+chr$(z+k%(k)*q)
```

After each encrypted character, the *k* counter must be incremented by 1 in order to read the next number from the code.

```
k=k+1
if k>3 then k=0
```

If *k* reaches a value greater than 3, it is reset to 0 for the next cycle.

```
db$(d$,i,j)=z$
```

After the entire string has been encrypted, it is written to the corresponding field of the current record and the *while...wend* loop continues running with the next field.

Once all the records have been encrypted in this way, the "Please wait ..." display is overwritten again with spaces and a "Database encrypted" message is output. Then the subroutine goes back to the main program.

## Decrypting the database

The decrypting of an encrypted database takes place in this procedure according to the same system as the encryption. With the same regularity, the code numbers must be subtracted in order from the ASCII values of the encrypted characters to get to the correct characters.

The example offers a solution: This is defined as 1 or -1 when tapping one of the two buttons and is stored in the *q* variable.

```
x%=asc(input$(1))
if (x%=14) then q=1:gosub encr
if (x%=15) then q=-1:gosub encr
```

This factor is used in the place where a numerical value must be added to or subtracted from the ASCII value of a character.

```
z$=z$+chr$(z+k%(k)*q)
```

That way you can use the same formula for both directions (encrypting and decrypting).

At the very end, the program uses this factor to decide which message to output.

```
if (q=1)
  print "Database encrypted"
else
  print "Database decrypted"
endif
```

*Different messages at the end*

# 8.3 Evaluating MobileDB databases

MobileDB is a relatively simple database system for the Palm. The data types are not new and all fields are basically the same, which simplifies importing to HotPaw Basic. They differ only in the width of the columns in the display.

Compared to JFile, this system has fewer advantages. However, to make up for it, hundreds of freeware databases are available with information on all different kinds of topics for MobileDB at http://www.mobilegeneration.com/databases.

## Operation of MobileDB

This program displays a list of MobileDB databases when you start it up. When you click a name, the database opens up. The records are displayed in rows. You navigate through the different columns using the arrows on the right.

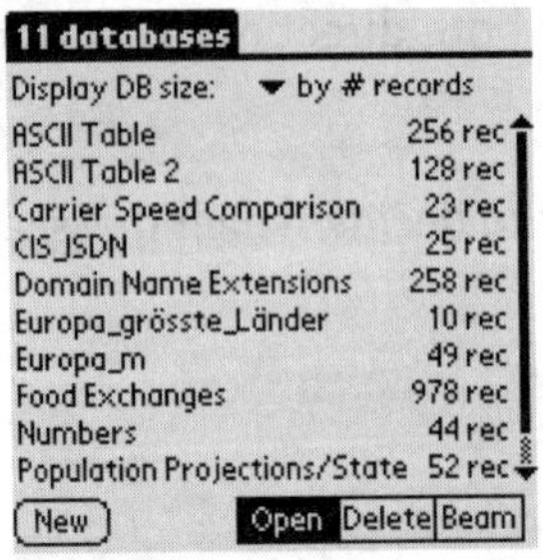


Database list in MobileDB

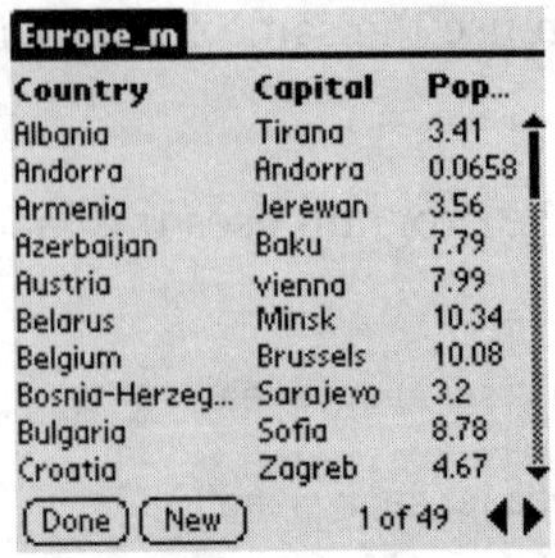


Database in MobileDB

Clicking one of the records puts you in Display mode. All the fields of this record are displayed. You can edit them by tapping the *Edit* button.

Display mode in MobileDB

Edit mode in MobileDB

**CD**

### Database on the companion CD

You can find the sample database shown here on the companion CD to this book as *Europe_m.pdb*. The data formats of JFile and MobileDB are not compatible, so you cannot use the database we described earlier in this chapter.

Using the *Record/Find Record* menu item or */F*, you can find a record in the database. Specify whether to search for the word in all data fields or only in a specific one.

After a search, a small button with an *R* appears in the upper right corner. Tapping this continues the search with the same search text.

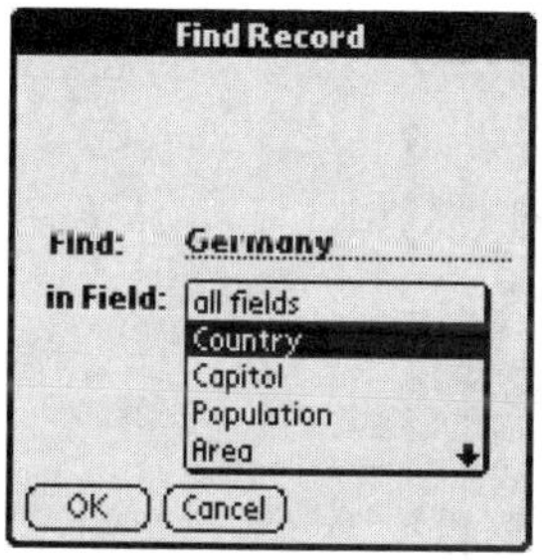


Inputting a search word

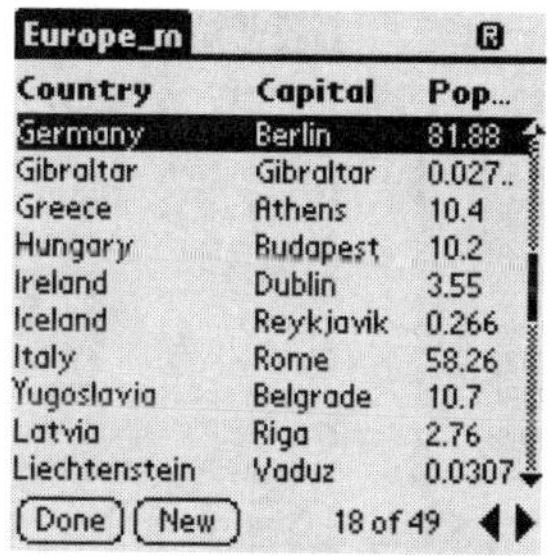


Display of the search result

## Sorting

You can sort the database using up to three criteria. Choose the *Record/Sort Records* menu item or */S*. The second sorting criterion can be applied within a group of records that are identical by the first sorting criterion.

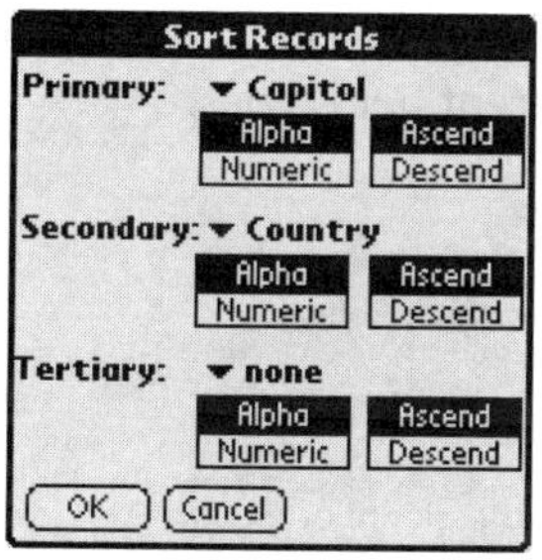


Inputting several sorting criteria

Sorted database

You do not have to specify all three criteria. For each column you can make settings determining whether to sort in descending or ascending order, alphabetically, or numerically. This selection is critical for columns with numerical values. If you sort numerical values alphabetically, they can be sorted like words, first by the first character, then by the second, and so on. No consideration is given to the length of the string, so no false result can occur. Short numbers are always smaller than long ones. However, MobileDB saves everything as strings; it does not recognize any numerical data fields.

Using the *Tools/Filter Records* menu item or */L*, you can limit the display to records that contain a specified term in a specified field or in all fields.

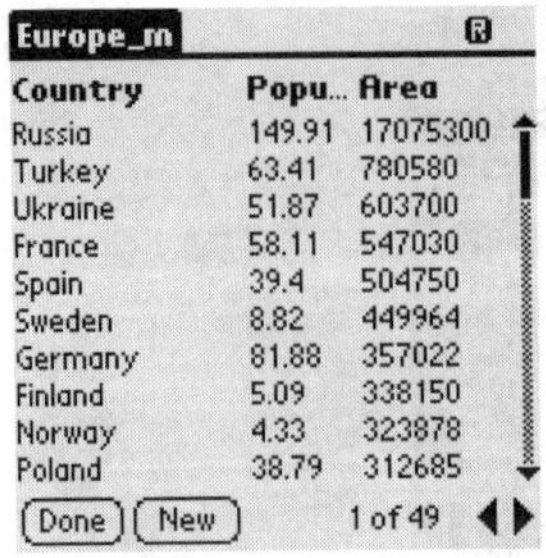


Numerical sorting

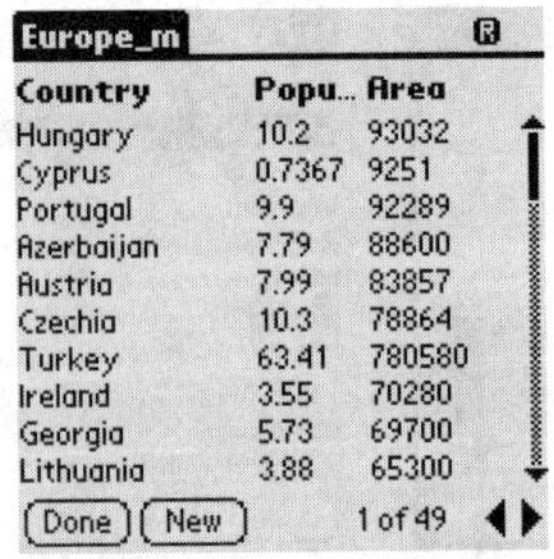


Alphabetical sorting

*Tools/Show All Records* or */A* disables the filter and displays all the records again.

## Creating custom databases

In the List overview of all databases, you can create a new database with the *New* option. You must name all the occurring fields. Don't specify any types because MobileDB does not recognize any different field types.

| **MobileDB** | **2.06** |
|---|---|
| Software manufacturer or programmer | Mobile Generation Software |
| Category | Database |
| Size | 51 KB |
| Hardware requirements | PalmPilot Professional or higher |
| Software requirements | PalmOS 2.x and higher |
| Language | English |
| Costs | US $ 14.95 |
| Download address | www.mobilegeneration.com |
| On CD | No |

# Record numbering in MobileDB databases

In JFile databases the individual records are numbered consecutively starting at 0. The order corresponds to the type of sorting that has been set. MobileDB is different. The database contains four records more than are displayed in MobileDB. They have the following contents:

- Field names.
- Widths of the fields in the column display.

- The word *"str"* in every field.
- Blank record.

These four records are entered in the database according to the sorting and must be correspondingly recognized and ignored by the respective HotPaw Basic program.

The following program makes it possible to browse through the database, whereby these four additional records can be recognized. Use *Europe_m.pdb* again as a sample database. This time it has been numerically sorted in MobileDB by numbers of inhabitants. The program shows how to access MobileDB databases from HotPaw Basic.

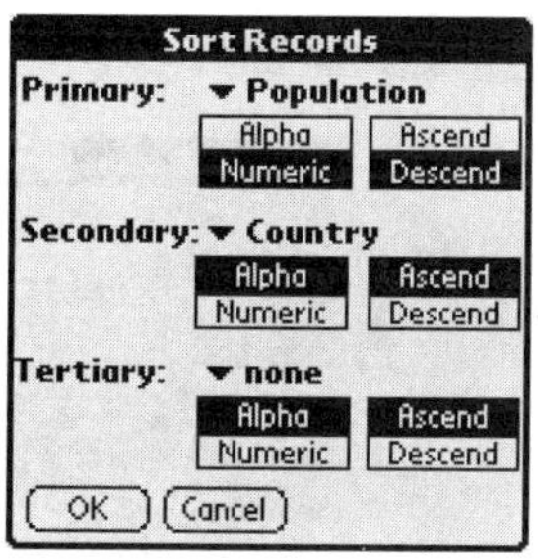


*Sorting*

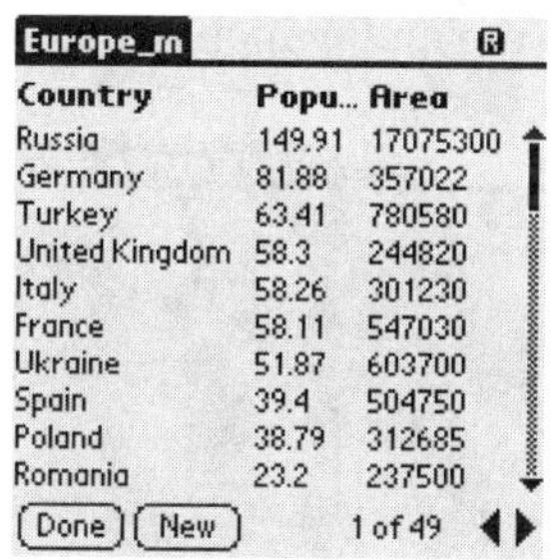


*Sorted database*

```
#MobileDB1.bas
draw -1
form btn 10,125,60,18,"< Back",1
form btn 80,125,60,18,"Next >",1
l$="                                        "
j=0
gosub displaydb

start:
x%=asc(input$(1))
if (x%=14) then j=j-1:gosub displaydb
if (x%=15) then j=j+1:gosub displaydb
goto start

displaydb:
for i=1 to 6
  draw db$("Europe_m",j,i)+l$,0,i*15
next i
draw "Record: "+str$(j)+"    ",0,105
return
```

**CD**

**Program on the companion CD**

You can also find this program on the companion CD to this book as *0806.bas.*

The same *db$()* function is used that was used to read JFile records.

```
for i=1 to 6
  draw db$("Europa_m",j,i)+l$,0,i*15
next i
```

This loop runs over the six fields of the database, reads the contents, and writes them below one another. To offset the variable field lengths, the *l$* string is always appended to the end, which consists of several spaces.

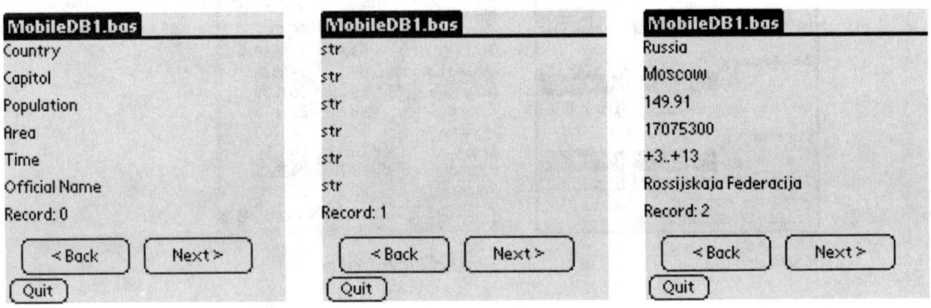


*Records 0 to 2 in the sorting by numbers of inhabitants*

The *Back* and *Next* buttons decrement and increment the counter by 1. If the counter reaches a value that is less than 0 or greater than the number of true records plus the four additional records, the word *"error"* appears in all of the fields.

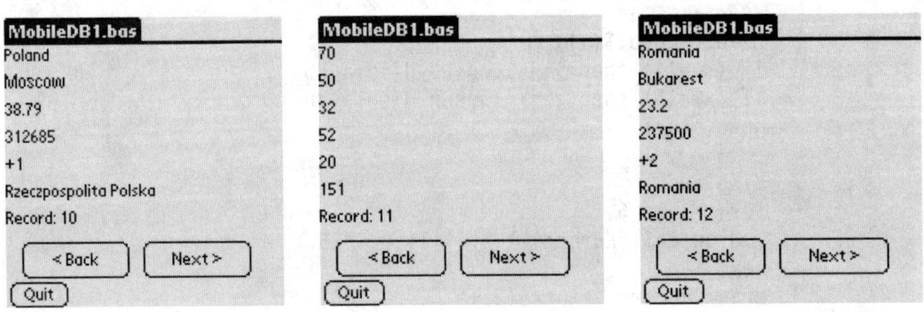


*Records 10 to 12 in the sorting by numbers of inhabitants*

The figures show three records following one another so that you can recognize exactly where the additional records are sorted.

## Business graphics and curves from databases

The following program example generates a bar chart from the values of a MobileDB database. In this program you can see how to access MobileDB databases from HotPaw Basic. The differences in working with JFile databases are not great. However, you can only read MobileDB databases with HotPaw Basic; you cannot make changes.

*List display*

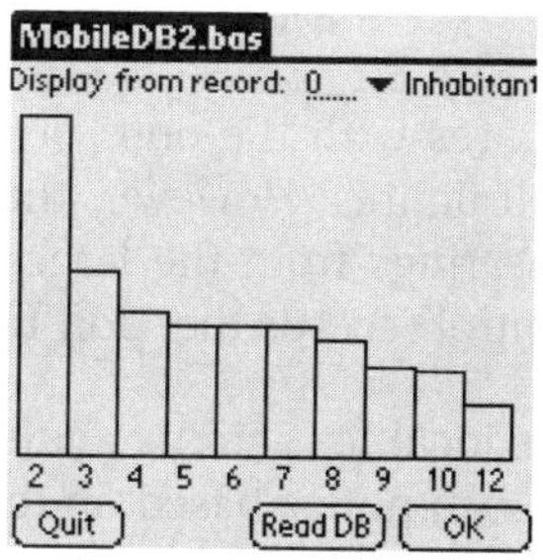


*Graphic display*

The program inputs the data of the *Europe_m.pdb* database. With minor adaptations you can graphically evaluate other databases in the same manner. On page 419 of Chapter 9, you can find a method for exporting graphics to the PC for further processing.

The order corresponds to the sorting that has been set in MobileDB. In the figures, the database is sorted in descending order by the number of inhabitants.

In the input field above, specify which record the data is to be read from. The four records of a MobileDB database that do not contain any true data are automatically skipped, as you can see from the record number in the first column of the table. In the list field in the upper right corner, select whether numbers of inhabitants or areas are to appear in the third column.

The *Read DB* button rereads the database starting with the specified record and then displays the list.

The *OK* button switches to the graphic and back to the list. The graphic is scaled in such a way that the largest of the displayed values fills the height of the display.

*List display*

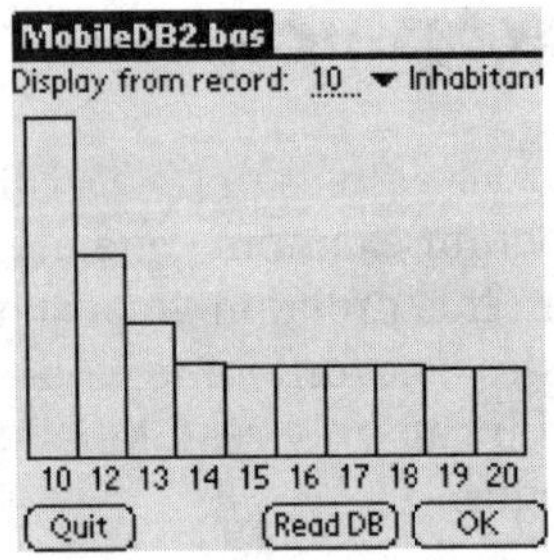


*Graphic display*

Compare these figures with the ones on the previous page. Records 10 and 12 are present in both figures. However, the scaling of the graphic is different because it gets its bearings from the largest displayed value. Record 11 contains one of the four control records that don't contain any real values.

Such programs are ideal for gaining additional information from a database that would not attract such notice based on the numerical values alone. In the example, the database is sorted in MobileDB by areas and then input into the HotPaw Basic program.

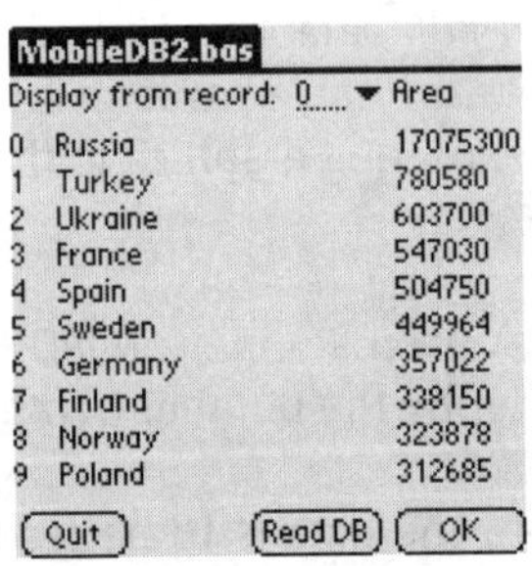


*List display by area*

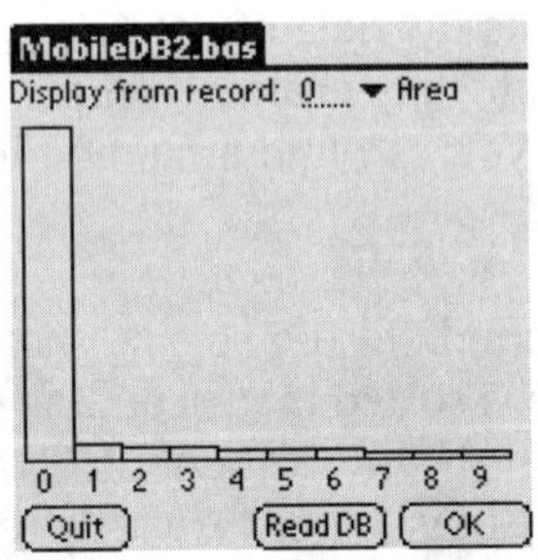


*Graphic display of the areas*

In the graphic the first bar is very large in comparison to the others because Russia appears in the database as total area, not just the European part.

Now select the *Inhabitants* option in the list field and tap the *Read DB* button again. After that the numbers of inhabitants of the countries are read out from the database, with the sorting order unchanged.

You immediately notice in the graphic that three of the ten largest countries in area have only very small numbers of inhabitants. On the basis of the record numbers that appear in the graphic, you can find the countries of Sweden, Finland, and Norway in the list view.

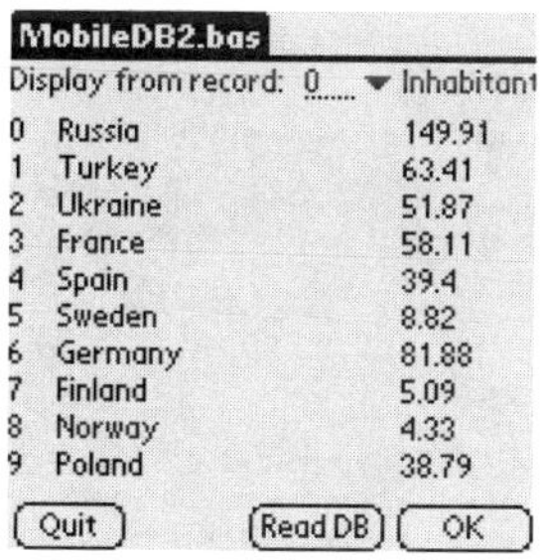


List display with numbers of inhabitants

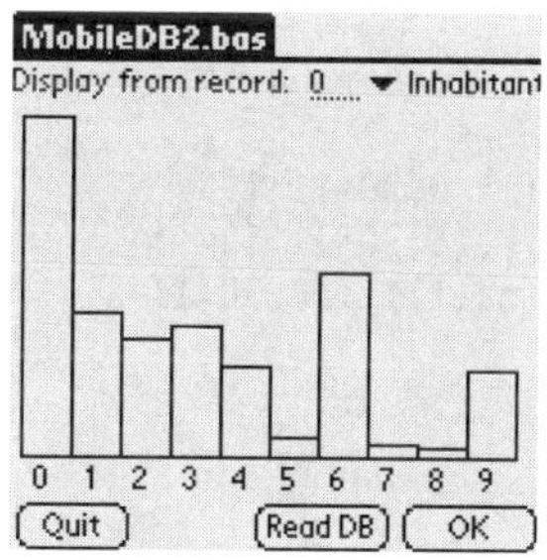


Graphic display of the numbers of inhabitants

Such evaluations are practical for many databases. It is true that our HotPaw Basic program is specially tailored to the *Europe_p.pdb* database. However, in the program description you can find corresponding notes for adapting the program to other databases.

```
#MobileDB2.bas
dim n1$(9),n1%(9),n2(9),a$(2)
draw -1
form btn 75,147,39,12,"Read DB",1
form btn 120,147,39,12,"OK",1
form fld 90,15,15,12,"",1
a$(1)="Population"
a$(2)="Area"
form lst 105,15,2,1,a$,1
draw "Display from record: ",0,15

start:
x%=asc(input$(1))
if (x%=14) then gosub list
if (x%=15) then if (g%=1) then gosub list else gosub graphic
goto start

list:
g%=0
draw 0,30,160,115,-7
for i=0 to 9
n2(i)=0
next i
```

```
j=val(s$(0))
i=0
while ((i<10)and(db$("Europe_m",j,1)<>"error"))
  n1$(i)=db$("Europe_m",j,1)
  if
((n1$(i)<>"Country")and(n1$(i)<>"str")and(n1$(i)<>"")and(not(val(n1$(i))
➥)>0))
    n2(i)=val(db$("Europe_m",j,val(s$(1))+2))
    n1%(i)=j
    draw str$(j),0,30+11*i
    draw n1$(i),15,30+11*i
    draw str$(n2(i)),120,30+11*i
    i=i+1
  endif
  j=j+1
wend
return

graphic:
g%=1
draw 0,30,160,115,-7
m=n2(0)
for i=1 to 9
  if (n2(i)>m) then m=n2(i)
next i
for i=0 to 9
  if (n2(i)<>0)
    y=int(n2(i)/m*100)
    draw i*15+4, 132-y, 14, y, 4
    draw str$(n1%(i)),i*15+7,133
  endif
next i
return
```

**CD**

**Program on the companion CD**

You can also find this program on the companion CD to this book as *0807.bas*. The indentation is only for readability and is not included in the original program on the CD, because it is difficult to display on memos.

At the beginning of the program, two buttons – the input field and the list field in the upper right area – are defined, and some variable fields are dimensioned. The following variable table gives an overview of the use of the variables in the program:

| Variable | Use in the program |
|---|---|
| a$(2) | Texts for the list field |
| g% | Mode: List = 0, Graphic = 1 |
| i | Loop counter |
| j | Counter for current record |
| m | Maximum of the values to be displayed in the graphic |
| n1$(9) | Country labels |
| n1%(9) | Record numbers |
| n2(9) | Values for Inhabitants or Area |
| s$(0) | Return value of the input field = Number of the first record to be displayed |
| s$(0) | Return value of the input field = Number of the first record to be displayed |
| s$(1) | Return value of the list field: Inhabitants = 1, Area = 2 |
| x% | Return value of the last tapped button |
| y | Height of the graphic bar |

**Tip**

**Adaptation to other databases**

To use this program with another database, perform the following adaptation in the beginning:

The list field must contain the names of the respective data fields from where data can be displayed. If more than two such data fields occur in the database, you must dimension the *a$()* field variable accordingly.

The actual main program starts and waits for the user to enter a number for the first record and then tap one of the buttons.

- The *Read DB* button calls the *list:* subroutine, which reads the records from the database and displays them in a list.
- The result of the *OK* button depends on whether a list or a graphic is currently displayed. This button switches between the list and the graphic. You can see all the form elements in both modes.

```
start:
x%=asc(input$(1))
if (x%=14) then gosub list
if (x%=15) then if (g%=1) then gosub list else gosub graphic
goto start
```

The *list:* subroutine sets the *g%* mode to 0. This mode is queried by the *OK* button to determine whether the list or the graphic is currently displayed. After that a rectangular screen area is deleted, to hide any possible graphic before displaying a list.

```
g%=0
draw 0,30,160,115,-7
```

Then the program sets the *n2()* numerical values all to 0 so that no invalid values appear later in the graphic.

```
for i=0 to 9
  n2(i)=0
next i
```

The contents of the input field for the first record to be input are stored in the *j* variable as a numerical value and the *i* loop counter is set to 0.

```
j=val(s$(0))
i=0
```

A *while...wend* loop fills the ten lines of the list but terminates if the *"error"* error message appears while reading a record. Then the end of the database is reached and no further lines can be displayed.

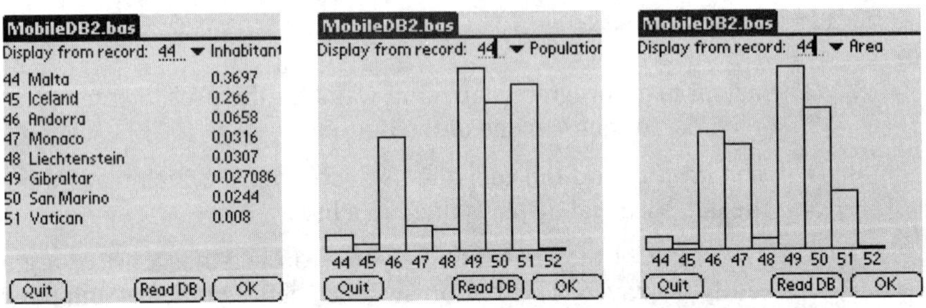


*Display of the smallest countries from Record 44 in sorting by numbers of inhabitants (Compared to the number of inhabitants, Iceland has a very large area.)*

```
while ((i<10)and(db$("Europe_m",j,1)<>"error"))
  ...
wend
```

The name of the respective country is read from the record.

```
n1$(i)=db$("Europe_m",j,1)
if
((n1$(i)<>"Country")and(n1$(i)<>"str")and(n1$(i)<>"")and(not(val(n1$(i))
➥)>0))
  ...
endif
j=j+1
```

The input value is checked by four criteria to exclude the four control records that appear in every MobileDB database:

- It cannot be the word *"Country"*. The current record would be the one with the field labels.
- It cannot be the word *"str"*. The current record would be the one with the *"str"* label in every field.
- It cannot be blank. The current record would be the blank control record.
- It cannot contain a numerical value. The current record would be the control record with the column widths.

If all the checks are positive, the record is further evaluated. Otherwise, only the record number is incremented so that the next record can be read.

```
n2(i)=val(db$("Europe_m",j,val(s$(1))+2))
```

The numerical value in the *n2(i)* variable depends on which option in the list field was selected, *Inhabitants* or *Area*. The return value of a list field is the number of the selected list element (1 or 2). To this, add 2 to obtain field numbers 3 or 4 for *Inhabitants* or *Area*.

```
n1%(i)=j
```

The current record number is stored in the *n1%(i)* variable, because when a control record is skipped, the record number no longer matches the loop counter. Then the three values Record number, Country, and Number of Inhabitants or Area are written to a line on the screen.

```
draw str$(j),0,30+11*i
draw n1$(i),15,30+11*i
draw str$(n2(i)),120,30+11*i
i=i+1
```

The loop counter is only incremented if a line has really been written so that no blank lines appear.

**Tip**

**Adaptation to other databases**

To use this program with another database, make the following adaptations in the *list:* subroutine:

The database name *Europe_m* must be replaced by the corresponding name.

The number that is added to the return value of the list field must be adapted in such a way that the program reads out the correct data field.

The *graphic:* subroutine is based on the graphic program introduced earlier.

At the beginning, the *g%* mode is set to 1 and a rectangular screen area is deleted to hide the displayed list. A loop then finds the maximum of the values to be displayed and stores it in the *m* variable, because the bars can be scaled on this basis.

```
graphic:
g%=1
draw 0,30,160,115,-7
m=n2(0)
for i=1 to 9
  if (n2(i)>m) then m=n2(i)
next i
```

Then a loop runs as long as a value is still stored in the *n2(i)* variable. If lines at the end are to be blank, no bars can be drawn for them either.

```
if (n2(i)<>0)
  y=int(n2(i)/m*100)
  draw i*15+4, 132-y, 14, y, 4
  draw str$(n1%(i)),i*15+7,133
endif
```

The height of the bars is calculated from the maximum, whereby the highest bar has a height of 100 pixels to allow enough room for the other displays.

The record numbers are displayed below the graphic so that you can assign the bars to the countries by toggling the *OK* button.

**Tip**

**Adaptation to other databases**

To use this program with another database, you do not need to make any adaptations in the *graphic:* subroutine. This program part reads only references the data that the *list:* subroutine has stored, not data from the database.

# 8.4 Free database design with DB

DB is a free database system pursuant to the GNU Public License. The program is in constant development. As of now, very few finished databases occur in the DB format. However, the program is available in English, German, and Dutch. Other than that, the features are still quite limited in comparison to other systems. The openness of this program and its data format are best appreciated for its interaction with HotPaw Basic. HotPaw Basic can create databases in the DB format as well as add records to existing DB databases. You can read records, just as you can with JFile and MobileDB.

## Operation of DB

DB databases appear, as in other systems, in a list. When you tap one of these databases, it is displayed in columns.

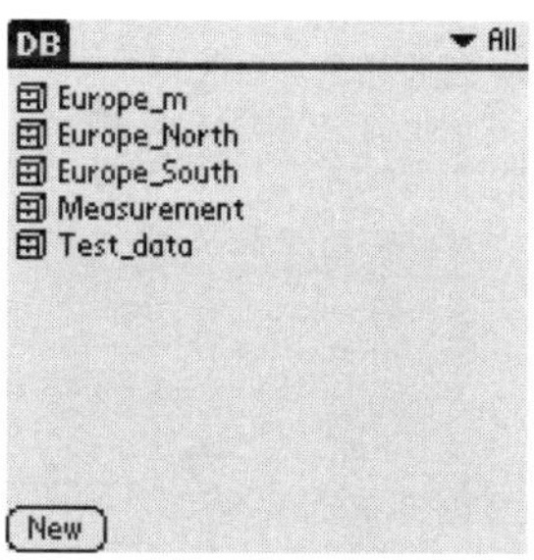


List of databases in DB

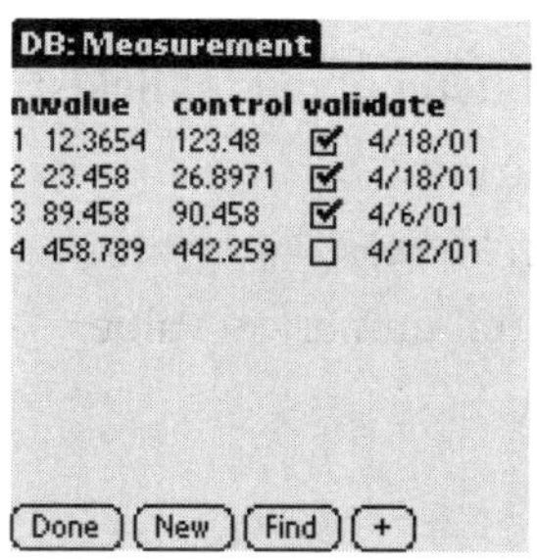


Column display of a DB database

Tap a record in the column display to see it in its entirety and edit it. Choose the *New* button to create a new record.

You can search the database for a specified character string. In the search, specify whether to search the entire database or only in a data field. Choose the + button to continue the search after a hit with the same settings.

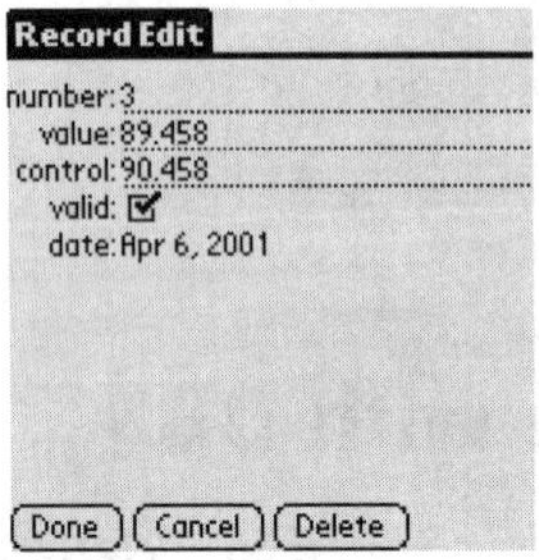


*Changing a record in DB*

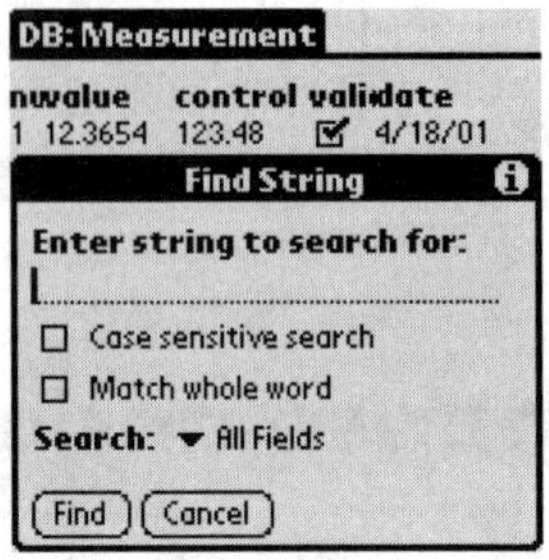


*Searching in a DB database*

Using the *Options/DB Design* menu item or */D*, you can change the field labels and field types of a database, add new fields, or delete fields.

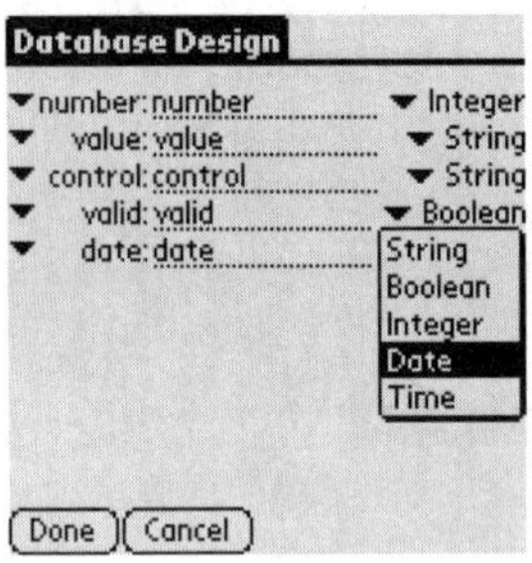


*Definition of the data fields*

DB supports five different types of fields:

- **String** - Any strings
- **Boolean** - Checkboxes
- **Integer –** Integral numerical values
- **Date** - Date
- **Time** - Time

In DB you can make settings determining which data fields appear in which order in the column display. To do this, choose the *Options/List Views* menu item or */W*.

*Changing the column display in DB*

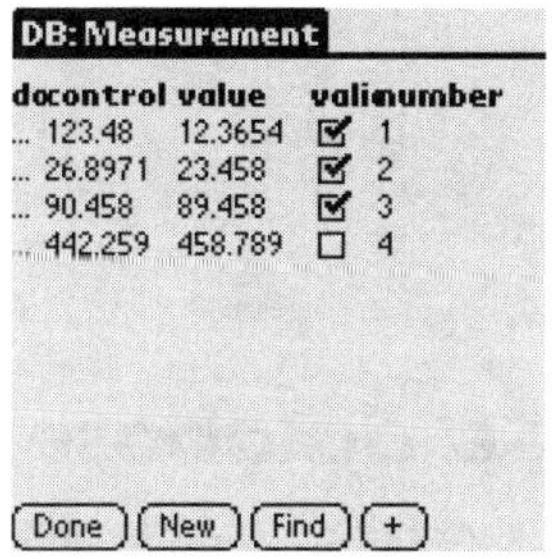


*Column display in the new format*

You can specify which fields are to appear and how wide the respective columns can be displayed. You don't have to always display all the fields of a database. This selection has no influence on the display mode of individual records in Edit mode.

In its current version, DB still does not offer a feature for sorting records by specified criteria.

In the list of the DB databases, tap the icon next to a database to display a menu. You can delete, rename, beam, duplicate the database, or display information about it.

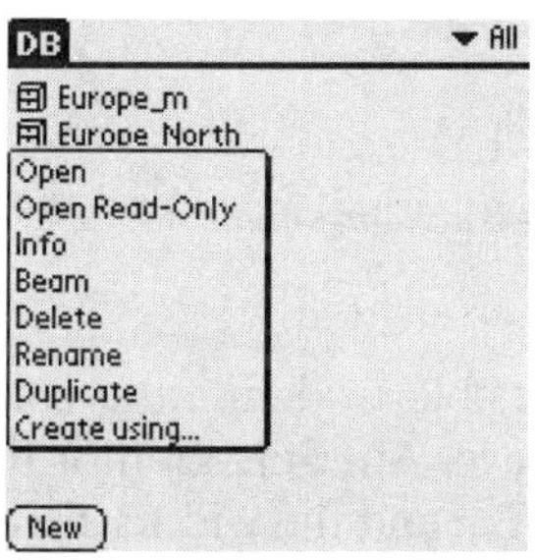


*Menu with functions of a DB database*

| DB | 0.3.0 |
|---|---|
| Software manufacturer or programmer | Tom Dyas |
| Category | Database |
| Size | 75 KB |
| Hardware requirements | Any Palm |
| Software requirements | Don't know |

| Language | German, English, Dutch |
|---|---|
| Costs | Freeware (GPL) |
| Download address | sourceforge.net/projects/pilot-db |
| On CD | No |

## Creating a database out of birthdays or appointments from the Date Book

Users often enter dates into the Date Book on a long term basis and don't look at the appointments until shortly before. It would be much more practical to have a database for all such appointments at your fingertips.

The next HotPaw Basic program writes trade show dates from the Palm Date Book to a DB database. The program generates the database itself, which you can then edit as you would any other DB database.

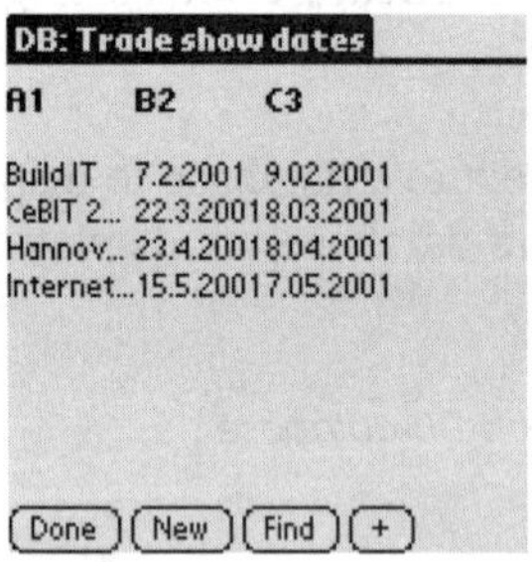


*The new database in DB right after creation*

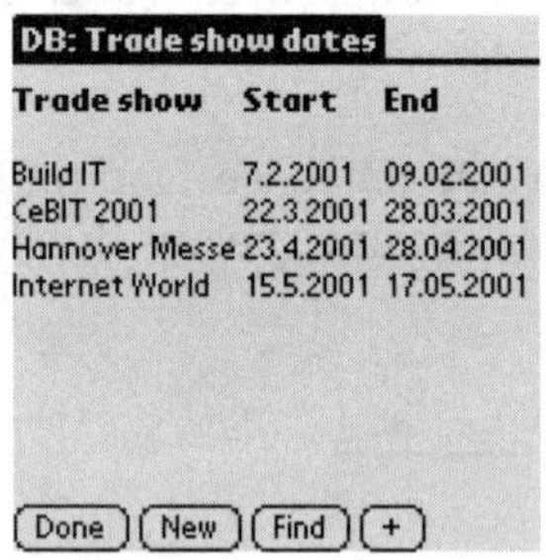


*Manually changed column widths and names*

Unfortunately, in HotPaw Basic it is not possible to define the column widths and names of the data fields for a DB database. After creation of the database, the fields have the standard labels A1, B2, C3, ... and the widths are all the same. However, you can easily change this using the DB functions.

**Tip**

**Finding the database**

It is possible that DB cannot immediately display a database created by HotPaw Basic in its list of databases. In this case, choose the *DB/Find Databases* option or */R.*

*Appointment in the Date Book*

*Note with the end date*

The program assumes that trade shows are entered in the Date Book with their starting date. The word *"Trade show:"* must be at the beginning. The end date is on a note about this appointment and starts with the word *"End: "*.

```
#Trade_show_dates.bas
d=db.open "Trade show dates" as new "DBOS", 3 else error
n%=0
while (get$("date",n%,10)<>"error")
  if (left$(s$(20),11)="Trade show:")
    s$(20)=mid$(s$(20),13)
    j$=s$(21)
    s$(21)=s$(23)+"."+s$(22)+"."+j$
    s$(22)=mid$(s$(29),6)+j$
    put d,new,(3)
  endif
  n%=n%+1
wend
print "Database created"
end

error:
print "Database could not"+chr$(10)+"be created"
```

**CD**

**Program on the companion CD**

You can also find this program on the companion CD to this book as *0808.bas.* The indentation is only for readability and is not included in the original program on the CD, because it is difficult to display on memos.

The program does not need a user interface. The appointments are read out from the Date Book and written to the database. The database is generated in the first program line.

### *db.open <Database> as new "DBOS", <Fields> else <Error>*

This function creates a new database in the DB format and returns a database ID that can be used later by other database functions. The function has three variable parameters:

- **Database** – Name of the new DB database. If a database with this name already exists, *db.open* returns its database ID and the program can use this database.
- **Fields** – Number of data fields in each record of the new database.
- **Error** – If the database fails to open, the program returns to the branch mark specified.

The program creates a database named *Trade show dates* and three data fields. These fields later contain the name of the trade show, the starting date, and the end date. If the program does not succeed in creating the database, the program goes to the *error:* branch mark and outputs a corresponding message.

```
n%=0
while (get$("date",n%,10)<>"error")
  if (left$(s$(20),11)="Trade show:")
  ...
  endif
  n%=n%+1
wend
```

A *while...wend* loop reads all the appointments from the Date Book. If the first eleven characters of the appointment label match the word *"Trade show:"*, this appointment is read and written to the database.

HowPaw Basic uses the same variables *s$(29) ...* for writing records to DB databases that it used to read appointments.

| Variable | Use for appointments | Use for databases |
|---|---|---|
| s$(20) | Text for appointment | 1st Data field |
| s$(21) | Year | 2nd Data field |
| s$(22) | Month | 3rd Data field |
| s$(23) | Day | ... |
| ... | Additional parameters of an appointment | ... |
| s$(29) | Note | ... |

The name of the trade show matches the text from the appointment starting with the twelfth character, because the word *"Trade show:"* is not supposed to be written to the database.

```
s$(20)=mid$(s$(20),12)
```

Because of the double use of the *s$()* variable, the year number from the appointment is temporarily stored in the *j$* variable. After that the appointment is put together in the *s$(21)* variable as it is to be written to the database.

```
j$=s$(21)
s$(21)=s$(23)+"."+s$(22)+"."+j$
```

The end date in the third data field of the database is read out from the note about the appointment. The buffered year number is added to its end.

```
s$(22)=mid$(s$(29),6)+j$
put d,new,(3)
```

Finally the *put* statement writes the record to the Database.

### *put <Database-ID>, new, (<Fields>)*

This function writes a record to the database. The contents of the individual fields are read from the *s$(20)* ... variables.

- **Database-ID** – the database-ID must be specified that the program generated while opening the database, not the name of the database.
- **Fields** – Specify the number of fields per record. This field number has to match with the true number of fields in the database. It determines how many of the *s$()* variables are read in the writing of a record.

## Adaptation to American date format

In the USA the date is written Month-Day-Year. The use of the *s$()* variables remains the same in HotPaw Basic. However, if you want to distribute your program in an American version, you must assume that the users have written their trade show dates on the notes in the American format. The newly created database should then use this format.

Note with the end date in the American date format

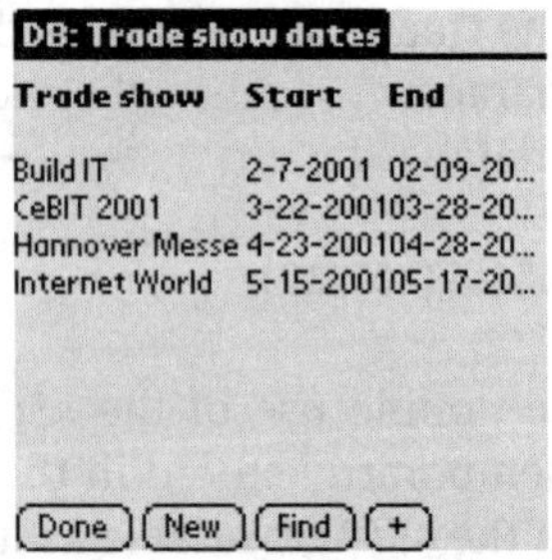


*Databasewith date specifications in the American format*

The date specifications in the American format occupy more space on the screen through the hyphens. Accordingly you must make the columns of the database wider or else you won't be able to see the entire date.

You must make a few small changes in the program.

```
#Trade_show_dates_US.bas
d=db.open "Trade show dates" as new "DBOS", 3 else error
n%=0
while (get$("date",n%,10)<>"error")
  if (left$(s$(20),11)="Trade show:")
    s$(20)=mid$(s$(20),13)
    j$=s$(21)
    s$(21)=s$(22)+"-"+s$(23)+"-"+j$
    s$(22)=mid$(s$(29),6)+"-"+j$
    put d,new,(3)
  endif
  n%=n%+1
wend
print "Database created"
end

error:
print "Database could not"+chr$(10)+"be created"
```

**CD**

**Program on the companion CD**

You can also find this program on the companion CD to this book as *0808us.bas*. The indentation is only for readability and is not included in the original program on the CD, because it is difficult to display on memos.

The only differences are in the two lines that write the date specifications to the database. The reading of the appointments contains no differences. The reading of the end date from the note doesn't need to be changed because the input string is written out as a string and is not evaluated as a date.

## Database for permanent storage of values from programs

A drawback to the HotPaw Basic programs is that their results are only available on the screen at the end of the program. If you start a different Palm program and then the HotPaw Basic program again, the results are no longer at your disposal.

Databases are ideal for this purpose as "permanent" temporary storage. The data stored in a database can be synchronized on the PC and passed on to other users. In addition, you can have HotPaw Basic input them again at the next program startup and continue processing them.

We described a program with which you can use the Palm as a counter device for counting all kinds of things. To circumvent the problem that all the input data is deleted whenever the program terminates, the program offers a feature for manually entering optional initial values. If you want to continue counting where you left off later, you must note the values in another way, for example by writing them on a memo and then re-entering them manually. This is laborious, subject to error, and no longer necessary with the next program version.

*Counter with database linking*

This new version of the counter program can simultaneously store the data of the three counters together with the current date and time in a separate database. The program can read the last record from this database again later and continue counting where it left off.

The database is written in DB format and can be evaluated at any time using the standard functions of DB. You can add the new functions from this program to other programs, where it is a matter of continuing to use the results of a calculation again the next time you start the program.

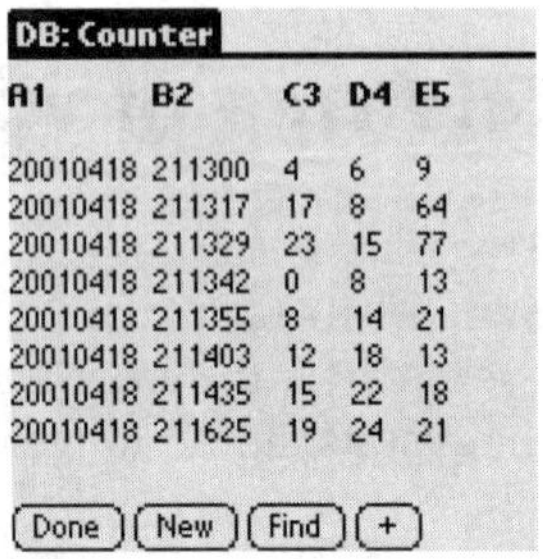


Database with data from the counter

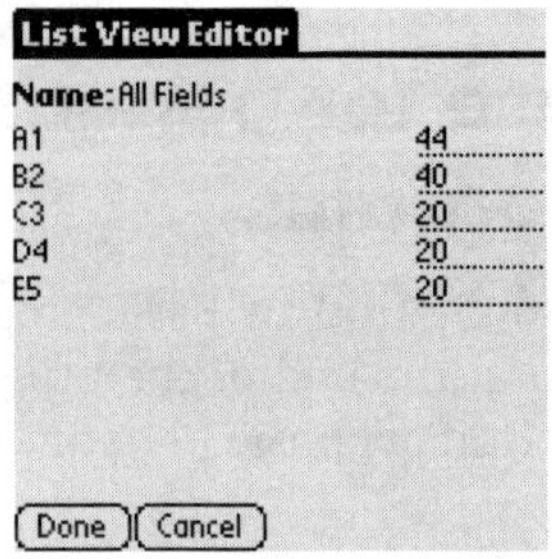


Setting the column widths

When HotPaw Basic creates the database, all the columns have a standard width. You can customize these widths for display in DB, which is unimportant for the pure functionality of the database for the HotPaw Basic program.

```
#counter4.bas
draw -1
form btn 10,40,40,60," ",1
form btn 60,40,40,60,"",1
form btn 110,40,40,60,"",1
form btn 10,125,40,15,"Set ",1
form btn 60,125,40,15," Set",1
form btn 110,125,40,15," Set",1
form btn 60,147,40,12,"DB read",1
form btn 110,147,40,12,"DB write",1
form fld 10,110,40,12,"0",1
form fld 60,110,40,12,"0",1
form fld 110,110,40,12,"0",1
dim n%(2)
d=db.open "Counter" as new "DBOS", 5 else error

start:
c=asc(input$(1))-14
if ((c>=0) and (c<=2))
  n%(c)=n%(c)+1
  draw str$(n%(c),5),10+c*50,20,2
endif
if ((c>=3) and (c<=5))
  c=c-3
```

```
    n%(c)=val(s$(c))
    draw str$(n%(c),5),10+c*50,20,2
  endif
  if (c=6) then gosub readIn:
  if (c=7) then gosub write:
  goto start

  readIn:
  z%=db.len("Counter",-16)
  for i=0 to 2
    n%(i)=val(db$(d,z%-1,i+3))
    draw str$(n%(i),5),10+i*50,20,2
  next i
  return

  write:
  s$(20)=fn date$(0)
  s$(21)=fn time$(0)
  s$(22)=str$(n%(0))
  s$(23)=str$(n%(1))
  s$(24)=str$(n%(2))
  put d,new,(5)
  return

  error:
  print "Database could not"+chr$(19)+"be created"
```

CD

**Program on the companion CD**

You can also find this program on the companion CD to this book as *0809.bas*. The indentation is only for readability and is not included in the original program on the CD, because it is difficult to display on memos.

You already have a detailed description of how the counter works. In the following section, you can only cover the additional functions for database linking.

Two new buttons are defined and a database named *Counter* is created in the initialization part of the program. If this database already exists, the *db.open* function automatically opens it.

```
d=db.open "Counter" as new "DBOS", 5 else error
```

Two additional possibilities now occur in the query of the buttons, namely that one of the two new buttons has been tapped.

```
if (c=6) then gosub readIn:
if (c=7) then gosub write:
```

In these cases a subroutine for reading and a subroutine for writing the database are called.

Before a database can be read, it must first be written:

```
write:
s$(20)=fn date$(0)
s$(21)=fn time$(0)
s$(22)=str$(n%(0))
s$(23)=str$(n%(1))
s$(24)=str$(n%(2))
put d,new,(5)
return
```

To write the five data fields, the five *s$(20) ... s$(24)* variables must be filled with the respective values. The current date and time are written to the first two data fields. We use the standard formats of the *fn date$(0)* and *fn time$(0)* functions. In contrast to the notations customary in Date Books, these formats can be automatically sorted, resulting in a chronological order.

In reading the last saved value, the number of the record in the database must be determined first. The last added record is always the one with the highest number.

```
readIn:
z%=db.len("Counter",-16)
for i=0 to 2
  n%(i)=val(db$(d,z%-1,i+3))
  draw str$(n%(i),5),10+i*50,20,2
next i
return
```

### *db.len( <Database> ,-16)*

This function specifies the number of records in a DB database. The *Database* parameter contains the name of the database.

The values of the three counters *n%(0) ... n%(2)* are read out in a loop one after the other.

### *db$(<Database-ID>, <Record>, <Data field>)*

Use this function to read out data from a DB database. The database must first be opened by *db.open*. The return value of the *db.open* function is the database-ID, which is then used here.

In our program, 1 is subtracted from the determined value of *z%* for the calculation of the last record number, because record numbers begin with 0, but *z%* contains the number of records in the database.

Data fields *3 ... 5* result from the loop counter +2. The first two data fields in the database contain the date and the time, both of which are not read out.

The read values are written up on the screen by the same *draw* statement that writes the numbers when the user taps one of the big buttons.

# 8.5 Merging and converting databases

None of the database systems we've described has a feature for converting data to a different database format. Moreover, none of the programs can merge two or more databases into a single database.

We can solve these problems with a couple of small HotPaw Basic programs. Even if a bit of extra manual work is necessary, it's still significantly faster than copying out the data.

## Converting JFile to DB

Conversion to the DB format can be done without manual preparatory work in DB, because HotPaw Basic can create DB databases on its own. After completion of the database, some extra work is still necessary for processing in DB:

- Finding the database for display in DB using the *DB/Find Databases* menu item.
- Creating the field labels in DB using the *Options/DB Design* menu item.
- Specifying the column widths in DB using the *Options/List Views* menu item.

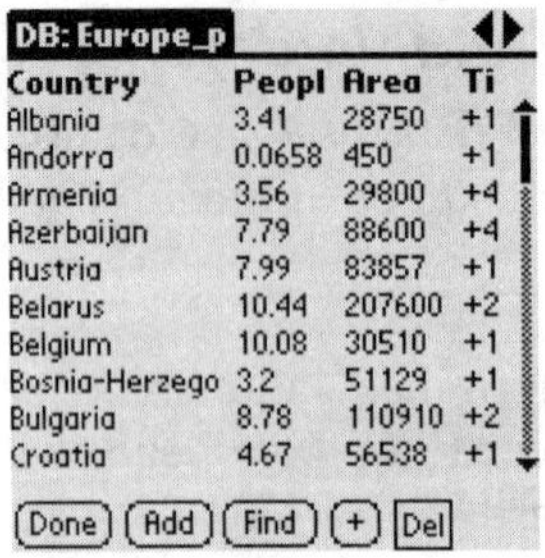


Original database in JFile

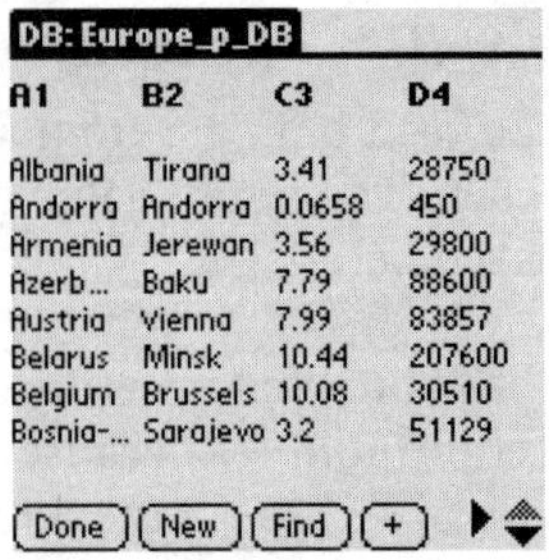


After conversion to DB

The following HotPaw Basic program queries a database name and creates a new database in the DB format that contains the same data as the JFile database. The original JFile database is preserved.

**Tip**

**HotPaw Basic processes only strings**

Keep in mind that HotPaw Basic only processes strings in database operations. Accordingly, all the fields of the new database are of the *Text* type.

```
#JFile2DB.bas
d$=input$("Name of the database:")
if (db$(d$,0,1)="error") then goto error1
z%=db.len(d$,-16)
s%=0
while (db$(d$,0,s%+1)<>"error")
  s%=s%+1
wend
if (s%>19) then goto error2
d1$=d$+"_DB"
d2=db.open d1$ as new "DBOS", s% else error3
for i=0 to z%-1
  for j=s% to 1 step -1
    s$(j+19)=db$(d$,i,j)
  next j
  put d2,new,(s%)
next i
print "DB database created"
end

error1:
print "JFile database not found"
end
```

```
error2:
print "Too many data fields"
end
error3:
print "DB database cannot"+chr$(10)+"be created"
```

CD

**Program on the companion CD**

You can also find this program on the companion CD to this book as *0810.bas*. The indentation is only for readability and is not included in the original program on the CD, because it is difficult to display on memos.

At the beginning, the program queries the name of a database and checks whether it is present by attempting to read the first field of the first record of this database.

```
d$=input$("Name of the database:")
if (db$(d$,0,1)="error") then goto error1
```

In the next step the program determines the number of records (rows) and data fields (columns) of the original database.

```
z%=db.len(d$,-16)
s%=0
while (db$(d$,0,s%+1)<>"error")
  s%=s%+1
wend
```

The number of rows can be determined using the *db.len()*function. A *while... wend* loop is used to determine the number of columns, running until an error occurs while reading a column.

HotPaw Basic can write DB databases with a maximum of 19 data fields. If the JFile database has more fields, a corresponding error message appears and the program terminates.

```
if (s%>19) then goto error2
```

The name of the new DB database matches the name of the JFile database with an appended "*_DB*" for differentiation.

```
d1$=d$+"_DB"
d2=db.open d1$ as new "DBOS", s% else error3
```

The reading and writing of the data occurs in two loops that are nested within each other.

```
for i=0 to z%-1
  for j=s% to 1 step -1
    s$(j+19)=db$(d$,i,j)
  next j
  put d2,new,(s%)
next i
```

The outer loop runs through all records beginning with 0. Within this loop an additional loop reads the fields of the respective record from the JFile database to *s$()* variables. The number of required variables depends on the number of fields in the database.

By default, the *db$()* function, which reads out the records, uses the *s$(20)* variable for temporary storage. However, this variable is needed for writing the first data field of each record. For this reason the loop runs backwards and reads *s$(20)* last. Then this variable can no longer be overwritten in further loop cycles.

After a complete record from the JFile database has been written to the *s$()* variables, a *put* statement writes the new record to the DB database.

After all the records have been written, a message is output. With longer databases, this process can take several seconds.

## Merging two DB databases

If you have several databases with similar subject matter, you cannot merge them automatically with any of the database systems we've described thus far. The only options are copying out or manually merging them and then converting them on the PC.

The next HotPaw Basic program uses a simple example to show you how to create a new database out of two DB databases.

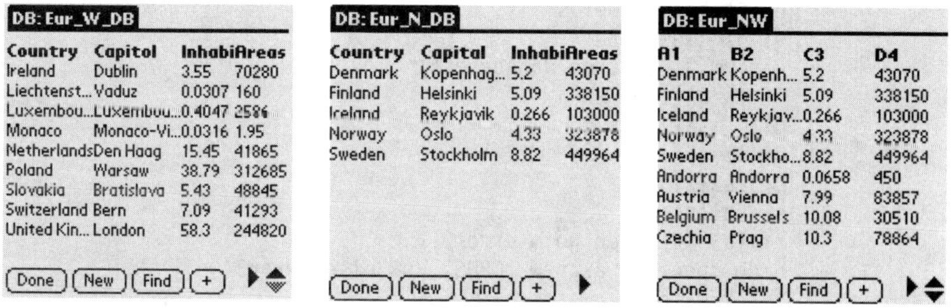


*Two single databases and the merged database*

> **CD**
>
> **Databases on the companion CD**
>
> On the companion CD to this book you can find four databases for this example with statistical information on European countries: *Eur_n_db.pdb* (North Europe), *Eur_w_db.pdb* (Central and West Europe), *Eur_o_db.pdb* (East Europe), *Eur_s_db.pdb* (South Europe).

The program creates a new DB database. First, all the records of the first database are input to this database, then all the records of the second database.

At the start of the program, you must specify the names of the databases to be read as well as the name of the new database. In addition, you must enter how many data fields the databases have because HotPaw Basic, in contrast to JFile, cannot automatically determine this from a DB database.

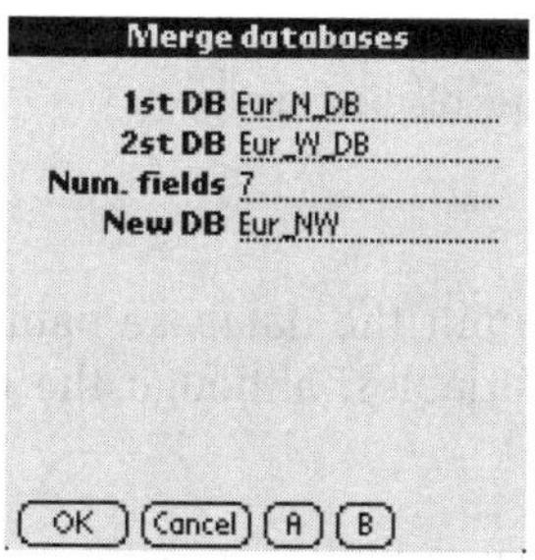


*Inputting the database names*

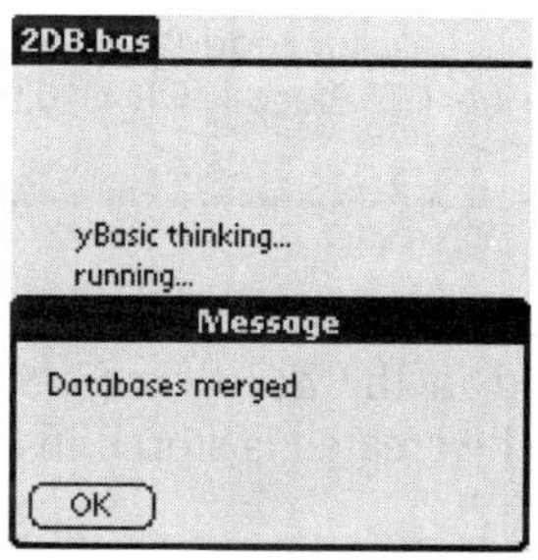


*Message after completion of the new database*

```
#2DB.bas
dim d$(1)
s$(0)="1st DB"
s$(2)="2st DB"
```

```
s$(4)="Num. fields"
s$(6)="New DB"
a=form(9,4,"Merge databases")
if (a=0) then end
d$(0)=s$(1)
d$(1)=s$(3)
dn$=s$(7)
s%=val(s$(5))
if (s%>19) then goto error2
d=db.open dn$ as new "DBOS", s% else error3
for k=0 to 1
  z%=db.len(d$(k),-16)
  for i=0 to z%-1
    for j=s% to 1 step -1
      s$(j+19)=db$(d$(k),i,j)
    next j
    put d,new,(s%)
  next i
next k
print "Databases merged"
end

error2:
print "Too many data fields"
end
error3:
print "DB database cannot"+chr$(10)+"be created"
```

**CD**

**Program on the companion CD**

You can also find this program on the companion CD to this book as *0811.bas*. The indentation is only for readability and is not included in the original program on the CD, because it is difficult to display on memos.

A HotPaw Basic standard form is used to input the database names. The two names are stored in the *d$(0)* and *d$(1)* variables, although the name of the new database to be created is stored in *dn$*.

Because HotPaw Basic can only write databases with a maximum of 19 fields, the input field number is checked, and if it is too large, an error message is output.

```
s%=val(s$(5))
if (s%>19) then goto error2
```

Then the program creates the new database.

```
d=db.open dn$ as new "DBOS", s% else error3
```

The reading and writing of the data occurs in three loops that are nested within one another. The outermost loop repeats the read operations for both databases. In so doing, the loop first determines the number of records for each database.

```
for k=0 to 1
  z%=db.len(d$(k),-16)
  ...
next k
```

The next inner loop runs through all the database records to be read. Another loop runs within this one, which reads the data fields to the *s$()* variables. These variables are then used for writing the record to the new database. The writing of the *s$()* variables occurs backwards again, as in the last example, to avoid overwriting the *s$(20)* variable with an incorrect value.

```
for i=0 to z%-1
  for j=s% to 1 step -1
    s$(j+19)=db$(d$(k),i,j)
  next j
  put d,new,(s%)
next i
```

After the two databases have been read and the records have been written to the new database, the program ends with a corresponding message.

```
print "Databases merged"
end
```

**Tip**

**Merging more than two databases**

You can merge more than two databases in the same manner. Change the input form so that more names can be entered. The *k* loop must then run more often.

# 8.6 Reading information from DOC documents

The Palm has memos for saving and editing texts. However, memos have the decisive drawback that they are limited to a length no greater than 4,000 characters. For this reason, soon after the appearance of the first Pilot, Doc format for large texts has gained ground, allowing you to use the Palm as an electronic book or electronic newspaper.

> **Note**
>
> **File extension .doc**
>
> Microsoft Word uses the *.doc* file extension for its documents. Except for the name, this has nothing to do with the Palm Doc format. On the PC, Palm documents have the *.prc* or *.pdb* extension.

Meanwhile, numerous display programs and utilities for this program are available for you to create such documents on the PC or on the Palm. The texts are PRC or PDB files on the PC and are transferred by the installation tool through HotSync. The corresponding display programs then list them on the Palm. For this purpose, every text can have a name, which does not necessarily have to match the filename on the PC. We introduce you to the most important converters of this type in Chapter 10.

The standard Doc format on the Palm knows nothing of character formatting, fonts, or font sizes. The entire text looks the same, which saves tremendous amounts of memory. In addition, Doc documents can be stored on the Palm in compressed form and can be decompressed in real time as you are reading it. Thus a Palm document has only a fraction of the size of a Word document.

## Doc display programs on the Palm

Numerous display programs have come into being for this Doc format on the Palm. Some of them have additional functions. The table gives you an overview of the most important Doc display programs.

| Program | Internet | Special features |
|---|---|---|
| AportisDoc | www.aportis.com | Automatic scrolling, PDF conversion on the PC |
| CSpotRun | www.32768.com/bill/palmos | Freeware (GPL), line spacing can be changed |
| Documents to Go | www.dataviz.com | Automatic data synchronization with the PC |
| HandBuch | www.digibuch.de | Freeware, German language |
| iSilo | www.isilo.com | Better compressed format, automatic HTML conversion on the PC, character formatting possible |
| J-Doc | www.tt.rim.or.jp/~tatsushi | Turning the display and Japanese characters possible |
| Mobile Link Doc | www.mobilegeneration.com | Links between documents possible |
| Panaread | www.panaread.com | Large display, automatic scrolling |
| RichReader | users.erols.com/arenakm/palm/RichReader.html | Formatting possible, turning the display |
| QED | visionary2000.com/qed | Editing documents on the Palm |
| Smartdoc | www.cesinc.com | Editing documents on the Palm |
| TealDoc | www.tealpoint.com | Graphics in texts, text linking, automatic scrolling, German version available |
| Z-Doc | www.geocities.com/Area51/7689/zman.htm | Editing documents on the Palm, Freeware (GPL) |

You can find other systems that work with their own document formats. However, because HotPaw Basic only works with standard Doc documents, you should not be concerned with them.

Using AportisDoc as an example, you can understand how Doc display programs work.

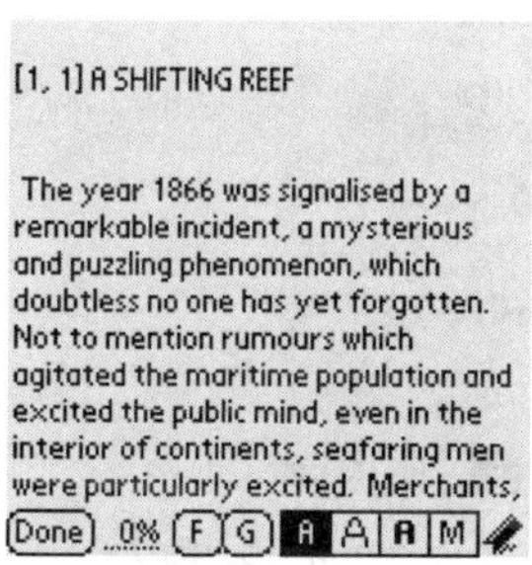


Displaying a document in AportisDoc

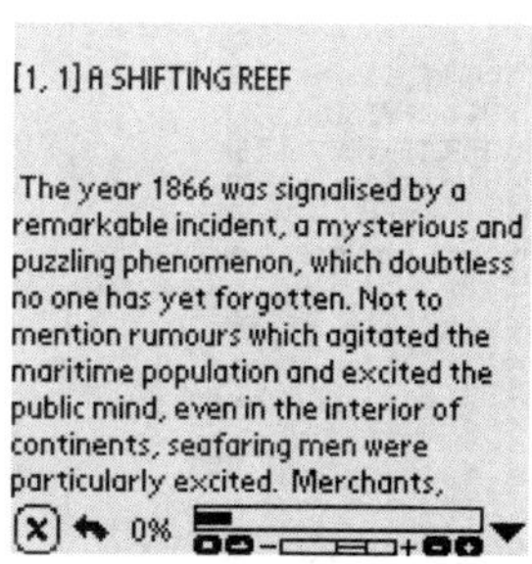


Displaying a document in TealDoc

**CD**

**Programs on the companion CD**

On the companion CD to this book, you can find shareware versions of the two best known Doc display programs for the Palm: AportisDoc and TealDoc.

In addition to standard Doc format, TealDoc supports its own special format in which lines, buttons, and graphics can be used in the texts. For more detailed information, please see *The Essential Palm User's Guide* from DATA BECKER.

# Reading HotPaw Basic programs from Doc documents

Various converters for converting normal texts on the PC to Doc documents are available. Transferring large amounts of Basic programs in source text to the Palm through the Doc format is easy, easier than copying them through the Clipboard to the Palm desktop on memos. The same applies for the use of the Palm OS Emulator. Here, too, it's much easier to install Doc files than memos. The only problem is that HotPaw Basic programs can only read memos, not Doc documents.

The next HotPaw Basic program inputs Doc documents and generates memos from them. This way you can write programs on your PC, convert them to Doc format, and install them on the Palm or on the Emulator.

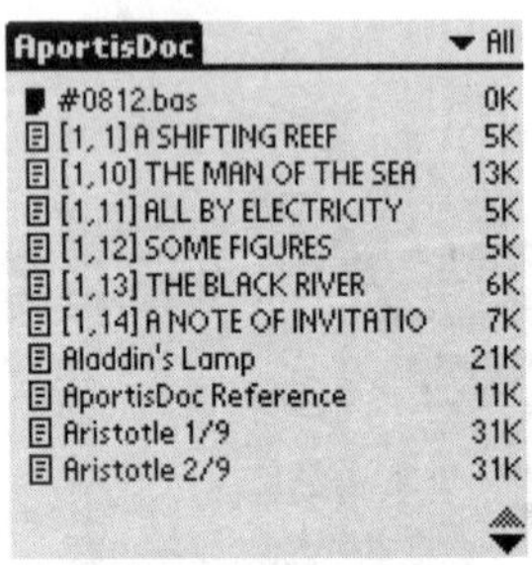


*List of documents in AportisDoc*

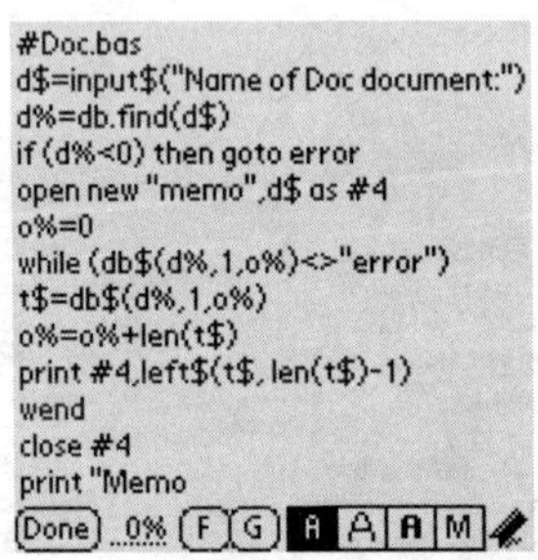


*HotPaw Basic program in AportisDoc*

As an example, the source code of this program has been converted to Doc format under the name of *#0812.bas*. You can view this text in AportisDoc or other Doc display programs.

**CD**

**File on the companion CD**

You can also find this file on the companion CD to this book as *#0812.pdb.*

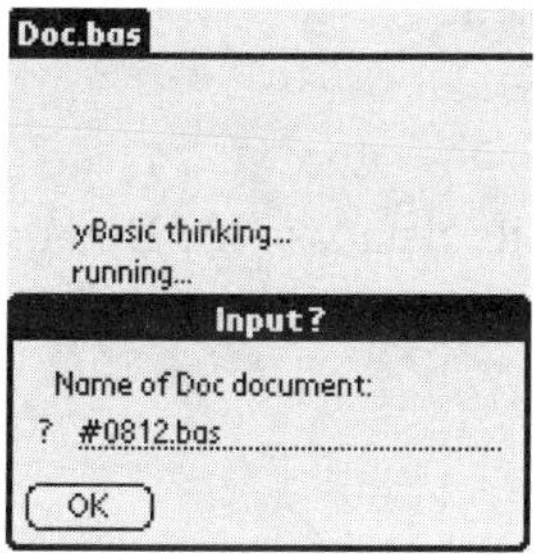


*Inputting the document name*

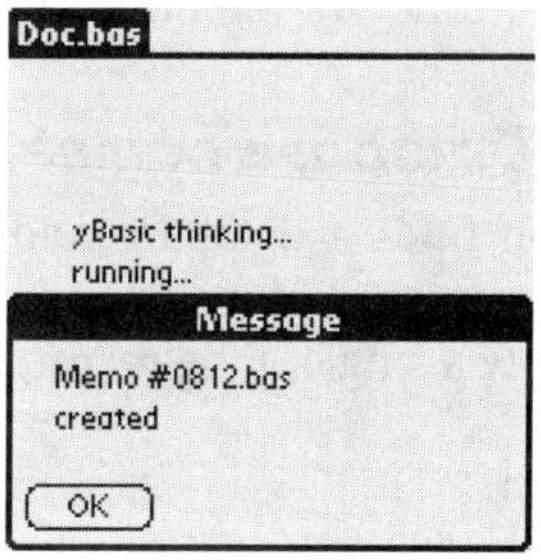


*Message after creating the memo*

```
#Doc.bas
d$=input$("Name of Doc document:")
d%=db.find(d$)
if (d%<0) then goto error
open new "memo",d$ as #4
o%=0
while (db$(d%,1,o%)<>"error")
  t$=db$(d%,1,o%)
  o%=o%+len(t$)
  print #4,left$(t$, len(t$)-1)
wend
close #4
print "Memo "+d$+chr$(10)+"created"
end

error:
print "Document not found"
```

**CD**

**Program on the companion CD**

You can also find this program on the companion CD to this book as *0812.bas.* The indentation is only for readability and is not included in the original program on the CD, because it is difficult to display on memos.

The program uses a simple prompt in which the user has to specify the name of the document that is to be converted; the program does not use a special user interface.

```
d$=input$("Name of Doc document:")
```

The *db.find()* function then finds this document.

### *db.find(<Database name>)*

This function finds a database and returns its database-ID. Doc documents on the Palm are nothing other than databases in a special format. These databases consist of only a single, long record.

```
d%=db.find(d$)
if (d%<0) then goto error
```

The database-ID of the document is stored in the *d%* variable. If it could not find the document, *db.find()* returns a negative number and the program displays an error message.

```
open new "memo",d$ as #4
```

If the function finds the document, a memo of the same name is created. A *while...wend* loop inputs the document line by line. The entire document consists of one record. Each character can be precisely addressed by its special offset.

```
while (db$(d%,1,o%)<>"error")
  t$=db$(d%,1,o%)
  o%=o%+len(t$)
  print #4,left$(t$, len(t$)-1)
wend
```

The program always continues reading a new line where the previous line ended. In accordance with the length of an input string, the offset for the next read operation is shifted ahead.

### *db$(<Database-ID>,1,<Offset>)*

This form of the *db$()* function reads a string from a Doc document. *db.find()* must first determine the database-ID of this document. If the offset value occurs after the end of the document, *db$()* returns the *"error"* string.

The offset is incremented by the length of the string input to the *t$* variable. The last character of this string is the carriage return at the end of the line. This should not be written to the memo because the *print #4* statement automatically ends a line and otherwise blank lines would appear between the lines. For this reason the string is shortened by one character when it is written to the memo.

At the end a message appears stating that the memo has been created. The name of the memo is included in the display.

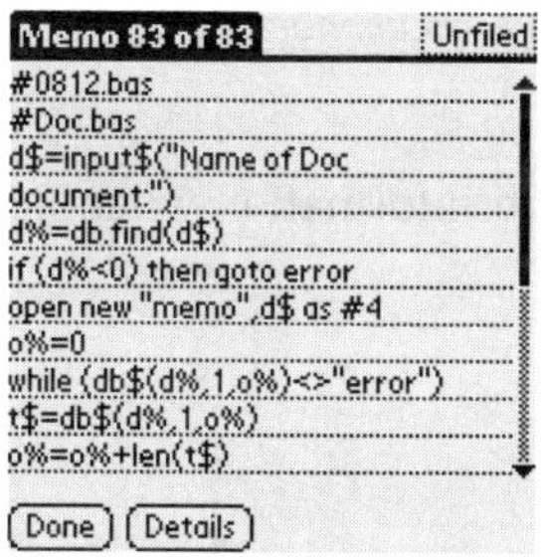


*The new created memo*

The name of the memo matches the document name of the Doc document. Thus, if you use this program to transfer HotPaw Basic program source texts, the document name appears in the first line and the program name entered in the document appears in the second line. You are now at liberty to delete one of the two names. If you leave both lines, the first line can be displayed in HotPaw Basic as the program name. The second line can be interpreted as a comment line because of the # character at the beginning and has no influence on the behavior of the program. Thus it can stay on the memo without creating problems.

## Creating a database from a formatted DOC document

You can find countless documents with interesting information formatted as tables on the different shareware and freeware servers on the Internet. Although no real tables in Doc format appear on the Palm, you can form them with spaces. As a result, they usually no longer look like a table in a Doc display program with the proportional Palm font. AportisDoc offers a non-proportional font for displaying formatted texts. To do this, tap the *M* button at the bottom border.

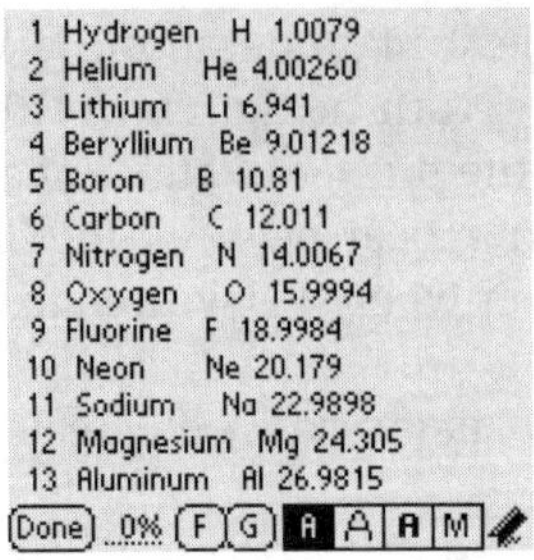

| | | | |
|---|---|---|---|
| 1 | Hydrogen | H | 1.0079 |
| 2 | Helium | He | 4.00260 |
| 3 | Lithium | Li | 6.941 |
| 4 | Beryllium | Be | 9.01218 |
| 5 | Boron | B | 10.81 |
| 6 | Carbon | C | 12.011 |
| 7 | Nitrogen | N | 14.0067 |
| 8 | Oxygen | O | 15.9994 |
| 9 | Fluorine | F | 18.9984 |
| 10 | Neon | Ne | 20.179 |
| 11 | Sodium | Na | 22.9898 |
| 12 | Magnesium | Mg | 24.305 |
| 13 | Aluminum | Al | 26.9815 |



*The periodic table of the elements in AportisDoc*

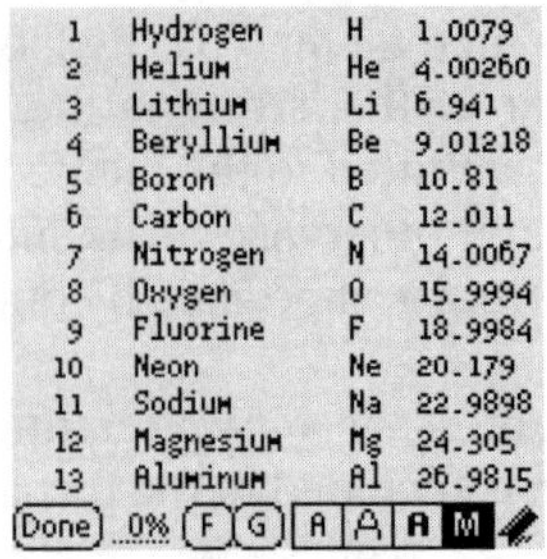

| | | | |
|---|---|---|---|
| 1 | Hydrogen | H | 1.0079 |
| 2 | Helium | He | 4.00260 |
| 3 | Lithium | Li | 6.941 |
| 4 | Beryllium | Be | 9.01218 |
| 5 | Boron | B | 10.81 |
| 6 | Carbon | C | 12.011 |
| 7 | Nitrogen | N | 14.0067 |
| 8 | Oxygen | O | 15.9994 |
| 9 | Fluorine | F | 18.9984 |
| 10 | Neon | Ne | 20.179 |
| 11 | Sodium | Na | 22.9898 |
| 12 | Magnesium | Mg | 24.305 |
| 13 | Aluminum | Al | 26.9815 |



*Display in non-proportional font*

Moreover, you can much better evaluate such information when it is stored in a database than in a text document.

**CD**

**File on the companion CD**

In the companion CD to this book you can find a document for this example named *Elemente.pdb* with a list of the first 107 elements with atomic numbers and mean atomic weights.

The next HotPaw Basic program can create a database with four fields out of this document. The data fields are determined from the position of the characters, because the document has a column structure.

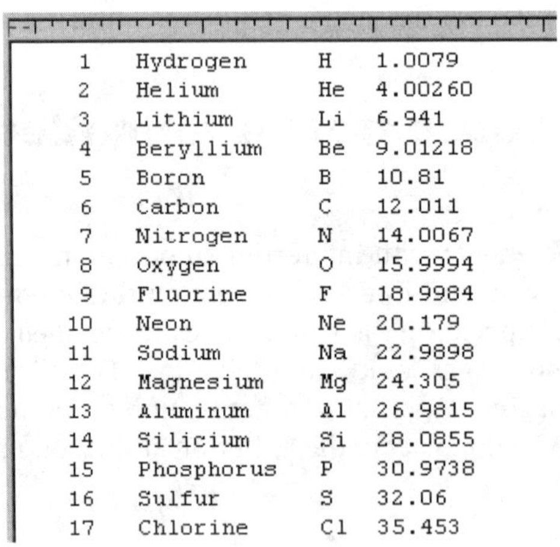

| | | | |
|---|---|---|---|
| 1 | Hydrogen | H | 1.0079 |
| 2 | Helium | He | 4.00260 |
| 3 | Lithium | Li | 6.941 |
| 4 | Beryllium | Be | 9.01218 |
| 5 | Boron | B | 10.81 |
| 6 | Carbon | C | 12.011 |
| 7 | Nitrogen | N | 14.0067 |
| 8 | Oxygen | O | 15.9994 |
| 9 | Fluorine | F | 18.9984 |
| 10 | Neon | Ne | 20.179 |
| 11 | Sodium | Na | 22.9898 |
| 12 | Magnesium | Mg | 24.305 |
| 13 | Aluminum | Al | 26.9815 |
| 14 | Silicium | Si | 28.0855 |
| 15 | Phosphorus | P | 30.9738 |
| 16 | Sulfur | S | 32.06 |
| 17 | Chlorine | Cl | 35.453 |

*In the text editor you detect the positions of the columns*

```
#Elements.bas
b=db.open "Elements_DB" as new "DBOS",4 else error1
d%=db.find("Elements")
if (d%<0) then goto error2
o%-0
while (db$(d%,1,o%)<>"error")
  t$=db$(d%,1,o%)
  o%=o%+len(t$)
  t1$=left$(t$,len(t$)-1)
  s$(20)=left$(t1$,4)
  s$(21)=mid$(t1$,8,12)
  s$(22)=mid$(t1$,21,2)
  s$(23)=mid$(t1$,25)
  put b,new,(4)
wend
print "Database Elements_DB created"
end

error1:
print "Database cannot be created"
end
error2:
print "Document Elements not found"
```

CD

**Program on the companion CD**

You can also find this program on the companion CD to this book as *0813.bas*. The indentation is only for readability and is not included in the original program on the CD, because it is difficult to display on memos.

First, the new database is created and opened. If you are working with several databases in a program, you can only open one database with write access. Opening one database can automatically close other databases, so always close a database before accessing other databases.

```
b=db.open "Elements_DB" as new "DBOS",4 else error1
d%=db.find("Elements")
if (d%<0) then goto error2
```

After that the program searches for the Doc document. If it is not found, the usual error message appears.

Then a *while...wend* loop runs over the entire document and reads one line of it. Using the character position in the line, four strings are read into the *s$(20)* ... *s$(23)* variables. A *put* statement then writes a new record from the variables.

When the offset reaches the end of the document, the *while...wend* loop ends and a message is output stating that the database has been created.

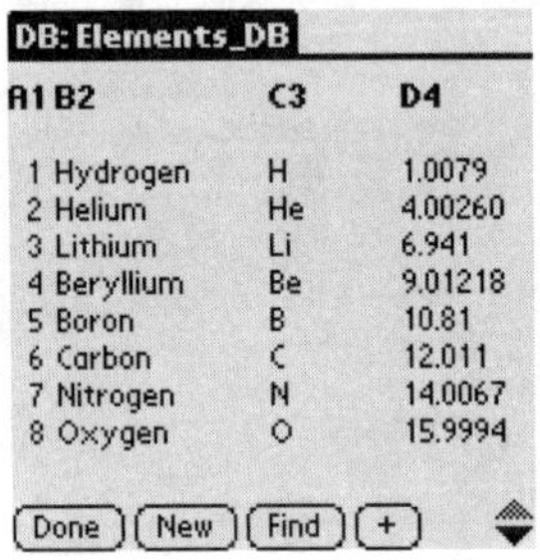


The newly created database ...

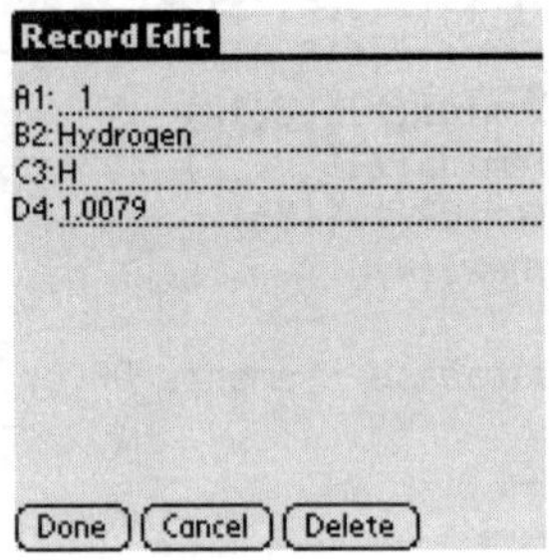


... and a single record from it

As always, you must name the data fields manually, because HotPaw Basic doesn't have a function for this.

# 9. Exchanging Data with the PC

HotSync offers an important advantage over other organizers by making a smooth exchange of data between the Palm itself and the Palm Desktop on the PC possible.

You can use this synchronization to transfer data created by programs on the Palm to the PC for further processing.

A favorite data-exchange method is to write the data to databases in standard formats, such as JFile or DB, as described in the preceding chapter. During HotSync these databases are transferred to the Backup directory of the Palm Desktop to be processed with special converters. You will find more on this in Chapter 10, "Programming Tools and Function Libraries."

## 9.1 Using memos to transfer data

Palm-OS memos are automatically transferred to the Palm Desktop, where the transferred memos can be exported to other programs. They must not be pure text files. A program can also write data to a memo in a way that permits it to be recognized by the corresponding program as its native file format. All formats based upon ASCII, for example, CSV, DXF, VRML, or PostScript are therefore possible.

The following examples show how HotPaw Basic programs generate memos that can be used by other programs on the PC.

### Stopwatch with data evaluation in a spreadsheet

When time intervals are recorded with a stopwatch, in most cases they are used further for some sort of analysis and evaluation. You write them down and later copy them from this note, but that is tedious and subject to errors. It is easier if the stopwatch exports your data directly to the PC.

You created a stopwatch program with HotPaw Basic on page 231 of Chapter 6. Expand this program now to write its data in a memo and in a format that can be evaluated by spreadsheets.

*The expanded stopwatch*

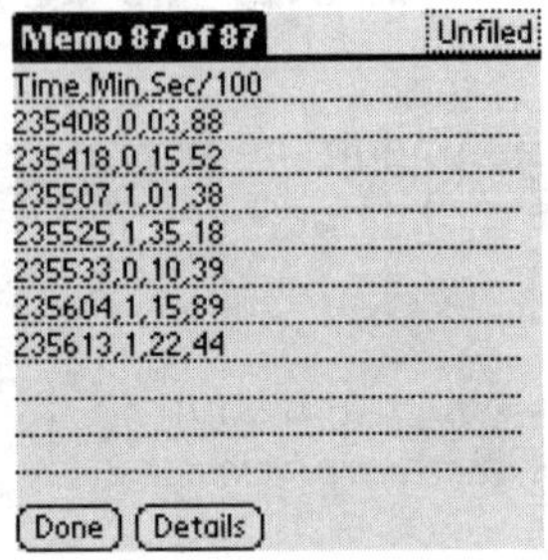


*Exported data in a memo*

The current time of the interval measurement as well as the measured minutes, seconds, and hundredths for each measurement are written to a separate line in a memo. A line is created in the memo each time you click the *Save* button.

```
#Stopwatch3.bas
draw -1
form btn 20,50,50,50,"Start",1
form btn 90,50,50,50,"Stop",1
form btn 90,120,50,20,"Reset",1
form btn 20,120,50,20,"Save",1
mz%=0

reset:
draw "0 : 00 : 00  ",20,20,2
while (asc(input$(1))<>14)
wend
a%=fn 17

start:
m$=str$(int(((fn 17)-a%)/6000))
s$=str$(int((((fn 17)-a%)mod 6000)/100))
if (len(s$)=1) then s$="0"+s$
h$=str$(int(((fn 17)-a%)mod 100))
if (len(h$)=1) then h$="0"+h$
draw m$+" : "+s$+" : "+h$+"  ",20,20,2
if (asc(inkey$)=15) then goto stop
goto start

stop:
b=asc(input$(1))-13
```

```
on b goto 110, 120, 130 ,140
110 a%=(fn 17)-6000*val(m$)-100*val(s$)-val(h$)
goto start
120 goto stop
130 goto reset
140 if (mz%=0)
  mz$="Time,Min,Sec/100 "
  open new "memo",mz$ as #4
  mz%=1
endif
print #4, fn time$(0)+","+m$+","+s$+","+h$"
goto stop
end
```

CD

**Program on the companion CD**

You can find this program on the companion CD to this book as *0901.bas.* Indentation is used only for readability and is not contained in the original program on the CD, because it is difficult to display in memos.

The program works essentially like the stopwatch described above. Only the new functions are described below for data exportation.

An additional button is defined right at the beginning, and the *mz%* variable is set to 0. Later this will indicate whether a memo was already generated for data export.

```
form btn 20,120,50,20,"Save",1
mz%=0
```

The next change in the program is in the line that queries the next button pressed after stopping the stopwatch. A further alternative is offered for the case where the new button, *Save*, is pressed.

```
on b goto 110, 120, 130 ,140
```

The program jumps to the new line number 140. Verification is done to determine whether the *mz%* is still at 0. In this case, the program has not yet created a memo, so you are still concerned with the first saved time measurement.

```
140 if (mz%=0)
  mz$= „time, min, sec,/100 "
  open new "memo",mz$ as #4
  mz%=1
endif
print #4, fn time$(0)+","+m$+","+s$+","+h$"
goto stop
```

The program creates a new memo whereby the first line contains the later column headings of the table. The variable *mz%* is now set to 1. Whenever this variable is at 1, the program assumes that a suitable memo already exists and writes a new line to this memo containing the current time, the measured minutes, seconds, and hundredths, respectively separated by commas.

## Transfer of the data to the PC

This memo is transferred to the PC automatically during the next HotSync.

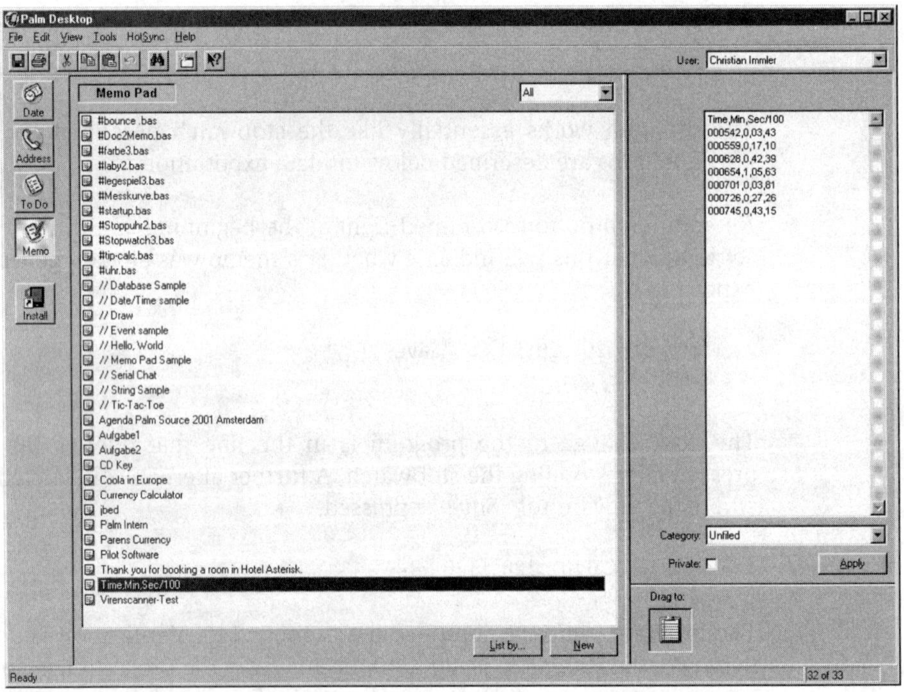


*The memo created by the program on the Palm Desktop*

Export this memo into a CSV file that can be read for spreadsheets.

**Tip**

**The CSV file format**

The abbreviation CSV stands for **C**omma **S**eparated **V**alue and means "values separated by commas". This pure ASCII format can be read by all spreadsheets and by most database programs. Each line in a CSV file represents a record in the database or a line in the spreadsheet. The individual data fields are separated from one another inside the line by commas or semicolons.

For that, two possibilities exist:

In the first method, you select the memo on the Palm Desktop and then select *File/Export* in the menu.

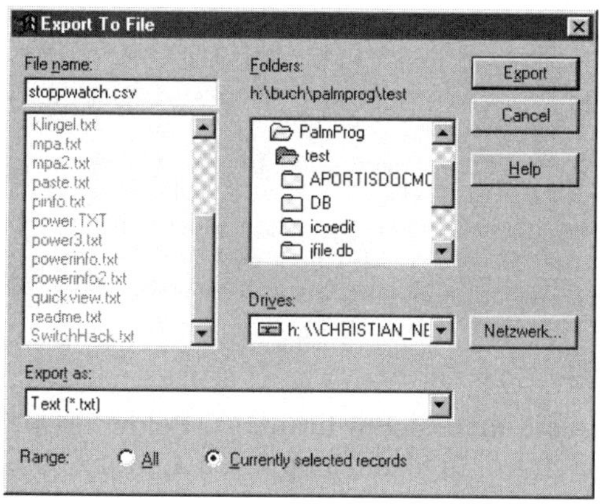


*Exporting a memo*

Pay attention to the following settings:

- The *Currently Selected Entries* option must be active.
- The *Text (*.txt)* option in the *Export* field must be selected, not the *csv* option.
- Enter a file name with the suffix *csv* in the *File Name* field.

When you click *Export*, a further dialog box for selecting the export fields appears.

*Selection of the export fields*

Select only the *Memo* field and then double-click the CSV file produced in Windows Explorer. It opens automatically with your set standard spreadsheet.

| | A | B | C | D |
|---|---|---|---|---|
| 1 | Time | Min | Sec | /100 |
| 2 | | | | |
| 3 | 000542 | 0 | 03 | 43 |
| 4 | | | | |
| 5 | 000559 | 0 | 17 | 10 |
| 6 | | | | |
| 7 | 000628 | 0 | 42 | 39 |
| 8 | | | | |
| 9 | 000654 | 1 | 05 | 63 |
| 10 | | | | |
| 11 | 000701 | 0 | 03 | 81 |
| 12 | | | | |
| 13 | 000726 | 0 | 27 | 26 |
| 14 | | | | |
| 15 | 000745 | 0 | 43 | 15 |

*The CSV file in Excel 2000*

Appearing in the first line are the column headings. Below them, as selectable values, the time measurements of the Palm stopwatch appear.

This process ran without problems up to version Excel 95, as well as in Lotus 1-2-3, because in Excel 97, blank lines appear between the lines.

The second method works somewhat differently but leads to the same result. Decide for yourself which method is simpler:

Mark the memo with the stopwatch measurements on the Palm Desktop and drag it, with the mouse button held down, to the Clipboard icon in the lower right of the Palm-Desktop window.

Start a simple text editor, for example, the Windows-Editor, and insert the Clipboard contents there using Ctrl+V.

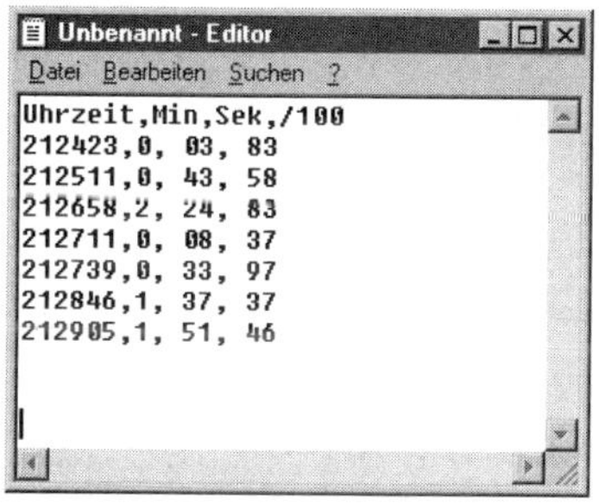


*The memo copied into the Editor from the Clipboard*

Save the text from the Editor as a file with the suffix *csv*. Double-click your spreadsheet and the file now opens.

## Exporting a graphic

Simple charts, bar graphs, and diagrams can be drawn in HotPaw Basic in vector form using the *draw* command. Such vectors are represented, as in vector-oriented CAD and graphics programs, as lines through starting and ending points. Vector graphics, in contrast to pixel graphics, can be easily scaled. That means a graphic produced on the Palm can be usefully employed on the PC with its significantly larger screen.

The standard HotSync function and Palm Desktop offer no option for exchanging graphics. However, the process can be done through the most important file format for vector graphics, DXF. DXF files are pure ASCII files without binary code and can therefore be written into a memo.

The next HotPaw Basic program is an expansion of the bar graph program from the previous chapter, which created a bar graph from a database. The new program version can write this graphic to a memo in the DXF format. It can then be converted into a DXF file on the PC after a HotSync. This program demonstrates how to export your other programs to the PC.

**CD**

**File on the companion CD**

This program, like the preceding version, also requires the *Europe_m.pdb* database from the companion CD to this book.

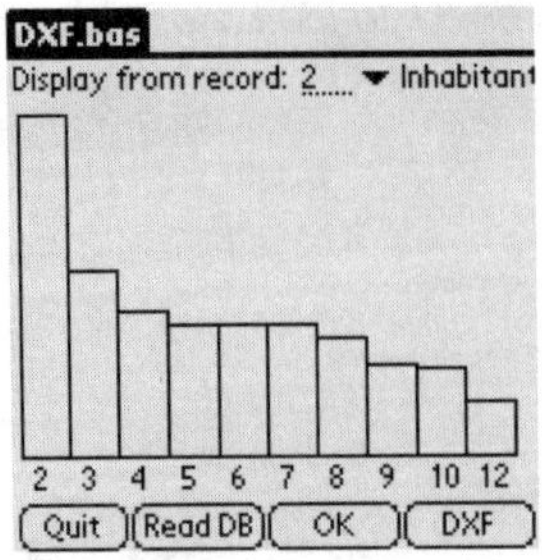


The graphic

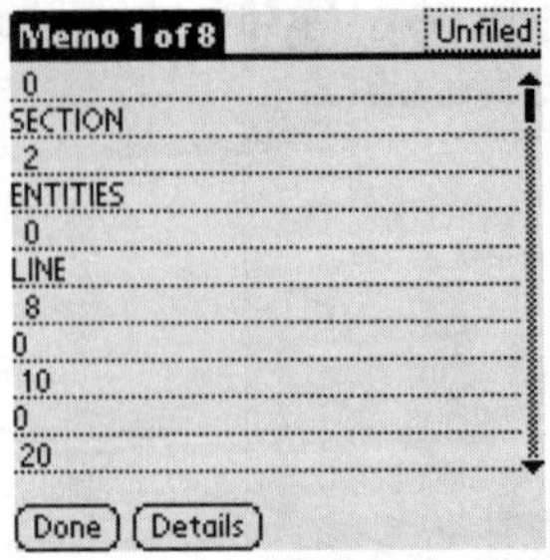


Beginning ...

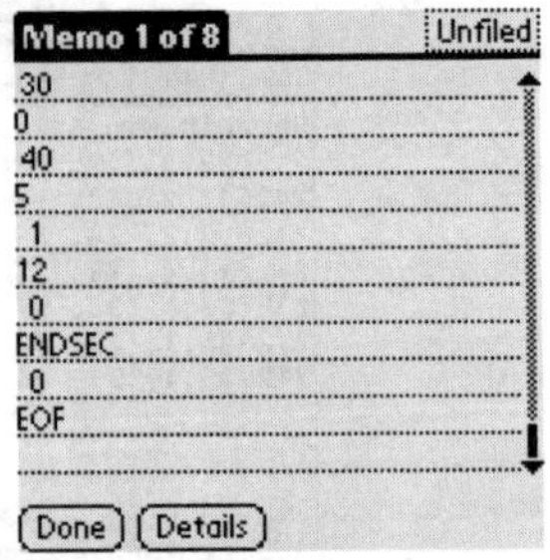


... and end of DXF output

**Tip**

**Watch out for the maximal memo size**

DXF files can be very long. Be aware that a memo can contain a maximum of 4,000 characters. The exported graphic from the example already has 3,494 characters. Either export only the important parts of a graphic or write several memos, as needed.

After the HotSync, proceed as follows in order to convert the memo into a DXF file:

Mark the memo on the Palm Desktop and drag it, with the mouse button held down, to the Clipboard icon on the lower right of the Palm-Desktop window. This memo has the simple name *"0"*. Read the description of the DXF format further below to find out why it has to be like that.

Start a simple text editor, for example, the Windows Editor, and insert the Clipboard contents using Ctrl+V.

Save the text from the Editor as a file with the *dxf*-suffix. Import this file to your graphics program.

**Tip**

**No File/Export**

In this case, do not use the *File/Export* function from the Palm Desktop. The function adds a character to the end of the line that is not permissible in DXF files. The DXF files can then no longer be imported into graphics programs.

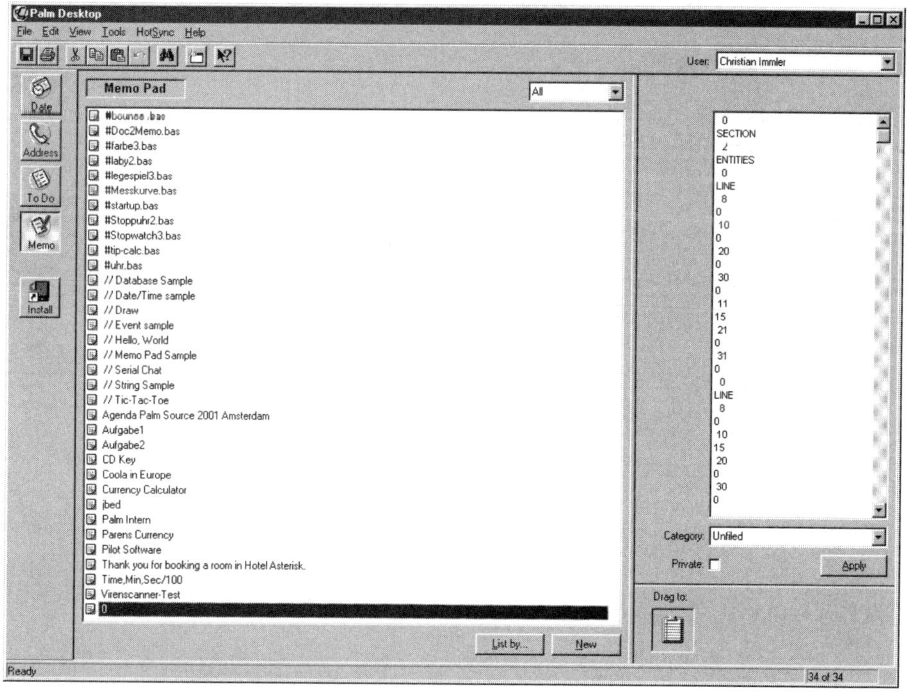


*The memo on the Palm Desktop*

**Tip**

### The DXF format

The DXF format was defined by Autodesk with the first version of AutoCAD and has been considered since that time to be the standard data exchange format for CAD and other vector-oriented graphics programs. The DXF format was developed further with each AutoCAD version, to permit the representation of the respective new AutoCAD-features. Today, any CAD program and even many other graphics programs such as, for example, Paint Shop Pro or Adobe Illustrator can read DXF files. Not all of these programs have however kept pace with the current developments of the DXF format. DXF version AutoCAD 12, which is only a few years old, is currently used most often for exchanging data with outside programs. Problems during importation into graphics programs arise only rarely. Moreover, this format produces smaller files than the DXF format from AutoCAD 2000.

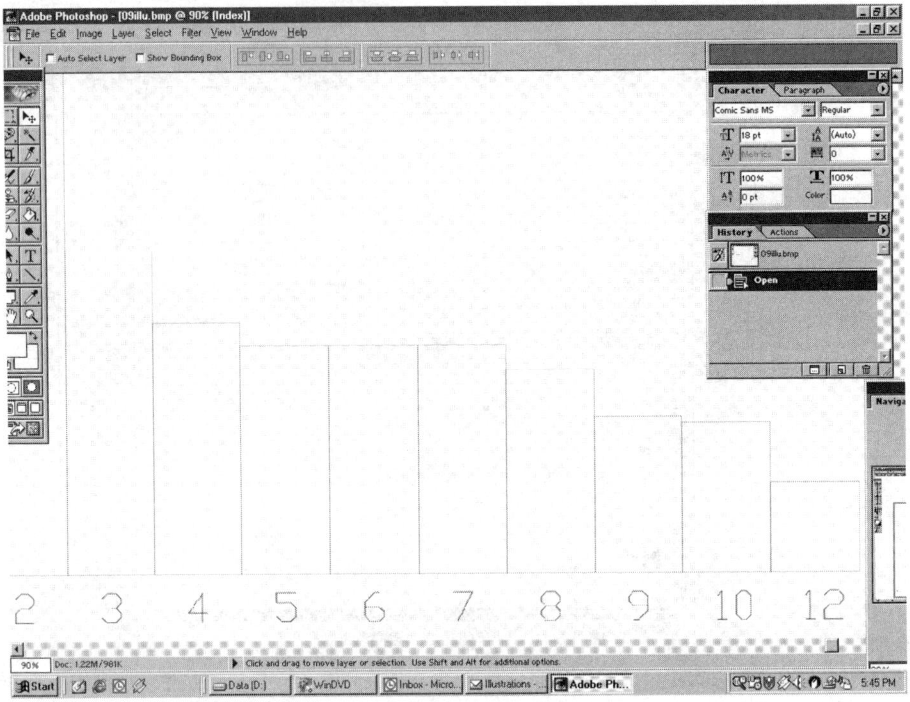


*The imported DXF graphic in Adobe Photoshop*

The HotPaw Basic program writes a very simple DXF format with no version number, which can be read by any graphics program supporting any DXF version.

**CD**

**File on the companion CD**

You will find the DXF file of the graphic shown as *0903.dxf* on the companion CD to this book.

DXF files consist of numerous groups of two lines following one after the other. The first line always contains a group number that indicates how the second line should be evaluated. Each object represented, whether it is a line, circle, text, or a 3D-body, consists of several such line pairs describing the various coordinates and properties of the object.

**Tip**

**Detailed information on the DXF format**

You can describe only the most important DXF elements needed for the example program.

The example program writes only the absolutely necessary DXF groups. Otherwise, the DXF file would rapidly become very large. The table provides an overview of the groups that must be available in any case.

| Group number | Object type | Content |
|---|---|---|
| 0 | | Beginning of an object or of a section |
| 2 | SECTION | Designation of a section in the Dxf file |
| 8 | | Layer |
| 10 | Line | x-coordinate, starting point |
| 20 | Line | y-coordinate, starting point |
| 30 | Line | z-coordinate, starting point |
| 10 | Text | x-coordinate, beginning of text |
| 20 | Text | y-coordinate, beginning of text |
| 30 | Text | z-coordinate, beginning of text |
| 11 | Line | x-coordinate, end point |
| 21 | Line | y-coordinate, end point |
| 31 | Line | z-coordinate, end point |
| 40 | Text | Text height |
| 1 | Text | Text content |

The group number is always indented by at least one space for the clear separation of the groups.

Each DXF file can consist of several SECTIONS. Absolutely necessary are the SECTION ENTITIES containing the actual objects. Other SECTIONS could, for example, contain layer tables of block definitions.

```
  0
SECTION
  2
ENTITIES
```

The first four lines of the DXF file contain a group 0 that establishes the beginning of the SECTION and a group 2 with the name of the SECTION.

Because the DXF format does not permit comment lines, the first line always contains a 0, so the memos appear on the Palm with the name "0".

Following after that are the objects. The next listing segment shows the display of a line.

```
  0
LINE
  8
0
 10
0
 20
0
 30
0
 11
15
 21
0
 31
0
```

The 0 group at the beginning defines the object as a line with the DXF-object type LINE. Following that is a group 8 with the layer specification 0. All objects in the example are drawn on the standard layer 0, because the DXF file must then contain no layer table.

The coordinates in groups 10, 20, 11, 21 indicate that this line extends from coordinate point 0,0 to point 15,0, making a two-dimensional graphic. Groups 30 and 31 for the z-coordinates are consequently 0 in all objects.

The example graphic always contains four lines, one after the other, for the representation of a bar and, after that, a text object with the assigned field number.

```
  0
TEXT
  8
0
 10
5
 20
```

```
-8
 30
0
 40
5
  1
2
```

The group 0 at the beginning defines the object as text with the DXF-object type TEXT. Following that is a group 8 with the layer specification 0.

The coordinates in groups 10, 20 indicate that this text begins at coordinate point 5,-8. Here, too, group 30 for the z-coordinate is 0.

Found in group 40 is the text height of five coordinate units and at the end, in group 1, the text that is in this case the number *"2"*.

Once all ten bars of the graphic have been formed in this way, two more groups follow, which indicate the end of the SECTION and the end of the file.

```
  0
ENDSEC
  0
EOF
```

The *EOF* line is always the last line of a DXF file.

## How the program works

Now that you understand how a DXF is structured, turn once more to the Hot-Paw Basic program on the Palm, which generates files according to the described plan and writes to a memo.

You can export any other vector-based graphic from the Palm to the PC using the principle of this program.

```
#DXF.bas
dim n1$(9),n1%(9),n2(9),a$(2)
draw -1
form btn 38,147,38,12,"Read DB",1
form btn 79,147,38,12,"OK",1
form btn 120,147,38,12,"DXF",1
form fld 90,15,15,12,"",1
a$(1)="Inhabitants"
```

```
a$(2)="Area"
form lst 105,15,2,1,a$,1
draw " Display from record: ",0,15
start:
x%=asc(input$(1))
if (x%=14) then gosub list
if (x%=15) then if (g%=1) then gosub list else gosub graphic
if (x%=16) then gosub dxf
goto start

list:
g%=0
draw 0,30,160,115,-7
for i=0 to 9
  n2(i)=0
next i
z=val(s$(0))
j=z
i=0
while ((i<10)and(db$("Europe_m",j,1)<>"error"))
  n1$(i)=db$("Europe_m",j,1)
  if
((n1$(i)<>"Country")and(n1$(i)<>"str")and(n1$(i)<>"")and(not(val(n1$(i))
➥)>0))
    n2(i)=val(db$("Europe_m",j,val(s$(1))+2))
    n1%(i)=j
    draw str$(j),0,30+11*i
    draw n1$(i),15,30+11*i
    draw str$(n2(i)),120,30+11*i
    i=i+1
  endif
  j=j+1
wend
return

graphic:
g%=1
draw 0,30,160,115,-7
m=n2(0)
for i=1 to 9
  if (n2(i)>m) then m=n2(i)
next i
for i=0 to 9
  if (n2(i)<>0)
    y=int(n2(i)/m*100)
    draw i*15+4, 132-y, 14, y, 4
    draw str$(n1%(i)),i*15+7,133
  endif
next i
return
```

```
dxf:
print " DXF export takes a few seconds. Please wait ..."
m=n2(0)
for i=1 to 9
  if (n2(i)>m) then m=n2(i)
next i
open new "memo","  0" as #4
print #4,"SECTION"
print #4,"  2"
print #4,"ENTITIES"
for i=0 to 9
  if (n2(i)<>0)
    y=int(n2(i)/m*100)
    x1=i*15
    x2=(i+1)*15
    px1=x1:py1=0:px2=x2:py2=0
    gosub drawline
    px1=x2:py1=0:px2=x2:py2=y
    gosub drawline
    px1=x2:py1=y:px2=x1:py2=y
    gosub drawline
    px1=x1:py1=y:px2=x1:py2=0
    gosub drawline
    print #4,"  0"
    print #4,"TEXT"
    print #4,"  8"
    print #4,"0"
    print #4," 10"
    print #4,str$(x1+5)
    print #4," 20"
    print #4,"-8"
    print #4," 30"
    print #4,"0"
    print #4," 40"
    print #4,"5"
    print #4,"  1"
    print #4,str$(n1%(i))
  endif
next i
print #4,"  0"
print #4,"ENDSEC"
print #4,"  0"
print #4,"EOF"
close #4
print " DXF file created "
return

drawline:
print #4,"  0"
print #4,"LINE"
```

```
print #4,"  8"
print #4,"0"
print #4," 10"
print #4,px1
print #4," 20"
print #4,py1
print #4," 30"
print #4,"0"
print #4," 11"
print #4,px2
print #4," 21"
print #4,py2
print #4," 31"
print #4,"0"
return
```

**CD**

**Program on the companion CD**

You can also find this program on the companion CD to this book as *0902.bas*. Indentation serves only for readability and is not contained in the original program on the CD, because it is difficult to display in memos.

The first part of this program corresponds exactly to the program described in the preceding chapter, with two small, but important differences:

- An additional button is defined in the button definitions at the beginning. The button coordinates were changed for ergonomic reasons. The buttons lie in a logical sequence, as you would normally click them: First select the database; then create the graphic with *OK* and, finally, the DXF output.
- An additional option occurs when the buttons are queried in the main program. If you click the new *DXF* button, the program calls the new *dxf:* subprogram.

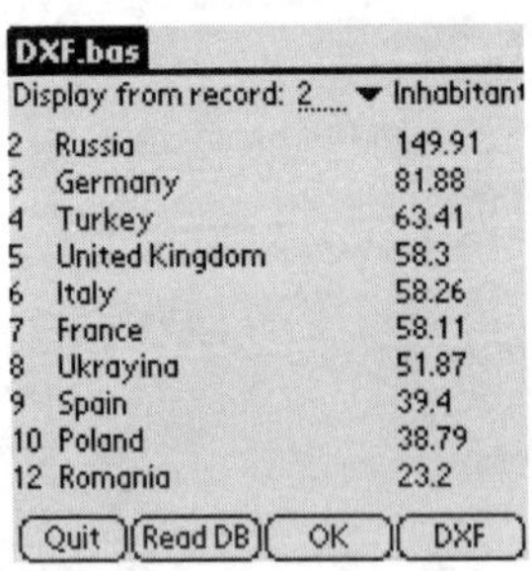


*The new program version*

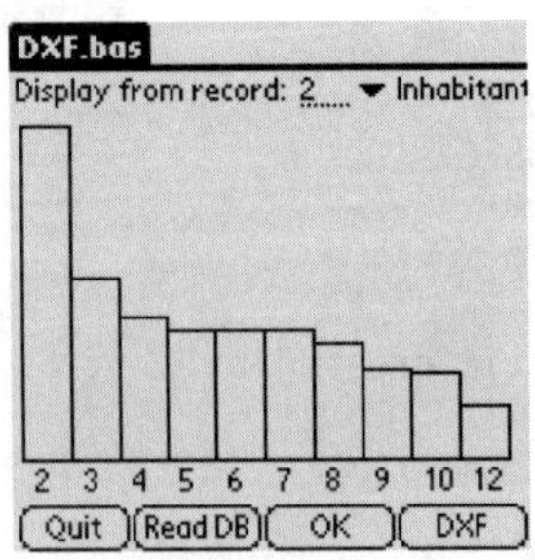


*The graphics display*

Restrict yourselves in the following description to the new *dxf:* subprogram. Find a detailed description of the basic program functions further below.

```
dxf:
print " DXF export takes a few seconds. Please wait ..."
m=n2(0)
for i=1 to 9
  if (n2(i)>m) then m=n2(i)
next i
```

The first thing displayed by the program is the message that generation of the DXF file can take some time.

*Message before the creation of a DXF file*

If the user has confirmed this message, the maximum of the displayed values for scaling the graphic must then be determined. The graphic uses the same size relationships in the DXF file as on the screen of the Palm. It can be scaled as desired on the PC after importation into a graphics program.

```
open new "memo","  0" as #4
print #4,"SECTION"
print #4,"  2"
print #4,"ENTITIES"
```

A new memo is created, and the first four standard lines of the DXF file are then written. The first line corresponds to the memo name and is always *"0"*.

```
for i=0 to 9
  if (n2(i)<>0)
  ...
  endif
next i
```

A loop then runs over all ten bars of the graphic, but the command to write the graphic will be executed only if the value of the respective bar is not 0. That prevents error messages at the end, if the entered number of the first record to be displayed lies just before the end of the database.

```
y=int(n2(i)/m*100)
x1=i*15
x2=(i+1)*15
```

The program calculates the y-coordinates of the upper point as well the x-coordinates of left and right side for each bar. The lower end of the bar always lies at 0.

```
px1=x1:py1=0:px2=x2:py2=0
gosub drawline
px1=x2:py1=0:px2=x2:py2=y
gosub drawline
px1=x2:py1=y:px2=x1:py2=y
gosub drawline
px1=x1:py1=y:px2=x1:py2=0
gosub drawline
```

The coordinates of the starting and ending point are specified from these coordinates for each of the four lines of a bar, and then the second subprogram draw line starts, writing the line into the DXF file.

```
drawline:
print #4,"  0"
print #4,"LINE"
print #4,"  8"
print #4,"0"
print #4," 10"
print #4,px1
print #4," 20"
print #4,py1
print #4," 30"
print #4,"0"
print #4," 11"
print #4,px2
print #4," 21"
print #4,py2
print #4," 31"
print #4,"0"
return
```

This subprogram writes all the required DXF groups, one after the other, and the respective values into separate lines of the memo.

```
print #4,"  0"
print #4,"TEXT"
print #4,"  8"
print #4,"0"
print #4," 10"
print #4,str$(x1+5)
print #4," 20"
print #4,"-8"
print #4," 30"
print #4,"0"
print #4," 40"
print #4,"5"
print #4,"  1"
print #4,str$(nl%(i))
```

After the four lines are drawn, the TEXT object with the record number of the respective bar is written to the DXF file in a similar manner. The sequence of the objects inside a SECTION of a DXF file can be arbitrary. It need not be in any relationship with the graphic arrangement of the objects.

```
print #4,"  0"
print #4,"ENDSEC"
print #4,"  0"
print #4,"EOF"
close #4
print " DXF file created "
```

At the end of the loop, when all bars are drawn, the four closing lines are written into the DXF file, the memo is closed with *close #4*, and a message appears that DXF exportation is finished.

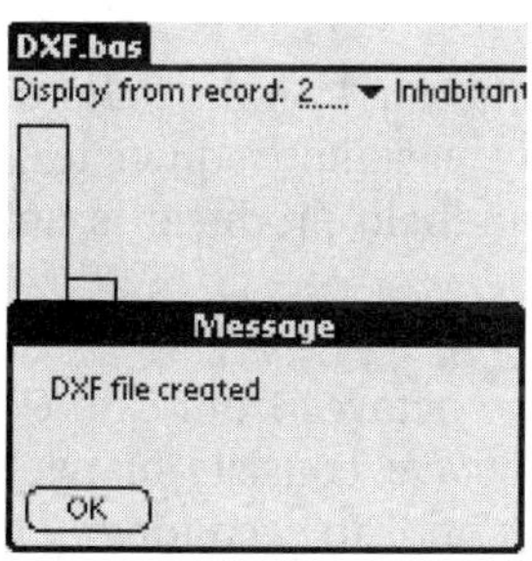


*Message following the completed DXF export*

The program jumps back again into the main program so that another region of the database can be displayed.

## Testing handheld ring tones on the Palm

If you walk around airports or large trade fairs, you can hear handhelds ringing at every turn. It is sometimes difficult to distinguish your own handheld from the others. Modern handhelds offer the option of entering personal ring tones, thereby giving your own handheld a distinctive ring.

Find ring tones on various Websites and CDs. You must type the text files into the handheld keypad and save them; then listen to the various ring tones. You can't identify the melody from the text file. Users frequently type various melodies on the tiny handheld keypad, but in the end the tones go unused because they do not correspond to one's taste in music.

The next program offers some help with the selection of ring tones. If you want to obtain a ring tone as a key sequence, type this text file into a memo on the Palm Desktop. After you HotSync, listen to the melody in the HotPaw Basic program on the Palm, trying out various melodies before you decide to type one of them on the handheld keypad.

**Tip**

**Watch out for different ring-tone formats**

Unfortunately, all manufacturers of handhelds use different formats for keying in ring tones. In the case of a few producers, even the method of writing differs among different types of handhelds. The example program uses the input format for Motorola handhelds. Motorola discloses its format for entering ring tones openly.

The program shows in general how to generate tones on the Palm using HotPaw Basic. The program can calculate with note values and frequencies. The conversion of the ring-tone format of a different handheld producer is not a big problem, once you know the format.

The tones in music are ordinarily indicated in octaves from C to C. Most handhelds count the octaves from A to A. An octave consists of twelve half-tone steps, so a precisely defined frequency corresponds to each tone:

| Tone (Handheld writing method) | Comment | Frequency (Hz) | Numbering of the basic tones | Numbering of all tones |
|---|---|---|---|---|
| G# | | 844 | | 11 |
| G | | 792 | 6 | 10 |
| F# | | 734 | | 9 |
| F | Corresponds to: E# | 704 | 5 | 8 |
| E | | 660 | 4 | 7 |
| D# | | 634 | | 6 |
| D | | 594 | 3 | 5 |
| C# | | 550 | | 4 |
| C | Corresponds to: B# | 528 | 2 | 3 |
| B | | 495 | 1 | 2 |
| A# | | 475 | | 1 |
| A | "Chamber tone" | 440 | 0 | 0 |

*Both right-hand columns in this table are required for the storage of the tones in the program and thus have nothing to do with musical notation*

**Tip**

**American notation**

Most handhelds use American notation for designating tones.

The pound sign (#) after a tone increases this tone by a half-tone step, which corresponds to a line in the table. No supplementary intermediate steps occur at two points in an octave, between E and F as well as between B and C, because the basic tones are only a half tone apart.

Additional octaves result from doubling the frequencies. For example, the next C tones are at 264 Hz and 1,056 Hz. On the handheld, the next octave begins at the next higher A with 880 Hz.

## The format of the Motorola ring tones

The first character of a ring tone establishes the speed of the music, from 1 (slow) to 4 (fast). Exactly one space must stand between this number and the first tone and likewise one space between the individual tones. Each melody can consist of up to 35 tones.

Each note in the melody begins with a capital letter from A through G, followed by a pound sign, if it is a half tone. The musical sign for lowering the sign by a half step (b) cannot be represented. These tones must be harmonically translated: The sound Eb corresponds for example to D#.

The tones thus indicated correspond to the octaves between A (880 Hz) and A (1,760 Hz). To raise a tone by one octave, write a + after it, to lower it by one octave, a -, respectively with no space after the tone designation. You can represent the tones between A (440 Hz) and A (3,520 Hz) in this way.

The duration is entered as the last character of a memo, as a number between 1 and 8, the larger the number, the longer the tone. The 8 thereby represents a half note, the 4 a quarter note, the 2 an eighth note, and the 1 a sixteenth note.

```
4 C2 D2 E2 F2 G2 G2 G2 G2 A+2 F2 C+2 A+2 G4 A+2 F2 C+2 A+2 G4 G2 F2 F2 F2 F2
E2 E2 E2 E2 D2 E2 D2 C2 E2 G4
```

*A Motorola ring tone in the key-notation format*

## The program

The program reads ring tones in the Motorola format from a memo and plays them on the Palm. You can edit the memo at any time and thus change the melody.

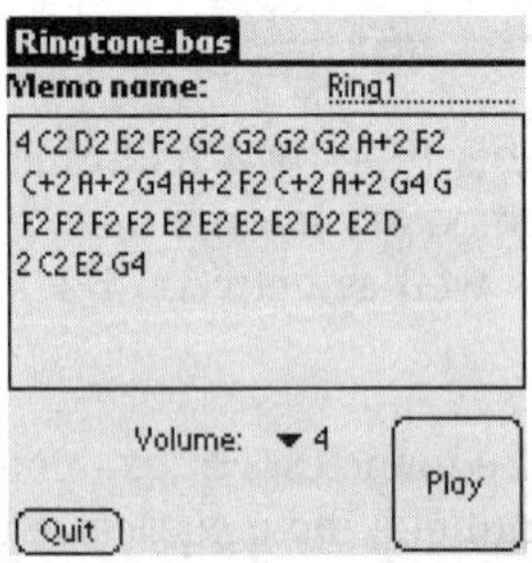


*Ring tone in the program*

The program assumes that the entire ring tone was received on the Palm Desktop as one line from the Clipboard, in other words, that it contains no wordwraps. Insert an additional line at the beginning to identify this ring tone clearly. The program searches the ring tones with the aid of the first line of each memo in the memo list.

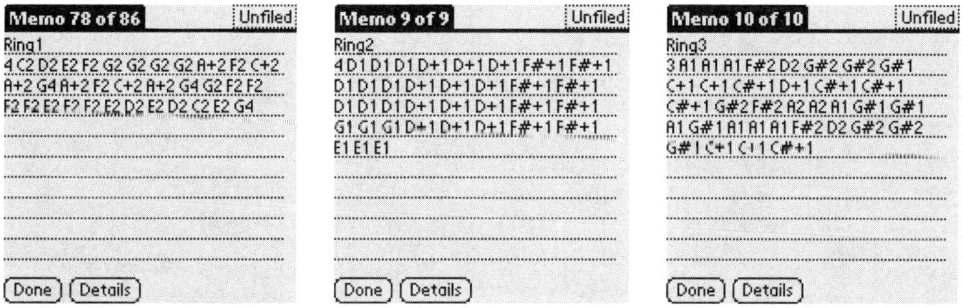


*Various ring tones in memos*

Enter the memo name to the upper right of the program, set the volume level in the *Volume* list box, and click *Play*. The memo will be read, displayed in the program, and played.

**Tip**

**Testing on the Emulator**

If you would like to test the program on the Palm OS-Emulator, first activate the sound function. To do that, select *Settings/Properties* in the context menu of the Emulator and activate the *Enable Sounds* switch.

```
#Ringtone.bas
draw -1
form btn 120,120,38,38,"Play",1
form fld 100,15,58,12,"",1
dim a$(6),t$(3),f%(35), u%(6)
for i=1 to 6
  a$(i)=str$(i)
next i
form lst 80,120,6,4,a$,1
draw "Memo name:",0,15,1
draw "Volume:",40,120
draw 1,30,158,80,4
data 440,475,495,528,550,594
data 634,660,704,734,792,844
for i=0 to 11
  read f%(i)
  f%(i+12)=f%(i)*2
  f%(i+24)=f%(i)*4
next i
data 0,2,3,5,7,8,10
for i=0 to 6
  read u%(i)
next i
```

```
start:
x%=asc(input$(1))
if (x%=14) then gosub play:
goto start

play:
v%=val(s$(1))*10
m=db.find("memo",s$(0))
if (m<0) then goto error
open "memo",m as #1
input #1,x$
draw 1,30,158,80,-7
for i=0 to 2
  t$(i)=""
next i
i=0
while (not(eof))
  input #1, t$(i)
  i=i+1
wend
for i=0 to 2
  for j=0 to 1
    draw mid$(t$(i),j*32+1,32),3,j*12+i*24+32
  next j
next i
s%=val(left$(t$(0),1))
j=3
for i=0 to 2
  l=len(t$(i))+1
  while (j<l)
    t1$=mid$(t$(i),j,1)
    if (t1$=" ")
      gosub ton
    else
      t2$=t2$+t1$
    endif
    j=j+1
  wend
  j=1
next i
gosub ton
return

ton:
f1%=asc(left$(t2$,1))-65
f2%=u%(f1%)+12
if (mid$(t2$,len(t2$)-1,1)="+") then f2%=f2%+12
if (mid$(t2$,len(t2$)-1,1)="-") then f2%=f2%-12
if (mid$(t2$,2,1)="#") then f2%=f2%+1
```

```
t%=f%(f2%)
d%=val(right$(t2$,1))*400/s%
sound t%,d%,v%
t2$=""
return

error:
print "Memo not found "
goto start
```

CD

**Program on the book CD**

You can also find this program on the companion CD to this book as *0904.bas*. Indentation serves only for readability and is not contained in the original program on the CD, because it is difficult to display in memos. You can find three ring tones on the CD: *0905.txt, 0906.txt* and *0907.txt*.

The elements of the user surface are defined in the first part of the program. The list box, *a$()*, receives the numerical values 1 through 6 as selection options through a loop.

```
data 440,475,495,528,550,594
data 634,660,704,734,792,844
for i=0 to 11
  read f%(i)
  f%(i+12)=f%(i)*2
  f%(i+24)=f%(i)*4
next i
```

A subsequent loop reads the tones of the lowest octave from *data* lines and writes them to the variables *f%(0) ... f%(11)*. The next two octaves, *f%(12) ... f%(23)* and *f%(24) ... f%(35)*, are produced by doubling or quadrupling the frequencies.

| Variables list | |
|---|---|
| a$() | Filed with selection options for the loudspeaker controller |
| d% | Tone length |
| f%() | Frequencies of the 36 tones used |
| f1% | Number of a fundamental tone |
| f2% | Number of the tone in the list (including half tone steps) |
| i | Loop counter |

| Variables list | |
|---|---|
| j | Loop counter |
| l | Length of a read-in text line |
| m | Index of the memo opened |
| s$(0) | Name of the memo (return value of the input field) |
| s$(1) | Return value of the loudspeaker controller |
| s% | Playing speed |
| t$() | Text lines read in from the memo |
| t% | Frequency of a tone |
| t1$ | Individual characters read in |
| t2$ | Character string for a tone |
| u%() | Conversion values for fundamental tones |
| v% | Sound volume |
| x$ | Dummy for reading in the memo name |
| x% | Return value of the button clicked |

```
data 0,2,3,5,7,8,10
for i=0 to 6
  read u%(i)
next i
```

The numbers of the seven fundamental tones, *A ... G,* which consist of only one letter, are read into the *u%()* variable field. These are used, because the tones are later determined with the aid of the ASCII values of the letters.

```
start:
x%=asc(input$(1))
if (x%=14) then gosub play:
goto start
```

The program runs in a loop, which waits for the user to click the *Play* button. In this case, the subprogram, *play,* is called.

```
play:
v%=val(s$(1))*10
```

The sound volume selected in the list box is multiplied by 10 and written into the *v%* variable. The sound volume on the Palm is defined in a numerical value between 0 and 63. The program returns the values: *10, 20, ... 60*. The very small sound-volume values below 10 are nearly inaudible.

```
m=db.find("memo",s$(0))
if (m<0) then goto error
open "memo",m as #1
input #1,x$
```

The program searches a memo according to the name entered and reads the first line from it into the *x$* variable. The latter is not used further but serves only to direct the position pointer to the second line, where the actual ring tone begins.

```
draw 1,30,158,80,-7
```

The display field in which the key sequence appears must now be deleted to prevent individual characters from the previously displayed ring tone from remaining there.

```
for i=0 to 2
  t$(i)=""
next i
```

The program deletes the *t$()* character string so that no residues of old ring tones remain behind if a new ring tone is clearly shorter than one previously used.

```
i=0
while (not(eof))
  input #1, t$(i)
  i=i+1
wend
```

The program automatically reads several character strings from the memo one after the other. A character string in HotPaw Basic can contain a maximum of 63 characters. This loop reads the entire memo independently and, at the end of a character string, automatically begins a new one. The entire character string of a ring tone must be written to the memo continuously, without additional line breaks.

```
for i=0 to 2
  for j=0 to 1
    draw mid$(t$(i),j*32+1,32),3,j*12+i*24+32
  next j
next i
```

In the display field in the program, only a maximum of 32 characters can appear on the screen. The display of the character strings read in therefore results in two nested loops. The inner loop displays the first 32 characters of a character string and then the remainder. The outer loop runs over a maximum of three read-in character strings.

A tone in the Motorola format can consist of five characters maximum: space character, letter, increase sign, (#), octave (+/-), and duration. With a maximum of 35 tones, that equals a maximum of 175 characters. In three character strings of up to 63 characters, it is even possible to display up to 189 characters.

```
s%=val(left$(t$(0),1))
```

After displaying the tone, the program reads the speed from the first character of the first character string.

```
j=3
for i=0 to 2
  l=len(t$(i))+1
  while (j<l)
    ...
  wend
  j=1
next i
```

Two nested loops now run, one after the other, over the maximum of three character strings read in and thereby reads characters continuously. It makes a difference whether the end of a character string appears exactly at the end of a tone or lies in the middle of a tone. The reading of the first character string begins with the third character, because the first character of this character string indicates the speed, the second being a space character. The following character strings are read from the first character.

```
t1$=mid$(t$(i),j,1)
if (t1$=" ")
  gosub ton
else
  t2$=t2$+t1$
endif
j=j+1
```

The program reads each character, one after the other. When it reaches a space character, the program calls the *tone:* subprogram that plays the tone, the tone read being otherwise appended to the *t2$* character string until it comes to a space character and the tone is complete.

The *tone* subprogram is called again at the very end of the last character string to play the last tone, because the latter does not necessarily end with a space character.

```
ton:
f1%=asc(left$(t2$,1))-65
```

The *tone* subprogram calculates the number of the respective fundamental tone *0 ... 6* from the ASCII value of the first character of the *t2$* character string:

```
f2%=u%(f1%)+12
```

With the help of this numerical value, the number of the corresponding tone in the second octave is determined from the u%() table:

```
if (mid$(t2$,len(t2$)-1,1)="+") then f2%=f2%+12
```

If the penultimate character is –, depending upon whether the tone employs a #, and if the second or third character in *t2$* – is a +, the tone is increased by one octave. The number will thus be twelve units higher.

```
if (mid$(t2$,len(t2$)-1,1)="-") then f2%=f2%-12
```

In the same way, the tone must be reduced by one octave, twelve units, in the case of a –.

```
if (mid$(t2$,2,1)="#") then f2%=f2%+1
```

If the second character is a pound sign, the tone is raised by a half-tone step, a number in the *f%()* field being increased.

```
t%=f%(f2%)
```

With the aid of the tone number thus determined, the program reads the frequency from the *f%()* field.

```
d%=val(right$(t2$,1))*400/s%
```

The duration of a tone corresponds to the indicated tone length, multiplied by 400 milliseconds and divided by that speed indicated at the beginning of the melody.

**Tip**

**Different speeds**

Actual Palms play the tone sequence somewhat slower than the Emulator. Moreover, the speeds on the various handheld types are not exactly the same. If you need to, you can change the factor 400 in the program.

```
sound t%,d%,v%
```

This line plays the tone.

### *Sound <frequency>, <duration>, <volume>*

The *sound* command in HotPaw Basic plays a tone on the Palm. To do that, you need to enter three parameters:

- Frequency - in Hz
- Duration - in milliseconds
- Volume - Integer between 0 and 63

After playing the tone, the program resets the *t2$* character string again to an empty string. The *tone* subprogram is thus ended, and the next characters are read in. The process is repeated until the last character in the last character string has been read.

**Tip**

**Editing ring tones**

Using this program, you can create ring tones in a memo yourself to try them out. The best approach is to use the SwitchHack (see page 40) or Task Hack (see page 480), in order to switch back and forth between the HotPaw Basic program and the memo more easily. The *yLaunch* tool, described on page 486, enables you to start the HotPaw Basic program with its own icon. That saves you the trouble of looking for the program in the yBasic interpreter each time.

# 9.2 Developing your own synchronization tools with CASL

Those procedures described so far are of course quite suitable for exporting data from the Palm to the PC. In addition, CASL gives you the possibility of a true data update. Data is not merely transferred but actually synchronized as in the case of the Address Book and Calendar.

Imagine the following scenario: You save your personal-best times from sports training or your high scores from a game in a list on the PC. You can add new high scores to this list at any time.

If you play somewhere else, you take this list on the Palm along with you, enter additional data there, and then synchronize the list again with the PC at home so that the new data can be available on the PC, and you can enter additional data.

In principle something like that would be possible with a Palm memo, although memos have some disadvantages:

- There is no possibility for entering data on the PC automatically, such as, for example, the current date. The data can be processed on the Palm Desktop only or copied there from other programs, using the Clipboard.
- Transfer to a different computer by exporting and importing is relatively tedious. You can continue working with your own data on another computer only with difficulty.

CASL offers its own synchronization conduit and its own database format. Use it to gather data in a CASL-program on the Palm, synchronize it during HotSync, and continue working with the same program (or even a different one) that runs on the PC with CASLwin-Runtime. The changed data is again synchronized on the Palm during the next HotSync.

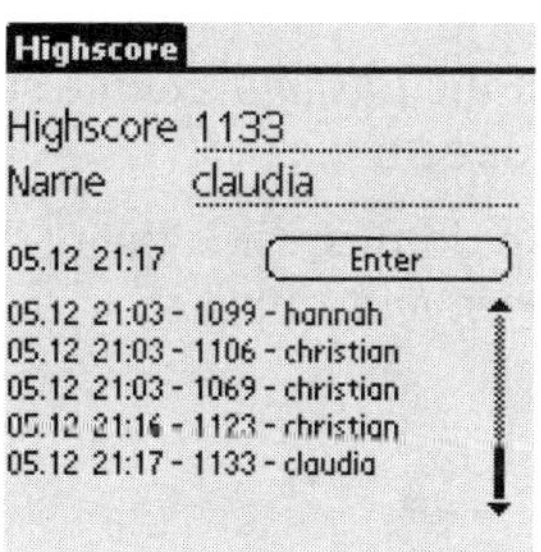

*Left: Entering high scores on the Palm*

*Right: After the HotSync, further data can be added on the PC*

# Software requirements for CASL programs on the PC

CASL programs, including the synchronization, run without further preparations on the PC on which the CASLide development environment is installed. However, if you would like to pass along your own program to other users for their own PCs, be aware of a few special things.

> **Tip**
>
> **CASL-Freeware components**
>
> Should you want to pass along a CASL program, you might pass along the following necessary components at no cost:
>
> - *CASLwin.exe* - Runtime module for Windows
> - *CASLrt_pro.prc* - Runtime module for Palm
> - *CASLCn20.dll* - HotSync Conduit
> - *CondReg.exe* - Program for installing the HotSync Conduit
> - *RemCond.exe* - Program for uninstalling the HotSync Conduits
> - *CASL*.fnt* - CASL fonts
>
> You will find more detailed information on rights under licensing in the file *License.txt*, which is installed with the CASLide.

Proceed as follows to install a CASL program on a PC on which no CASLide is installed (skip these steps if CASLide is installed):

- Generate a CSP file of your program in the CASLide with the *Windows Release* setting on your development computer. This appears in the *Windows release* subdirectory, below the directory in which the CPJ file of the program is saved.
- Create a *CASL* subdirectory on the foreign PC below the *\Palm\<User name>* directory.
- Copy the CSP file with your program and the *Caslwin.exe* file supplied with CASL into this *\Palm\<Username>\CASL* directory.
- Register the CSP file type in Windows. To do this, click the CSP just copied in the Windows-Explorer. A dialog box *Open with* appears.

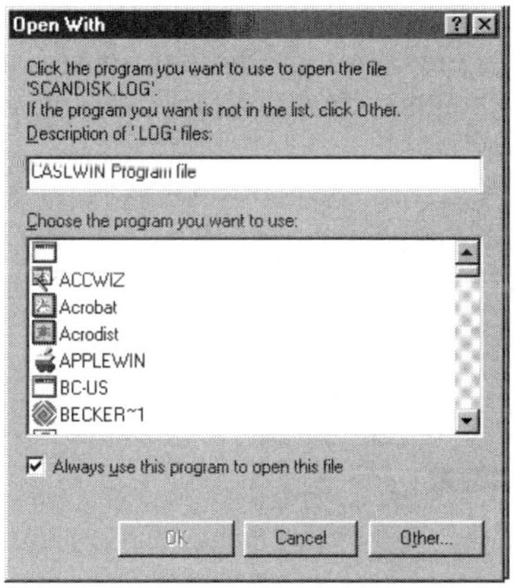


*The Open- with dialog box with an unknown file type*

- Enter an expressive name for the CASLwin file type program files in the upper field of this dialog box. Then click the *Others* button.
- Select the previously copied program *Caslwin.exe* and check to make sure that the *Always open this file with this program* switch is on.

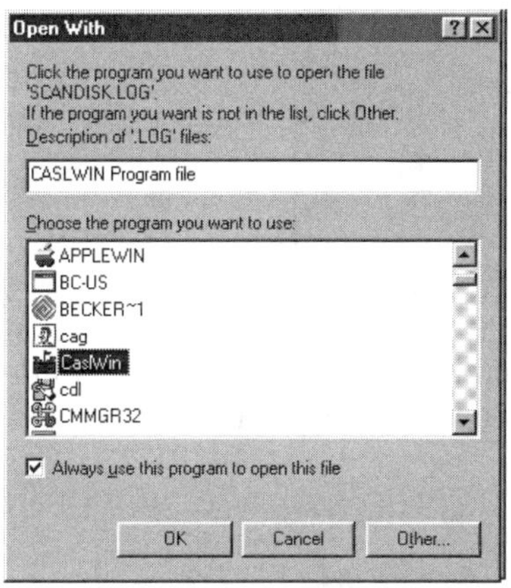


*The newly entered CASLwin program*

- If you click *OK*, the CASL program starts in Windows. Close it again right away, because the HotSync Conduit must still be installed.
- End the HotSync Manager.
- Copy *Caslcn20.dll* file into the *\Windows* directory and the *Condreg.exe* file into any temporary directory. Now start this program as follows:

```
condreg \windows
```

- If Windows is installed in a different directory on the computer you are using, for example, *\Winnt*, you must change the parameters accordingly. You can delete the *Condreg.exe* file again. Then restart the HotSync Manager and select the *User defined* option.

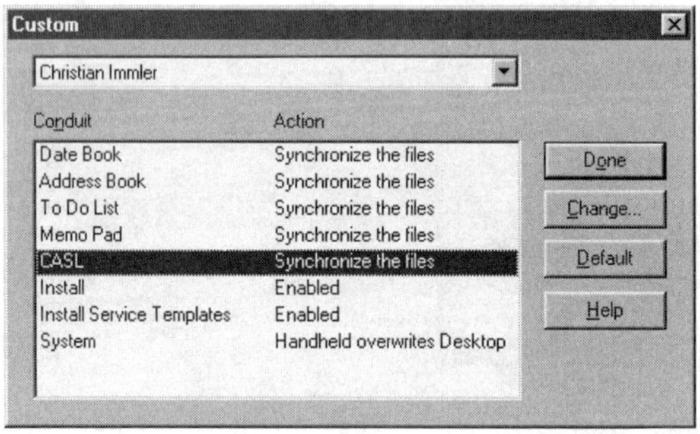


*The CASL Conduit iin the HotSync Manager*

- Select the new CASL Conduit and click *Change*.

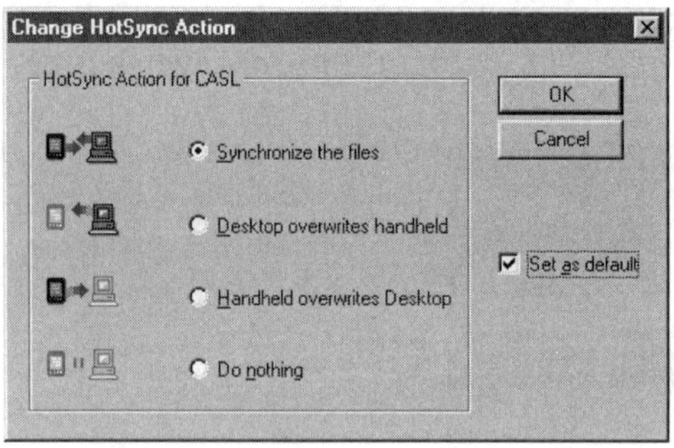


*Settings for the CASL Conduit*

- Select the *Synchronize files* option and turn on the *As standard* switch. Then exit this dialog with *OK* and the next one with *Done*.

**Tip**

**Start programs first on the Palm**

Whenever you use a CASL program that updates Palm files with the PC through the CASL Conduit, start it for the first time on the Palm, not on the PC. CASL creates the database with the information to be exchanged on the Palm and then transfers it to the PC. Entering data on the PC first won't work because the CASL Conduit would not register the database. This is true only the very first time you start a program. Once the database is set up and synchronized, data can be entered alternately on the Palm and on the PC.

If the CASL-programs appear too small in Windows, start them with the *ScreenSize* command-line parameters from a DOS window:

```
\CASL\CASLwin highscor.csp -ScreenSize 320 320
```

This command line starts the example program, *Highscor.csp*, with a 320 x 320 pixel window, that is to say, with a surface four times as large as the 160 x 160 pixel Palm display.

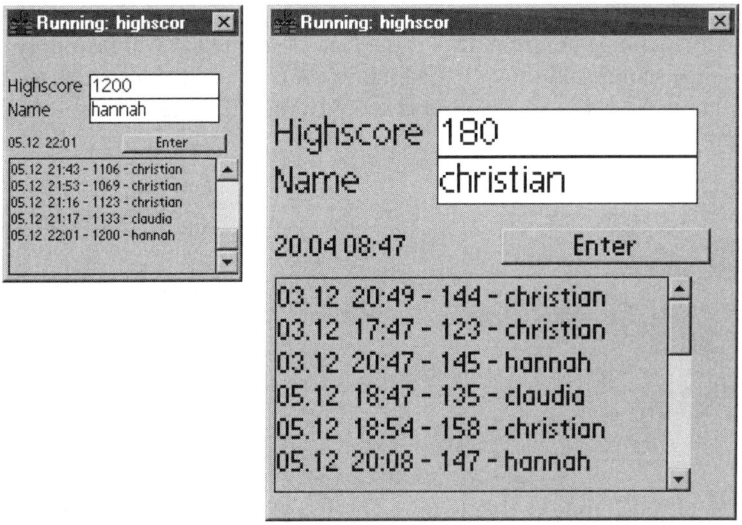


*Size comparison between 160 x 160 und 320 x 320 pixels*

The standard Windows elements, such as the title bar or scroll bars, do not change size.

## Synchronization of a Highscore-list

Now you can create an actual program from the example described previously. In this program, you can record your personal high scores on the Palm, synchronize the data on the PC, and enter new data. The new data is written back again to the Palm during the next HotSync.

Cheating, that is to say, changing high scores after they have been entered, is not an option with this program.

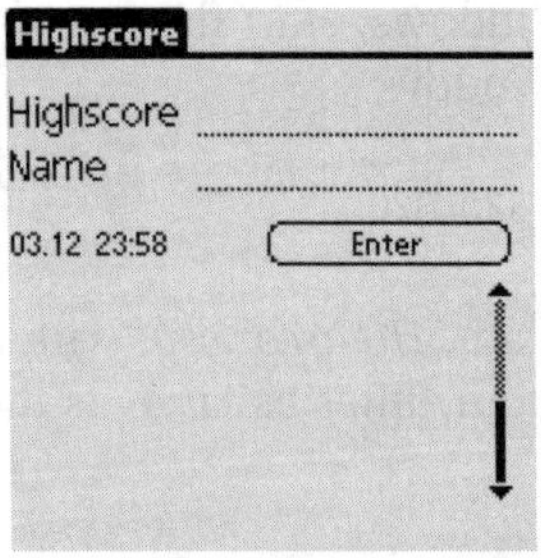


*The program after the first start on the Palm*

When you start the program for the first time, the list will be empty. You can enter high scores and the assigned names. A clock will always run to the left in the program. The time will be inserted in the list along with the respective high score.

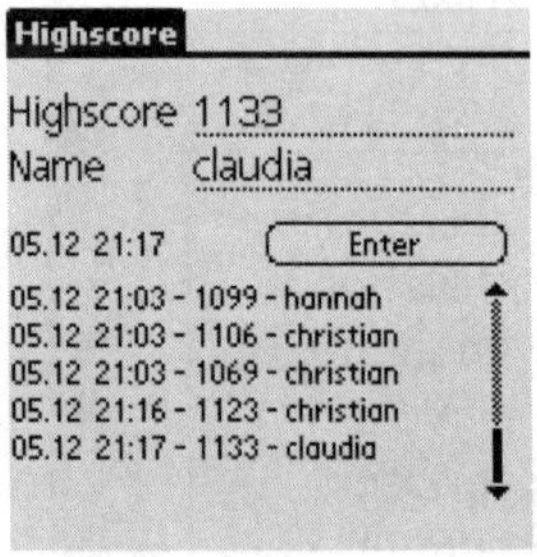


*List with several high scores entered*

This list is a database that is stored on the Palm. It is read in again with each new start of the program, so the data will not be lost.

The database is transmitted to the PC during synchronization so that it can be further processed with the same program in a version compiled for Windows.

*You can enter additional data in Windows*

If the list is longer than the window, scroll it up and down using the screen scroll bar. The new entries will always be attached at the end.

The source code of the associated program appears as follows:

```
label high1;
  font "largefont";
  position 10,150;
  display "Highscore";
  end;

label name1;
  font "largefont";
  position 10,250;
  display "Name";
  end;

label time1;
  position 10,400;
  end;

text high2;
  font "largefont";
  char_size 9,1;
  position 360,150;
  end;

text name2;
  font "largefont";
  char_size 9,1;
  position 360,250;
  end;

button ok;
  char_size 9,1;
  position 500,400;
  display "Enter";
  end;

text list;
  char_size 18,6;
  position 10,500;
  no_input;
  scrollbar bottom;
  end;

variables;
  string time;
```

```
  string high;
  string name;
  string listtxt;
  string time2;
  end;

dbfile highscoredb;
  field time;
  field high;
  field name;
  sync_pref merge;
  end;

function readIn;
  listtxt="";
  errorcode=0;
  seek_start highscoredb, 0;
  while errorcode=0;
    get_fields highscoredb;
    if errorcode=0;
      listtxt=listtxt+time+" - "+high+" - "+name+char(10);
    end_if;
  end_while;
  put list, listtxt;
  end;

function ok;
  get high2, high;
  get name2, name;
  time=time2;
  seek_end highscoredb,0;
  put_fields highscoredb;
  listtxt=listtxt+time+" - "+high+" - "+name+char(10);
  put list, listtxt;
  end;

function clock;
  time2=string(day(),"00")+"."+string(month(),"00")+" "+string(hour(
➥),"00")+":"+string(minute(),"00");
  put time1, time2;
  timer clock, 1000;
  end;

function startup;
  open highscoredb, "Highscores";
  readIn;
  clock;
  end;
```

**CD**

**Program on the companion CD**

You can also find this program on the companion CD to this book as *0908.csl.*

The *label, text,* and *button* objects of the user surface are defined in the first part of the program. You don't need to concern yourself with it further. The only peculiarity is the scrollbar list box that displays the high-score list:

```
text list;
  char_size 18,6;
  position 10,500;
  no_input;
  scrollbar bottom;
  end;
```

This field must be defined as a *text* object , even though no entry is possible. Used otherwise for static texts are *label* objects, but they don't support scrollbars.

### *text*

Three parameters determine the form and behavior of such a field:

- **no_input** – Indicates that no entry is possible in this field.
- **char_size** – Designates the size. The first value stands for the width in letters, the second for the number of visible lines. The width is measured with a font that is not proportional. Significantly more characters fit into the field in the case of the proportional font of the Palm.
- **scrollbar** – Indicates where the standard position of the scrollbar is to be. Where new list elements are to be added to the bottom, it should be dragged all the way to the bottom, if the list doesn't fit into the window entirely. The other option, *top,* is used for example when displaying relatively long texts that are read from the top.

Five string variables are defined in the variable-declaration part.

| Variable | Use in the program |
|---|---|
| time | Time entry for storage in the list |
| high | High score for storage in the list |

| Variable | Use in the program |
|---|---|
| name | Name for storage in the list |
| listtxt | The complete text of the list for display in the *text*-field |
| time2 | Running time for the time indication in the *label time1* |

Following that is the declaration of a new object type, *dbfile*.

## *dbfile*

A *dbfile* object is a variable structure in the program, which serves to receive data from a database. This object represents the interface between the program and the separately stored database, comparable to the *s$()* variables in HotPaw Basic.

The object can have two different parameters:

| Parameter | Values | Meaning |
|---|---|---|
| Field | Variable name | Indicated here for each field of the database is a previously defined variable for data exchange with the program. It is necessary to enter just as many *field*-parameters as there are fields in the database. |
| Sync_pref | | Type of synchronization. |
| | Merge | True synchronization with the transmission of new records in both directions. |
| | Pda_to_pc | The Palm data overwrite the data on the PC. |
| | PC_to_pda | The PC data overwrite the data on the Palm. |
| | None | This database is not synchronized. |

The database in the program has three fields, corresponding to the variables *time, high*, and *name.*

```
dbfile highscoredb;
  field time;
  field high;
  field name;
  sync_pref merge;
  end;
```

The *dbfile* object has the name *highscoredb*. This object is used for reading and writing the database and corresponds roughly to the database ID in HotPaw Basic.

The database should be synchronized with the PC in both directions.

The startup function, *startup*, is called at program startup:

```
function startup;
  open highscoredb, "Highscores";
  readIn;
  clock;
  end;
```

The first thing opened by the *startup* function is the *Highscores* database.

### *open <dbfile object>, <database name>;*

This function opens the database with the name indicated and links it to that *dbfile* object indicated first. If the database is not yet available on the Palm, it will be created automatically. If the database was already open, it is closed and reopened.

You don't normally need to worry about closing the database. CASL closes all open databases automatically, when a CASL program is ended.

**Tip**

**The database position pointer**

CASL manages an internal position pointer for each opened database, indicating which point in the database is to be read or written next. The *open* function automatically sets the database position point to the very beginning.

Once the database is open, the *startup* function calls the *read* function.

```
function readIn;
  listtxt="";
  errorcode=0;
  seek_start highscoredb, 0;
  while errorcode=0;
    get_fields highscoredb;
    if errorcode=0;
      listtxt=listtxt+time+" - "+high+" - "+name+char(10);
    end_if;
  end_while;
  put list, listtxt;
  end;
```

First the *read* function sets the *string* variable *listtxt* to an empty character string and the *errorcode* variable predefined by CASL to 0.

### *errorcode*

This variable is predefined in CASL and thus does not need to be declared in the program. If any error does arise in the program, CASL writes an error number into this variable automatically.

As the next step, the database position indicator is set to the beginning of the database. That would not be necessary in this case, because it of course still stands at the beginning on opening. That is important when the *read* function is later called.

### *seek_start <dbfile object>, <position>;*

This function moves the database position pointer to a specific database record number, counted from the beginning of the database. The database is identified through the corresponding *dbfile* object.

A *while...end_while* loop runs until an error occurs. If the end of a database is passed over when records are being read, CASL will write an error number into the *errorcode* variable. The database records are read inside this loop.

### *get_fields <dbfile object>;*

This function reads a record from the database, which is identified with its associated *dbfile* object. The individual data fields are written into the variable indicated in the *dbfile* object.

The record at the position toward which the database position pointer is currently pointing is always read. The pointer is always moved back by one record after reading to allow the next record to be read.

When the *errorcode* variable in the program still stands at 0 after the reading of a record, that means that data was still being read and that the end of the database has not yet been overstepped.

In this case, a character string is formed from those data fields read in, which were stored by *get_fields* in the *time, high* and *name* variables, and *listtxt* is appended to the character string. A wordwrap character *char(10)* is also attached at the end.

**Tip**

**Wordwraps in long text fields**

A single character string is always shown in a multiple-line *text* field. The wordwrap normally takes place automatically with the aid of the field width. In the example, however, the lines are written below one another in such a way that columns result.

The already known *put* function writes the contents of the *listtxt* character string into the *text* field, *lists*, at the end of the *while...end_while* loop.

During the initial start of the *read* function from the *startup* function, an already present database is written completely into the *text* field to read all the data. If the program is started for the very first time on a Palm, only the database will be created, but nothing will be written into the *listtxt* variable, because CASL reads a record immediately on the first try, which will set the *errorcode* variable to an error.

After the *read* function has written the database into the *text* field, the *startup* function calls the *clock* function, which inserts the time into *label time1*.

```
function clock;
  time2=string(day(),"00")+"."+string(month(),"00")+"  "+string(hour(
  ➥),"00")+":"+string(minute(),"00");
  put time1, time2;
  timer clock, 1000;
  end;
```

The *clock* function forms a character string, *time2*, with the aid of the current time and the date. This is written into the *label time1* with *put* and then updated again, through the CASL *timer*, to 1,000 milliseconds. The *timer* was already used on page 233 for a stopwatch.

The date and the time are determined with four standard functions of CASL:

### *day()*

Returns the current day as a numerical value between 1 and 31.

### *month()*

Returns the current month as a numerical value between 1 and 12.

### hour()

Returns the current hour as a numerical value between 0 and 23.

### minute()

Returns the current minute as a numerical value between 0 and 59.

All numerical values are converted into character strings and set for two places with the formatting command, *"00"* so that the database entries will later all have the same length and appear in columns, one over the other, in the list display.

This time entry in the *label time1* is automatically updated each second. The *Startup* function has run and the program awaits an event.

The only object triggering an event is the *OK* button, which starts a function with the same name.

```
function ok;
  get high2, high;
  get name2, name;
  time=time2;
  seek_end highscoredb,0;
  put_fields highscoredb;
  listtxt=listtxt+time+" - "+high+" - "+name+char(10);
  put list, listtxt;
  end;
```

This function serves for the entry of a new high score in the list. First of all, the *text* objects *high2* and *name2,* in which users enter their names and high scores, are read into the *high* and *name* variables. Likewise, the current time entry from the *label time2* is written into the *time* variable.

As the next step, the database position pointer is set to the very end of the database.

### seek_end <dbfile object>, <position>;

This function sets the position pointer of a database to a specific record number, counted from the end of the database. The database is thereby identified through the corresponding *dbfile* object, as with *seek_start*.

At this position, a new record should be inserted after the last record.

### *put_fields <dbfile object>;*

This function writes a record into the database, which is identified with its assigned *dbfile* object. The individual data fields are read from those variables indicated in the *dbfile*- object.

The record is always written to that position indicated by the database position pointer. After writing, the pointer is again set back by one record, so that the next database can be written directly after it.

The new data is appended to the *listtxt* character string, and that is in turn written into the *text*-field *list*. The high score entered also appears there.

On leaving the program, note that the database is closed automatically and synchronized with the PC during the next HotSync. You can then enter data there with the same program.

## The data format of CASL databases

The databases created by CASL on the Palm are converted during synchronization with the CASL Conduit into a special ASCII format with the suffix.*cdb*. You can edit these files on the PC with different programs.

```
#CDBID: CASL
#MAJREV: 2
#MINREV: 0
#FLDCNT: 3
#RECCNT: 17
#SYNCMODE: MERGE
#FLDNUM:1 TYPE:S SIZE:0
#FLDNUM:2 TYPE:S SIZE:0
#FLDNUM:3 TYPE:S SIZE:0
0x00128009,0x0000,"03.12  20:49","144","christian"
0x0012800E,0x0000,"03.12  17:47","123","christian"
0x0012800A,0x0000,"03.12  20:47","145","hannah"
0x00128008,0x0000,"05.12  18:47","135","claudia"
0x0012800C,0x0000,"05.12  18:54","158","christian"
0x0012800B,0x0000,"05.12  20:08","147","hannah"
0x0012800D,0x0000,"05.12  20:49","158","claudia"
0x00128007,0x0000,"05.12  20:59","163","christian"
0x00128002,0x0000,"05.12  21:01","1021","claudia"
0x00128001,0x0000,"05.12  21:03","1011","christian"
0x00128003,0x0000,"05.12  21:10","1067","claudia"
0x00128005,0x0000,"05.12  21:40","1099","hannah"
0x00128006,0x0000,"05.12  21:43","1106","christian"
```

```
0x00128004,0x0000,"05.12  21:53","1069","christian"
0x0012800F,0x0000,"05.12  21:16","1123","christian"
0x00128010,0x0000,"05.12  21:17","1133","claudia"
0x00000000,0x0008,"05.12  22:01","1200","hannah"
```

This listing shows a CASL database from the last example program.

These databases consist of a header with general information on the database. A separate line for each record then follows.

The following table describes the parameters in the header.

| Parameter | Meaning |
|---|---|
| #CBID: | CASL (identifies the file as a CASL database). |
| #MAJREV: | Database version number, in CASL 3.x immer: 2. |
| #MINREV: | Secondary version number, reserved for intermediate updates. |
| #FLDCNT: | Number of data fields. |
| #RECCNT: | Number of records. |
| #SYNCMODE: | HotSync mode: MERGE, PC_TO_PDA, PDA_TO_PC, NO_SYNC corresponds to the *sync_pref* parameter in the *dbfile*-object in the CASL-program code. |
| #FLDNUM: | A line is indicated here for each data field. This contains a field number at the beginning, starting at 1, then two additional parameters.<br>TYPE: S = character string, N = number, NA = array of numbers, BA = byte array.<br>SIZE: Element number, if the data field is an array. |

Following after the header is the identical number of lines indicated in the *#RECCNT* parameter. These lines contain two parameters for control at the beginning, separated by commas, one value for each data field.

The Palm uses the first, eight-place hex number for internal management. Because there is no file system comparable with Windows there, all data and even programs are available instead in database form. If a database is created on the PC, *0x00000000* is contained there.

The second, four-place hex number indicates the status of the record. The value is assembled from a hex addition of the following four values:

| Value | Meaning |
|---|---|
| 0x0001 | Was used during HotSync |
| 0x0002 | Marked for deletion |
| 0x0004 | Record was changed |
| 0x0008 | New record |

**Tip**

**International number formats**

Numbers in the data fields must be enclosed between quotation marks, like character strings, if they contain commas as decimal separators. Whenever a database from the Palm is synchronized on the PC, the CASL Conduit converts the numbers automatically into the number format set in Windows. If this number format uses commas, the quotation marks are automatically inserted.

You can read and edit the CDB files at any time with a Windows program. The files must be available in the *\Palm\<Username>\CASL* directory for synchronization. Don't forget that a CASL database must always be created on the Palm first.

# 10. Programming tools and function libraries

Using the programming languages HotPaw Basic and CASL, you can write applications for various purposes, assuming you have ideas and creativity. You cannot do it well without tools to assist you, however. This chapter includes some tools that will make your daily programming easier and solve some problems that the programming languages alone cannot manage.

## 10.1 Including external functions in CASL

If you write a lot of programs, you probably find yourself using certain functions repeatedly. You can use the Clipboard to copy them from one program to the next, but a more efficient process would be to include the complete standard functions from another file. Doing so has two critical benefits:

- The additional standard functions do not significantly increase the size of the program source code. The new part of the program therefore remains more transparent. By not having to scroll through the standard functions so much, you reduce the risk of inadvertently changing something.
- When you want to make only general changes to the standard functions for all programs, you need do this only once. The changes are then available in all the affected programs.

CASL also provides the option of categorizing objects, variables, and functions into so-called package files with the extension *.cpk*. These can be added to the beginning of a program using the *include* instruction.

### *include <filename>;*

This line includes a CPK file in the program.

CPK files have the same syntax as normal CASL programs. They may contain objects, variables, and functions. The following example shows you how.

## About menu in programs

You are probably familiar with the Windows convention of finding a menu called *Help*, usually at the upper right. This menu always contains an item called *About*, where you can find a short reference to the program author. Many Palm programs now include a similar function. Because these messages are always the same, it makes sense not to reprogram them for every program. The example shows how to use CASL to build an *About* message into all your programs.

The new menu

The About message

In a CPK file that functions for all programs, a menu is defined together with a menu item as well as a *message_box* that displays a predefined message. These functions work on the Palm and in Windows.

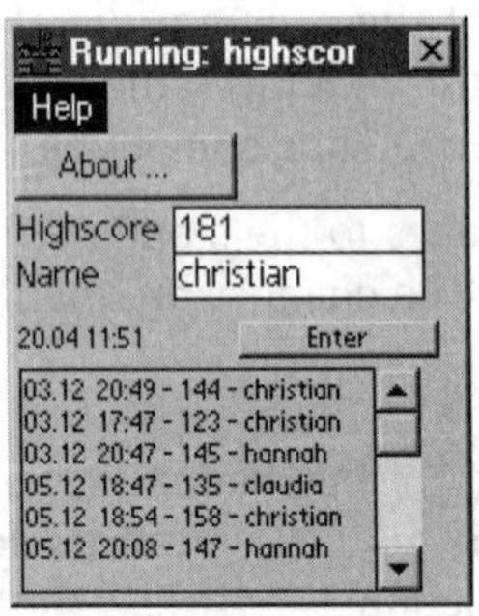


The new menu

The About menu in Windows

For example, you can use the program for the High Score list from the last chapter, for another CASL example program from this book, or even your own program.

The only change to the program is the following line, which appears at the beginning:

```
include "about.cpk";
```

**CD**

**Program on the companion CD**

You will find the new program on the companion CD as *1001.csl.*

After making this small program change, you must create the file *About.cpk*, which contains the actual new functions.

Click this icon and select the option *Package File.* A new window appears in CASLide, which at first is named simply *CASLide32.*

Now click this icon to give the file a name. Select the file format *CASL Package* and enter the file name *About.cpk.* Then write or copy the displayed listing to this window:

```
menu_top help;
  display "Help";
  end;

menu_item about, help;
  display "About ...";
  end;

variables;
  numeric msgbox;
  string msgtxt="program example from:"+char(10)+"    \"The Big
  ➥Book"+char(10)+"    Palm programming \""+char(10)+"    www.
  ➥databecker.com";
  end;

function about;
  msgbox=message_box(0,"DATA BECKER",msgtxt,"OK","","");
  end;
```

Note that the long line *string msgtxt ...* must be written in one line, even if printing constraints show it here in three lines.

**CD**

**File on the companion CD**

You will find this file on the companion CD to this book as *1001.cpk.*

Select the option *Project/Update includes* in CASLide menu. This includes the CPK file into the project so that the next time you open the project it automatically appears in its own window. A new folder appears in the left window of CASLide, containing the name of the CPK file.

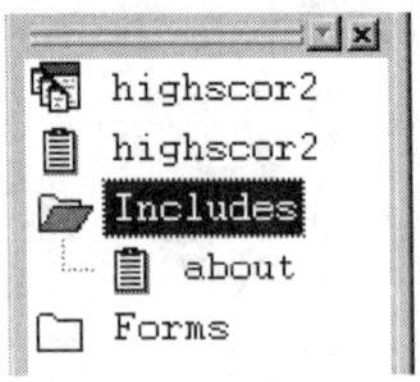


*Includes shown in the left CASLide window*

In this include file a menu is defined for the *menu_top* object *help*, which displays the word *Help* in the menu line. This menu contains a single menu item *About*, which is filled with the *menu_item* object *about*.

Clicking this menu item opens the function of the same name, showing a *message_box* that displays the string *msgtxt*, which is defined in the *variables* section.

This string consists of several lines separated by the character *char(10)*. Three spaces appear at the beginning of all the lines except the first. Insert the strings for all *message_box* messages that can be displayed in Windows, because the symbols (*info, Warning ...*) in the *message_box* windows in Windows are so large that they cover up the first part of the displayed string. You will find a detailed explanation of the *message_box* function on page 200 of Chapter 5.

**Tip**

**Displaying special characters in string**

If quotation marks (") appear within a string, you must represent these with the character combination \", because a normal quotation mark ends a string. The backslash character (\) is represented by the character combination \\.

# CASL error numbers

Whenever an error occurs in CASL, it is written as a negative number between -1 and -15 in the variable *errorcode*. Palm OS error messages write positive numbers in this variable.

| Error name | Error no. |
|---|---|
| ce_div_0 | -1 |
| ce_array | -2 |
| ce_not_open | -3 |
| ce_fld_mis | -4 |
| ce_eof | -5 |
| ce_fmode | -6 |
| ce_file_nf | -7 |
| ce_file_del | -8 |
| ce_serial_open | -9 |
| ce_serial_comm | -10 |
| ce_file_open | -11 |
| ce_rec_not_found | -12 |
| ce_put_record_error | -13 |
| ce_file_delete_error | -14 |
| ce_bad_number_error | -15 |

To process the error, you must always know the corresponding error numbers. Being able to work directly with the error names would simplify the writing of programs and also make the programs easier to read.

CASL therefore provides a special include file *Caslerr2.cpk*, which allows you to use error names. Variables are defined with the error names that contain the associated error number.

```
variables;
  ce_div_0 = -1;
  ce_array = -2;
  ce_not_open = -3;
  ce_fld_mis = -4;
  ce_eof = -5;
  ce_fmode = -6;
  ce_file_nf = -7;
  ce_file_del = -8;
  ce_serial_open = -9;
  ce_serial_comm = -10;
```

```
ce_file_open = -11;
ce_rec_not_found = -12;
ce_put_record_error = -13;
ce_file_delete_error = -14;
ce_bad_number_error = -15;
```

You can now create more understandable queries, such as:

```
if errorcode=ce_eof;
```

This query asks whether the error "End of File„ occurred, which is easier to understand in the source code than:

```
if errorcode=-5;
```

The function of both variations is completely identical.

In addition, the *Caslerr2.cpk* file contains an array with error messages in plain text:

```
ce_errors[16] = "No Error", "Divide by 0", "Invalid array index",
  "File not open", "DB Field mismatch", "File EOF",
  "Invalid file mode", "File not found", "Record deleted",
  "Serial Port Error", "Serial Comm Error", "File Already Open",
  "Record Not Found", "Put Record Error", "Delete Record Error",
  "Bad Number Error";
```

This array allows you to create error messages and assumes a *label* object *display* is defined in the program for displaying any errors that occur. The line:

```
put display, string(errorcode,"##");
```

would, for example, show the number -5 when an "End of File" error occurs, which would be nearly meaningless to most users.

But by using the file *Caslerr2.cpk*, you could write this program line as follows:

```
put display, ce_errors[-errorcode];
```

Hereafter when the same error occurs, the text *File EOF* appears. Because all error messages have negative numbers but arrays always need positive numbers for the individual elements, a minus sign is inserted in front of the variable *errorcode*.

**CD**

**Addrpack.cpk, Barpack.cpk, Memopack.cpk, Todopack.cpk**

CASL supplies four additional include files containing functions for working with the Palm address book, bar graphics, bookmarks, and the ToDo list. You will also find these include files on the companion CD to this book. They are not normally supplied with the CASL demo version, because they are too large for the demo compiler and therefore won't run.

# 10.2 Creating your own icons for programs

Each program on the start interface has, in addition to its name, a graphical icon. Many programs also contain symbols on buttons, because simple symbols often say more than a description in a short word.

## Symbols for CASL programs

CASL programs can be started not only from the CASL runtime menu on the Palm but also by using their own icons on the Palm's program startup screen. The programs generally use the standard CASL ("castle") icon, which is somewhat wider than the icon for CASL runtime.

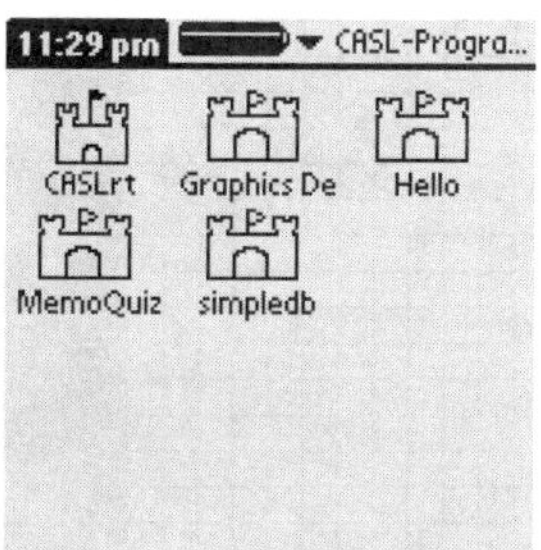


*Programs with CASL icons*

You can personalize a program's appearance by assigning it an icon. Users remember a program icon just as easily as a program name and automatically associate such icons with the corresponding program even if – or perhaps because – the program names are similar. You can create these icons for CASL programs directly in CASL.

For example, create an icon for the currency calculator on page 53 of Chapter 3, which will clearly identify it as such.

**CD**

**Program on the companion CD**

You can also find this program companion CD to this book as *0316.csl.*

If you still have the project file from that exercise, open it or create a new project with the name *0316.cpj*.

Then click this icon in CASLide, and in the dialog box, check the option *ICON File*.

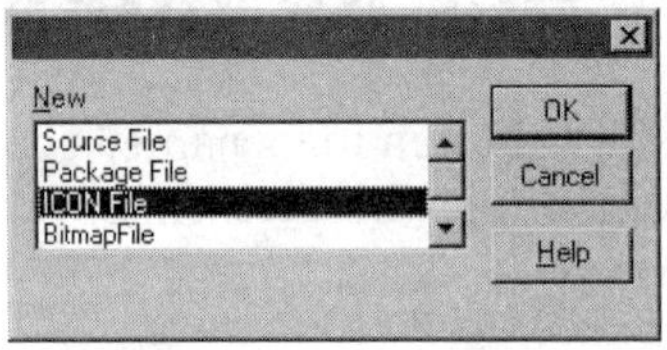


*New file types for a CASL project*

A new window appears in CASLide with a grid consisting of 32 x 32 fields.

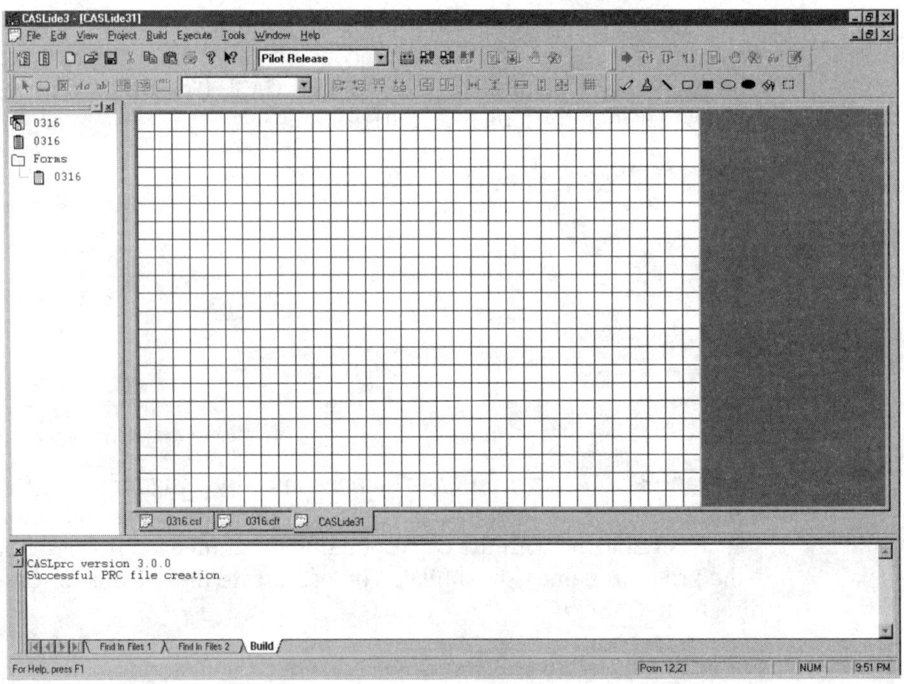


*The new icon window inCASLide*

In this window, use the symbols in the Image toolbar to draw a new icon for the program.

**Tip**

**Showing the Image Toolbar**

If the Image toolbar is not visible, enable the *View/Image Toolbar* option in the menu.

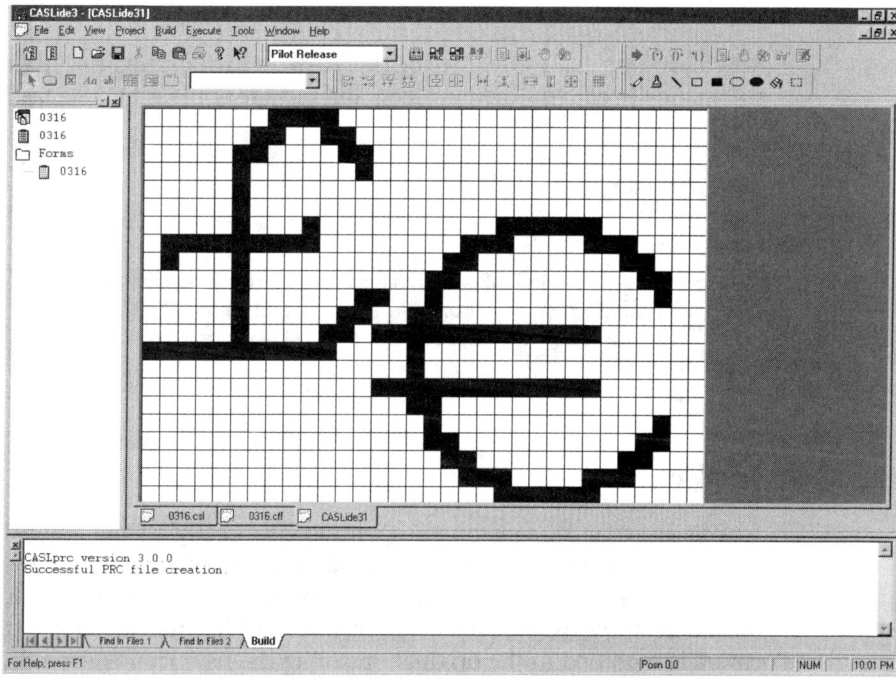


*Icon for the currency calculator*

Once you have finished drawing the icon, click *Save once.*

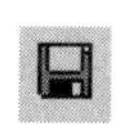

The icon is saved as a CIC file. Give the file the same name as the project file; then the icon is automatically included into the project. In the window at left, a new *Images* folder appears containing the icon.

**CD**

**File on the companion CD**

You will find the icon file on the companion CD to this book as *0316.cic*.

*The new icon has been included in the project*

Now if you create a PRC file for the Palm from the program, it will automatically contain the new icon and not the standard CASL castle icon.

**Tip**

**CIC file format**

The CIC file format for icons in CASL is nothing more than a standard BMP format with 1 bit of color depth and an exact size of 32 x 32 pixels. This means you can view and edit the CIC files with any graphics-editing program in Windows.

## IcoEdit

IcoEdit is a tool for changing program icons directly on the Palm. The icons for the Palm standard applications cannot be changed, because they are stored in ROM. As opposed to the various program starters with their own icons, such as SilverScreen (www.pocketsensei.com), IcoEdit has the advantage that the application is modified in the original, meaning the new icon is even available if IcoEdit is not installed.

IcoEdit can edit both the normal large icons as well as the smaller ones for the list view of the Palm Program startup screen.

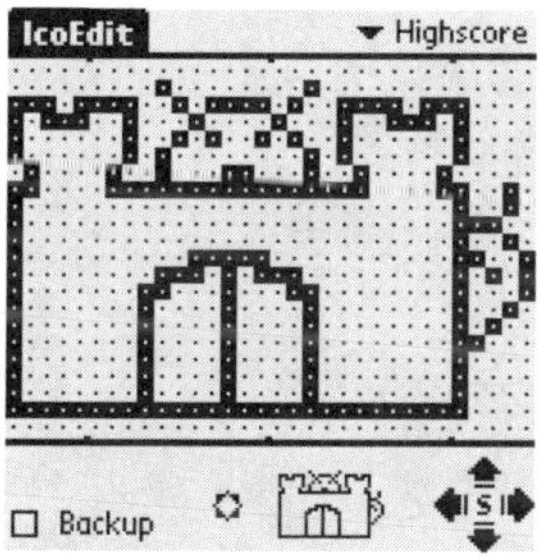


*Modifying a program icon with IcoEdit*

| **IcoEdit** | **1.31** |
|---|---|
| Software manufacturer or programmer | MapleTop |
| Category | Development tools |
| Size | 27 KB |
| Hardware requirements | Any Palm |
| Software requirements | none |
| Language | English |
| Cost | US $ 10.00 |
| Download address | www.mapletop.com |
| Available on CD | Yes |

## Bitmap editor for HotPaw Basic

HotPaw Basic stores graphics binary-coded in the source code. This means creating such graphics requires some computing. The bitmap editor BitMan is a HotPaw Basic program that provides a graphical interface for drawing bitmaps, which can then be exported as bookmarks in the format for the HotPaw Basic source code.

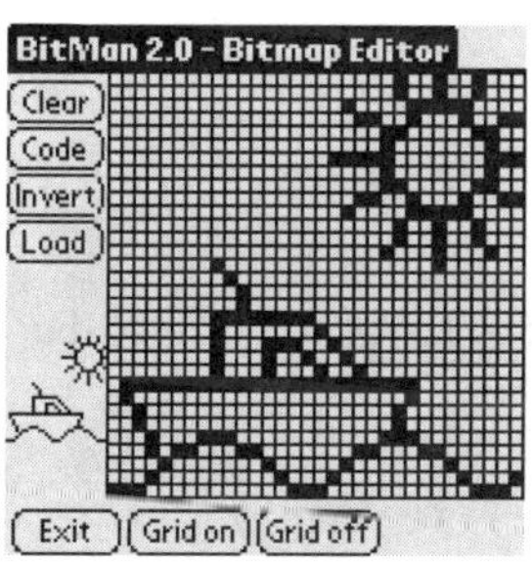


*Creating a bitmap graphic with BitMan*

| BitMan | 2.0 |
|---|---|
| Software manufacturer or programmer | Magnus Wohlen |
| Category | Development tools |
| Size | 5 KB |
| Hardware requirements | Palm III and higher |
| Software requirements | HotPaw Basic |
| Language | English |
| Cost | Freeware |
| Download address | www.palmgear.com/software/showsoftware.cfm?prodID=6331 |
| Available on CD | No |

# 10.3 Useful tools on the PC

If you program your Palm, chances are you're programming elsewhere as well. You are likely also involved with some kind of conversion and installation work on the PC. Various programs that might be useful to you follow.

## My Little Buddy – Desktop enhancer and installation tool

You would think that the connection between the Palm and the PC desktop would be perfect by now, but in fact it could be even better. My Little Buddy collects all the typical applications (for example, Pilot Desktop, HotSync, and Install) together in one place and adds additional functionality:

- Accessory programs on the PC
- Installing programs on the Palm
- Managing Web sites
- File viewer for various Palm formats

*The My Little Buddy taskbar*

My Little Buddy consists essentially of a taskbar on the desktop and a symbol in the systray, behind which is a context menu with the same options. Multiple users are also supported. The taskbar can be configured to run continually in the background.

Starts the Palm desktop or another desktop program, which can be entered in the configuration settings.

Opens the My Little Buddy installation tool. This supports Drag & Drop, favorites directories, simultaneous installation of multiple files, notes for installed files, and simultaneous installation for multiple users.

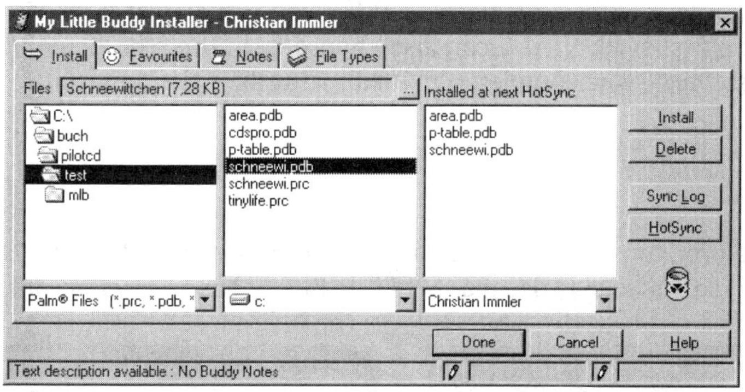


*The My Little Buddy installation tool*

Select any file or drag them into the window. At the bottom right, select the Palm user for whom you want to install the selected file.

The *Notes* tab can be used to store additional information about the files. Some programs already come with such a notes file for My Little Buddy.

This symbol brings up a menu in which you yourself can enter accessory applications for the Palm on a PC, such as a database converter, text editors, or the Palm OS emulator. This menu then gives you direct access to these programs.

Your most frequently used Palm WWW sites can be collated here. My Little Buddy comes preconfigured with regularly used sites. My Little Buddy can also read in sites you already have set up in your favorites folder for most popular browsers.

My Little Buddy offers a plug-in interface for external file viewers, with which you can view Palm files and export them into different formats. The manufacturer of My Little Buddy offers viewers for Doc, HanDBase, JFile, MobileDB, PiMC, TealPaint, as well as a text editor. Manufacturers of programs can add their own viewers for their file formats. This feature makes My Little Buddy of special interest for developers, because you directly view the documents and databases that are synchronized on the Palm. The same is true for databases that are restored to the backup directory during a HotSync.

The configuration tool and its screen allows total control of My Little Buddy's functions from the installer or organizer you want to use through location of key files. For example, if you want to synchronize your data with Lotus Organizer or ACT!, you can start it from My Little Buddy using the first symbol. You can also choose from three basic toolbar styles, one of which gives you complete flexibility regarding the appearance of My Little Buddy.

## Skins

Today's programs offer more and more ways of completely changing the look and feel, so it's no surprise that My Little Buddy has an interface for skins.

The *Toolbar* tab of My Little Buddy allows you to select various skins; the default installation set providing 10 skins to choose from. The program shows you which My Little Buddy functions it supports for each skin.

*My Little Buddy with the Palm look*

| **My Little Buddy** | **2.63** |
|---|---|
| Software manufacturer or programmer | Precise Solutions |
| Category | Desktop |
| Size | 8 MB |
| Hardware requirements | Any Palm |
| Software requirements | Windows 95/98/NT |
| Language | English |
| Cost | US $ 20.00 |
| Download address | www.precise-solutions.cix.co.uk |
| Available on CD | No |

## Pilot Install

Are you annoyed when you want to install a file on the Palm but must wait while the entire HotSync procedure runs? Are you irritated if you can't place a Palm file on a friend's computer because no Palm desktop is installed there or if no profile for your name is there?

It's no coincidence the freeware tool *Pilot Install* has been rated tops by all the Palm software providers in the Internet. This little program lets you transfer Palm files from the PC to any connected Palm without requiring that the Palm desktop be installed or that an appropriate Palm user is set up on the PC. Furthermore, only the specified data is sent from the PC to the Palm. No actual HotSync occurs.

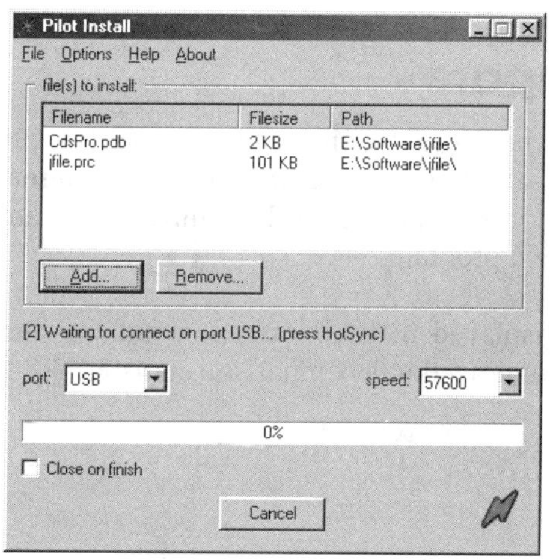


*Pilot Install installs Palm files without HotSync*

Just specify the interface and the transmission speed. The HotSync manager is automatically turned off when you start Pilot Install. Thereafter, when you press the HotSync button on the docking station, Pilot Install is opened instead of the HotSync manager. When you quit Pilot Install after a successful installation of the files, the HotSync manager automatically activates itself again.

**Tip**

**Synchronizing time of day with the Palm**

Enable the option *Options/PDA Date/Set time* in the Pilot Install menu. This automatically sets the time of day on the Palm according to the PC system time. This is particularly useful if you want to calibrate your PC automatically to a time server. The Palm will also change itself over to daylight savings time.

| **Pilot Install** | **1.9** |
|---|---|
| Software manufacturer or programmer | Envicon |
| Category | Desktop |
| Size | 397 KB |
| Hardware requirements | Any Palm |
| Software requirements | Windows 95/98/NT |
| Language | English/German |
| Cost | Freeware |
| Download address | pinstall.envicon.com |
| Available on CD | Yes |

## Norton File Compare

Users of Norton SystemWorks, Norton Commander, or Norton Utilities have a practical tool at their disposal: *Norton File Compare* finds differences between two files. This allows you, for example, to easily compare program versions or even files created by your own program.

The two files are clearly displayed in two adjacent windows. Differences are highlighted in color and summarized in a comparison statistic.

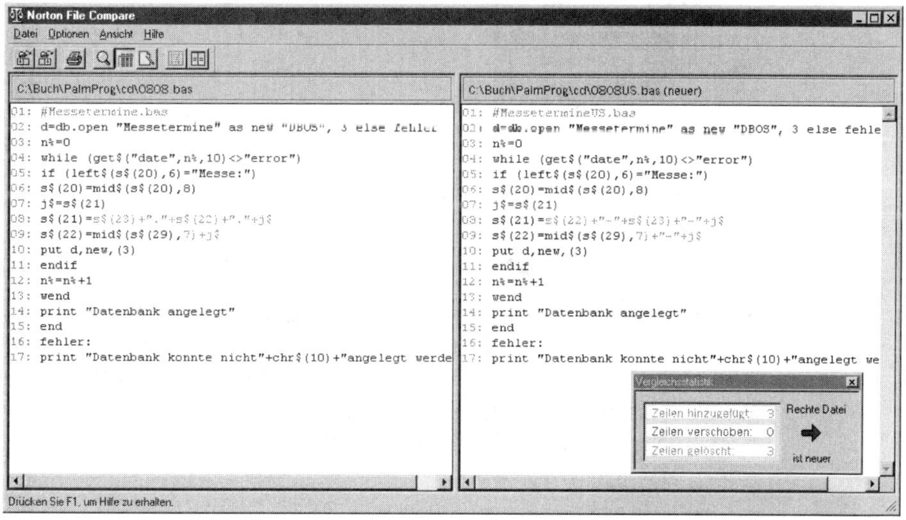


*File comparison with Norton File Compare from Norton SystemWorks 2001*

# 10.4 Systemhacks simplify everyday work

Hacks are Palm system expansions that reach deep into the operating system and can therefore directly change the Palm user interface and standard functions. Earlier we touched on this topic briefly when we discussed how to install SwitchHack, a tool for switching back and forth between the two last used applications using a graffiti line.

In this section you learn some more hacks that you as a programmer can put to good use and on your own programs. Additional useful hacks for various purposes can be found in the DATA BECKER book *Essential Palm Users Guide* as well as on the CD *Essential Palm Packet 2*.

## EVPlugBase

EVPlugBase, like Hackmaster, is a tool for configuring and enabling hacks on the Palm. As opposed to Hackmaster, EVPlugBase also offers, in addition to the hack interface, other options for managing system plug-ins in other formats. One more advantage: EVPlugBase is freeware.

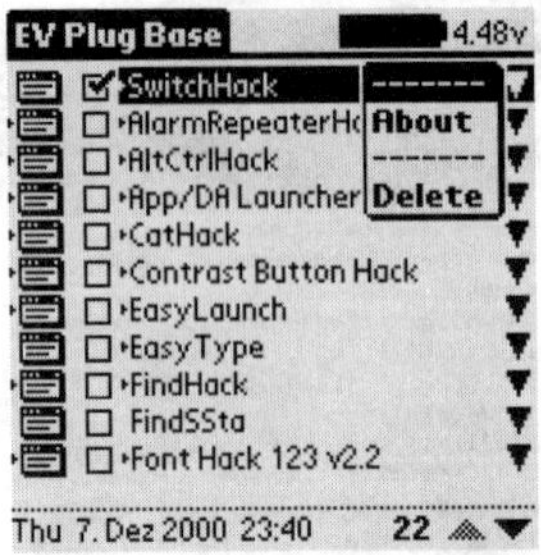


*Listing of all hacks in EVPlugBase*

To enable an installed hack under EVPlugBase, select the corresponding checkbox. Each installed hack that is configurable is highlighted by EVPlugBase. In the symbol view, find a small triangle on the left side of the symbol. In the list view the triangle appears at left in front of the entry. Click the symbol for the hack to open the associated configuration field.

**Tip**

**All at once**

Use the menu command *Unplug* or */U* to disable all the hacks and other plug-ins at one time.

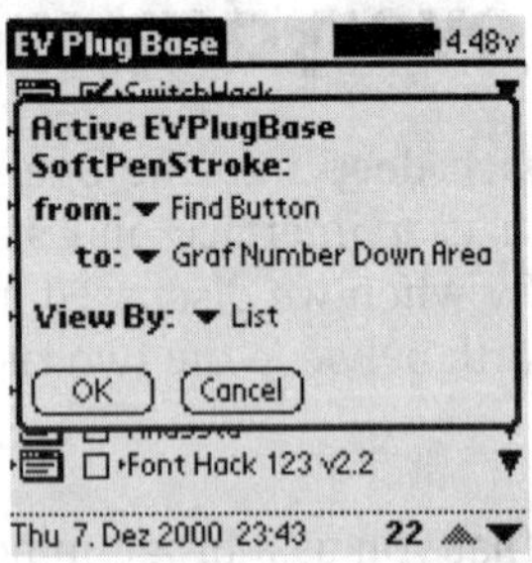


*Use the Options/*Preferences *menu or /*P *to specify a Graffiti for using to open EVPlugBase*

| EVPlugBase | 1.0b1 |
|---|---|
| Software manufacturer or programmer | EVSoft |
| Category | Hacks |
| Size | 20 KB |
| Hardware requirements | Any Palm |
| Software requirements | none |
| Language | English |
| Cost | Freeware |
| Download address | www.evscl.com/en/en_home.html |
| Available on CD | Yes |

# Easy Launch

Programming in HotPaw requires that you constantly switch back and forth between various applications, bookmarks, the HotPaw Basic interpreter, a database, a document viewer, and so on. Having to go to the program start interface of the Palm OS to find the desired application can be very tedious, especially if the list of installed applications is long.

Easy Launch can make this process a lot easier. In this hack you can specify 16 different Graffiti from among the four soft buttons and the Graffiti area, each of which starts a certain program. These Graffiti strokes are available anytime without having to switch to the program start interface.

*Configuring EasyLaunch*

Be sure the Graffiti strokes you configure are not already in use by, for example, SwitchHack, as described above on page 40 of Chapter 2 or as start commands for EVPlugBase.

| EasyLaunch | 0.02 |
|---|---|
| Software manufacturer or programmer | Hynek Syrovatka |
| Category | Hacks |
| Size | 3 KB |
| Hardware requirements | Any Palm |
| Software requirements | Hackmaster or EvPlugBase |
| Language | English |
| Cost | Freeware |
| Download address | www.mujweb.cz/www/hysy/elaunch |
| Available on CD | Yes |

# Task Hack

Yet another very interesting method of switching between different programs is Task Hack, though it only functions on Palm V series organizers. Pressing the contrast button at the upper border multiple times switches you between multiple, previously defined applications.

The list of applications to use can be determined using the Task Setup program. Enter only the applications you use often. Otherwise, scrolling through the list may take you as long as switching between two programs.

This configuration program also allows you to set whether or not you want the contrast setting to appear at the same time when pressing its key.

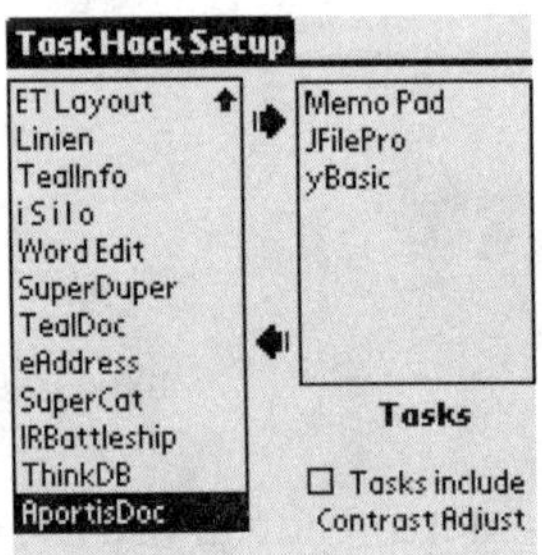


*Program list configuration for TaskHack*

| Task Hack | 1.1 |
|---|---|
| Software manufacturer or programmer | Horace Ho |
| Category | Hacks |
| Size | 4 KB |
| Hardware requirements | Palm V, Vx |
| Software requirements | Hackmaster or EvPlugBase |
| Language | English |
| Cost | US $ 5.95 |
| Download address | palm.pair.com |
| Available on CD | Yes |

# Lchars

Programs that convert units often use special mathematical characters, such as the superscript 2 in m² or the percent sign, and many games use the card symbols ♣, ♦, ♥, ♠. None of these characters can be entered using Graffiti or with the onscreen keyboard, but they are part of the Palm OS character set.

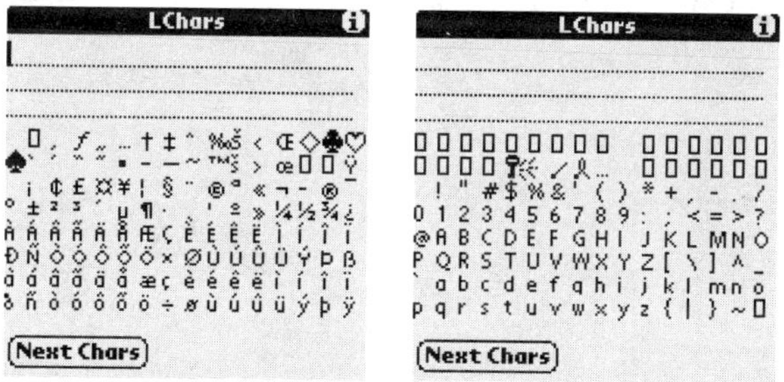


*The complete Palm OS character set in LChars*

The freeware program LChars offers a small editing window in which you can enter all the characters available on the Palm and then copy them to the clipboard for pasting in any other program. The program runs fully independently, requiring neither Hackmaster nor EVPlugBase.

| Lchars | |
|---|---|
| Software manufacturer or programmer | Laurent Thaler |
| Category | Tools |
| Size | 6 KB |
| Hardware requirements | Any Palm |
| Software requirements | none |
| Language | English |
| Cost | Freeware |
| Download address | lthaler.free.fr |
| Available on CD | No |

# Your own welcome screen with important appointments or the quote of the day

Some users like to have their Palm welcome screen display their current appointments or a witty saying. Some clever manipulation of a HotPaw Basic program using a shareware hack makes this possible.

*Current appointments and a clever saying every day*

The program reads the day's appointments from the date book and displays them together with the current date and time of day in the upper part of the screen. In the lower half , a saying appears, which is read out of a JFile database by a random generator. You can add your own sayings to this database whenever desired.

The program demonstrates the cooperation between various Palm tools such as a HotPaw Basic program, a JFile database, the start tool *yLaunch*, and a shareware for the Hackmaster or EVPlugBase.

```
#startup.bas
draw -1
draw 0,90,160,90
d%=db.find("quotations")
if (d%<0)
  draw "No quotations found",10,100
  goto appointments
endif
n%=rnd(db.len("quotations",-16))
draw "Saying of the day",10,95,1
draw db$(d%,n%,1),0,110
draw db$(d%,n%,2),0,122
draw db$(d%,n%,3),60,145

appointments:
d1$=right$(fn date$(0),2)
```

```
d2$=mid$(fn date$(0),5,2)
d3$=left$(fn date$(0),4)
draw "Dates today "+d1$+"."+d2$+"."+d3$,10,15,1
x=find("date",0,val(fn date$(0)))
gosub appointment2
for i=1 to 4
  x1=x
  x=find("date",-12,val(fn date$(0)))
  if (x>x1) then gosub appointment2
next i

start:
a$=fn time$(0)
s=val(mid$(a$,5,2))
draw left$(a$,2)+":"+mid$(a$,3,2)+":"+right$(a$,2)+"  ",120,1
goto start

appointment2:
get$("date",x,10)
if (s$(20)<>"")
  t1$=s$(24)
  if (len(t1$)=1) then t1$="0"+t1$
  t2$=s$(25)
  if (len(t2$)=1) then t2$="0"+t2$
  t$=t1$+":"+t2$+" "+s$(20)
  draw t$,0,i*12+30
endif
return
```

**CD**

**Program on the companion CD**

You can also find this program on the companion CD to this book as *1002.bas.* The indentation is for purposes of clarity only and is not contained in the original program on the CD, because it is difficult to render on memos.

The source code for the program contains no functions that you would not already recognize. In the first part the JFile database, *Quotations* is searched for and a random number used to extract a data record. The random generator depends on the number of records in the database so that the program will still function if you add your own sayings to the database.

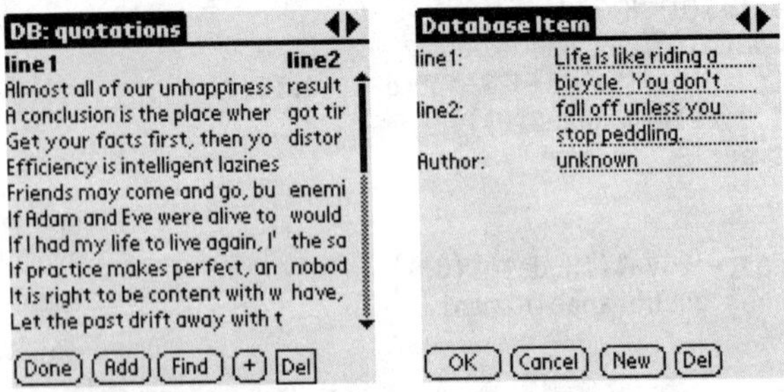


*The quotations database in JFile*

**CD**

### File on the companion CD

You can find this database on the companion CD to this book as *Quotations.pdb.*

The database contains three fields. The first two contain a line each of text. For shorter quotes, the second field may be empty. The third field is for the author or other attribution.

```
n%=rnd(db.len("Quotations",-16))
draw "Quote of the day",10,95,1
draw db$(d%,n%,1),0,110
draw db$(d%,n%,2),0,122
draw db$(d%,n%,3),60,145
```

The program reads all three lines of the randomly selected record and writes them to the corresponding positions on the screen. If no suitable database is found, the program goes directly to the jump label *dates:*, where the dates are read out and displayed.

At the same point the program continues to run even after displaying a saying and retrieves the current data, showing it together with the string *Dates today.* The calendar date is converted from three partial strings of the calendar date number into the format customary for Europe.

**Tip**

### Adapting to the American calendar date format

To display the current calendar date in American format, you won't need to do the conversion from the date number. HotPaw Basic offers its own function *fn date$(0,1)*, which returns the current date in American format as a character string. Example: Jan 11, 2001.

The *find ("date",0,val(fn date$(0))* function determines the first appointment for the current day. Each appointment has its own number in the date book database. This number is transferred to the subroutine *appointment2* in the variable *x*, and the subroutine uses *get("date", ...)* to write the individual fields of the appointment into the variables *s$(20) ... s$(29)*.

```
appointment2:
get$("date",x,10)
if (s$(20)<>"")
  t1$=s$(24)
  if (len(t1$)=1) then t1$="0"+t1$
  t2$=s$(25)
  if (len(t2$)=1) then t2$="0"+t2$
  t$=t1$+":"+t2$+" "+s$(20)
  draw t$,0,i*12+30
endif
return
```

When the program creates the string to be displayed, the hours and minutes are always formatted to 2 places so that the display has visually integrity.

After this first appointment for the day, a loop starts, which reads up to four additional dates for the same day. If you use the number *-12* as the second parameter in the function *find ("date"...)*, the function looks for additional dates after the first one of the day.

```
for i=1 to 4
  x1=x
  x=find("date",-12,val(fn date$(0)))
  if (x>x1) then gosub appointment2
next i
```

Successive dates always have successive numbers. If the *find("date"...)* function returns a negative value, this means no other date was found for the same day. Only if another valid date was found is the subprogram *date2* started. It reads this date from the calendar and displays it. The loop counter always moves the display position down by one line.

```
start:
a$=fn time$(0)
s=val(mid$(a$,5,2))
draw left$(a$,2)+":"+mid$(a$,3,2)+":"+right$(a$,2)+"  ",120,1
goto start
```

Once all the dates have been displayed, the program runs in an endless loop that displays the time of day in the upper right corner and continuously updates it.

## Starting the program

Up to this point the program is a normal HotPaw Basic program that has to be started from the yBasic interpreter. This means it does not yet accomplish the task of automatically starting at power-up.

The manufacturer of HotPaw Basic does offer a small freeware tool called *yLaunch* that allows you to start a HotPaw Basic program from the Program startup screen of the Palm OS, using an icon. This program must have the name *#startup.bas* on the bookmark. If yLaunch finds no bookmark by this name, an error message appears.

| yLaunch | |
|---|---|
| Software manufacturer or programmer | HotPaw |
| Category | Tools |
| Size | 2 KB |
| Hardware requirements | Palm III and higher |
| Software requirements | HotPaw Basic |
| Language | English |
| Cost | Freeware |
| Download address | www.hotpaw.com/rhn/hotpaw |
| Available on CD | No |

## Automatic start with Power Launch

*Power Launch* is a shareware hack that automatically starts any program having its own icon in the Program startup screen whenever the Palm is turned on using the power switch.

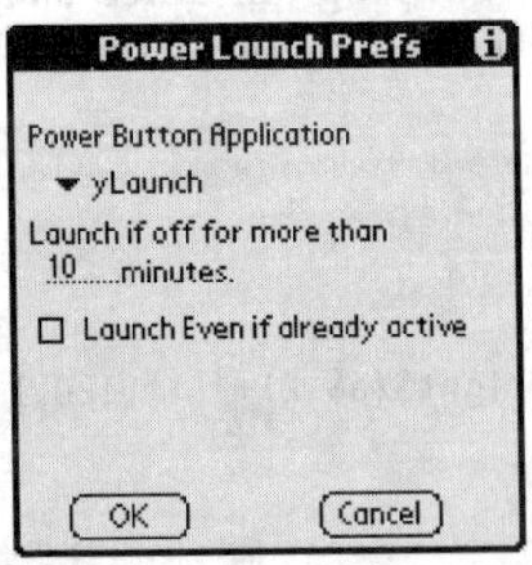


*Settings for Power Launch*

In the list of applications that is part of the configuration for this hack, select the program *yLaunch*, which will start the HotPaw Basic program.

In addition, you can specify that the program only starts automatically if the Palm was turned off for a certain length of time. This prevents the start program from being opened each time the organizer automatically turns itself off after a short inactive time.

| **Power Launch** | **1.4** |
|---|---|
| Software manufacturer or programmer | Ron Gouldner |
| Category | Hacks |
| Size | 4 KB |
| Hardware requirements | Any Palm |
| Software requirements | Hackmaster (supplied) or EVPlugBase |
| Language | English |
| Cost | US $ 5.00 |
| Download address | www.rgps.com |
| Available on CD | Yes |

The combination of *Power Launch*, *yLaunch*, and a HotPaw Basic program enables you to create any desired start programs of your own.

# 10.5 Compatibility between yBasic and cbasPad

Before HotPaw Basic was released, the same manufacturer offered a Basic interpreter for the Palm called cbasPad. As opposed to today's HotPaw Basic, this program also runs on organizers having the old Palm OS 2.x.

**Tip**

**cbasPad download**

If you are interested in testing your program for compatibility with the old cbasPad, you can download the program (now freeware) at the following URL: www.palmgear.com/software/showsoftware.cfm?prodID=1.

The syntax of the two languages is, for the most part, identical. You can often move cbasPad programs directly into HotPaw Basic. You should, however, note the following differences:

- cbasPad does not do calculations using Mathlib. This means trigonometric and logarithmic calculations must be programmed yourself, which may result in significantly less accurate results. The normal floating decimal calculations are based on the internal procedure of the Palm OS 2.x and will provide only inexact results on today's Palm OS.
- cbasPad has no database functions.
- cbasPad contains only limited functions for date and time calculation.
- cbasPad cannot read data using *read...data*.
- *if...then* queries are only allowed to occupy one line in cbasPad.
- cbasPad cannot use the graphics functions *moveto, lineto* and *draw*.
- cbasPad can only use *print* and *msbox* for outputting.
- cbasPad provides no color support on the Palm IIIc.
- Programs running under cbasPad must have line numbers.

Some functions had even fewer parameters or other names in cbasPad than in HotPaw Basic. This means you should always test an old cbasPad program before using it in HotPaw Basic.

| **cbasPad** | **097b4** |
|---|---|
| Software manufacturer or programmer | Ron Nicholson |
| Category | Tools |
| Size | 67 KByte |
| Hardware requirements | Any Palm |
| Software requirements | none |
| Language | English |
| Cost | Freeware |
| Download address | www.nicholson.com/rhn |
| Available on CD | No |

# 10.6 Database and text converters

In the preceding sections, you worked with HotPaw Basic texts in Doc format, but these texts first must be created on the PC. For this purpose, some practical tools are included on the CD.

**Tip**

**Converting with Pilot Install**

Users of the Pilot Install program described on page 475 have it especially easy. They cannot only transfer PRC and PDB files to a Palm but also ASCII text files in TXT format. These are automatically converted into Doc Format when they are transferred.

## DocReader

DocReader is a small Windows editor that allows you to convert ASCII-TXT files into Doc format and back. The documents can be edited directly in the editor allowing you to copy texts from other programs to the editor window through the clipboard and then convert them into Doc format for the Palm. You can also place bookmarks in the documents, which can be used in the display programs on the Palm.

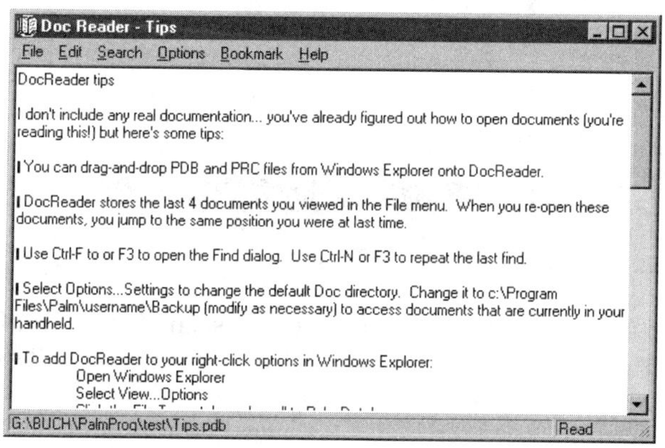


*DocReader for viewing and converting Doc files in Windows*

| Doc Reader | 0.69 |
|---|---|
| Software manufacturer or programmer | Mike Pickering |
| Category | Tools |
| Size | 522 KB |
| Hardware requirements | Any Palm |
| Software requirements | Windows 95/98/NT |
| Language | English |
| Cost | Freeware |
| Download address | www.crosswinds.net/~mpicker0 |
| Available on CD | Yes |

## AportisDoc PDF Converter

Aportis offers a converter to convert PDF files into the standard Doc format for the Palm. Graphics and formatting are automatically removed, leaving only the simple text.

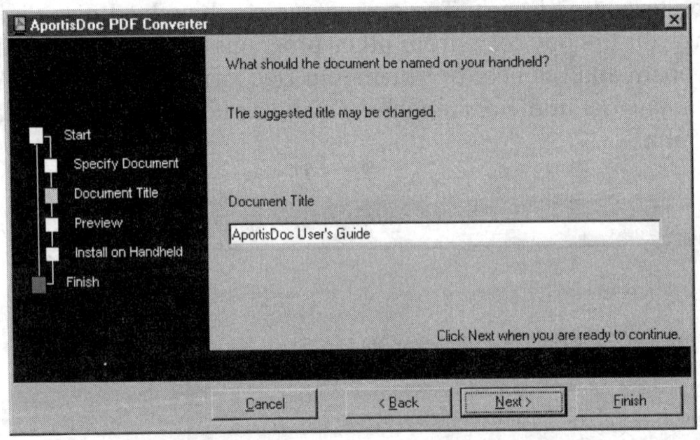


*The AportisDoc PDF Converter*

Aportis plans to introduce a new product in the second quarter of 2001 to replace this converter. This means the current freeware version will expire and no longer function.

| ApportisDoc PDF Converter | |
|---|---|
| Software manufacturer or programmer | Aportis |
| Category | Tools |
| Size | 1.1 MB |
| Hardware requirements | Any Palm |
| Software requirements | Windows 95/98/NT |
| Language | English |
| Cost | Freeware (until March 2001) |
| Download address | www.aportis.com |
| Available on CD | Yes |

# JFEdit Pro

JFEdit Pro is a program for editing Jfile-4.x databases in Windows. This gives you all the options for modifying records, adding new ones, or even altering the structure of the database by inserting or deleting columns or changing the field types. The sort, search, and filter functions of JFile were included in the program with the same functionality. Numeric values can be automatically summed by lines or columns. The databases do not have to be converted, as the program works with the original data format of JFile. In addition, JFile files can be automatically synchronized with the Palm after editing. You can also use the program independently of the Palm as a pure data manager in Windows, because it is a full-blown database.

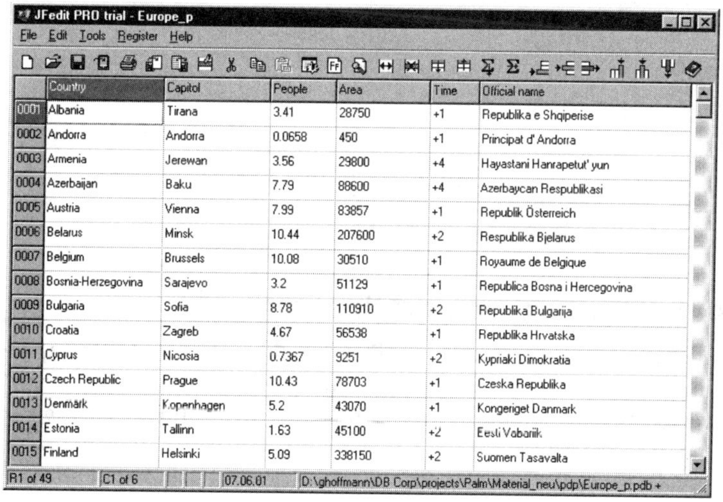


*JFEdit Pro edits and converts JFile 4 databases*

| JFEdit Pro | 3.23 |
|---|---|
| Software manufacturer or programmer | Christoph Muenzer |
| Category | Database |
| Size | 659 KB |
| Hardware requirements | Any Palm |
| Software requirements | Windows 95/98/NT |
| Language | English |
| Cost | US $ 22.95 |
| Download address | www.hugoland.de |
| Available on CD | Yes |

# JFile 4.x Converter

JFile 4 Converter is a converter running in Windows for JFile databases to CSV and back. The converted file is saved in the same directory as the source file and receives the same name (except for the file extension). You can also choose to create an Info file.

When converting from PDB to CSV, decide whether to use a decimal point or semicolon to separate the data fields. When converting from CSV to PDB, you are prompted to give a name for the database on the Palm.

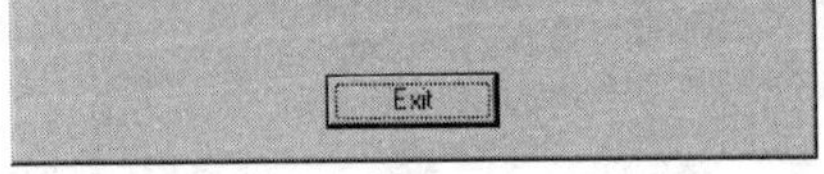


*JFile Pro Converter - converting in Windows*

## Jconvpro as command line converter

If you want to convert multiple JFile 4 databases to CSV format and back or to automatically start the conversion from within a program, you can also use this converter as a command line version. Use the command *jconvpro* and the following parameters.

### Converting from CSV to PDB

```
jconvpro.exe <1|3> <input_file> <output_file> <database_name>
[<OPTIONAL_INFO_FILE>]
```

| *<1>* | CSV file with decimal points |
|---|---|
| *<3>* | CSV file with semicolons |
| *<input_file>* | Name of the CSV file |
| *<output_file>* | Name of the PDB file |
| *<database_name>* | Database name on the Palm |
| *[<OPTIONAL_INFO_FILE>]* | Name of an optional Info file |

### Converting from PDB to CSV

```
jconvpro.exe <2|4> <input_file> <output_file>
[<OPTIONAL_INFO_FILE>]
```

| *<2>* | CSV file with decimal points |
|---|---|
| *<4>* | CSV file with semicolons |
| *<input_file>* | Name of the PDB file |
| *<output_file>* | Name of the CSV file |
| *[<OPTIONAL_INFO_FILE>]* | Name of an optional Info file |

| **JFile 4.x Converter** | **1.0k** |
|---|---|
| Software manufacturer or programmer | Land-J Technologies |
| Category | Database |
| Size | 180 KB |
| Hardware requirements | Any Palm |
| Software requirements | Windows 95/98/NT |
| Language | English |
| Cost | Freeware (comes supplied with JFile 4.x) |
| Download address | www.land-j.com |
| Available on CD | Yes |

## JFTrans

JFTrans converts JFile databases into Access 2000 databases and back. The data and also the database structure may be modified beforehand in a separate editor window. When you import a JFile database, the field types must first be assigned.

Note that Access is much more particular about field types than JFile. In the Access database, each field must really agree with the type of data contained in it. No exceptions are allowed.

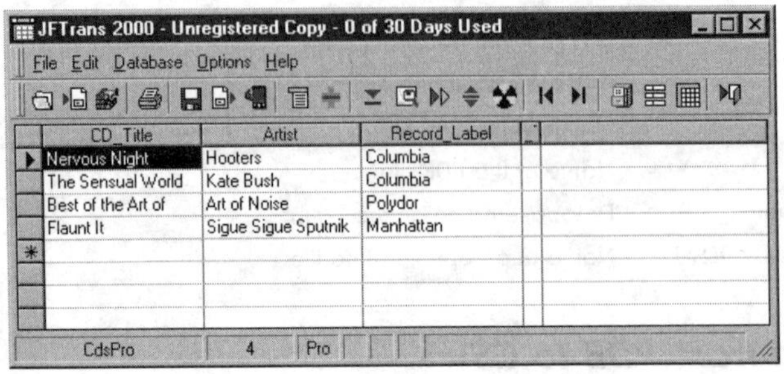


*The JFTrans 2000edit and display window*

Once you have determined the data types, the database appears in JFTrans. Search, sort, and filter functions are also available. You can edit the data values and even modify the database structure. The latter is much easier than in Access. In JFTrans it is easy to create new databases using templates and export them as Access or JFile.

JFTrans 2000 automatically installs a demo version of JFile 4. You can also use this program without Access 2000 to edit JFile 4 databases in Windows.

If you do not have Access 2000 installed, you must go to www.microsoft.com/data/download.htm?RLD=377 and download and install **M**icrosoft **D**ata **A**ccess **C**omponents (MDAC) before you can install JFTrans 2000.

| **JFTrans** | **1.52** |
|---|---|
| Software manufacturer or programmer | Steven Hawkins |
| Category | Database |
| Size | 4.2 MB |
| Hardware requirements | Any Palm |
| Software requirements | Windows 95/98/NT |
| Language | English |
| Cost | US $ 19.95 |
| Download address | home.ica.net/~shawkins/jftrans.htm |
| Available on CD | Yes |

**Note**

**JFTrans for Access 97**

Due to numerous problems and incompatibilities in Access 2000, many users prefer Access 97. Here again a version of JFTrans, which is continuously updated, is parallel to JFTrans 2000. No Microsoft Data Access Components are required for Access 97.

# Index

# Index

## E



## F

## I



## J



## L



## M

## U



## V



## W



## Y



## Z

# PUMP UP YOUR PALM™

## 150 Essential Programs™ for Palm OS

## Special Offer

## Only $9.99 each – You Save 50%

Originally $19.95

For $9.99 each, receive over 150 popular freeware and shareware programs. Choose from 3 collections that best fit your lifestyle. Compatible with Palm, IBM, Visor, Sony, and TRGpro. Visit *www.databecker.com* for more product information.

Quantity

______ *150 Essential Programs™: Executive Edition*

______ *150 Essential Programs™: Home & Family Edition*

______ *150 Essential Programs™: World Traveler Edition*

*Data Becker reserves the right to substitute Editions, while supplies last.

Name ______________________________

Address ______________________________

City ______________________________

State ______________ Zip Code ______________

Phone ______________________________

Email Address ______________________________

Please mail (1.) this completed form (2.) your book sales receipt (3.) $9.99 for each collection and (4.) $3.95 for shipping and handling to: (MA residents add 5% sales tax)

Data Becker<br>
Palm Software Offer<br>
210 Highland Avenue<br>
Needham Heights MA 02494

Not responsible for lost, late or misdirected mail. Not valid with any other offers. Void where prohibited. One request per household. Valid to end-user only with purchase of Data Becker's Palm book. Offer good in US only. Check or money order accepted payable to DATA BECKER (no cash please). This form may not be reproduced. Allow 3-4 weeks for processing. If product not received in 4 weeks, please email reception@databecker.com.

**Visit *www.databecker.com* for more great product ideas and solutions**